An Intellectual History of Liberal Catholicism in Western Europe, 1789–1870

An Intellectual History of Liberal Catholicism in Western Europe, 1789–1870

Edited by
Aude Attuel-Hallade

BLOOMSBURY ACADEMIC
LONDON • NEW YORK • OXFORD • NEW DELHI • SYDNEY

BLOOMSBURY ACADEMIC
Bloomsbury Publishing Plc, 50 Bedford Square, London, WC1B 3DP, UK
Bloomsbury Publishing Inc, 1385 Broadway, New York, NY 10018, USA
Bloomsbury Publishing Ireland, 29 Earlsfort Terrace, Dublin 2, D02 AY28, Ireland

BLOOMSBURY, BLOOMSBURY ACADEMIC and the Diana logo are
trademarks of Bloomsbury Publishing Plc

First published in Great Britain 2024
Paperback edition published 2025

Copyright © Aude Attuel-Hallade, 2024

Aude Attuel-Hallade has asserted her right under the Copyright,
Designs and Patents Act, 1988, to be identified as Editor of this work.

Cover Image © agefotostock / Alamy Stock Photo

All rights reserved. No part of this publication may be: i) reproduced or transmitted in any form, electronic or mechanical, including photocopying, recording or by means of any information storage or retrieval system without prior permission in writing from the publishers; or ii) used or reproduced in any way for the training, development or operation of artificial intelligence (AI) technologies, including generative AI technologies. The rights holders expressly reserve this publication from the text and data mining exception as per Article 4(3) of the Digital Single Market Directive (EU) 2019/790.

Bloomsbury Publishing Plc does not have any control over, or responsibility for, any third-party websites referred to or in this book. All internet addresses given in this book were correct at the time of going to press. The author and publisher regret any inconvenience caused if addresses have changed or sites have ceased to exist, but can accept no responsibility for any such changes.

Every effort has been made to trace the copyright holders and obtain permission to reproduce the copyright material. Please do get in touch with any enquiries or any information relating to such material or the rights holder. We would be pleased to rectify any omissions in subsequent editions of this publication should they be drawn to our attention.

A catalogue record for this book is available from the British Library.

A catalog record for this book is available from the Library of Congress.

ISBN: HB: 978-1-3503-7107-1
PB: 978-1-3503-7103-3
ePDF: 978-1-3503-7104-0
eBook: 978-1-3503-7105-7

Typeset by Integra Software Services Pvt. Ltd.

For product safety related questions contact productsafety@bloomsbury.com.

To find out more about our authors and books visit www.bloomsbury.com
and sign up for our newsletters.

To my parents, Patrick and Cynthia

Contents

List of contributors	viii
Bio-bibliographies	ix
Acknowledgements	xii

Liberal Catholicism/Catholic Liberalism: A non-sense? *Aude Attuel-Hallade (ed.)* 1

Part One Theology, truth and the philosophy of history

1 Political Modernity-Christianity: Interpretative circles *Bernard Bourdin* 11
2 John Henry Newman, an anti-liberal? *Frédéric Libaud* 29
3 Edmund Burke, T.B. Macaulay, Lord Acton and the French Revolution: The Church, the State and the individual *Aude Attuel-Hallade* 41

Part Two Catholicism and liberty(/ies)

4 Liberties before liberalism: Ultramontane political thought in England, c. 1835–50 *Colm O'Siochru* 73
5 Historical and ecclesiological foundations of Spanish Catholic liberalism. From the Jansenist imprint to the Constitution of Cádiz of 1812 *Bernard Callebat* 93
6 Between Sinai and Calvary: Spanish Catholicism in the face of freedom of worship in 1869 *Francisco Javier Ramon Solans* 111

Part Three Temporal and spiritual power and education

7 Sin, grace and secular history: Pierre Paul Royer-Collard's criticism of the anti-sacrilege law of 1825 *Daniele Giuseppe Palmer* 129
8 'A free Church in a free state'. The relationship between Church and State in the thought of Charles de Montalembert *Arthur Hérisson* 149
9 J. H. Newman facing the spirit of the day: A focus on the idea of education in the Victorian context *Maud Besnard* 169

Conclusion: Contested faith or contested liberty? – Contexts and strategies of Liberal Catholicism *Peter Schröder* 183

Bibliography	192
Index of names	213

List of Contributors

Aude Attuel-Hallade, Institut Catholique d'Etudes Supérieures (ICES)/Sorbonne Université/Panthéon Sorbonne, France

Maud Besnard, Institut Catholique de Rennes, France

Bernard Bourdin, Institut Catholique de Paris, France

Bernard Callebat, Institut Catholique d'Etudes Supérieures (ICES), France

Arthur Herisson, Ecole française de Rome, Italy

Frédéric Libaud, Université de Strasbourg, France

Colm O'Siochru, Dulwich College, London, UK

Daniele Palmer, King's College Cambridge, UK

Francisco Javier Ramon Solans, Casa de Velàsquez/Universidad de Zaragoza, Spain

Peter Schröder, University College London (UCL), London, UK

Bio-Bibliographies

Aude Attuel-Hallade is University Lecturer at the Institut Catholique d'Etudes Supérieures (ICES) in Modern British and French History and Researcher at CRICES (ICES) and at the Centre d'Histoire du XIXe siècle (Sorbonne Université/Panthéon Sorbonne). She holds a 1st class PhD in British and American History, Literature and Language from the Sorbonne Nouvelle (Paris III) and specialises in the history of ideas and in political science. She has taught British, American and French history and civilisation in France and in the UK (Université Paris-Est Créteil (AEI international School), Sorbonne Nouvelle (Paris III), Ecole Polytechnique, Université de Versailles St-Quentin-en-Yvelines, University of St Andrews) and ran her own research Seminar on 'Religion, Liberalism and Democracy in 19th UK and France' at the Institut Catholique de Paris. Her research work hinges on British and French liberal thought in the long 19th century. For the last few years, she's been working on the links between religion and liberty in post-revolutionary Europe. Recent publications include a monograph on *T.B. Macaulay et la Révolution française: la pensée libérale whig en débat* (Paris: Michel Houdiard éditions, 2018), the aim of which was to propose a redefinition of British liberal thought in light of the French Revolution, and articles on Lord Acton's conception of liberalism.

Maud Besnard is Doctor in English-speaking World Studies. She has been Director of the ENGLISH Department and lecturer at the Catholic Institute of Rennes since 2007. She defended her thesis on *The University Idea according to Cardinal John Henry Newman: education, religion, culture and development of the person* in 2015. Her research focuses on the history of ideas in the 19th century with a particular interest in the transmission of knowledge and its influence on the human formation. She has published several articles in this direction in Les Etudes newmaniennes and participated in the colloquium on Education and Christian Educators, organized by ICR in 2011. The proceedings of the colloquium were published in the work *Éducation et éducateurs chrétiens* (Paris, edition L 'Harmattan, 2013).

Bernard Bourdin is Professor of Political Philosophy and History of Ideas at the Institut Catholique de Paris (Faculty of Social Sciences, Economics and Law). He has a doctorate in philosophy, theology and the history of religions, and specializes in the relationship between politics and religion (Christianity). His most recent book is entitled 'Le chrétien peut-il aussi être citoyen' (Paris: Editions du Cerf, 2023).

Bernard Callebat is Faculty Professor and part-time Lecturer and Associate Researcher (CRICES) at the Institut Catholique d'Etudes Supérieures (ICES). He teaches in the two Faculties of Law in Toulouse, that of the Catholic Institute of

Toulouse and that of the University of Toulouse 1 Capitole. He is also a Full Professor at the Faculty of Canon Law of Toulouse, where he also directs doctoral studies. He is visiting professor at the law faculties of Tunis, Constanza and Pamplona. He specializes in particular in the history of Latin sources from the High Middle Ages.

Arthur Herisson A former student of the *École normale supérieure* (Paris), Arthur Hérisson is currently a scientific member of the *École française de Rome*. In November 2018, he defended a Ph.D. thesis entitled *Les catholiques français face à l'unification italienne (1856–1871). Une mobilisation internationale de masse entre politique et religion* at the Université Paris 1 Panthéon-Sorbonne. He also edited with Pierre-Marie Delpu and Vincent Robert the book *Médias, politique et révolution en 1867: les échos européens de la bataille de Mentana*, to be published by Classiques Garnier. He is currently pursuing research on counter-revolutionary internationalism in Western Europe during the pontificate of Pius IX.

Frédéric Libaud holds a degree in spiritual theology from the Gregorian University of Rome (2004). He is a priest of the diocese of Strasbourg, has a doctorate in theology from the Faculty of Catholic Theology of Strasbourg and is vice-official of the diocese. The theme of his doctorate was the invisible world in the Parochial and Plain Sermons of John Henry Newman, published in 2016 under the title "Seeing the invisible". Since then, he has continued to work on the works of Cardinal Newman. In addition to numerous articles, he has also published "Filling Eternity – Holiness according to John Henry Newman" (2019). Currently, he is working on a second doctorate in canonical criminal law.

Colm O'Siochru is Head of History at Dulwich College, London, a leading independent school. He holds a 1st class MA in Modern History & International Relations from the University of St Andrews, and an MPhil in Intellectual History from the University of Cambridge. He has written a DPhil thesis (not yet submitted) on ultramontane political theology in England, ca. 1830–1914. It confronts the myths surrounding 'Ultramontanism' – deployed by most contemporaries as an invidious epithet, and by most historians as a 'shibboleth of reproof' (Robert Sullivan, *Catholic Historical Review*, 1998). It locates the causes of this distortion in the historiography and hagiography of different varieties of liberal Catholicism, from 1850s to the present day: from the disciples of Lord John Acton to the disciples of Prof John Bossy. It seeks to recover the lost aspects of this ultramontanism – its Roman and Mennaisian incarnationalism; its Görresian and O'Connellite commitments to constitutional pluralism and 'liberty consecrated'; its anti-Malthusian political economy; its anti-positivist philosophy; its internal tensions over the possibility of integralism in the modern world – by situating 'English' debates between recusants, converts, and migrants (Irish and ecclesiastical) in their transnational contexts. Drawing primarily on a wide range of printed sources – periodicals, papers, sermons, tracts, hymns, meditations, etc. – it emphasises that ultramontanism was an intellectual and rhetorical construct as much as it was an institutional power-grab. Aspects of this project and approach can be found in O'Siochrú's engagement with one species of Victorian liberal Catholicism, "'Edward

Semper Augustus": E. A. Freeman on Rome, the Papacy, and the Unity of History', in G. A. Bremner and Jonathan Conlin, eds., *Making History: Edward Augustus Freeman and Victorian Cultural Politics*, Proceedings of the British Academy, 202 (Oxford, 2015), 47–63.

Daniele Palmer is working on a doctorate in history at King's College, Cambridge. His work focuses on the reception of Giambattista Vico's writings in the work of French historians and political theorists of the first half of the nineteenth century, concentrating principally on questions in the history of classical scholarship and the development of historiography.

Francisco Javier Ramon Solans is Ramón y Cajal Researcher at the University of Zaragoza, Spain. He received his PhD in History from the University of Zaragoza and the University of Paris 8. He has been a research fellow in EHESS (Paris), New York University and University of Paris I and University of Münster. He is the author of *Más allá de los Andes. Los orígenes ultramontanos de la Iglesia latinoamericana* (UPV 2020); *Historia global de las religiones en el mundo contemporáneo* (Alianza 2019) and *La Virgen del Pilar dice... Usos políticos y nacionales de un culto mariano en la España contemporánea* (Prensas Universitarias de Zaragoza, 2014) and he has coedited with Roberto Di Stefano, *Marian Devotions, Political Mobilization, and Nationalism in Europe and America* (Palgrave Macmillan, 2016); with Pedro Rújula, *El Desafío de la Revolución. Reaccionarios, antiliberales y contrarrevolucionarios (siglos XVIII y XIX)* (Comares, 2017); and with Olaf Blaschke, *Weltreligion im Umbruch. Transnationale Perspektiven auf das Christentum in der Globalisierung* (Campus Verlag, 2018). He has published several articles in peer-reviewed journals such as *Historia y Política, Ayer, Mélanges de la Casa Velázquez, Hispania, Religions, European History Quarterly, Atlantic Studies, Journal of Ecclesiastical History, Annales Histoire Sciences Sociales* and *Annales Historiques de la Révolution française*; and book chapters on Marian devotions, National-Catholicism, political prophecies, miracles, and Ultramontanism. His current research is on the relationships between Latin American and European Catholicism and the role they played in the making of a centralized and globalized Catholic Church.

Peter Schröder is Professor of the History of Political Thought at University College London. He was visiting professor at universities in Seoul, Rome and Paris and held numerous senior research fellowships. Recent publications include a monograph on *Trust in Early Modern International Political Thought, 1598–1713* (Ideas in Context 116) Cambridge University Press 2017 (paperback 2019), as well as four edited volumes: Two German editions (both Meiner Verlag) of R. Filmer, *Patriarcha*, Hamburg 2019 and of T. Hobbes, *Dialog zwischen einem Philosophen und einem Juristen über das Common Law*, Hamburg 2021 and two collections of essays: *Der Staat als Genossenschaft. Zum rechtshistorischen und politischen Werk Otto von Gierkes*, Nomos Verlag Baden-Baden 2021 and *Concepts and Contexts of Vattel's Political and Legal Thought*, Cambridge University Press 2021.

Acknowledgements

Invaluable has been the unfailing and selfless support, help, advice and encouragement that Professor Franck Lessay has given me for so many years. I could not have had a finer mentor. His intellectual training and belief in my research projects and in this current book, in particular, have meant much to me. I am, above all, much indebted to him.

I would like to extend my warmest thanks to Professor Stéphane Guy and to Professor Marie-Claude Esposito for their constant faith in and support of my scientific and academic projects. I owe much to them too.

I am also most grateful to *The Britain and Ireland Association for Political Thought* (APT) for having rallied round and hosted the international panel I organized and chaired as part of the Annual Political Thought Conference of 2021 and from which this manuscript is taken. And much obliged I am to the directors of the *Centre d'Histoire du XIXe siècle* (Sorbonne Université/Panthéon Sorbonne), the professors Jacques-Olivier Boudon, Dominique Kalifa and Bertrand Tillier, to the AEI International School (Université Paris-Est Créteil), to Professor Miles Taylor and Professor Richard Bourke, to Emily Jones and Pierre-Marie Delpu and to the former and current presidents of the Institut Catholique d'Etudes Supérieures (ICES), Eric de Labarre and Eric Ghérardi for their support and trust.

Last but not least, I pay high tribute to my parents Patrick and Cynthia Attuel; my uncle and aunt Jean-Claude and Josiane Attuel; my sister and brother, Frédérique and Guillaume Attuel; my children, Louise, Romane and Timéon; and above all, my husband, Sébastien Hallade, without whom this project could not have seen the light of day.

Liberal Catholicism/Catholic Liberalism: A non-sense?

Aude Attuel-Hallade (ed.)
(CRICES, Institut Catholique d'Etudes Supérieures)
(Centre d'Histoire du XIXe siècle, Sorbonne Université/Panthéon Sorbonne)

A new era, opposed to the Christian order, did not begin until 1789. Its charter on the Declaration of the Rights of Man and of the Citizen, understood these rights as negative to the rights of God. Not to reject them absolutely and bring the world back to atheism; but only to maintain that the citizen, as a citizen, was not, in society, subject to the law of God. Man, the individual, the private individual remained subject to religious faith and his Christian conscience; Christianity was still the law of man as a man; It was no longer the law of man as he lived in society. Civil and political society was sovereign in its own right; it was no longer the sovereignty of Jesus Christ. Jesus Christ became a stranger in France; the Gospel no longer had any rights, no shares, no role in the constitution of the French people. This exclusion of the Church and Christ was what is called liberalism
(*Revue du Monde Catholique*, 15 February 1902[1])

To Article X of the Declaration of the Rights of Man and of the Citizen (26 August 1789), which asserts that religion is an opinion, the First Vatican Council (1869-70) responded with the dogma of papal infallibility against the background of the Franco-Prussian War and Italian unification. Between these two dates, Europe underwent profound upheavals, religiously as well as politically, economically and socially. In its western part – with problematic contours – understood here as Catholic and Protestant for the most part, the reaffirmation of monarchical legitimacy and the borders drawn by the Congress of Vienna in 1814-15 did not prevent the birth of new states – in the form of monarchies – Belgium in 1830, Italy in 1861 and Germany in 1871. Nor did it prevent the instability of political regimes in France (the Restoration, the July Monarchy, the Second Republic, the Second Empire and the Third Republic) as in Spain (the absolutism of Ferdinand VII, the *trieno liberal*, the Carlist wars, the putsch of 1868 and the First Republic), nor the liberal, democratic and national claims, notably in 1830-31 and during the Springtime of the People, nor the colonization in Africa and the decolonization in America. This period was also illustrated by the questioning of the temporal and spiritual sovereignty of the papacy. Though the prerogatives of the latter were null in the predominantly Protestant countries – even if they were a source of concern ('the Papal Aggression' of 1850 in the UK) by the presence of a strong Catholic minority (the 'Irish question' in the UK) or even by the emergence of a Catholic party (the *Zentrum* in Germany) – they were also limited in predominantly Catholic countries (Napoleon Bonaparte's Concordat in 1801, the Belgian constitution of 1831, 'Jansenism' in Spain, Cavour's anticlerical policy in Italy). In addition, the States of the Church were considerably reduced between 1861 and 1870 during the Italian Wars of Independence. Finally, the property of the Church was nationalized in France (2 November 1789) as in Spain (the depreciation from the end of the eighteenth century to the beginning of the twentieth century). Admittedly, the threats to the spiritual and temporal sovereignty of the Catholic Church do not date from the French Revolution and the nineteenth century, including for the 'eldest daughter of the Church', as Gallicanism and Jansenism testify. And yet, within about a decade, the constitutional monarchy, then the Republic and finally the French Consulate made religion an opinion (26 August 1789), decreed the nationalization of the property of the clergy (2 November 1789) and the Civil Constitution of the clergy (12 July 1790), separated the Church and the State (1795) and finally deconfessionalized the French State by the Concordat (1801–2). The French revolutionaries thereby opened a particular sequence for Catholicism. The intransigence of Pius IX and the fourfold rejection of the Reformation, the Enlightenment, the liberal state and the Revolution were nourished by the revolutionary persecution of Catholicism under the French Revolution. In his encyclical *Quanta cura* of 1864, Pope Pius IX reviewed eighty modern errors. After the refusal of an ecclesiastical power to exercise its authority with the consent of all-powerful civil governments, of national Churches not subject to papal authority, of the exclusion of the Church on the matrimonial level and in the field of education, the pope concluded his *Syllabus* of 8 December 1864 with an eightieth and last error stated as follows: 'The Roman Pontiff can and must reconcile and compromise with progress, liberalism and modern civilization.' Does this mean that to be a Catholic was to refuse or deny 'Year 1 of liberty'?

Following the Protestant Reformation of the sixteenth century, Christian Europe was divided. The pacification of the wars of religion resulted in the action, the arbitration of monarchs, intending to overcome religious cleavages by the establishment of national Churches – *cujus regio ejus religio* (as the prince, so the religion) – and the proclamation of edicts. The Catholic Church, universal, was concerned not only about religious fragmentation but also about the strengthening of sovereign prerogatives in religious matters. The affirmation of the modern state thus became, under the pen of Catholic writers, the illustration of a new absolutism, which threatened Catholic universality, the freedom of Christians and the spiritual and temporal sovereignty of the Church. Nevertheless, the French Revolution added to the traditional conflict between civil and religious power, between Church and State, between Church and Emperor – already germinating at the first Christian Council, that of Nicaea (325), convened by the Roman Emperor Constantine and epitomized by the Investiture Controversy in the Middle Ages (notably between Pope Gregory VII and the Holy Roman Emperor Henry IV) – the question of the place of religion in society. The links between the throne and the altar were no longer questioned alone, but also the role of religion, as a belief, a dogma, an institution and a morality, in social and political education. It was actually not until the French Revolution that the Christian foundations of civil society and government were truly called into question. The most striking factor of civilization or, on the contrary, a civilizational catastrophe breaking with the history of humanity, the so-called capital letter Revolution, was effectively the most astonishing event the world had ever known, as expressed by the British philosopher Edmund Burke, the father of political conservatism, as early as 1790. By posing freedom as a universal principle and by proclaiming the sovereignty of the individual, it definitively modified the historical,[2] political, religious and moral paradigms on which the liberal societies of the *Ancien Régime* were based and imposed *de facto* a reflection on the (new) relations between the 'Rights of Man' and the 'Rights of God'. Although the liberal current asserted itself in the seventeenth century around the struggle against absolute power, of kings as well as of the pope, the French Revolution divided liberal writers. In this respect, Edmund Burke was highly concerned by the revolutionary uprooting, by the policy of wiping the slate clean of the past. If his work is not exempt from criticism of the French Catholic Church of the *Ancien Régime*, the liberal and conservative Member of Parliament nevertheless vehemently condemned the questioning of the Catholic mores of France, of religion as a social bond. For his part, if the father of Whig history – liberal, Protestant and progressive – Thomas Babington Macaulay deplored, like Burke, the abstraction of human rights, he nonetheless applauded the loss of political and moral power of the Catholic Church in France and the secularizing policy of the French revolutionaries. As for the counter-revolutionary, Joseph de Maistre, for his part a Catholic and anti-liberal, the destructive revolutionary violence allowed for 'washing' the sins of the monarchical and Catholic France and announced its regeneration. Does this then imply that to be a liberal was to have a utilitarian approach to religion, as a guarantor of morals and order, as long as it did not disturb public order and that to be a Catholic was to reject any questioning of religion, as an institution and social bond?

Nonetheless, it is still necessary to agree on the definitions of *Catholicism* and *liberalism*, plural notions calling for contextualization and territorialization. To be a Catholic is, at the same time, to adhere to a set of beliefs, to share a Book, the Bible, to respect a dogma of which the Pope, at the top of the ecclesiastical hierarchy, is the guarantor, and a morality, that of the Decalogue, but it is also to be part of a centuries-old history, to belong to a majority or minority religion. To be a liberal is to fight political and religious despotism, to defend religious tolerance, to prefer the separation or balance of powers but also to affirm the prerogatives of the State and/or defend individual freedoms. However, these simple definitions need to be nuanced, clarified in the light of political and religious events and controversies. In any case, Catholicism, as Truth and act of faith, as a centuries-old history, as universalism, as the announcement of the reign of Christ, as a majority or minority religion, dialogued with liberalism, as a current and political party born during religious and civil wars, as a State guaranteeing freedom of worship, as a political and moral philosophy based on the rights and autonomy of the individual.

A number of Liberal writers and Catholic writers did not systematically condemn the French Revolution, either by distinguishing between the Revolution of 1789 – giving birth to a constitutional monarchy – and the Terror of 1793 – leading to an anticlerical Republic – or by explaining revolutionary violence by the national and international context, or by inscribing the French Revolution in a liberal philosophy of history or in the essence of Christianity. A *liberal Catholicism* (primacy of the liberal matrix) or a *Catholic liberalism* (primacy of the catholic matrix) was then emerging. Despite the condemnation of liberalism, of democracy, of secularization by the Catholic institution (Papal Rome), a dialogue was hence established among these historians, theologians and political actors around the link between Catholicism, revolution and liberalism. For if the concept of freedom is ancient, and goes back to Antiquity (Greeks, Stoics) and Christianity (St Paul), as is that of free will (Saint Augustine, *On Free Choice of the Will (De libero arbitrio)*), the novelty with the Revolution is that it substituted the sovereignty of God, this 'highest power of all', by the sovereignty of the individual. But how then to reconcile the irreconcilable, from a dogmatic and theological point of view, the liberal individualism of the Revolution and the doctrine of the Church? The questions of authority and truth on the one hand and that of the Christian conception of liberty on the other arise. Is man/the individual, capable of attaining the truth by himself or is this truth pre-existing to the individual? Can he reach salvation as he sees fit? Is the ecclesiastical (papal) authority only able to determine the contents of the Christian faith and the divine truth as the guarantor of the Word of God? How to reconcile the dogma of the universal Roman Church with the freedom of conscience proclaimed by the Declaration of the Rights of Man and of the Citizen? How to reconcile religious truth and historical progress – or modernity? Divine sovereignty and individual sovereignty? Sin, salvation and freedom? Are these expressions just oxymorons? Would they only cover intellectual exercises and political actions doomed to failure? What is more, are they interchangeable?

In France, Catholic Liberalism was born in 1828.[3] Among the most frequently studied figures of this Catholic Liberalism: Félicité de Lamennais, Charles de Montalembert and Henri Lacordaire, all three editors of *L'Avenir* in 1830–1, and representatives of the people under the French Second Republic. In Germany, Ignaz von Döllinger followed the same trajectory as Felicité de Lamennais: from ultramontane to the refusal of papal sovereignty.[4] In the UK, John Emerich Edward Dalberg-Acton (Lord Acton) rose up like Döllinger against the dogma of papal infallibility. However, is it possible to speak of an intellectual? Philosophical? Political? movement and/or current? – by evoking a few isolated figures? Besides, if these latter corresponded, met, read each other's work, they did not agree on the role of the Church, the Pope, on history, on education, on freedom of conscience. Would the consistency of Catholic Liberalism only hold in the blacklisting and excommunication of Catholic writers or the fear of condemnation by the Church? Did the proclamation of the dogma of papal infallibility by Vatican I signify the death of Catholic Liberalism? Would the freedom of religion guaranteed by Vatican II (*Dignitatis Humanae*) underscore the late triumph of Catholic Liberalism? Or perhaps should we accept that the definition of liberty is plural, including among Catholic writers? The Middle Ages, often mobilized to exemplify the defence of freedom and good government by the Church, through the pacification of morals (the 'peace and truces of God' seeking to limit and control feudal violence) and the opposition to the growing pretensions of the monarchical state, was as well studied by the liberal

Catholic, Acton, as by the ultramontane, Nicholas Wiseman or Montalembert. But does the exercise of freedom – of expression, of demonstration, of association – as with the Spanish Catholics in 1869, that a liberal constitution offers, represent a first step towards the acceptance of a liberal or even democratic regime? And did talking about liberty, like John Henry Newman did, amount to espousing liberal theses? In 1863, the Congresses of Mechelen and Munich brought together, among others, the Catholics, Acton, Döllinger and Montalembert. But the *Syllabus* of 1864 condemned the liberal demands of these Congresses. Would Catholic liberalism, the religion of Truth, seeking to reconcile the Bible, theology, the Church, religious freedom – even freedom of conscience – and a representative government, or liberal Catholicism, a philosophical and political movement based on Catholic morality, the Decalogue, then be the religion of the exit from religion, to paraphrase Philippe Boutry about spiritualism?[5]

This volume, bringing together nine contributions divided into three parts – a first entitled 'Theology, Truth and the Philosophy of History', a second, 'Catholicism and Liberty(ies)', and a last one, 'Temporal and Spiritual Power and Education' – intends to explore the paths of Catholic writers who wished to absorb the French Revolution, and more broadly to reconcile universal religion, based on Truth and eternity with liberal modernity premised on experience, observation and adaptability. It is proposed as an excursus and not as an exhaustive sum. Not all liberal Catholic or Catholic liberal writers nor all Western European countries have been included here. However, it intends to sow milestones for a better understanding of Liberal Catholicism. It aims at questioning a specific liberal approach through Catholicism. It is not so much a question of looking at the process of secularization understood as the decline of religious institutions, practices and beliefs in Western Europe in the nineteenth century, nor of questioning the consubstantiality of the exit from religion to Christianity (Marcel Gauchet).[6] Nor is it so much a question of returning to the secularization of the idea of salvation in the philosophy of history (Karl Löwith) or to a diverse and plural religiosity while ancient religions decline (Charles Taylor) or to dwell on the existence or not of a Catholic liberalism (René Rémond).[7] Above all, it is a question of appreciating how and why European Catholic and liberal thinkers, historians, theologians and political actors, 'the new clerics', the scientist and the politician – to use the title of two lectures by Max Weber (1919)[8] – relied on, studied, questioned dogma, history and religious morality, while fighting or not religious institutions, in order to build the post-revolutionary society and state. Liberal Catholics still endeavoured to define liberalism by virtue of their Catholic faith which has hence entailed a reflection on the possible Catholic roots of modern and contemporary liberalism. What new liberal order, socio-political and religious model they proposed, what philosophy of history and what moral doctrines, glorifying or condemning the new era or the ancient order and honouring anew the themes of decadence and of a golden age, of sin and salvation, they offered and why these liberals were so attached to pursuing a dialogue with the 'ancient beliefs' are the main questions raised and addressed in this book. By choosing an intellectual history, this volume sheds light on the liveliness but also the complexity of the debates on the essence of liberalism and Catholicism, on the definition of liberty, on the links between churches and states, between religion and citizenship. It highlights sociability, the circles, the networks, – the correspondence (as between Acton and Döllinger), the personal relationships (as between the Frenchman, Montalembert and the Belgian, Adolphe Deschamps) – and the media coverage – works, reviews (as *The Home and Foreign Review*, *The Rambler*), petitions, demonstrations, speeches, congresses, schools and universities across the Europe of liberal Catholicism, in other words, the channels through which ideas circulated, were transformed and encouraged dialogue between liberalism and Catholicism in the nineteenth century, against a backdrop of political and cultural democratization. It gives prominence to the pivotal period that the years 1789 to 1870 represented for Liberal Catholicism – especially around the years 1790–1800, with, at the heart, the European upheaval caused by the French Revolution, then the years 1830–60, with, at their core, the threats weighing on the temporal sovereignty of the pope following the Springtime of the Peoples and the Italian unification and which led to the doctrine of papal infallibility at the First Vatican Council – and for a better understanding of the religious roots of liberalism and the ever-present tensions between liberty, dogma and the Church.[9] The initial premise is accordingly that the French Revolution should no longer be studied so much as a major step in the secularization of the French, even European, society, opening a secular paradigm, but understood as the inauguration of a particular, even unprecedented, sequence of dialogues between European 'public moralists',[10] the new and the former clerics, representatives of the official majority or minority churches. More broadly, this book invites the reader to uncover the political, ideological and philosophical tensions that the religious question entails in the redefinition of European, post-revolutionary liberalism.

Notes

1   'Une nouvelle ère, opposée à l'ordre chrétien, ne commença qu'en 1789. Sa charte sur la Déclaration des Droits de l'homme et du citoyen, entendait ces droits comme négatifs des droits de Dieu. Non pas pour les rejeter absolument et ramener le monde à l'athéisme; mais seulement pour soutenir que le citoyen, en tant qu'il est citoyen, n'est pas, dans la société, soumis à la loi de Dieu. L'homme, l'individu, le simple particulier reste assujetti à la foi religieuse et à sa conscience chrétienne; le christianisme est encore la loi de l'homme en tant qu'homme; il n'est plus la loi de l'homme en tant qu'il vit en société. La société civile et politique est souveraine en son espèce; elle ne relève plus de la souveraineté de Jesus-Christ. Jésus-Christ devient un étranger en France; l'Evangile n'a plus aucun droit, aucune part, aucun rôle dans la constitution du peuple français. Cette exclusion de l'Eglise et du Christ, c'est ce qu'on appelle le libéralisme'. See Rousseau, J.J, *Du Contrat Social ou Principe du droit politique* (Amsterdam : Marc Michel, 1762), livre IV, Chapter VIII, 296–305.
2   'The Most Astonishing [circumstance] That Has Hitherto Happened in the World'. Edmund Burke, *Reflections on the Revolution in France*, ed. J.G.A Pocock (Indianapolis: Hackett Publishing Company, 1987), 230, 9.
3   Lucien James, 'La place du catholicisme libéral dans la culture politique française', in *Charles de Montalembert. L'Eglise, la politique, la liberté*, ed. A. de Meaux and E. Montalembert (Paris: CNRS éditions, 2012), 59–77.

4   As Philippe Boutry emphasized, ultramontanism, referring to Catholics obeying 'beyond the mountains' (which is to say to the papacy), became in the nineteenth century the nominee and the carryall of European anti-Catholicism. Cf 'Papacy and Culture in the Nineteenth Century, Magisterium, Orthodoxy, Tradition', *Revue d'histoire du XIX siecle*, no. 28; 'Religion, Politics and Culture in the Nineteenth Century', dir. Jacqueline Lalouette and Michèle Riot-Sarcey, 2004/1, 31–58.
5   Philippe Boutry, 'La gauche et la religion', in *History of the Left in France*, vol. 1, *The Legacy of the Nineteenth Century*, ed. Jean-Jacques Becker and Gilles Candar (Paris: La Découverte, 2005), 317–41.
6   Marcel Gauchet, *Le Désenchantement du monde. Une histoire politique de la religion* (Paris: Gallimard, 1985).
7   Charles Taylor, *L'Age séculier* (Paris: Edition du Seuil, 2011); Karl Löwith, *Histoire et Salut. Les présupposés théologiques de la philosophie de l'histoire*, translated from the German by M.C. Challiol-Gillet, S. Hurstel and J.F. Kervegan (1949/1953). (Paris: Gallimard, 2002). René Rémond, *Lamennais et la démocratie* (Paris: Presses Universitaires de France, 1948).
8   Max Weber, *Le Savant et le politique* (Paris: Plomb, 1959).
9   Cf 'Pope Francis Faces Another German Reformation', *The New York Times*, 11 May 2021.
10 Stefan Collini, *Public Moralists. Political Thought and Intellectual Life in Great Britain, 1850–1930* (Oxford: Oxford University Press, 1993).

Part One

Theology, truth and the philosophy of history

1

Political Modernity-Christianity: Interpretative circles

Bernard Bourdin
Catholic Institute of Paris
Text translated from the French by Aude Attuel-Hallade and Cynthia Attuel

Introduction

Christianity and political modernity is a subject extensively treated by historians, sociologists, philosophers and theologians. But putting Christianity and political Modernity face to face by the coordinating conjunction 'and' would amount to predetermining what both links and unlinks two political and religious realities. Either they would be antithetical or, conversely, they would be the *recto-verso* of each other. In the first scenario, Modernity would signify the renunciation of the Christian matrix which marked the European and Western hemisphere in depth. In the second scenario, Modernity would have no specific meaning since it would only be the secularization of Christian spiritual and moral content. I therefore propose to abandon this approach in favour of the noun *Modernity* followed by a hyphen with the other noun *Christianity*. By this choice, it will be a question of verifying, on the one hand, how Modernity carries, in its case of political application, a break with the very idea of religion (and especially with Christianity), as the collective structuring of European societies. It will be a question of verifying, on the other hand, how it is also linked with Christianity. It should be added that if Modernity owes a debt to Christianity, Christianity has not been without being reconfigured by the ideals of Modernity. This is why the very heart of my work will be to propose criteria for defining what it is now agreed to designate by *Modernity*. But do these criteria justify the classic theorems of secularization (Max Weber, Carl Schmitt, Karl Löwith ...), or do they not rather call for a whole other theorem already announced by that of *interpretative circles?* Thanks to these definition criteria, the impact of the denominational plurality of Christianity on the constitution of political Modernity can be assessed as a consequence. Finally, these criteria will shed light at the end of this work on what makes the difference between classical Modernity and Neo-modernity (a substantive that I prefer to post-modernity). But the first question that should be borne in mind is whether Modernity, independently of its political side, designates only an era or is it also a normative philosophical truth that has unfolded over a long historical temporality? This first question is at the heart of the interpretative circles that I propose.

I Modernity: Between historical epochs and normative philosophical truth

To answer this question, we must first ask two preliminary questions: the first is of a chronological nature, and the second, more subtle, is to know if it is declined from its beginning in the singular or on the contrary in the plural. With regard to the first question, it calls for no more precise an answer than to claim to date the end of Antiquity and the Middle Ages, then the beginning of modern times, with exactitude. The chronology is useful for giving benchmarks, but it always risks being reductive by essentializing the eras by designations that are, moreover, very relative. This is the case with the *Middle Ages,* long considered an era of religious obscurantism. For this reason, it would be by definition the perfect antithesis of Modernity. It will be a good reason to stop at the Middle Ages because this long period is in fact the ideal historical framework to account for the genesis of Modernity. I say *genesis* and not *birth,* in other words Modernity is procedural before being *an* era born at a precise moment in history. I will come back to this question in more detail in connection with the historiographical stakes raised by a philosophical-political definition of Modernity. Correlatively to the historiographical issue, I come to the question of the naming of Modernity. Although it is a process, nothing as such prohibits speaking of *the* Modernity as a global human phenomenon animated by the guiding idea of renouncing any religious structuring of the political condition. But the definite personal pronoun is the tree that hides the forest of a multiplicity of meanings. The origin of the noun *Modernity* probably comes from the literary and artistic circles of the first half of the nineteenth century.[1] And so it was only during the twentieth century (and it seems to me in the second half) that the noun *Modernity* was adopted in the philosophical, theological milieu and in the human and social sciences, to the point of now belonging to the lexical field of anyone endowed with a general culture. And that is the problem. When a word is part of the *koiné* of the daily language of an era, the false evidence of its meaning is the very proof that it is seriously lacking in the criteria for defining it in order to know what we are talking about and what it designates. *Modernity* being one of them, at the risk of appearing presumptuous, my ambition is to provide some clarifications on this false evidence that is *Modernity*. It will be understood, *to see clearly* is already to recognize that there cannot be a chronological moment determined in an unequivocal way. In other words, there is no *birth* of Modernity, but a *genesis* which itself unfolds in several spheres of human existence (astronomical, geographical, political, religious, artistic). What will appear obvious to many, nevertheless, constitutes a useful methodological detour because it has fundamental consequences in the relationship (or correlation) between political modernity and Christianity. First of all, Modernity is more than an era as it crosses several. Christianity is nodal in its interpretative function of Modernity to such an extent that the latter cannot be explained without certain topical modalities of Christianity. Consequently, can we leave Modernity as we leave one era among others? The European-Western world has undeniably come out of classical Modernity, that which extends from the sixteenth to the twentieth century, and which should moreover be subdivided. But have we left Modernity as such? It is difficult to think so, as evidenced by the use of notions that are more approximate than rigorous such as post-modernity, ultra-modernity, the rarer is that of neo-modernity.[2] So many syntagms to express the exit from classical Modernity and at the same time the impossibility of leaving Modernity as a way of inhabiting and structuring the world outside of all politico-religious norms. To define itself, if Modernity does not therefore avoid being classified into epochs (or else it would be outside history, which would be absurd), it is nevertheless not reduced to a single regime of historical temporality. Because it travels, this notion is therefore of great flexibility in its mode of historical expression, while being in reality constraining in its philosophical truth because of its normative ambition. Hence the importance of the criteria for defining Modernity. To achieve this, it is from its opposite that it is necessary to proceed, namely Christianity in its late medieval period.

II Political Modernity-Christianity: A philosophical interpretation (Hans Blumenberg) and an anthropological interpretation (Louis Dumont)

1 Political modernity through a certain type of Christianity: An interpretative circle of the end of the Middle Ages

Choosing to propose criteria for defining political Modernity starting from the end of the Middle Ages amounts to considering that Modernity is a regime of historical temporality which could not have arisen outside of its opposite, which is the late medieval Christianity. Conversely, it becomes by way of return possible to consider that medieval Christianity would not have been completed if it had not produced its opposite. It is through this interpretative circle that criteria for defining political Modernity can be developed, which simultaneously allow the development of those that define this *Middle Age* of European-Western history. The founding act of the Political Modernity-Christianity link was played out in this crucial moment of the fourteenth and fifteenth centuries. The mirror effect that occurs between Christianity, in its multiple theological, political, legal, economic and artistic dimensions, and Modernity, is what can just as much authorize the theorems of secularization, to paraphrase the philosopher Blumenberg, as it can challenge them by appealing to what Blumenberg considered to be *The legitimacy of modern times* (that is to say, for him Modernity and not just an era).[3]

2 The philosophical interpretation of Hans Blumenberg: The legitimacy of modern times

According to Blumenberg, if we follow the theorems of secularization, Modernity is defined as being the secularization of theological categories specific to Christianity which have become worldly. From extra-mundane, the salvation of man is now realized on earth.[4] Modernity thus understood is therefore only accomplished Christianity[5] and because it is accomplished, it therefore no longer has any reason to exist in the historical form of the Church that the Middle Ages knew in particular. Modernity is in this perspective only the earthly eschatology of Christianity, which implicitly strikes it with a strong theological coefficient. Consequently, Modernity has no legitimacy apart from its Christian references. By this interpretation of the mirror effect produced by the theorems of secularization, confusion inevitably arises between what pertains to the proper good of Christianity and what pertains to the proper good of Modernity:

> On the contrary, however, we must consider the theorem of secularization as a mediately theological use of the difficulties that have historically appeared during the philosophical attempt to found a beginning of modern Times ... But modernity resorts less to what is given to it here than opposes it and responds to its challenge. This difference ... makes secularity the characteristic feature of modernity without it necessarily being the result of secularizations.[6]

On the other hand, if, as Blumenberg thought, Modernity has its legitimacy, the mirror effect with the end of the Middle Ages takes on a completely different meaning. It is only a certain type of Christianity that has produced Modernity, that of the theological absolutism of William of Ockham, and another that has been dismissed, that of Thomasian scholasticism. For Blumenberg, the nodal moment of the modern crisis and rupture was that of the doctrine of the *potentia absoluta Dei*. The reversal of this doctrine into a capacity for man to dispose of himself is therefore the paradoxical consequence of the 'theological absolutism' of nominalism. This has its counterpart in the process of 'human self-affirmation'. This transformation into its opposite of theological absolutism was made possible by the crisis of the scholastic conception of theology, the latter being disqualified in its function of 'science', capable of articulating human intelligence to faith. This crisis had two consequences: on the one hand, the impossibility of pursuing the rational understanding between the Greek conception of the cosmos (the hierarchical organization of the terrestrial order whose keystone is God) with the theological understanding of creation and salvation through Christianity; on the other hand, by virtue of this epistemological and metaphysical break, the autonomous deployment of scientific activity has been freed from all theological and teleological allegiance. These two consequences mean that the crisis of Thomasian scholasticism was decisive in the rise of Modernity, from nominalist theological absolutism to the[7] scientific and political revolutions of the seventeenth century, passing through the religious Reforms of the sixteenth century, marked by a certain form of nominalism. Hence the nodal importance for Blumenberg of the theological absolutism of William of Ockham to defeat the idea that Modernity is the fruit of the secularization of Christianity. If

Modernity has a *debt* to Christianity, it is in reality only to better oppose it in order to assert itself. What is true of the deployment of the autonomy of scientific activity is also true of that of the foundation of modern politics. Thus, theological absolutism paved the way for political absolutism. The expression 'lieutenant of God on earth' testifies to this. In analogy with divine omnipotence, this expression was first attributed to papal power, and then was transferred for the purposes of the cause of political sovereignty, to the absoluteness of monarchical power in the sixteenth and seventeenth centuries. Let us note that analogy, a highly prized concept in Thomasian thought, is the object of a change in metaphysical status. In the field of political theories, as is the case with Bodin, analogy must promote the sovereignty of the state. Thus sovereign power is a delegation of divine power.[8] The same is true with the natural laws in Hobbes, the content of which is in every way divergent with the analogy of the law in the theology of Saint Thomas.[9] Their task, however, is that of a function of framing the finality of the sovereign's field of action, like the natural law in the *Aquinas*. For Blumenberg, this meant that content identities and function identities should not be confused. For this reason, these two concepts are crucial for the legitimacy of Modernity. Contrary to the theorems of secularization, the distinction established between identity of content and function does not allow us to consider political absolutism as the secularization of divine omnipotence. The first is not foreign to its original theological substance, but it cannot be reduced to it, it is not just its secularized version ... By its self-affirmation, political absolutism has freed itself from its theological dependence and therefore fully belongs to the secular political sphere. The concept of sovereignty has acquired its own legitimacy. Let's summarize. If a certain type of Christianity (Ockhamism then nominalism) was the means by which Modernity was possible, this also means that it could not constitute itself. An apologetics of Modernity is therefore not possible. And on the side of Christianity, also against all apologetics, the end of the Middle Ages cannot be evaluated in its entirety as the historical phase heralding Modernity. Rather, the Middle Ages came to an end because Christianity was less and less homogeneous and could no longer be transmitted without generating another understanding of itself. The interpretative circle that I propose to make the relationship between political Modernity and Christianity intelligible is only possible on condition of renouncing any relationship of antecedence (not chronological) but in the status of interpretation. And because there is no relation of antecedence, there is, on the contrary, miscegenation: Modernity is at work within a certain type of Christianity (the theological absolutism of William of Ockham) and consequently gives it its founding configuration. Such is the mirror effect of secularity, which for Blumenberg was the opposite of secularization. If I made the choice to reverse the precedence in favour of the noun *Modernity* in order to counter with Blumenberg the theorems of secularization, it is also inversely to recognize that Modernity is the fruit of a work of Christianity on itself. This is why it is an interpretative circle establishing an inclusive relationship between a secular modality of being in the world and a Christian modality of being in the world. This interpretative circle is consequently the architectonic keystone of the criteria for defining political Modernity by Christianity. Four criteria are to be retained: the individual, freedom, equality and a common power by contract. In order to elucidate them, it is necessary to continue my genealogical investigation while passing from a philosophical interpretation to an anthropological interpretation, namely that of Louis Dumont. Wouldn't the modern individual, freedom, equality and common power by contract be conditioned by the Christian paradox of 'the individual-outside-the-world to the individual-in-the-world'?

3 The anthropological interpretation of Louis Dumont: From 'the individual-outside-the-world to the individual-in-the-world'

When Louis Dumont published his work *Essais sur l'individualisme. Une perspective anthropologique sur l'idéologie moderne*,[10] the French anthropologist had to his credit important works on the Indian world, the best-known work being *Homo hierachicus. Le système de castes et ses implications.*[11] The Indian anthropologist, specialist in a civilization structured by the hierarchy of castes, wondered about what he called *modern ideology*, a phenomenon very specific to the modern West. How was it able to move from a hierarchical and holistic social organization to an individualistic and egalitarian social organization? The absence of castes cannot explain everything. This is why Dumont strongly emphasized Christianity as a guiding thread with two central issues. The first is that of 'the individual-outside-the-world to the individual-in-the-world'. The second is that of the state. It is at the crossroads of the genesis of the individual and the State 'from the 13th century' that Dumont was interested as an anthropologist in the major determining role of the metaphysics of William of Ockham. It is the originality of his *Essais* to establish cross-cutting relationships between theology, metaphysics, history of ideas and political philosophy, with a view to highlighting an anthropology specific to modern Western civilization. What Dumont designated by *modern ideology* is none other than Modernity, to which he brought criteria of definition that distanced him, just as much as Blumenberg, from any theorem of secularization.[12] On the other hand, he deduced no consequence in terms of legitimacy or 'historical illegitimacy' of Modernity. But like Blumenberg, the theological absolutism of William of Ockham is central as a historical and metaphysical moment of the shift of the Christian world from 'the individual-outside-the-world' to the modern ideology of 'the individual-in-the-world'. Dumont's anthropological interpretation corroborates what I call the interpretive circle of Modernity through a certain type of Christianity. This Christianity was at the heart of a profound crisis of the universal in the fourteenth century to which it intended to respond: In Ockhamist metaphysics, it is impossible to designate secondary substances directly, as Thomas Aquinas thought.[13] Only the primary substances can be designated, hence the primacy of the singular over the universal. This results in a decisive consequence in the relationship to the law. The analogical theory of the law (Eternal, natural and positive law …) in Thomas Aquinas which supposes an objective and universal rational order no longer has any justification. It is replaced by the primacy of the 'absolute power' of God who knows only his own limit. In this voluntarist perspective 'The law … becomes in its totality the expression of the "power" or the will of the legislator … Moreover, while the law was conceived as a just (objective) relation between social beings, it becomes the recognition of the social power (*potestas*) of the individual'.[14] In this context of his demonstration, Dumont clearly highlights the correlation between the primacy of the omnipotence of God and that of the singular, both signifying the renunciation of a universal capable of being designated by secondary substances to the benefit of a universal elaborated by primary substances which are the double voluntarism of the omnipotence of God and that of the singular which Dumont designates a little too quickly by 'the individual'. This concept, on which Dumont insisted so much, must be understood as the consequence of the new modern anthropological ordering, namely the passage from the holistic conception of the social bond (*universitas*) to the individualistic one (*societas*):

> When there is nothing more ontologically real beyond the particular being ... this particular being becomes an individual in the modern sense of the term. An immediate corollary of transformation is the emphasis on the notion of 'power' (*potestas*) which appears as a modern functional equivalent of the traditional idea of order and hierarchy.[15]

To the notion of a hierarchical universal *ordo*, the Franciscan theologian opened the way to that of future political philosophies of the contract which only recognize individuals, free and equal by natural law and governed by a State (sovereign or executive power) wanted by themselves. The modern political concept of power is to Modernity ('modern ideology') what the hierarchy was to Christianity before William of Ockham. Voluntarism and Ockhamist singularism are undeniably at the heart of the interpretative circle of Modernity by a certain type of Christianity. But if the anthropologist Dumont converges with the philosopher Blumenberg on the nodal role of the Ockhamian moment, he nevertheless inscribed this moment within a dialectical process intrinsic to Christianity, namely the passage from 'the individual-outside-of-the-world' to 'the individual-in-the-world'. If with Ockham, Christianity radically reconfigured this dialectical relationship, there remains the need to know its pre-Ockhamian dynamic within Christianity. To this end, Dumont had to first define what opposed holistic social structuring and individualistic social structuring:

> Where the Individual is the supreme value I speak of *individualism*; in the opposite case, where the value is in society as a whole, I speak of *holism*. Basically, the problem of the origins of individualism is how, from the general type of holistic societies, a new type was able to develop which fundamentally contradicted the common conception. How was this transition possible, how can we conceive of a transition between two antithetical universes, these two irreconcilable ideologies.[16]

Unlike India,[17] it is this transition which was possible in the West that Dumont set himself the intellectual task of explaining *from* the Christian matrix of the 'individual-outside-the-world' which produced 'the individual-in-the-world':

> Is it possible to think that individualism began like this in the West? This is precisely what I am going to try to show; ... There is no doubt about the fundamental conception of man born of the teaching of Christ: as Troeltsch said, man is an *individual-in-relation-to-God*, meaning, for our use, an essentially out-of-the-world individual.[18]

Following in the footsteps of Troeltsch, Dumont could conceive of the specifically Christian conception of 'the individual-outside-the-world'. The paradoxical dynamic that it generated through the centuries of Christianity first devalued the world in the name of its privileged relationship with God through Christ, to invest it better to the point of generating 'the individual-in-the-world' which turned against Christianity. Let us briefly examine the stages of this paradoxical dynamic. First of all, this devaluation of the world is so intrinsic to Christianity that it was expressed from the primitive Church[19] by the eschatological awareness of the imminent end of time. This depreciation was continued by the 'individual-outside-the-world' of the monastic type (which reinvested the world through the economy) and the rise in power of the hierarchical dualism of spiritual and temporal powers[20] which only made explicit in its political meaning the Christian paradox of the 'individual-outside-the-world' engendering 'the individual-in-the-world':

> Then, in the eighth century, a dramatic change occurred. By a historic decision, the popes severed their link with Byzantium and assumed temporal power in the West ... The Church then claimed to rule, directly or indirectly, over the world, which meant that the Christian individual was now engaged in the world to an unprecedented degree.[21]

Finally, the last stage, absolutely decisive for Dumont, before entering the era of the political philosophies of the contract was: Calvin's Reformation. This brought the accomplished Christian version of the individualism of 'the individual-outside-the-world' engendering 'the individual-in-the-world'. The reason is that, for the anthropologist, Calvin radicalized the heterogeneity of Christianity in the world, no longer through mediating institutions as practised by the medieval Church, then by Catholicism resulting from the Council of Trent (monasticism, active religious life), but centring it on 'the will of the individual'.[22] By this very fact, Calvinism allowed for the passage from the Christian version of the 'individual-outside-the-world' to the modern version of the 'individual-in-the-world'.[23] Dumont drew from this all the necessary anthropological consequences in the passage from a traditional holistic society to a modern individualistic society:

> There is therefore a greater continuity between the two types of individualism than we had supposed at the beginning, with this consequence that a hypothetical direct transition from traditional holism to modern individualism no longer appears to us as improbable, but as impossible.[24]

After Ockhamian singularism, Calvinian individualism corroborated the idea that modern individualism would not have been possible without this double theological filiation of Christianity. For Dumont, it was through the channel of a certain type of Christianity that 'the individual-in-the-world' was able to unfold. But this Christianity of the singular, then of the individual, was able to constitute itself only in relationship and reaction to the medieval fact – Church: 'It is clear that, until the Reformation, the Church had been the great agent of transformation that we are studying, a kind of active mediator between the individual-outside – the-world and the world, that is to say society and in particular the Empire or the State'.[25] This other Christianity, in opposition to which the primacy of the singular and then of the individual could be generated, is that of Catholic institutionalism without which the corollary of the individual that is the State would not exist. Dumont does not resort to this notion of institutionalism and even less to the dialectic of 'institution-outside-the-world' (the Church) to 'institution-in-the-world' (the State), symmetrical to the individual ... However, these two Christianities constitute the theological-political matrix of the exit from the holistic social structuring, an exit thanks to which the modern version of the 'individual-in-the-world' has been possible. By this anthropological (or rather anthropological-theological) interpretation, Dumont dismissed the thesis of self-empowered Modernity, to paraphrase Blumenberg, but as I have already underlined, he also dismissed the thesis of the theorem of secularization in favour of an anthropological interpretation of Modernity, as much through the Christianity of the individual-framework as that of the institution – *plenitudo potestatis* – State one. We will recognize, once again, that of William of Ockham, the theologian through whom the genesis of political Modernity was possible by the criteria which define it: the individual as heir to the singular ockhamist, the sovereignty of the State as heir to the Omnipotence of God, freedom and equality being the corollary of the individual antithesis of a hierarchical conception of the universal. But if the anthropologist Dumont, like the philosopher Blumenberg, recognized the Ockhamian moment as the key moment which tilted Christianity towards Modernity ('The modern ideology'), he stood out from it in that he was primarily interested in the Christian matrix of the 'individual-outside-the-world' as the condition of the theological possibility of the 'individual-in-the-world'. This matrix at work in Ockham's metaphysics was all the more so in Calvin's Reformed theology. This means that from the fourteenth to the sixteenth centuries, Christianity swung historic Christianity from a holistic structure (*universitas*) to an individualist structure (*societas*) of the socio-political organization.[26] The genesis of 'the individual-in-the-world' and that of the State proceeded from the same freedom from a holistic conception of the social bond. The individual, with what it entails in terms of freedom and equality, and the State are indeed the epicentre of a definition of Modernity.

4 The genesis of the individual and the state: The historiographic stake of an interpretative circle of the sixteenth century

Following the philosophical and anthropological interpretations of Blumenberg and Dumont, the Protestant Reformation posed a real historiographic challenge for the history of Christianity, and with it, in the relationship that *modern Europe* maintained with Christianity. Asking the question in these terms is tantamount to distancing oneself from an essentialist approach declining 'the' Protestantism in the singular, the latter being moreover presented as the 'cause' or 'origin' of political or economic Modernity.[27] This causal approach is encouraged by the chronological division that we know: Antiquity, Middle Ages, Renaissance, modern times or Age of Enlightenment. This division creates a blind spot which underestimates the considerable changes at work between the fourteenth and sixteenth centuries. Luther was, for this historiographical reason, the most important Reformer. Because the first of them, he was at the junction of medieval heritage (and even of Christian antiquity with the Augustinian heritage) and modernity in the process of affirmation. From Luther, the notion of 'reform' took on a capital 'R', which corroborates by this other historiographical model, the philosophical and anthropological interpretations of Blumenberg and Dumont. This other historiographical model makes it possible to evaluate the 'continuous' reformist tropism in the West since the fourteenth century and, at the same time, the historical break established from the beginning of the sixteenth century. In the light of these continuities and ruptures, the historical division could be redefined over a long period extending from the eleventh century with the Gregorian reform until the eighteenth century,[28] passing through the rise in power of the Roman pontificate in the thirteenth century and its contestation by the pre-reform movements of the fourteenth century, in which Jan Hus, John Wycliffe, Marsilius of Padua and William of Ockham took part. In other words, these pre-reform centuries saw the genesis of two Modernities in tension, but also correlative: that of the individual and that of the State. This is the reason why the unity of this period is characterized by the very polysemous meaning of the notion of 'reform'.[29] By this proposed division, it is not a question of contesting the originality of the Protestant Reformation by absorbing it into a vast whole, but on the contrary of situating the decisive rupture which it operated, from within a dynamic inherent in Christianity.[30] A Dynamic, whose common feature is the constantly ambivalent relationship that Christianity has maintained since its primitive moment with the political powers. This ambivalent relationship is determined, following the event of the Incarnation, by a specifically Christian institutional fact, that of the Church. Always vis-à-vis the political power (imperial, royal, etc.), the Church was faced with a dilemma: either to free itself from it for its own freedom by reinforcing its hierarchical structure (Reform of Gregory VII for the *libertas ecclesiae* in relation to the Germanic Empire: *Dictatus papae*[31]), or conversely to free itself from the weight of its hierarchy which compromised its fidelity to the Gospel and to the primitive Church (pre-reforms of the fourteenth century and Protestant Reformation). According to this other reformist logic, the emphasis is placed on Christian freedom, which paradoxically allowed for the rise in power of the individual and of the State, as Dumont clearly explained by his anthropological interpretation. The historiographical issue is therefore capital because it has an impact on the role played by the various types of Christianity in the sixteenth century in the rise of the individual and the State. Modernity by the Lutheran-Calvinist individual, Modernity by the Lutheran (*Obrigkeit*: authority), Anglican and Catholic-Gallican temporal reign. It should be noted that these two sides of modernity by the individual and the state have undeniable denominational ties, but these are complex enough not to reduce them to a binary denominational typology. This is why Protestant Modernity cannot be opposed to Catholic[32] *anti-modernity* via the Median Modernity of the Anglican Church. The Protestant Reformation could not be reduced to the primacy of the individual over the State, as was clearly the case with Luther. Conversely, Catholicism cannot be reduced to the primacy of the State over the individual (royal Gallicanism) and that of the Roman Church over the State (Cardinal Bellarmine's doctrine of the pope's indirect temporal power). Consequently, after the metaphysical rupture introduced by Ockham, the interpretative circle accounting for Modernity through a certain type of Christianity (the omnipotence of God and the singular) becomes more complex due to the diversity of Christianity. From the sixteenth century, Modernity entered a second phase. After its speculative Ockhamist foundation, it became operational on a theological-ecclesiological register with the Protestant and Catholic Reforms. And within these reforms of very opposite types, the fact 'national Church' asserted itself with the Anglican Church and the Gallican Church. The operational theological-ecclesiological register of Modernity therefore took on a political dimension. Following it in the seventeenth century, the four criteria for defining the foundations of political Modernity, namely the individual, freedom, equality and common power by contract, then entered fully into their philosophical meaning to implement the autonomy of modern political rationality.

III Christianity at grips with the philosophical criteria of Modernity: The inversion of the interpretative circle of the fourteenth to sixteenth centuries

1 The political revolution of contract theories: What future for Christianity?

If Blumenberg shed essential light on a philosophy of the *legitimacy* of Modernity which was neither self-empowered nor a simple secularization of Christianity, if Dumont accounted through anthropology for the theological conditions for the realization of 'modern ideology', it is now necessary to verify this in the political philosophies of the contract of the seventeenth and eighteenth centuries. Although political contractualism was formulated in very specific terms in Hobbes, Spinoza, Locke and Rousseau, it nevertheless espoused the common schema of a contract by which individuals pass from the state of nature to the state of politics in the form of the sovereignty of the State (Hobbes and Spinoza), of the people (Rousseau) or of a legislative and executive power (Locke). Through this common framework, these four political philosophers were thus able to think about the foundations of modern politics independently of Christianity. It is by virtue of this autonomy that the criteria which define political Modernity reached their philosophical maturity: individual, freedom, equality in the state of nature found their extension in the political state. But in this new secular configuration of autonomy, what became of Christianity? Contrary to a prejudice (probably specific to French history), political Modernity neutralized the monopoly of the Churches much more than it dismissed Christianity as such. It was even reclassified within the contract which could not stand on its own. The paradox of a political society based on a contract is that it needs what it has separated itself from: religion. It must therefore both free itself from society's foundation in God while calling for a Christianity that can be *assimilated* to the contract that allows society to hold together thanks to a common belief. This is why Hobbes thought of the Republic as a Christian Republic under the aegis of the sovereign-Leviathan; Spinoza thought of the right to sacred things (*Jus circa sacra*) also under the aegis of the sovereign; Locke appealed to a *commonwealth* in which each contracting party was free in his way of believing, but was not free not to believe; Rousseau, more radical than his three predecessors, denied Christianity any ability to be a civil religion, which is why he proposed his own. To paraphrase Max Weber, and closer to us, Marcel Gauchet, the disenchantment of the world that occurred in this great revolutionary century, the seventeenth century, did not lead to the end of Christianity, but rather to that of the historic Christianity of Christendom. With the political philosophies of the contract, Christianity was bound to reinvent itself according to the criteria for defining Modernity. It had therefore to reconcile its status as a religion of salvation with the free and equal individual, obeying a common power. This common power was that of the society built by men and for men with no other end than the earthly one. If Christianity of Christendom was definitively extinct, apart from its perennial heritage (Churches, cathedrals, …), Christianity nevertheless had a future, but on the condition of becoming *modern*. Hence the reversal of the interpretative circle of the fourteenth to sixteenth centuries: Whereas Modernity had been realized in its foundations by a certain type of Christianity, it was now up to Christianity to be realized by a certain type of Modernity.

2 The authority of history in Benjamin Constant: What new relevance of Christianity?

If Christianity had a future within the political philosophies of contract, it is essentially as morality or as the basis of moral obligation (Locke). But the experience of the French Revolution showed the impossibility of reconciling Christianity (Catholicism) with revolutionary contractualism. More attractive is the political philosophy of Hegel which offered Christianity, through the mediation of the State, to accomplish history. But this other path turned Christianity into atheism through the Marxist criticism of religion. More relevant was the positive function of religious sentiment, the best ally of liberal states, as the liberal thinker Benjamin Constant expounded. The advent of the modern world translated for him into a historic break between the freedom of the Moderns and that of the Ancients.[33] A rupture that he designated by 'the authority of history'. It is within this rupture that Constant's theory of religious feeling found its place as the source of the freedom of the Moderns. Belonging to what is intimate to man, religious feeling was the ally of individual freedom, with all the political consequences that result from it for Constant.[34] But the religious feeling manifested itself in human history by religious forms which Constant distinguished into sacerdotal and non-sacerdotal types. Corresponding much better to the requirements of modern freedom and equality by the non-existence of a priestly hierarchy, the second type was favoured by the liberal thinker:

> By studying all the epochs when the religious feeling triumphed, we see everywhere that freedom was its companion … the first Christians resuscitated the noble doctrines of equality and fraternity among all men … Protestantism preserved Germany, under Charles V, from the universal monarchy. Current England owes it its constitution.[35]

The third criterion that allowed religious feeling to bring a guarantee to freedom was quite naturally the separation of State and Church. Because of these three criteria, religious feeling, non-priestly form and the separation of State and Church, the constantian *via moderna* was that by which Christianity had a future. If the interpretive circle now turned to the advantage of Modernity, the constantian approach to religions inserted non-priestly Christianity within the movement of modern freedoms (the authority of history) and allowed it not to be reduced to a single function of social utility within a political contract, or even to have to occupy a teleological function of intramundane history. Free from any political allegiance, it was by way of return a factor of freedom. Modernity through a certain type of Christianity had imposed its trademark. It was therefore not just a simple secularization of the Christian theological substance. For its part, although emerging from Christendom, Christianity itself had not lost its specificity by being a vector of transcendence within the framework of very immanent political regimes. But as theoretically attractive as this new interpretative circle may be, calling for the future of a certain form of Christianity (and more broadly of non-priestly religions) through a certain type of Modernity, the reality was quite different. The criteria that defined the foundations of political Modernity could turn against themselves. A historical moment attests to this: that of totalitarianism.

IV Political Modernity against itself: The subversion of the interpretative circle of the seventeenth to eighteenth centuries

1 Political Modernity in the age of totalitarianism

The totalitarianisms of the twentieth century have been the subject of numerous studies after the fall of Nazism, Hannah Arendt, being certainly the finest analyst of this unprecedented political phenomenon in the history of humanity.[36] It was its novel character that rightly suggests that it was the *product* of Modernity. To use the language of Dumont, holistic conceptions of the social bond had experienced tyranny, but they had never engendered the two forms of totalitarianism that are Nazism and Communism. They are paradoxically the inverted image of individualistic societies by their refusal of the *normative version* of political Modernity that are liberal democracies. They are therefore the dissident version. Instead of the individual, of freedom, of equality in law and of a common power at the service of all, totalitarianisms prefer power as encompassing domination with what that implies as *going beyond* the individual, to the benefit of the organic and hierarchical unity of the *total* political community. It is this aspiration for the unity of the whole that has led to the analysis of totalitarianisms through the prism of the return of religion, but an eminently political[37] (Eric Voegelin) and therefore secular (Raymond Aron) religion. What can such oxymorons mean if not that the totalitarian phenomenon is in reality, on the one hand, the expression of the unfinished process of the foundations of political Modernity, and on the other hand, the expression of the destabilization of Christianity by this same Modernity which nevertheless issued from it. In this hybrid context, the conjunction of the two facilitated the advent of the hybrid system of totalitarian beliefs. Because Nazism and Communism are ideologies with intramundane realization, they are fully part of modern secularity (and not of simple secularizations of Christian substance), amply freed from Christianity. But Nazism and Communism also belong to an ancient religious world, pre-Christian (return to a cosmic and hierarchical unity) and post-Christian because of their neopagan or atheist emancipation from Christianity. This is what made Voegelin and Aron say that totalitarianisms were political (Nazism) or secular (communism) religions. These two syntagms, in the form of an oxymoron, perfectly illustrate the hybridity of these two totalitarianisms with regard to the epicentre of the foundations of *the* political Modernity, namely democracy and liberalism, which are the two faces of the political regime resulting from the individual and from the modern State, without which there is neither liberty nor equality *in law*. Nazi and Communist totalitarianisms were the first experience of shaking *normative* political Modernity. Largely relieved of the heritage of the Christian symbolic apparatus (dogmatic theology, Church, liturgy, etc.), the paradox of this moment of political Modernity is that it was sufficiently freed from Christianity to exist by itself, but that at the same time it still needs heteronomous references that liberal democracy does not provide and that post-Christian Christianity can no longer provide. Hence its attempt to remedy this by creating political theologies that should not be confused with political religions.

2 Twentieth-century political theologies: Powerless attempts to rehabilitate a new interpretive circle

The first designer, Carl Schmitt, is the typical case of the thinker who attempted to reinstate Christianity (in its Catholic form) by challenging the capacity of liberal democracy to be truly democratic. This radical conservative opposition to the philosophical presuppositions of liberal-bourgeois democracy, through recourse to a theological-political conceptuality, reappeared in the 1970s through the intervention of left-wing political theology. It is appropriate to retain three essential remarks on these two currents of thought of political theology. On the one hand, whether conservative or progressive, it did not aim to establish a new Christian society, but rather to develop theological concepts bearing another conception of democracy (Schmitt) or another conception of a just society (Metz). These two types of political theology also had as a common struggle the refusal of the loss of political meaning of Christianity engendered by liberal democracy.[38] A second remark follows from this: political theology is a modern creation which seeks to bring another configuration to political Modernity, which greatly opposes it to what was the revolutionary project of political or secular religions in complete rupture with the Christian referent.[39] Finally, as a third remark, with their claims to Christianity (notably Catholic), the political theologies of both the right and left participated, on the contrary, in a new implementation of the interpretative circle Political Modernity-Christianity stemming from the end of the Middle Ages. But too deeply linked to the tensions inherent in the Christianity of that time, this interpretative circle could be renewed: The theological-political mimicry State-Nation-Church (if we take at least the English and French scenarios) has not been more operative since the nineteenth century. Hence the impossibility for a conservative political theology to open anew the doors of history to Christianity. But progressive political theologies have shown little more promise because they are too locked into a logic of protest against the modern liberal-democratic order. Restoring to Christianity its driving force which would make it enter history again inevitably requires being able to inject new meaning into political Modernity. In other words, how could it get out of the dilemmas in which political Modernity finds itself after the totalitarian experiences? This will give meaning to my conclusion.

Conclusion

I have proposed from a philosophical model, that of Hans Blumenberg, and an anthropological model, that of Louis Dumont, a first interpretative circle making it possible to make political Modernity intelligible in the light of a certain type of Christianity: in the fourteenth century, that of Ockhamian theological absolutism, and in the wake of the Protestant Reformation of the sixteenth century, in particular the Reform of Calvin. Converging on this point with Blumenberg, this first interpretative circle rejects any theorem of the secularization of Christianity to define Modernity. Consequently, it does not aim to promote an apologetics of Christianity, but to assert the theological conditions of the genesis of political Modernity. This was defined around the four most decisive criteria: the individual, freedom, equality and common power (state sovereignty or executive power). The result is a second interpretative circle, which turns against the previous one to the benefit of the nascent Modernity. Hence the importance of the historiographical issue which involves another chronological breakdown. But rejecting the theorems of secularization does not amount to endorsing Blumenberg's thesis according to which Modernity could be legitimate. If Modernity undeniably has its specific structure of intelligibility, while being linked to a certain type of Christianity which has allowed for its own understanding of the political condition, the concept of legitimacy does not have any justification. It even seems contradictory to define Modernity in terms of the concept of legitimacy, a concept that belongs to an age that is far too theological to have any relevance for this philosophical-political regime that calls for autonomy and legality. The anthropological model of Louis Dumont is for this reason very fruitful. If the individual is a central criterion of political modernity, it can only oppose the holistic structuring of the premodern social bond. The question is therefore not to seek to legitimize a philosophical-political regime, that for Dumont, of 'modern ideology', but to account through this interpretative circle, for the passage of the primacy of the whole over the parts (holism) to the opposite primacy (individualism). Moreover, Modernity is so difficult to define in terms of legitimacy that it has itself produced its own contestation through the unprecedented advent of totalitarianism. Whether they are qualified as political or secular religions, they undeniably express the attempt to rediscover the primacy of the holistic social structuring over the individualistic one. The attempt was certainly a failure, but it nonetheless radicalized the inversion of the interpretative circle of the fourteenth to sixteenth centuries with the philosophical foundations of modern politics. But by *radicalized inversion*, we must understand that totalitarianisms have subverted the raison d'être of the interpretative circle of the seventeenth and eighteenth centuries. They even constitute a double subversion: on the one hand, that of the founding principles of Modernity, on the other hand, that of Christianity. In other words, by leaving the definitional frameworks of normative Modernity, totalitarianisms have also disqualified the symbolic apparatus of Christianity to the point that the attempts of political theologies to put Christianity back on the path of history have been of no effect.

Within the framework of the conclusion of this work centred on the correlation Political Modernity-Christianity and its interpretative circles, it is not possible to propose a precise analysis of the consequences of this double subversion, but I would like briefly to draw attention to two confusions which post-totalitarian political Modernity has not resisted to the point of dragging Christianity into it: the confusion between heteronomy and transcendence, between autonomy and self-foundation. These two confusions are the two founding marks of the subversion of Modernity into neo-modernity, and of Christianity into neo-Christianity. In the first case, totalitarianisms have been producers of heteronomy (political or secular religions) within political Modernity whose purpose is exactly the opposite. The foundations of political modernity were therefore initially subverted in their project by the confusion between totalitarian heteronomy and what they come from: a critical relationship to Christian[40] *transcendence*. A Confusion which is not without consequence on what is meant by autonomy. This is precisely the whole problem of the second scenario: the liberal democracies of the post-totalitarian age have become, from the end of the 1960s, producers of self-foundation instead of autonomy; that is to say of an individual referred to himself and of a State providing rights. Neo-modernity came out of it as a caricature of Modernity. In this new context, Christianity must no longer ensure its future according to the requirements of the foundations of modern politics, but stick to social norms of which it is not the producer, either to contest them or to support them. It therefore no longer has to *dialogue* with Modernity, which is only the shadow of its former self. As much as Modernity could not ignore Christianity (the first two interpretative circles), for Neo-modernity historical Christianity is an obstacle unless it becomes neo … in turn. But does neo-modernity have a future? Probably little more than totalitarianisms … Can we get out of Modernity anyway? Since this concept is not linked to an era, it is more relevant to affirm that we can only emerge from a historical moment of Modernity, as has already been the case … and as it will be again with neo-modernity. As for emerging from Modernity as a normative philosophical truth that has freed humans from all politico-religious norms, such a hypothesis seems very inconceivable until proven otherwise. However, Modernity is not immune to these contestations, as I argued with totalitarianisms. Doesn't the guarantee of its durability still reside (at least in the European-Western sphere) in further elaborating the fruitfulness of a new interpretative circle with Christianity?

Notes

1. From a historical perspective, see Bernard Plongeron, *Histoire du Christianisme. Les défis de la modernité (1750–1840)* (Paris: Desclée), T. 10.
2. Yet it is the latter to which I shall resort.
3. Hans Blumenberg, *La Légitimité des temps modernes* (Paris: Nrf Editions, Gallimard, coll. 'Bibliothèque de philosophie', 1999).
4. Karl Löwith, *Histoire et Salut, les présupposés théologiques de la philosophie de l'histoire* (Paris: Nrf Gallimard, 2002).
5. About Hegel and the 'reconciliation of Christianity with modern-day society …': Jean-Claude Monod, *La querelle de la sécularisation de Hegel à Blumenberg* (Paris: Librairie Philosophique J. Vrin, 2002), 62.
6. Blumenberg, *La Légitimité des temps modernes*, 86.
7. Ibid., 168. Systemic comparison of the crises of Antiquity and the Middle Ages, see the pages from 156 to 201.
8. Jean Bodin, *Les Six livres de la République*, text revised by Christiane Frémont, Marie-Dominique Couzinet and Henri Rochais (Paris: Fayard, 1986), Book I, chap. X, 295.
9. See 'Critique du thomisme et construction de la loi naturelle chez Hobbes', in *Hobbes, Spinoza or the Politics of Speech*, edited under the supervision of Julie Saada (Lyon: ENS Editions, 2009), 63–91. See notably 'Les effets politiques de la transformation de la loi naturelle', 82–8. On the difficulty of interpreting the concept of substance, see Monod, *La querelle de la sécularisation*, 154–7.
10. Louis Dumont, *Essais sur l'individualisme. Une perspective anthropologique sur l'idéologie moderne* (Paris: Seuil, coll. Points Essais, 1991).
11. Louis Dumont, *Homo hierarchicus. Le système des castes et ses implications* (1967 Paris: Gallimard, 1975).
12. Moreover, Louis Dumont never resorted to this notion of secularization.
13. Hence the famous assertion of William of Ockham, during his controversy with the Pope, that there was no Franciscan order but Franciscans: Ibid., 86.
14. Ibid., 87.
15. Ibid., 88.
16. Ibid., 37.
17. On the comparison between the Indian and Christian 'renouncer': Ibid., 38.
18. Ibid., 39.
19. Ibid., 43–6.
20. Ibid., 69.
21. Ibid., 71. In this context of his *Essais*, Louis Dumont gives the impression of underestimating the importance of the Gregorian Reform of the eleventh century when he situated the rupture in the eighth century.
22. Ibid., 77.
23. Taking a distance from Troeltsch (to whom Dumont referred a lot) and Weber, Dumont preferred 'to speak of an ascetic intra-worldliness' in connection with 'the individual-in-the-world': Ibid., 75–6.
24. Ibid., 77.
25. Ibid., 80.
26. Ibid., 85.
27. Max Weber, *L'Ethique protestante et l'esprit du capitalisme suivi de Les sectes protestantes et l'esprit du capitalisme* (Paris: Plon, 1964), 103. What applied to the capitalist economy applied to the genesis of the modern state.

28 The year 1789 constituted a symbolic date with the beginning of the French Revolution.
29 There was nothing in common between the pontifical reform of Gregory VII and that of Luther. Yet it is the word 'reform' that is used, and in both cases for justified reasons.
30 Ernst Troeltsch, *Protestantisme et modernité*, translated from German and prefaced by Marc B. de Launay (Paris: Nrf Editions Gallimard, coll. 'Librairie des Sciences Humaines', 1991), 111.
31 In 1075, by the *Dictatus papae*, Pope Gregory VII proclaimed the bishop of Rome absolute sovereign of the Church. He also recognized his right to depose princes and bishops in the universal Church, to release subjects from the oath of fidelity and affirmed that he could not be judged by anyone.
32 If, by virtue of its hierarchical and top-down conception of power, Roman Catholicism does not meet the two criteria of modernity, namely freedom and equality, it has nonetheless amply contributed to the emancipation from feudal relations of dependence by the implementation, in the thirteenth century, of its specific concept of sovereignty, namely, the *Plenitudo potestatis*.
33 See Pierre Manent, *Les libéraux* (Paris, Gallimard, coll. 'tel', 2001, De la liberté des Anciens comparée à celle des Modernes), 438–61.
34 Benjamin Constant, *De la religion* in *Oeuvres complètes* (Berlin/Boston: De Gruyter, 2013), vol. 1, 138–9.
35 Ibid., 135–6.
36 Hannah Arendt, *The Origins of Totalitarianism* (New York: Schocken Books, 2004).
37 Eric Voegelin, *Les religions politiques* (Paris: Editions du Cerf, col. 'Humanités', 1988).
38 In Schmitt, the emphasis is on the superiority of Catholic representation over that of liberalism: Carl Schmitt, *La visibilité de l'Egl`ise, Catholicisme romain et forme politique, Donoso Cortés* (four essays), presented by Bernard Bourdin, *Carl Schmitt: quelle théologie politique?* (Paris: Editions du Cerf, coll. 'La nuit surveillée', 2011). For Metz, the focus is on the criticism of the privatization of faith: Jean-Baptiste Metz, *La foi dans l'histoire et la société* (Paris: Les Editions du Cerf, coll. 'Cogitation Fidei', 1979).
39 Schmitt is the typical case of this equivocation by his rallying to Nazism in 1933. His attempt to de-catholicize his thought was a failure and led to his disgrace by the dignitaries of the regime. Schmitt very quickly rediscovered the whole issue of political theology in Christianity at the end of the war.
40 The Christian-Germans under the Nazi regime are an example of this.

2

John Henry Newman, an anti-liberal?

Frédéric Libaud
Université de Strasbourg
Text translated from the French by Aude Attuel-Hallade and Cynthia Attuel

Introduction

On 12 May 1879, at the Palazzo della Pigna, in Rome, John Henry Newman (1801–90) received the *Biglietto* by which Pope Leo XIII (1810–1903) elevated him to the rank of Cardinal. At the heart of his response, the *Biglietto Speech*, Newman stated: 'For thirty, forty, fifty years I have resisted to the best of my powers the spirit of liberalism in religion.'[1] The enemy he fought throughout his life and in each of his works finally bore a name: that of liberalism in religion. But what did Newman mean by such a formula? Because we must recognize with Franck Lessay, that 'liberalism is not easily understood, defined, or "laid out" for the needs of historical or philosophical analysis.'[2] And in the British nineteenth century, the term 'liberalism' undoubtedly had a multitude of realities.

From the Oxford Movement, of which he was one of the main actors, with the many Tracts, including Tract 73 entitled 'On the Introduction of Rational Principles into Religion', to his Letter to the *Duke of Norfolk* (1875), in which he returned to the Syllabus (encyclical *Quanta Cura* of 8 December 1864) and to the papal infallibility affirmed by the First Vatican Council in the dogmatic constitution *Pastor Aeternus* of 18 July 1870, Newman did not indeed cease to oppose liberalism in religion. Referring to the encyclical letter of 1864, Newman said:

> No one mourns, for instance, more than I, over the state of Oxford, given up, alas! to 'liberalism and progress', to the forfeiture of her great medieval motto, 'Dominus illuminatio mea,' and with a consequent call on her to go to Parliament or the Heralds' College for a new one; but what can we do? All I know is, that Toryism, that is, loyalty to persons, 'springs immortal in the human breast'; that religion is a spiritual loyalty; and that Catholicity is the only divine form of religion. And thus, in centuries to come, there may be found out some way of uniting what is free in the new structure of society with what is authoritative in the old, without any base compromise with 'Progress' and 'Liberalism'.[3]

Liberal Catholicism and Catholic Liberalism are two notions with still vague contours, many defenders and detractors. In view of the context of the nineteenth century in which liberalism developed in various forms (economic, political, philosophical, …), it seems relevant to deepen this notion of 'liberalism in religion' denounced by Cardinal Newman. Understood in the form of an anti-dogmatic principle, liberalism in religion refers to the question of transcendence and its inherent truth, to the personal, intellectual and spiritual bond maintained by the believer with his God and to the sensitive question of freedom in religious matters and especially in its relationship to authority. All these aspects deserve to be developed at length, but that would take us far beyond the scope of our framework. Moreover, as Jean-Guy Saint-Arnaud explained in his thesis,[4] this liberalism in religion, in Newman's eyes, took on various faces, including that of rationalism or scepticism, both equally opposed by our thinker.

As we will develop in our presentation, the definition of liberalism in religion given by Newman at the time of his elevation to the cardinalate was the fruit of a lifetime of a struggle against a groundswell that was then sweeping through European intellectual society. This Newmanian conception of liberalism (I) has its deepest roots in his conversion of 1816 (II) and is deployed in particular in a specific form of this liberalism, namely the rationalism regularly denounced by Newman (III).

I The liberalism combated by Newman

After affirming that liberalism in religion was the object of his lifelong struggle, in the continuation of the speech delivered in 1879 at the *Biglietto* reception, John Henry Newman clarified his remarks:

> Liberalism in religion is the doctrine that there is no absolute truth in religion, but that one creed is worth another, and this is the teaching that is gaining every day in substance and strength. It does not admit that any religion can be considered true. It teaches that they must all be tolerated, because they are all matters of opinion, that revealed religion is not a truth, but a matter of feeling and taste, that it is neither an objective nor a miraculous fact, and that each person has the right to make it say only what strikes his imagination. Devotion is not necessarily based on faith. One can attend Protestant and Catholic churches, and profit from both, without belonging to either. One can exchange spiritual thoughts and feelings fraternally, without having the slightest project of common doctrine, nor without seeing the necessity of it. Therefore, since religion is such a personal and private matter, it should not at all be taken into account in human relationships. If a man dresses in a new religion every morning, what does it matter? It is as insolent to meddle with someone's religion as with the source of his income or the government of his family. Religion is in no sense the bond of society.[5]

In the whole of Newman's work, this is the most complete definition of liberalism in religion. In these lines, liberalism appears as the negation of a revealed religion and therefore as the refusal of any truth in matters of religion. It is presented as the leaven of a religious relativism, according to which all religions are equal; therefore, for liberalism, no truth exists, except what everyone considers true, except the truth that everyone forges. It is then the open door to religion *à la carte*, where everyone can believe in what suits him, adhering to this or that religious doctrine and rejecting this or that other aspect of religion. Newman strongly opposed such an approach to religion that called into question the very foundations of religion and its inherent truth. This is why he summed up the notion in a succinct and powerful formula: 'Liberalism is the anti-dogmatic principle.'[6]

Already in 1833, in Palermo, Newman had written a poem devoted to liberalism, in which these various elements are found:

Jehu destroyed Baal out of Israel. Howbeit from the sins of Jeroboam Jehu
departed not from after them, to wit, the golden calves that were in Bethel, and
that were in Dan.
YE cannot halve the Gospel of God's grace;
   Men of presumptuous heart! I know you well.
   Ye are of those who plan that we should
   dwell,
Each in his tranquil home and holy place;
Seeing the Word refines all natures rude,
And tames the stirrings of the multitude.

And ye have caught some echoes of its lore,
   As heralded amid the joyous choirs;
   Ye mark'd it spoke of peace, chastised
   desires,
Good-will and mercy, – and ye heard no more;
But, as for zeal and quick-eyed sanctity,
And the dread depths of grace, ye pass'd them by.
And so ye halve the Truth; for ye in heart,
   At best, are doubters whether it be true,
   The theme discarding, as unmeet for you,
Statesmen or Sages. O new-compass'd art
Of the ancient Foe! – but what, if it extends
O'er our own camp, and rules amid our friends?

Palermo. 5 June 1833[7]

In this poem we can clearly see Newman's reproach of liberalism, namely that of breaking the Truth in two, that is, of undermining the unity of faith and the Gospel message. Newman became aware of this theological attitude when he worked on the question of Arianism in the fourth century and it became clearly evident to him on the eve of his conversion to the Roman Catholic Church, when he wrote in his *Essay on the Development of Christian Doctrine* (1845):

That there is a truth then; that there is one truth; […] that the search for truth is not the gratification of curiosity; that its attainment has nothing of the excitement of a discovery; that the mind is below truth, not above it, and is bound, not to descant upon it, but to venerate it; that truth and falsehood are set before us for the trial of our hearts; that our choice is an awful giving forth of lots on which salvation or rejection is inscribed; that before all things it is necessary to hold the Catholic faith.[8]

Breaking the Truth is also breaking the divine unity; it leads to constituting a patchwork of God, taking this or that aspect of a divinity present in a religion and rejecting the unpleasant aspects not approved by the individual conscience. Thus, everything that can disturb, everything that may seem unpleasant or demanding in a defined religion is crushed by liberals. The defenders of liberalism in religion choose to retain from the biblical message only what suits them, only what is pleasing to their personal state of mind. And Newman was aware, as early as 1833, of the risk that liberalism would spread widely and also reach the most fervent believers, each ending up constituting a religion *à la carte* and according to his own aspirations. Now, faced with such a liberal option, Newman opposed divine Revelation, as expressed in the Bible, preserved by Tradition and expounded by the magisterial teaching of the Church. Truth is received as a single revealed gift in the face of which an attitude of humility is required. Does this mean that liberalism is inherently something bad? This is not the case. Newman acknowledged in the same speech the positive aspects of liberalism:

> [T]here is much in the liberalistic theory which is good and true; for example, not to say more, the precepts of justice, truthfulness, sobriety, self-command, benevolence, which, as I have already noted, are among its avowed principles, and the natural laws of society.[9]

Moreover, according to Owen Chadwick, Lord Acton himself recognized in Newman three aspects of the much-decried liberalism, this Newmanian liberalism being reflected in his attitude towards science and the temporal power and in his theological notion of 'dogmatic development'.[10] Furthermore, in his *Apologia pro vita sua* written in 1864, he cited the Count of Montalembert and Father Lacordaire as two models of Catholics using and defending the concept of liberalism in religion. But he hastened to point out that

> If I hesitate to adopt their language about Liberalism, I impute the necessity of such hesitation to some differences between us in the use of words or in the circumstances of country; and thus I reconcile myself to remaining faithful to my own conception of it, though I cannot have their voices to give force to mine.[11]

Thus, Newman's opposition to liberalism in religion was not a general and principled opposition. He contested liberalism in religion as he himself understood and defined it and as it presented itself in the English nineteenth century, aware that others may conceive of it in other ways and thereby find advantages in it.

However, we must be careful not to let Newman's status shift from that of an opponent of liberalism in religion to that of an advocate of conservatism in religion. The exclamation of Pope Leo XIII prevents us from doing so: 'My Cardinal! It was not easy, it was not easy. They said he was too liberal, but I was determined to honour the Church in honouring Newman. I always had a cult for him. I am proud that I was able to honour such a man.'[12] The whole life of the Oxford convert and his works such as The *Oxford University Sermons* (1843), *An Essay on the Development of Christian Doctrine* (1845), *The Idea of a University* (1852) and *A Letter Addressed to the Duke of Norfolk* (1875) make clear that Newman showed no conservatism in theology but was animated by an uninterrupted quest for truth perceived in its historical and dogmatic unity.

II At the source of Newmanian anti-liberalism

To fully understand Newman's anti-liberalism, it is necessary to delve into his personal history and refer, above all, to the experience lived in 1816. This conversion, recorded in the *Apologia pro vita sua*, is at the root of his spiritual and intellectual development:

> When I was fifteen, (in the autumn of 1816,) a great change of thought took place in me. I fell under the influences of a definite Creed, and received into my intellect impressions of dogma, which, through God's mercy, have never been effaced or obscured. [The doctrine of final perseverance] had some influence on my opinions, in the direction of those childish imaginations which I have already mentioned, viz. in isolating me from the objects which surrounded me, in confirming me in my mistrust of the reality of material phenomena, and making me rest in the thought of two and two only absolute and luminously self-evident beings, myself and my Creator[13]

To approach this episode in the childhood of the Oxford convert from a purely spiritual angle would be to ignore its theological implications. This conversion was undoubtedly marked, according to Olivier de Berranger's formula, by an 'imprint of dogma'[14] because, for Newman, dogma was not only a truth to be believed but above all God to be honoured.

The conversion of 1816 allowed Newman not only to become aware of the personal relationship he was called to maintain with God, who was now really a person for him, but also of the theological implications that flowed from it, as he himself made clear in the last chapter of his *Apologia*:

> Starting then with the being of a God, (which, as I have said, is as certain to me as the certainty of my own existence, though when I try to put the grounds of that certainty into logical shape I find a difficulty in doing so in mood and figure to my satisfaction,) I look out of myself into the world of men, and there I see a sight which fills me with unspeakable distress. The world seems simply to give the lie to that great truth, of which my whole being is so full; and the effect upon me is, in consequence, as a matter of necessity, as confusing as if it denied that I am in existence myself. If I looked into a mirror, and did not see my face, I should have the sort of feeling which actually comes upon me, when I look into this living

busy world, and see no reflection of its Creator. This is, to me, one of those great difficulties of this absolute primary truth, to which I referred just now. Were it not for this voice, speaking so clearly in my conscience and my heart, I should be an atheist, or a pantheist, or a polytheist when I looked into the world.[15]

This personal encounter with God is the foundation of all Newmanian theology and, in his view, should form the basis of all theology. In this, the conversion of 1816 undoubtedly has a dogmatic dimension: it is God as a personal God who revealed himself to him in all his uniqueness and truth. 'What makes the essence of John Henry Newman's conversion is the doctrinal character of a religious certainty; more than a consolation, the young man receives the shock of an addiction.'[16] Through these few lines appears clearly the link between Newman's spiritual experience and the dogmatic impact produced by this encounter on his mind. For him, the heart of every dogmatic principle was this personal relationship with God himself. We can affirm that what animated Newman throughout his lifetime was this personal relationship to divine transcendence, this intimacy with the living God. God is not merely an object of study, he is above all the subject of a personal encounter. In this, it is not possible to split God and adhere to this or that article of faith while neglecting others. This is why he repeats several times, as in response to liberalism in religion: 'Many a man will live and die upon a dogma: no man will be a martyr for a conclusion.'[17] Thus, the spiritual dimension and the intellectual dimension are inseparable in the person and thought of Newman.

The God encountered by John Henry Newman is the God of Christians, that is, the God who became incarnate in Jesus Christ and who, after thirty-three years of earthly life, died and rose again to bring salvation to mankind. Excluding this kerygma from any theological study inevitably led, according to Newman, to falling into liberalism in religion, as it constitutes the very heart of the Christian faith from which all theological reflection can be conducted. This then makes it possible to understand the general principles of theological liberalism, as identified by Newman and reported by Yearley: 'Nevertheless, Yearley identifies six characteristic principles in Newman's understanding of liberal religion: (1) human nature is good; (2) private judgment is obligatory; (3) deity is a principle discoverable through examination of evidence; (4) revelation is a manifestation not a mystery; (5) useful goods are primary; and (6) education is salvatory.'[18] These six principles enunciated by Yearley can be united in a single principle: liberalism in religion is characterized by the negation of divine transcendence and its active grace. If we have in mind the dogmas of the Catholic faith, we easily understand why Newman struggled all his life against such a liberalism which, by denying God, denied the sinful nature of man, omitted the great principles of the moral life, challenged the mystery of divine Revelation and denied the salvation obtained on the wood of the cross by the death of Christ. Such an intellectual approach led inexorably to a religious relativism, which Newman identified, in his *Biglietto Speech*, with liberalism in religion: 'Liberalism in religion is the doctrine that there is no absolute truth in religion, but that one creed is worth another, and this is the teaching that is gaining every day in substance and strength.'[19] This remark might seem surprising from a man who went from Anglicanism to Catholicism after having flirted with evangelicalism, if it were not for the fact that throughout his life John Henry Newman never ceased to seek the truth, and having found it, he defended it. 'For it is our plain duty to preach and defend the truth in a straightforward way.'[20]

While for many liberals, as we shall see, reason and science prevailed over faith, for Newman, the driving force of all theological reflection was the intimate knowledge of God, through a life of meditation on God's Word, prayer and sacraments. Setting aside Newman's spiritual dimension and his clerical state prevents us from accurately understanding Newman's life, his theological work and his relationship to liberalism in religion. It is in the unity of the human mystery that the unity of the mystery of God is found, as Newman evoked in his 1833 poem on liberalism, in which he reproached liberals for wanting to 'halve the Gospel of God's grace'.[21] However, his conversion in 1816 was not the only reason for his anti-liberalism in religion, even if it is, in our eyes, one of the essential and too often ignored factors, because it is his visceral attachment to God that prevented him from succumbing to the siren song of liberalism and that made him a fervent opponent. The fact of having frequented, at a crucial moment in his life, anti-liberals, such as John Keble or Hurrell Froude, and having nourished his prayer and his thought in the school of the Fathers of the Church also strengthened his apprehension of this phenomenon and supported him in his fight against this liberalism in religion.

III An example of this liberalism in religion: Rationalism

Although he was tempted on several occasions to embrace liberalism in religion, Newman was able to resist it each time. Aware of this personal tendency and the means of seduction used by this liberalism, he took a lucid look at it. Regularly in his writings, whether in the *Oxford University Sermons*, *The Idea of a University* and *The Grammar of Assent*, Newman returned repeatedly to a specific form of this liberalism, namely rationalism, constantly reflecting on the relationship between faith and reason.

In the note at the end of his *Apologia pro vita sua* on liberalism, Newman made the connection between liberalism in religion and rationalism. He warned against the false freedom of thought that gives the human being the presumptuous illusion of being able to address by reason alone any question, even religious. Man, a created being, has the pride to believe that he can make a personal judgement on God, his creator.

> Liberty of thought is in itself a good; but it gives an opening to false liberty. Now by Liberalism I mean false liberty of thought, or the exercise of thought upon matters, in which, from the constitution of the human mind, thought cannot be brought to any successful issue, and therefore is out of place. Among such matters are first principles of whatever kind; and of these the most sacred and momentous are especially to be reckoned the truths of Revelation. Liberalism then is the mistake of subjecting to human judgment those revealed doctrines which are in their nature beyond and independent of it, and of claiming to determine on intrinsic

grounds the truth and value of propositions which rest for their reception simply on the external authority of the Divine Word.[22]

'Rationalism is the great evil of the day.'[23] One of Newman's struggles against liberalism took the form of a struggle against rationalism in religion, which he defined as 'rationalism is the exercise of reason instead of faith in matters of faith'.[24] His study on *The Arians of the 4th Century* (1833) already confronted him with this intellectual grip of reason disconnected from faith:

> But far greater was the evil, when men destitute of religious seriousness and earnestness engaged in the like theological discussions, not with any definite ecclesiastical object, but as a mere trial of skill, or as a literary recreation; regardless of the mischief thus done to the simplicity of Christian morals, and the evil encouragement given to fallacious reasonings and skeptical views.[25]

Sensitized to rationalism by this study of the Arians, Newman approached contemporary theological discussions with a keen eye. Thus, in the *Essay on the Development of Christian Doctrine*, he denounced the tendency of certain theologians, including Ignaz von Döllinger in Germany or John William Colenso in England to name but two, to want to apply to theological questions a scientific approach inherited from the so-called hard sciences, consisting of a system of proofs and reasoning. 'To the extent that theology is a science, where it uses formal reasoning, a rigorous logical method, it always runs the risk of making reductions.'[26] Faced with this tendency, Newman favoured, in the words of Pope Benedict XVI, a 'theology on its knees',[27] that is, a theology steeped in a spiritual life nourished by meditation on the Word of God and by frequenting the sacraments.

Rationalism claims to believe that faith can be acquired, consolidated and discussed only by resorting to explicit reasoning and by applying the tools of the scientific approach. It therefore overlooks the fact that faith is the fruit of Revelation, and that it is received in Tradition and is nourished by meditation on the Scriptures. Rationalism believes that it can erase any supernatural dimension from the act of faith.

> Rationalism is a certain abuse of Reason; that is, a use of it for purposes for which it never was intended, and is unfitted. To rationalize in matters of Revelation is to make our reason the standard and measure of the doctrines revealed; to stipulate that those doctrines should be such as to carry with them their own justification; to reject them, if they come in collision with our existing opinions or habits of thought, or are with difficulty harmonized with our existing stock of knowledge. And thus a rationalistic spirit is the antagonist of Faith; for Faith is, in its very nature, the acceptance of what our reason cannot reach, simply and absolutely upon testimony.[28]

This in no way means that Newman evacuated any intellectual and reasoned approach to faith. On the contrary, when we go through his works, we discover how much the intellectual approach is present and how much his theological discourse is structured by always being enlightened by faith. In Tract 73, Newman already presented the essential role of reason in religious matters, but always subordinated it to revealed truth.

> As regards Revealed Truth, it is not Rationalism to set about to ascertain, by the exercise of reason, what things are attainable by reason, and what are not; nor, in the absence of an express Revelation, to inquire into the truths of Religion, as they come to us by nature; nor to determine what proofs are necessary for the acceptance of a Revelation, if it be given; nor to reject a Revelation on the plea of insufficient proof; nor, after recognizing it as divine, to investigate the meaning of its declarations, and to interpret its language; nor to use its doctrines, as far as they can be fairly used, in inquiring into its divinity; nor to compare and connect them with our previous knowledge, with a view of making them parts of a whole; nor to bring them into dependence on each other, to trace their mutual relations, and to pursue them to their legitimate issues. This is not Rationalism; but it is Rationalism to accept the Revelation, and then to explain it away; to speak of it as the Word of God, and to treat it as the word of man; to refuse to let it speak for itself; to claim to be told the *why* and the *how* of God's dealings with us, as therein described, and to assign to Him a motive and a scope of our own; to stumble at the partial knowledge which He may give us of them; to put aside what is obscure, as if it had not been said at all; to accept one half of what has been told us, and not the other half; to assume that the contents of Revelation are also its proof; to frame some gratuitous hypothesis about them, and then to garble, gloss, and colour them, to trim, clip, pare away, and twist them, in order to bring them into conformity with the idea to which we have subjected them.[29]

This makes it clear that Newman was not opposed to all reflection and study in religious matters. Quite the contrary. As he recalls in *The Idea of a University*, theology must be studied, not in opposition but, in connection with all known knowledge, in order to allow a mutual enrichment and to acquire 'a connected view or grasp of things'.[30] Indeed, according to him,

> I purposely take instances within and without the Catholic pale, when I would speak of the intellect as such, is one which takes a connected view of old and new, past and present, far and near, and which has an insight into the influence of all these, one on another; without which there is no whole, and no centre. It possesses the knowledge, not only of things, but also of their mutual and true relations; knowledge, not merely considered as acquirement, but as philosophy.[31]

The mystery of faith, studied by theology, does not belong only to the earthly world but constitutes an opening to the invisible world. This is the reason why it cannot be studied with human methods alone but must integrate the whole supernatural dimension. In this, reason can be a good means when it is accompanied and enlightened by faith.

Conclusion

As early as 1865, Newman asked: 'The vital question was how we were to keep the Church from being liberalized.'[32] All his life, in most of his writings, he worked, moved by a personal attachment to God, against liberalism in religion, defending the faith and the Church. At the same time, he always challenged theological discourse, summoning it to explain itself, in order to help it develop according to a rational method. The *Sermons*, the *Idea of a University* or *The Grammar of Assent* are proof of this. Driven by the constant quest for truth and supported by the teaching of Tradition, John Henry Newman was able to demonstrate innovations in theological matters. Think, for example, of the *Rambler*'s article published in July 1859 on 'Consulting the Faithful in Matters of Doctrine'.[33] This article caused him many setbacks and it took all the intelligence and discernment of Pope Leo XIII to succeed in removing the label of liberal that some, following this publication, had attributed to Newman. Thus, while demonstrating anti-liberalism in religion, Cardinal Newman always reflected his faith in order to elaborate a rational discourse on it.

As Pope Benedict XVI recalled at the Prayer Vigil for the Beatification of Cardinal John Henry Newman in Hyde Park on Saturday, 18 September 2010: 'Today, where intellectual and moral relativism threatens to undermine the very foundations of our society, Newman reminds us that, as men and women created in the image and likeness of God, we are made to know the truth, to find in this truth our ultimate freedom and the fulfilment of our deepest human aspirations. In a word, we are destined to know Christ, who is himself "the way, the truth and the life."'[34]

Notes

1. John Henry Newman, 'Biglietto Speech', in *Addresses to Cardinal Newman with His Replies* (London: Longmans, Green and Co., 1905). The works of John Henry Newman, from which the quotes are taken, can be found at www.newmanreader.org.
2. Franck Lessay, 'Regards sur le libéralisme', *Commentaire* 2, no. 6 (1979): 324.
3. Newman, *Lettre au Duc de Norfolk* (Paris: Desclée de Brouwer, 1970), 273.
4. J-G. Saint-Arnaud, *Newman et l'Incroyance* (Paris: éditions Desclée et Cie, 1972).
5. Newman, 'Biglietto Speech'.
6. Newman, *Apologia pro vita sua* (Note A, Ad Solem, 2003), 479.
7. Newman, *Prayers, Verses and Devotions* (Poem LXXXIII), 563.
8. J.H. Newman, *Essay on the Development of Christian Doctrine* (1845), 429.
9. Newman, 'Biglietto Speech'.
10. Owen Chadwick, 'Acton et Newman', *Etudes Newmaniennes*, no.11 (1995): 178–9.
11. Newman, *Apologia pro vita sua*, 480.
12. Newman, *The Letters and Diaries of John Henry Newman* (Oxford: Clarendon Press, 1976), tome XXIV, 426.
13. Newman, *Apologia pro vita sua*, 121.
14. O. Berranger, 'Conscience et infaillibilité dans l'*Apologia* de Newman', *Nouvelle Revue Théologique* 129, no. 2. (Béranger), (2007): 180.
15. Newman, *Apologia pro vita sua*, 424–5.

16 J. Honoured, *Itinéraire spirituel de Newman* (Paris: Seuil, 1963), 24.
17 Newman, 'The Tamworth Reading Room', in *Discussions and arguments on Various Subjects* (Leominster: Gracewing, 2004), 293. We find the same formula in *La Grammaire de l'Assentiment* (Ad Solem, 2010), 153. A similar formula is found in *Sermons Catholiques – La puissance de la grâce* (Paris: Cerf, 2019), 193: 'No one becomes a martyr for a conclusion, no one is a martyr for an opinion; It is faith that makes martyrs.'
18 M.C. Hawley, 'Newman's Immanent Critique of Liberalism: A Philosophical Argument against Liberal Hubris', *Philosophy and Theology* 1, no. 27 (2015): 192.
19 Newman, 'Biglietto Speech'.
20 'For it is our plain duty to preach and defend the truth in a straightforward way', J.H. Newman, *Discussions and Arguments* (III – Holy Scripture in its relation to the Catholic Creed), 1872.
21 Newman, *Prayers, Verses and Devotions* (n° LXXXIII – Liberalism) (San Francisco: Ignatius Press, 2000).
22 Newman, *Apologia*, 482–3.
23 Ibid., 300.
24 Newman, *Essay on the Development of Christian Doctrine*, 240.
25 Newman, *Les Ariens du quatrième siècle (Arians of the 4th Century)* (1833; Paris: Téqui, 1988), 48.
26 'Dans la mesure où la théologie est une science, où elle utilise des raisonnements formels, une méthode logique rigoureuse, elle encourt toujours le risque d'effectuer, elle aussi des réductions'. J.G. Saint-Arnaud, *Newman et l'incroyance* (Paris: Les éditions Desclée et Cie, 1972), 167.
27 Benedict XVI, Speech during the visit to Heiligenkreuz Abbey, 9 September 2007, http://www.vatican.va/content/benedict-xvi/fr/speeches/2007/september/documents/hf_ben xvi_spe_20070909_heiligenkreuz.html.
28 Newman, *Tracts for the Times* (Leominster: Gracewing, 2013), Tract no. 73.
29 Newman, *Tracts for the Times*.
30 Newman, *L'Idée d'Université (The Idea of a University)*, (Ad Solem, no.15 (2007)), 45.
31 Ibid., 6, 18.
32 Newman, *Apologia pro vita sua*, 164.
33 Newman, *Thoughts on the Church* (Paris: Cerf, 1956), 402–39.
34 Benedict XVI, *Trip to the United Kingdom, 16–19 September 2010* (Paris: Salvator, 2010), 99. (Jn 14:6).

3

Edmund Burke, T.B. Macaulay, Lord Acton and the French Revolution: The Church, the State and the individual

Aude Attuel-Hallade
CRICES (Institut Catholique d'Etudes Supérieures)
Centre d'Histoire du XIXe siècle (Sorbonne Université/Panthéon Sorbonne)

Introduction

For over a century, three eminent thinkers and/or historians sought to expound the British liberal model and set forth its political, religious and moral foundations. All heir to the whig history, tradition and culture, and probably the most prominent exponents of modern British liberal thought, they addressed 'the most astonishing [circumstance] that ha[d] hitherto happened in the world'[1] and devoted most of their political and historical careers to comprehending and apprehending it as part (or not) of civilization and of the history of humanity. From the *Reflections on the Revolution in France* (1790) to the *Lectures on the French Revolution* (1910), the French Revolution ignited a deep reflection on the conditions and perpetuation of liberty in modern liberal societies. Paving the way for the rise of radical claims and protests in Ireland, notably, while giving impetus to the intellectual tightening of the Pope from the 1850s after Pius IX recovered his papal states, the Revolution, the Napoleonic wars and the ensuing affirmation of the Nation-states in Europe following the Springtime of the People (1848) not only questioned the ties between territory, power and religion but also those that existed between the individual, religion and history. 'What does Mr Southey mean by saying that religion is demonstrably the basis of civil government,'[2] wondered T.B. Macaulay in the review he devoted to the *Colloquies* of Robert Southey, one of Edmund Burke's disciples, in the 1830s. This question clearly epitomizes the tensions and divisions stemming from the religious issue that existed among the liberals, conservative or not, Protestant or Catholic, who all pondered on whether religion laid the foundations of customs and more generally of civil society, on the secularization of the State and on the religious and/or philosophical origins of the French Revolution. For beyond the traditional antagonism between Catholicism and Protestantism, inherent to Anglican theology, and the dislocation of Church and State, the 'irreligion' and 'atheism' of the French revolutionaries imposed hindsight on the role and place of religion in society and on the relationship between the 'city of God' and the 'city of men'.

Born to an Irish mother and a converted Anglican father, educated in his childhood in Dublin and married to a Catholic, Edmund Burke (1729-97),[3] who was a Whig MP from 1765 to 1794 (most part of which he spent in the opposition), adhered to 'conservative whiggism' which dominated the historiographical and political domain since the beginning of the eighteenth century. In 1790, he was the first to introduce the comparison between two, according to him, inseparable traditions, the French and the British, and to devote his life and work to the French Revolution which he systematically opposed to the British liberal model. In breaking away from its own history and religion in the name of reason and of the natural rights of man, in disrupting the legitimacy of law and order and the conditions for changing it, in the proclamation of the sovereign rights of the people as the founding principle of the new political regime, the French Revolution was considered by the counter-revolutionary thinker as totally extraneous to the British liberal tradition which originated in the Glorious Revolution and which successfully linked tradition and innovation, historical and religious continuity in the defence of inherited rights and of an immemorial constitution – embodied in shared sovereignty between the King and the Houses.

The son of one of the founders of the Evangelical Clapham Sect and educated in Scotland and England, Thomas Babington Macaulay (1800-59),[4] 'more burkean than Burke himself',[5] was a Whig MP in the majority and in power from 1830 to 1856 (1830-41; 1846-7, 1852-6) and is considered to be the father of what came to be known, after Herbert Butterfield's work, the whig interpretation of history. The first volumes of his masterpiece, *The History of England from the Accession of James II* (1848-61), were published a few months after the revolutions of 1848 shook France and its European neighbours for the third time since the French Revolution. And it was in reply to David Hume's scepticism that he was credited with having allowed whig history and its interpretation, which lasted well into the twentieth century, to rise from its ashes by consecrating a history defined as progressive, liberal and Protestant. After Rapin de Thoyras, a French Huguenot and first whig historian, Macaulay was the first to rekindle a history that, from Edward Coke to Herbert Butterfield, along with Edmund Burke, made a success story of the English past: an all providential history of an elected people whose institutions were seen as part of an evolving process, that of the constitutional progress of ancient liberties and the affirmation of a parliamentary government – common law and the Glorious revolution forming then the foundations of British liberal thought. Devoting his entire career as a historian and politician to the French Revolution and the English revolutions of the seventeenth century and their consequences on the (re)definition of British liberal thought, Macaulay restored meaning to English history at a time when, less than half a century after Burke, he had in turn to defend again the British model and to reassert that the British nation was 'the most brilliant ever known in the world'.

Born to a Catholic mother and bred in a whig and European aristocratic milieu, Lord Acton (1834-1902)[6] was a devout Catholic and a fervent liberal. He was a historian and a Liberal MP from 1859 to 1865. 'Stuffed with Macaulay', whom he considered to be the 'greatest writer of the age' along with Burke, he spearheaded the political, philosophical and intellectual principles and premises on which Liberal Catholicism was to evolve in England in the nineteenth century and led the way for a thorough reflection on a possible reconciliation between the tenets of Liberalism and the doctrines of Catholicism in post-revolutionary modern societies, while he significantly animated and influenced the Prime Minister Gladstone's liberal policies and thought (notably on Ireland). Founding and participating in the major organs which fuelled and propagated Liberal Catholic thought/ideology, *The Rambler (1848–1862), the Home and Foreign Review (1862–1864), The Chronicle (1867–1868)* and *the North British Review (1869–1871)*, he became Regius Professor at Cambridge in 1895 and edited the *Cambridge Modern History*. Though he was pervaded with his Catholic breeding, aristocratic and cosmopolitan background, he was above all marked by his intellectual apprenticeship and education in Paris (with Felix Dupanloup (1802–78)[7]) and most notably in Munich by the liberal Catholic Church historian and theologian, Johann Joseph Ignaz Von Döllinger (1799–1890). Published at the time when the Springtime of the People, the unification of Italy and the annexation of papal territories deeply questioned the temporal and spiritual power of the Pope, most of his work was devoted to the theorizing of a Catholic approach to Liberalism with the French Revolution as its focal point.

The work of these three thinkers needs to be understood as political and/or historical essays and pamphlets. As historians and/or statesmen, with due knowledge of the writings of the *philosophes* and the situation in France, they tackled the religious issue from a political and/or historical point of view without expressing any intent to propound theological precepts or doctrine. Their main objective was both to recall what needed to be understood by a British liberal thought and to propose the best political and religious means to maintain peace, stability and the Union of the kingdom. Though all were imbued with whig mythology and constitutionalism bequeathed by their predecessors, they proposed a very different interpretation of the *Ancien Régime* and solutions to the religious problem posed by the Revolution. Contrary to Edmund Burke, whom both admired, Macaulay and Acton accepted the French Revolution despite the terrorist episode. Witness to the fall of the *Ancien Régime* in France and confronted with the Penal laws and Disability Acts in Ireland, Burke strengthened his standpoint on the Establishment while T.B. Macaulay, fighting for the enforcement of the Catholic Emancipation Act of 1829 and facing up to the emergence of the Oxford Movement and the papal move known as the 'Papal Aggression', set out to redefine the links that existed between the State and the Church in the post-revolutionary UK. Lord Acton, who was in Rome before and during the first Vatican Council and who played a major role in the debate which opposed the Ultramontane bishops to the liberal bishops, by providing the minority with an impressive knowledge of ecclesiastical history, defended the place and role of the Roman Catholic Church while justifying the revolutionaries' actions.

The aim of this chapter is therefore to reflect on to what extent the French Revolution induced the three most influential proponents of the British constitutional model in the nineteenth century to investigate the role of the Roman Catholic Church in France, the links between the State and the Church, and the role and place of the individual in civil society and history.

I The Roman Catholic Church of France: A necessary destruction?

1 Antireligiosity and anticlericalism

What distinguished the French Enlightenment from the German or 'English' Enlightenment was its strong aversion to the religion of France. Often 'anticlerical' in their fight for the civil and even political emancipation of the people, the French Enlightenment attacked not only the beliefs but also the political role of the Church, soon confusing (the Catholic) religion with prejudice and distinguishing more clearly State and Church.[8] Without being atheists[9] and even rather deists, French philosophers adopted an anti-religious sentiment which was expressed through acerbic criticism of the Church and the French clergy, as evidenced by Voltaire's fierce fight against superstitions and abuses of religious power. This anticlericalism was found in the tradition and the foundations of whig thought, as Mark Goldie has shown, with the exception of Edmund Burke, who, as such, fell outside this whig philosophy by declaring that customs still remained in the Church and in chivalry, and by making the clergy or clerics the protectors of knowledge and culture.[10] Having debated the religious question in the Parisian *salons* and whose discussions found an echo in a speech he delivered to the House of Commons shortly after his return to England, Burke attacked atheism, like Voltaire and Rousseau.[11] But, he was, above all, particularly severe with regard to a society which would be dispossessed of its institutions and its religious authorities, vectors of political, social and moral stability, according to him. In a letter, dated 1 June 1791, which he addressed to the Viscount of Rivarol (1762–1848),[12] he expressed, a few months after the publication of his major work on the French Revolution, his scepticism and his condemnation of the attacks against the Christian tradition inaugurated by revolutionary France, which the new Emperor Leopold II seemed to wish to imitate.[13] Questioning the Emperor's promise to commit himself, from his accession on 20 February 1790, to the restoration of the traditional institutions of the kingdom,[14] Burke warned against the danger of following the policy of the French revolutionaries in religious matters. In his *Reflections*, he had already denounced the attack on the French clergy and castigated the disastrous consequences for Christianity, which would follow this disrepute of the Church and its religious personnel. 'The present ruling power has shown a disposition only to plunder the Church', he wrote. 'This new ecclesiastical establishment is intended only to be temporary and preparatory to the utter abolition, under any of its forms, of the Christian religion, whenever the minds of men are prepared for this last stroke against it, by the accomplishment of the plan for bringing its ministers into universal contempt.'[15] These ministers or this much slandered body, of which France had said 'a great deal of evil', was yet composed of virtuous and disinterested men and had not committed themselves to crimes which 'merited confiscation of their substance, nor those cruel insults and degradations, and that unnatural persecution which have been substituted in the place of meliorating regulation'.[16]

Echoing Macaulay's anticlericalism significantly present in his work and expressed through a condemnation of the Catholic Church of France and its clergy, Lord Acton exposed a completely different image of the clergy and of the Church of France a century later in his *Lectures on the French Revolution*. As he stated, two things chiefly made the memory of monarchy odious, dynastic wars and religious persecution. If wars had ended, the 'odium of persecution remained'. It was not always 'assignable to the influence of clergy, it was largely due to them' and 'they had attempted to renew it down to the eve of the Revolution'.[17] Land grabber, exploiting the feudal system, ruling by superstition, the religious institution, as Macaulay showed, was only the mirror of the French monarchical regime and its feudal society of orders (judged as archaic), and became a rebel against the emancipation of the people of France. 'The reduction of the royal power', Acton contended, 'was sure to seriously modify the position of men upon whom the royal power, in its excess, had so much relied, and who had done so much to raise up and to sustain it'. The French Enlightenment, as radical as they were on religion and political philosophy, had only revealed the failings of an *Ancien Régime* society where only a few privileged people monopolized the public fortune and left the rest of the nation, poor and ignorant, only one solution, revolt. Expressing the iniquity of the French political and social state, the French philosophers could therefore, for Macaulay, only help in the necessary undermining and in the extirpation of all the established opinions, old truths and errors of Old Regime France. As Lord Acton pointed out, 'the clergy, being a privileged order, like the nobles, was involved in the same fate'. 'People had come to believe that the cause of liberty demanded not the emancipation but the repression of the priesthood.'[18] Addressing the young Gladstone, then a Tory deputy, to whom he replied in a long essay devoted to the relationship between Church and State, Macaulay wrote, in support of the French example,

> if there were in any part of the world, a national church regarded as heretical by four fifths of the nation committed to its care, a church established and maintained by the sword, a church which, though possessing great wealth and power, and though long backed by persecuting laws, had, in the course of many generations, been found unable to propagate its doctrines [...] a church so odious, that fraud and violence, when used against its clear rights of property, were generally regarded as fair play, a church whose ministers were preaching to desolate the walls, and with difficulty obtaining their lawful subsistence by the help of bayonets, such a church, on our principles, could not, we must own, be defended.[19]

By comparing the Catholic Church of France and the Anglican Church of Ireland Macaulay pinpoints here the thorny question and the reasons for keeping or not a religious institution, a subject on which his predecessor and successor strove to respond in their works.

2 An inevitable conflict: Disestablishing the Church?

One of the most ambiguous standpoints in Burke's political thought may have been his plea for both toleration for Irish Catholics and for the Anglican Established Church of Ireland. As Stewart J. Brown has pointed out, the first three decades of the nineteenth century were marked by the state's desire to give the established churches a leading role in the work of consolidating the Union. As they were to be bulwarks against the spirit of revolution and republicanism, they were considered as major forces for national unity and for preserving peace.[20] Burke had already insisted on this point in his *Reflections on the Revolution in France*. The English people, he maintained, 'consider [their church establishment] as the foundation of their whole constitution, with which, and with every part of which, it holds an indissoluble union'.[21] Decrying the religious policies of the French Revolutionaries, Burke emphasized the national support that the Church enjoyed. 'The English people do not consider the establishment of their church as a simple commodity, but as an essential element of the state.' For Burke, the established church, representing in principle the customs and morals of the majority of its subjects, was an instrument of moderation and restraint, a moral check on the abuse of power. It prevented incremental and hasty changes. In Ireland though, the situation was peculiarly different as the Established Church represented only the minority of the Irish people. Although he did recognize in private correspondence that the Church of Ireland was not national and therefore posed a major political and religious problem, Burke did not however envisage the establishment of a majority church in Ireland as was the case in Scotland (the Kirk), let alone the idea of a disestablishment. It was politically impractical. Granting political and religious emancipation to Catholics was already a major step in the recognition of the Roman Catholic worship at a time when anti-Catholic feeling and the political, economic and social domination of the Protestant minority were strong, the Catholics not yet being eligible and becoming electors only from 1793. Religious uniformity was therefore the only possible means to maintain political unity that the disestablishment would necessarily have weakened by loosening the ties between England and Ireland while the spiritual sovereignty of the Pope over the Catholic church would have conflicted with the power of the King, head of the Anglican Church and bound to it by the English constitution.[22]

In comparing the Church of Ireland and the Catholic Church of France, Macaulay shared, at first, Burke's uncertainties and reservations about the consequences of the destruction of a religious institution, centuries-old, but also popular, such as the Catholic Church of France, particularly in terms of public order and security. Fearing political and moral disorder that would be provoked by the disappearance of the Church which 'intertwines its roots with the very foundations of society', Macaulay agreed on Burke's ascertainment that

> to a man who acts under the influence of no passion, who has nothing in view in his projects but the public good, a great difference will immediately strike him between what policy would dictate on the original introduction of such institutions and on the question of their total abolition, where they have cast their roots wide and deep, [...] that the one cannot be destroyed without notably impairing the other.[23]

He considered that it was, in effect, preferable not to destroy an already-established institution, especially when time and (popular) religious customs had sanctioned its existence.[24] Certainly, for Burke, the Church of France was not irreproachable nor the religion exempt from superstition but one could 'derive from superstition itself any resources which may thence be furnished for the public advantage' or at least find 'something else than the mere alternative of absolute destruction or unreformed existence' as he stressed in his *Reflections*.[25] It was the hope that Lord Acton sustained in his *Lectures* insisting on the original rallying of a part of the Catholic clergy to the Revolution. 'The majority of the clergy were true to the new ideas and on some decisive occasions, June 19 and August 4, promoted their victory'[26] in renouncing their feudal and seigniorial rights. Many prelates were enlightened reformers and 'even Robespierre believed that the inferior clergy were, in the bulk, democratic'.[27] As Michel Biard and Pascal Dupuy underscored, it was only after a period of unanimity, of a 'honeymoon' between revolution and religion that the detachment and the schism came and ushered in the separation of Church and State in France. Unfortunately, the Assembly 'turned the clergy into implacable enemies' as Acton put it. The gradual but determined change of front, improbable at first, was for the Liberal Catholic historian the true cause of the disastrous conflict that ensued. And it was by slow degrees that the full force of aversion at last predominated. But, contrary to Burke, the collision between the Church and the prevailing ideas was made inevitable for both Macaulay and Acton who explained and justified the destruction of the Roman Catholic Church by the revolutionaries, though Acton seemed to regret it at the end of his career.[28] From the Civil Constitution of the Clergy to the Concordat, the degree of abuse of the old regime clergy accounted, for both, for the attacks on the worship of the Catholic faithful, the dispossession of the property of the French Catholic Church and more broadly the religious policy of the French revolutionaries. Contrary to Burke, who called on any wise man to perhaps prefer the superstition which builds to that which tears down, Macaulay and Acton argued conversely as Macaulay put it in 'Walpole' that 'while he [would] condemn[ed] their hostility to religion [a wise man] would have acknowledged that it was the natural effect of a system under which religion had been constantly exhibited to them in forms which common sense rejected and at which humanity shuddered'.[29] To the question posed by the liberal conservative philosopher as whether to choose between 'the ancient monastic superstition and that of the so-called philosophers of the day', Macaulay and Acton naturally leaned towards the second option. In revolutionary France, both historians stressed, the absolutist, superstitious and pluri-secular abuses of the Catholic Church justified its destruction even though it represented the cult of the majority. As Macaulay made clear, it not only became a political and institutional obstacle but also an excellent receptacle for the anti-enlightenment and counter-revolutionary ideas. In Ireland, the Anglican Church criticized as being just as absolutist and violent as the first, although not a majority creed, was also attacked by both historians who inveighed against the intolerance and persecution of the Protestant Ascendency in Ireland against the Catholic majority and the exclusivity of a minority church. In both cases, it is the religious institution that Macaulay and Acton condemned. The only church in the world to enjoy an exclusive establishment, the Church of Ireland, was an aberration, 'a bad institution',[30] its establishment having been 'the occasion of the most atrocious persecution that ever disgraced the Protestant religion in my country and in the world',[31] Acton assessed. Accusing the Protestant priests of having 'gorged [themselves] with wealth and sunk in indolence'[32] at the beginning of the eighteenth century, Macaulay reproached the clergy for inappropriate proselytism as a vector of political and social unrest in a society identified with a Catholic majority. A minority church could not, in any case, replace a majority church. As Acton made plain in his review of Goldsmith's 'Irish History':

> No Catholic government ever imposed a Catholic establishment on a Protestant community, or destroyed a Protestant establishment. Even the Revocation of the Edict of Nantes, the greatest wrong ever inflicted on the Protestant subjects of a Catholic State, will bear no comparison with the establishment of the religion of a minority [...] a state church can only be justified by the acquiescence of the nation. In every other case it is a great social danger, and is inseparable from political oppression.[33]

Its disestablishment was consequently largely conceivable or even desirable for both historians.[34] The Church of Ireland was so 'odious and its vicinage so much endangers valuable parts of our polity', Macaulay contended, 'that, even if it were in itself a good institution, there would be strong reasons for giving it up'.[35] But being in the majority was not a sufficient guarantee either if the Church over-rode its social (to assemble and not to divide the community of the faithful) and moral (to guide and not obscure reason) functions (not to become a home for superstitions). According to them, the French Catholic Church, at the roots of the French society and state, had made religion and superstition synonymous. Though its destruction effectively threatened order, public security and political stability, its destruction was inevitable under the French Revolution so that the state could regain its independence, and that religion could become the ally of reason again.

At the heart of this opposition, two antagonistic readings of the French *Ancien Régime* were exposed by the three liberal thinkers. For the counter-revolutionary pamphleteer Burke, the irreligion of the French Enlightenment was a part of the political and 'cultural origins' of the French Revolution. If he defended prejudice, including religious prejudice and the state churches, he did so for he believed that they were the vectors of social and political cohesion as was the French Catholic Church, reformable from the inside according to him. For Macaulay and Acton, the failure of the French clergy to fill their social and political role accounted for the rapid, and at times violent, dechristianization of the French Revolutionaries. It explains both historians' defence and justification of the action of the French Revolutionaries against the Church which, by overriding its social, political and even moral role, had excluded itself from national interest and history.

It follows that the relationship between the Church and the State that they set forth in their work was fundamentally divergent and had to be (re)defined.

II The links and power of Church and State

1 Union or separation of Church and State/Erastianism or independence?

As the *Church and State* system implies, the close ties that the Church and the State had enjoyed ever since the Reformation had rendered the division of their powers even more complex as the sovereign would, from then on, incarnate the alliance between the State and the Church and embody national and religious affiliation based on the Latin maxim *cujus regio ejus religio* in force since the Augsburg and Westphalia treaties (1555, 1648). For Burke, as part of a gradual historical development, the *union*, rather than the *alliance*, between Church and State had always been the best means of guaranteeing the political and religious stability of civil societies as it ensured continuity with the established traditions of society that the French Revolution had destroyed in France. As he made clear, the Church and State did not represent two distinct entities, one being dependent on the other but one and the same thing being integral parts of the same whole. For both Macaulay and Acton, the union between the Church and State had, on the contrary, 'caused all persecution'.[36] As Macaulay maintained in 'Southey's Colloquies' regarding the *High Tories*, 'it would be desirable that they should remember how little advantage of honour the religious power formerly derived from the closest alliance with power'.[37] The example of ancient Greece and Rome had amply demonstrated for Acton that 'the vice of the classic State was that it was both Church and State in one. Morality was undistinguished from religion and politics from morals; and in religion, morality and politics there was only one legislator and one authority'.[38] For both, the union had, more recently, ignited the political and religious instability, tensions and violence that had raged in France as well as in Ireland where tyranny and persecution had prevailed and all the more so as since the Act of Union of 1801.[39] The political union and religious peace could only be maintained if the principle premised on a Church-State identity was abandoned as was the case in France since the Revolution and the Napoleonic era. In Ireland, Macaulay asserted, it had not only fuelled the traditional antagonism between Protestantism and Catholicism but it had also threatened the Empire and the Union of implosion. The anti-popery cry that the Tory parliamentarians fanned long after the adoption of the reforms of 1828 and 1829 and the illegal trial brought against O'Connell in 1844 only aggravated a situation that was all the more unsustainable that the demands of the Irish Catholics became increasingly pressing in the 1840s. In France, the separation between Church and State, first established by the Civil Constitution of the Clergy in 1790 and put in practice by Napoleon's Concordat of 1801, allowed for the reconciliation of the 'two Frances' and for the guarantee and security of individual liberties.

But, this separation that both historians advocated ended, however, in proposing opposed solutions. As Roland Minnerath explained, the problem of the relationship between Church and State is posed by the way in which the Christian community understands its social role and by the degree of control that the State intends to exercise over religious life.[40] From the sixteenth century, the State and the Church were considered as forming a single national body in which a quasi-episcopal king replaced the pope. Analysing the origins and roots of the Anglican Church in his work, Macaulay recalled that 'the most prominent and extraordinary phenomenon which the Reformation presents to us is the gigantic strength of the government contrasted with the feebleness of the religious parties'.[41] The Reformation had indeed inaugurated the subordination of religious power to political power, as the result of the will of the sovereigns to divest themselves of the papacy and to adopt a so-called Erastian policy, understood as the subordination of the Church to the interests of the State or the right of civil power to interfere in religious matters. Nothing so strongly 'distinguished the

Church of England from other Churches as the relation in which she stood to the monarchy'.[42] 'There was once a time', Acton put forward, in the article he devoted to the Count of Montalembert, 'when it was the common belief both of churchmen and statesmen, that the Church had great need of the State, and that her prosperity was proportioned to the favour she received from it'. And the pious protection extended to her by Catholic monarchs 'was deemed a prodigious security for religion'.[43] Precisely for Macaulay, the control of the Church by the State was the only solution to the problem posed by the religious tensions and conflicts and a precondition for peace and stability as Erastianism acted as a rampart against religious fanaticism, intolerance and an 'usurping clergy'. 'I will never put the State under the feet of that Church which it feeds out of the common funds of the Empire',[44] he insisted. In the controversies, around the appointment of clerics by the State – the most famous of which was around Hampden and Gorham – the patronage in Scotland[45] or the allocation granted to the Maynooth Catholic College, which opposed Macaulay to the *High Churchmen*, he never ceased to reaffirm the supremacy of the State in ecclesiastical matters. He recalled, in that respect, in his *History of England*, that since the Reformation, the English bishops had only been agents of the State. Before him, Burke had defended this and consequently lost his seat, just like Macaulay, on the question of the financing of Maynooth college, one of the largest seminaries worldwide dedicated to the education of Irish Catholic priests. But, Burke appeared, nonetheless, unusual in his upholding of the union of Church and State while supporting the independence of the Church against an 'erastian' policy. This is particularly evident in his condemnation of the confiscation of the church properties by the revolutionaries in France, an event to which he devoted a whole chapter in his *Reflections*. Being independent meant for Burke being independent from political affairs and financial needs. Politics and the pulpit were terms that agreed on little for Burke as he observed in his pamphlet. The cause of civil liberty and civil government gained as little as that of religion by this confusion of duties. To obtain independence, the Church needed to be endowed with sufficient private property in order not to depend on the individual or on the state's changing motivations or mood as had been the case in revolutionary France. In his essay, 'the Roman Question', Acton reiterated the same idea in his defence of the independence of the Pope. If he has not his own revenues, he argued,

> he must live upon the contributions either of governments or of the faithful. None, of course, can be expected from those states that are not Catholic; and there can be no security for their continuance in Catholic states […] Such a plan would render the Head of the Church dependent for his maintenance on powers almost all of which have despoiled the Church at home.[46]

What was crucial for both Burke and Acton was to prevent the State from infringing upon the Church's prerogatives, from controlling the Church as Erastianism entailed. As Acton expounded, Erastianism was not conceivable as 'consequently, religion was strong only in the strength of the State and the decline of the monarchy deprived the Church of her chief support'. 'When the revolution came', he affirmed, 'she was its first and easiest victim. The result of that old *regime* was, that the king of France was beheaded and the Pope died in a French prison'.[47] For Acton, in placing the English Church under the domination of the king, the Anglican Reformation drastically reduced its influence in society as it was from then on at the service of political power.[48] Yet, this influence was absolutely necessary for the Cambridge historian since 'one of its most important but delicate duties is to act as an [...] impartial and dispassionate mediator'[49] between the churches, the states and nations. It is its independence from political power that allowed it to act as such. As theologians have made clear, the Church could not be subordinated to the authority of the State as it had the absolute right to independence (financial, political and spiritual). Faced with the despotic power of the modern state, the Church appeared, for Acton, as the only force that could thwart it. Its very organization made it possible to constrain the absolutist tendencies of the State by acting as a check and balance upon the state powers, providing immense security for individual liberty.[50]

This is the reason why Acton defended the temporal power of the pope, an issue that had aroused strong reactions since the publication of Dollinger's *Kirche und Kirchen* at the time when the papal territories were annexed in Italy and when the distinction between spiritual power and temporal power (still) stirred spirits in the tense context of the rise of nationalisms in Europe.

2 Church and State: Temporal power vs spiritual power

As Jean-Louis Gazzaniga and Philippe Segur highlighted, the theological affirmation of the independence of the Church as a constitutive and characteristic feature of the religious institution resumes in a concise form a whole part of the Gospel message[51] that Acton upheld very clearly in his work and more precisely in 'Political Thoughts on the Church' (1859) as in his *History of Freedom in Antiquity* (1877) where he evokes the position of Jesus: 'render unto Caesar the things that are Caesar's and unto God the things that are God's'.[52] Acton reckoned very clearly that this separation of the spiritual and the temporal represented one of the essential contributions of Christianity and its novelty, compared to Antiquity, lied in the fact that the idea came from the religious authorities themselves. It gave the State a legitimacy it had never enjoyed before and set bounds to it that it had never yet acknowledged.[53] It bestowed, accordingly, to a universal Church the perpetual charge of limiting the potentially despotic or absolutist power of the State. 'Those words were the repudiation of absolutism and the inauguration of freedom', as he put it. But as the head of a universal church, the Pope had, for Acton, the right to both powers. His independence from State(s), nation(s) and/or country(ies) as the Head of a Universal Church demanded that he exert both a spiritual and temporal power in order to be able to act as this real and 'dispassionate mediator' between States and Nations, whether Protestant or Catholic. As he encouraged his compatriots to understand, the temporal power of the Pope was a matter of 'European interest'.[54] Every statesman had to perceive how important it was to recognize that the Pope had to be independent but also that the world be convinced and satisfied of his independence.[55] The universality of the papacy would be compromised if the duty of protecting it should become the permanent and exclusive privilege of any single country.[56] The immunity from the predominant influence of national and political divisions and of the 'indifference to the attachment of particular States and races – the security of unity and universality-consists in the existence of a single, supreme, independent head' whose primacy is the 'bulwark or rather the cornerstone of Catholicism' but whose mission is 'to all mankind',[57] as the institution which Christ founded in order 'to collect all nations together in one fold under one shepherd, while tolerating and respecting the natural historical distinctions of nations and of States, endeavours to reconcile antagonism, and to smooth away barriers between them instead of estranging them by artificial differences, and erecting new obstacles to their harmony'.[58] The loss of the Pope's liberty would thence be both a 'danger to the state and to the peace of the world', especially in the UK where the pressure of Catholic agitation, notably in Ireland, would be more severely felt than elsewhere. It would also represent an infringement on the inalienable rights of conscience which are the sacred foundation of all public liberties,[59] the only valid ground on which the Pope and every Christian 'can claim that his religion shall be free'. Temporal dominion then arose as the necessary foundation of this liberty and independence of the Church in ages when property was the indispensable condition of liberty and sovereignty the only security for independence. It was founded 'on the most sacred of human institutions', on the rights both of property and of sovereignty. The Holy See's sovereignty 'virtually began at the same time as the freedom of the Church' in order that the head of the Catholic Church might never henceforth be impeded in the free exercise of his supreme authority by the presence of any other sovereign authority in Rome. The course of events since then had rendered the temporal sovereignty of the Holy See more and more necessary and has gradually extended its dominion. And yet, it was not absolutely essential to the nature and ends of the Church. It had 'its source in causes which were external to her in the temporal condition of the world, not the spiritual aims of the Church; and as the world becomes impregnated with her ideas, the necessity of the temporal power would probably disappear'.[60] It was to pass away 'when the spiritual dominion [wa]s acknowledged by all nations'.

This delicate and complex relative autonomy of the temporal and spiritual powers that Acton supported can be found in the Hobbesian Erastianism that Macaulay advocated in the years 1830–40 against the two disciples of Burke, Robert Southey and the young Gladstone. The latter wished to recall the need for an intimate alliance between the temporal and spiritual powers in the name of religious truth, following the dislocation of the relationship between Church and State which had been presupposed by the emancipation of Catholics and non-conformists and the threat linked to religious indifferentism or disaffection.[61] If, in accordance with the Erastian principles amended in modern times by Hobbes in secularized states, the right to legislate in religious matters, whatever the religion individually professed by the prince, was a requirement, it did not imply for Macaulay the capacity of the state to propagate a religion as maintained by Southey and Gladstone and before them by Burke. 'All who administer the government of men, in which they stand in the person of God himself, should have high and worthy notions of their function and destination',[62] the philosopher claimed in his *Reflections*. In the service of God, the statesman had to profess the established religion whose consecration by the State necessarily inspired to free citizens a salutary respect. As a reasonable and public agent, he acted as part of a body, his very existence implying moral duties and moral responsibility by virtue of his public and collective character, as the young Gladstone explained in *The State in its Relation with the Church* (1839). But if this reverence due to the State allowed for state proselytism in Burke's opinion, it did not entail imposing a religion on recusant subjects nor claim its entitlement to religious truth as Gladstone would maintain. As Macaulay put forward in his response to Southey's colloquies regarding, as it seems, the *Civil Constitution of the Clergy* 'does [Southey] not know that the danger of states is to be estimated not by what breaks out of the public mind, but by what stays in it? Can he conceive anything more terrible than the situation of a government which rules without apprehension over a people of hypocrites?'[63] As such, Macaulay overturns the theory of a paternalistic state, spiritual guide of the people, promoted by his opponents who feared the outbreak of a revolution that would be worse than that 'which had brought together the States General'[64] and pinpointed the functions of an Erastian state against the pretensions of a state propagating the 'true religion'. To admit such a theory would amount to annihilating and dissolving all civil society. The example of the French Revolution, notably the Massacres of September, just as the politics of Queen Elizabeth I and Charles I and of the Tories during the revolution in Ireland, had, for Macaulay, sufficiently demonstrated that professing a religion led inevitably to chaos, persecution, intolerance and fanaticism. The example of the army displayed, for its part, all the absurdity of such an undertaking. If, as a collective being, the army, representing a strong unity of action, obeying one mind and acting as one man, had to profess one religion, it would have been led to defeat in 1704. 'Was it', Macaulay wondered, 'imperatively necessary that the Army should, as an army, have one established religion, that [the Prince] Eugène should be deprived of this command for being a Catholic, that all the Dutch and Austrian colonels should be broken for not subscribing the Thirty-Nine Articles'.[65] This confusion between spiritual and temporal interests which had led 'respectable men' in the UK to misunderstand the affairs of the state and to develop false and dangerous political theories clearly showed that the state, for Macaulay, had a strictly temporal role. As such, he is particularly severe in his work with regard to the revival of the High Church spirit, initiated by the Oxford movement, heir to theologians like William Laud and the restored Church under Charles II, whose influence on the Anglican Church foreshadowed the clerical resurgence.

3 The power of the State: Religious tolerance, emancipation and liberty

'Without being blind admirers either of the French or of the American institutions, we think it clear that the persons and property of citizens are better protected in France and in New England than in almost any society that now exists, or that has ever existed', wrote Macaulay in his essay devoted to refuting Gladstone's position. Referring to the neutrality of the State in religious matters of Concordatory France and the July Monarchy, Macaulay paid homage to the First Consul who spared France religious conflicts and brought political and religious peace to the country. Like Macaulay, Burke and Acton always stood for religious tolerance and fought against intolerance or persecution. Even if Acton was able to defend persecution for a time as a historical necessity when he was young,[66] the three liberal thinkers were particularly active in the defence of religious minorities, particularly Catholics, and worked to have the state recognize this. As Acton made plain, it was by the treatment of its minority that one could judge a free country. The case of revolutionary France and its impact on Catholic Ireland was particularly obvious for the three thinkers. As McConnell pointed out, the aversion to Catholicism was widespread and shared by both the 'establishmentarians' and the 'secularists'.[67] In that respect, Macaulay levelled a blatant criticism against two of the most renowned champions of toleration, John Locke and Tillotson, in his essays on the civil disabilities of the Jews, for being anti-Catholic and anti-Semitic. Burke had attacked the hypocrisy of those who condemned the persecution of Protestants in Catholic France while excused the persecution of Catholics in Ireland. For the three liberal thinkers, persecution was not only intolerable and unjust, it was also ineffective as evidenced by Burke's unpublished *Tracts Relative to the Laws against Popery in Ireland* (1760–5). Quoting and taking up Burke, Acton specified that

> persecution is the vice of particular religions, and the misfortune of particular stages of political society. It is the resource by which States that would be subverted by religious liberty escape the more dangerous alternative of imposing religious disabilities [...] But the system applied to Ireland, which uses religious disabilities for the purpose of political oppression, stands alone in solitary infamy among the crimes and follies of the rulers of men.[68]

Burke, who suffered from persecution himself and whose life was even endangered during the Gordon Riots (1780) underpinned, in a letter he wrote to his son regarding the Protestant Ascendancy in 1795, that 'persecution was purely destructive'. At the time, the Penal Laws, 'worse than any scheme of religious persecution' that ever existed,[69] kept the Catholic majority in submission to the Ascendancy and served the political and economic interest of the dominant protestant minority which had exclusive control of the Irish Parliament. For the whig philosopher, the intransigence of the Protestant authorities was driving the Catholics to violence, Jacobinism and rebellion. It was inciting Irish Catholics to embrace the revolutionary principles exalted in France. He feared tyranny and anarchy embodied in the Protestant minority and the principles of the French Revolution respectively would spark a revolution in Ireland. Catholicism, only, as a long-lasting tradition in Ireland, represented the 'most effectual barrier against Jacobinism'. In Ireland, most certainly, Catholicism had to be cherished as a good. Its suppression would turn Catholics into allies of revolution. Published a few months after the pacific demonstration of O'Connell's Association for the Repeal of the Union had gathered more than two thousand people in Ireland in 1843, Macaulay's 'State of Ireland' brought into focus the accountability of the Tory government for the political and religious disorders of Catholic Ireland which was mainly due to its religious intolerance. The 'anti-Papism' that the Tory MPs continued to kindle even after the enforcement of the Catholic Emancipation Act participated in worsening a most unstable situation. Toleration was accordingly for the three liberal thinkers a central tenet that they urged the government to advocate, a prerequisite for peace, order, stability and liberty. One of the main causes of Acton's disillusionment at the end of his life stemmed precisely from the profound disappointment he felt by the indulgence given to characters or events pertaining to religious intolerance, persecution or murders from the part of Liberal Catholics.[70] Protecting religious minorities from persecution or persecuted religious communities was the first requirement the Church and State had to conform to in liberal societies. Liberty of conscience and of religion equated with ruling out the potential tyranny of a Church and called for the political and religious emancipation of the Irish Catholics for which both Macaulay, as a Whig politician, and Acton, as a close friend and source of inspiration for Gladstone's Home Rule scheme, played an active part. As early as 1778, Burke had already made it a priority though the American and French Revolutions transformed it into a pressing need. For Burke, the right to vote would give security and strengthen the State as a greater number of people would be interested in the conservation of the constitution. For Macaulay and Acton, it was part of a larger scheme of necessary reforms of the British political system. For all, though, it would allow for the protection of the liberties of Irishmen. But just as the Protestant Ascendancy's intransigence drove Catholics to rebellion in Ireland, according to Burke, the events unfolding in France profoundly altered Burke's toleration policy as the Establishment was in danger of implosion. His defence of Catholic emancipation, that most of the Establishmentarians refused, could be perceived as the acceptance of a form of deconfessionalization of the State and yet Burke attempted to reconcile toleration and Establishment, contrary to Macaulay and Acton. As such, just as dissent had been transformed into a political faction in the 1790s, the aim of which after the French example was only to destroy the Establishment, according to him, he refused to endorse the repeal of the Test and Corporation Act that he had been prepared to defend ten years earlier. Unlike Burke, for whom the maintenance of the Establishment was a priority, Macaulay and Acton made toleration and religious emancipation an absolute principle. As Seamus Deane has clearly set out, the achievement of toleration and the dismantling of the institutional apparatus of the persecuting Protestant system in Ireland were for Acton entirely congruent with one another. The long battles over emancipation, tithes, education and church disestablishment in Ireland in the nineteenth century were part of a difficult transition that the UK had to make from being in effect a sectarian State that pretended to unity of religion – which the inclusion of Ireland in the federal system had rendered wholly false – to being a State in which Liberty prevailed.[71] As Benjamin Constant had clearly expounded as an unfailing principle, religious liberty was the first of liberties for both Macaulay and Acton. It explains their condemnation of the Church of France and Ireland and Macaulay's admiration for the Napoleonic Concordat. For Macaulay, in addition to the abolition of the principle *cujus rejus ejo religio*, and the imposition of the neutrality of the State in spiritual matters, the political and religious emancipation of all recognized religions, Christian or not, for the first time in Europe, which Napoleon put in place, was a model to follow and which could well have solved the Irish problem. When pondering over the outcome of the Civil Constitution of the Clergy, Acton indirectly drew the same conclusion. If the constitution thwarted the Revolution by creating a strong current of hostile feeling, the problem was 'to discover why the National Assembly and the committee that guided it, did not recognize […] that they were in flagrant contradiction with the first principles of the Revolution, why in that explosion of liberal sentiment, there was no room for religious freedom'.[72] That the patronage could not be left in the hands of the king absolutely, as it was by the Concordat of Leo X, was obvious, Acton contended, but if it had been given to the king acting through responsible ministers, then much of the difficulty and danger would have been overcome and the arrangement that grew out of the Concordat of Napoleon would have been anticipated.[73] It was the office of the King 'to negotiate with the Pope' and to negotiate wisely to save the Revolution and his own life. What was conceded by Pius VII to Bonaparte could well have been conceded by Pius VI to Louis XVI.[74] But instead, the unresolved conflict 'thus instituted between the Revolution and the Church hastened the fall of the throne and persecution and civil war'.[75]

III The omnipotence of Almighty God or the all powerful individual

1 Faith and history

In *Le Désenchantement du monde*, Marcel Gauchet submits from the first pages the choice that the Revolution imposed: 'either the commitment to the anteriority of the world and the law of things, or the commitment to the anteriority of men and of their creative activity. Or the submission to an order received in its entirety, determined before and outside one's will; or else the responsibility of a recognized order proceeding from the will of individuals'.[76] This choice between 'transcendence' and 'immanence', between two visions of the world, one 'beyond' human life, the other 'within' it, is particularly difficult to materialize. For, as Lucien Jaume remarked, the fact that sovereignty, this power which is 'higher than everything else' had, in its very genesis, to image something higher than itself, is an initial data the consequences of which, still present today according to him,[77] were well measured by the liberal thinkers of the nineteenth century and more particularly by the three liberal thinkers under study who accepted or not the French Revolution. If the theological problem which has opposed 'the City of men' to the 'City of God', free will to divine providence, is an old issue, the Revolution invited, above all, to redefine the place and the role of the individual in civil society and history, this individual who henceforth lost 'the place which had been reserved for him' (in the cosmos) by imposing a reflection on his power, as a man (and/or a citizen), his omnipotence or his relative submission to a 'higher' entity. The difficulty is all the more intricate as a large part of the liberals who accepted the French Revolution and this new individual sovereignty also and perfectly well conceived of the existence of a 'beyond history' to use the expression of Franck Lessay about Burke, of a 'beyond' the individual.[78] Under the French Revolution, Burke already insisted on this singular articulation in English history between the particular and the universal, which he wanted to set up as an example against the French revolutionaries.[79] Like de Maistre, Burke had shed light on the religious and Christian content of a human community 'delivered to the vagaries and sufferings of life in expiation of its faults'.[80] In a spirit as religious as that of the British philosopher, he could not elude the possibility of a divine condemnation striking the old world.[81] The purification by fire and blood of a culpable monarchy, nobility and clergy, revealed in de Maistre the divine will 'which is the law of laws and the sovereign of sovereigns'.[82] Going back to Antiquity, Acton paid tribute to this 'immutable' and 'divine' law that de Maistre referred to by praising the Hebrew nation for having been the first to have laid down the principle that all political authorities had to be tested and reformed according to a code which was not made by man, that there was a will, as the Stoics made later known, superior to the collective will of man, and a law that overruled those of Solon and Lycrugus, that 'law which is perfect and eternal as God himself, which proceeds from his nature, and reigns over heaven and earth and over all nations'.[83] As Karl Löwith elucidated in Weltgeschichte und Heilsgeschehen, the existence of a power above men was common both to Christians, who believed in divine Providence, and to pagans who believed in an inevitable and predetermined fate. It is comparable to the divine will if it is understood as the recognition of a higher power inaccessible to man. In Macaulay, we find this idea of an 'invisible hand' acting for the benefit of humanity, the idea that the action of men would be guided by an 'extra-human' (but not divine) power. It is inaccessible to the individual but contributes to his development and emancipation. 'In peace or in tumult, by means of old institutions, where those institutions are flexible, over the ruins of old institutions, where those institutions oppose an unbending resistance, the great march of society proceeds.'[84] Any effort to enforce this law would be 'lost and swept away in the mighty wish that the species goes onward'. The French Revolution had precisely been that great movement of the human mind which no government could have arrested. As early as 1796, Benjamin Constant called on the counter-revolutionaries to put an end to a vain and futile fight by inviting them not to fight against 'the necessity that drags us down'.[85] Those who seem to lead the movement are, in fact, only 'whirled along before it, those who attempt to resist it, are beaten down and crushed beneath it'.[86] And this was the great error of the counter-revolutionaries, to believe that, as Acton contended, 'the Revolution of the last century repudiates history. […] the unexpected truth, stranger than fiction, is that this was not the ruin but the renovation of history',[87] of the history of freedom, which the Revolution turned into a principle. Liberalism, Acton stated, had to be understood 'not only as a principle of government but also as a philosophy of history',[88] a history of progress which begins with 'the strongest religious movement […] and terminates in the equal claim of every man to be unhindered by man in the fulfillment of duty to God'.[89] And this constancy of progress, 'of progress in the direction of organized and assumed freedom is the characteristic fact of Modern History, and its tribute to the theory of Providence',[90] as, for Acton, 'liberty occupies the final summit, it profits by all the good that is in the world and suffers by all the evil, it pervades strife and inspires endeavor, it is almost if not altogether the sign and the price and the motive in the onward and upward advance of the race for which Christ was sacrificed' so much so that the revolutionary episode only sanctioned an intrinsically Christian principle. Even though, as Marcel Gauchet pointed out, what survived of the Christian faith had nothing to do with the role according to which its great inflections and rifts were played, it revealed itself in the hope of a horizon determining human existence.[91] The 'confident faith in a future full of promise is incomprehensible if we do not refer to the Christian faith which made the future the decisive horizon of our thought after Christ',[92] Karl Lowith insisted. A life oriented towards a future eschaton is not only characteristic of those who, in faith, live in hope and expectation, but also of those who are nourished by faith in history as such. And because the future only exists by anticipation, hope is 'an evil that seems good, because hope is always waiting for something better'[93] as he put forward. This is exactly what Macaulay espoused, interpreting the present events as harbingers, not of the last judgement but of the future advent of democracy. If he rejected faith in a transcendent finality and faith in God, unlike Acton, as the driving principle of history, he believed in the secular forces of progress the historical order replacing the natural and divine one. History was thus conceived as the very essence of the future to the extent that he recognized both the historicity of Salvation as an invention of Christianity and its withdrawal metaphorized in the concept of progress assuming thenceforth the functions of Providence. It was accordingly quite possible to make predictions about the future of liberal societies and to make the advent of democracy a providential necessity. As Tocqueville aptly put it in *De La démocratie en Amérique*, 'the gradual development of equality of conditions is a providential fact, it has its main characteristics; it is universal, lasting, it escapes human power every day'.[94] But, it remained to be determined whether this Christian or secular faith in the future could be placed in man or only in God.

2 Authority and power: Individual will against divine will?

In his *Reflections,* Burke clarified the relationship between human society and eternal society. Explaining the inextricable links between the terrestrial sphere and the celestial one, the British philosopher intended to show that the contract was nothing more than 'a clause in the great primeval contract of eternal society, [...] connecting the visible and invisible worlds, according to a fixed compact sanctioned by the inviolable oath which holds all physical and all moral natures, each in their appointed place'.[95] Laying down the conditions for the existence of human communities, Burke submitted the idea of an 'order of the world' presiding over 'the historical evolution of nations as well as that of the cosmos, both reflecting each other mutually because they were subject to the same mode of duration which gives its true significance to the notion of heritage'.[96] For Burke, the existence of such a 'transcendent Creator' supposed that human laws evoked those of the cosmos. As for the thinkers of Antiquity, the activity of men revealed for the British philosopher the laws of nature. 'Society is a natural order independent of individuals and in which the legitimization of human works and political institutions comes about through slow and spontaneous work, which empirically accumulates and selects the experiences of different generations',[97] as Massimo Boffa has underlined. Man, the State and the political institutions translated therefore the plan of the creator. They belonged to the natural order, willed by God and manifested by tradition. Man did not choose his obligations towards Humanity; he was not a signatory of a pact.[98] Nor was he the author, nor the master of the instruments of his improvement. Franck Lessay attested that for Burke the perfectibility of man was essentially of a spiritual nature and took 'the form of a *regressus* – at least in its intention – towards a prelapsarian state of union in God'.[99] As Marcel Gauchet reminded us, a heteronomous structure of society, which Burke adopted, implied an organization of the world being characterized by the obedience to the past, subjection and submission to tradition. This 'religious' society illustrating a collective and hierarchical structure of relations between men and submitting man to the immutable laws of nature made the individual incapable of founding his own society. United to God, men could not pretend to shape their society by a decree of their legislative will. As Gérard Gengembre explained, the revolutionaries had for Burke usurped the right of God by interfering with an inalienable project. And this claim had become sacrilege. It 'took humanity down a fatal slope'[100] since nothing could survive of these human institutions. By claiming the voluntarist character of the individual, the revolutionaries forgot human fragility and divine omnipotence and thus broke the ancestral links of man with himself, society and God.[101] For Burke, no decree of an assembly could found a freedom that was not already present in the national mores.[102] What legitimized for Burke the established constitution, as Stéphane Rials underscored, was 'less an initial *convention* than the prescription, the consolidation of a delegation of power to the rulers by the passage of time, the strengthening of the wise customs that ended up establishing themselves for the greatest common advantage'.[103] In this sense, the idea of prescription rejected that of arbitrary institutions acting as judges rather than conforming to the eternal order of things. It certified that the system in place was good and adapted to the specific conditions of a given country.[104] If Burke invoked nature like the revolutionaries, it was not to legitimize 'a regime deliberately constructed by a conscious act of will, starting from the supposed nature of man and by making a clean sweep of the past'[105] but to sanction the natural regime, the one that Providence had gradually engendered over the long term.

Against this theocentric vision that circulated among counter-revolutionaries, Macaulay eschewed the idea that it had to inform political practice and human activity. His attachment to the British tradition was not accompanied by a vertical and religious perception of the universe and its immutable laws so that if he made an apologist argument for the English constitution, he did not necessarily endorse the only constitutions established and legitimized by time. Unlike his illustrious predecessor, the post-revolutionary liberal historian did not conceive of the exercise of power as having to conform to the laws of nature. The state was not a sacred temple; its representatives were not in God's stead, as he repeated to the young Gladstone in 1839. Like Constant, the whig historian gave primacy to history over nature. The historical order he advocated made the individual the product of his time. He denied both the idea of the vanity of all human action and that of a human action which would obey the divine will by respecting order, tradition, customs and religion. The revolutionaries therefore did not break the natural and divine order by making a clean sweep of the past and their history, according to him. If his work echoes the Burkean criticism of revolutionary political voluntarism, it did not so much intend to condemn the legislative will as to, above all, rise up against an absolutization of the general will. For him, the regime built by a conscious act of will was fully commendable since it freed France from absolutism, prescription in France having given birth to an anti-liberal regime and the French monarchy of the *Ancien Régime* having been unable to reform and give birth to a liberal regime in France. So, by defending not only the *tabula rasa* and the act which allowed this emancipation while accepting the constitutional and political work of the French revolutionaries, Macaulay vindicated the individual capacity to act in the name of reason. Burke maintained that in the eternal and immutable law 'will and reason coincide' so that 'if what is but submission to necessity must become the object of choice, the law is broken, nature is disobeyed'.[106] This choice is, conversely, supported by Macaulay for whom individuals could not be defined by the community to which they belonged within a hierarchical, hereditary society encompassing individual components and drawing its legitimacy from divine sanction, as Burke claimed. It was the autonomy of the individual that he upheld, the part for the whole, by reversing the general interpretation of the human condition which 'prior to modernity placed man within an order in which he 'did not occupy the highest rank'.[107] The individual occupied, on the contrary, this reserved place, according to him, and if he accepted the political order instituted by the revolutionaries, it was also because he accepted change not according to 'the model of the *auctoritas* replaced in an older framework and which must always be preserved from ruptures' [108] but following that of an 'autonomous' society. Like Constant, Macaulay invested the individual with a real power of action. As rational agents, men had the power to produce laws and to found society in their image because the individual was endowed with the great capacities necessary for the progress of human societies. 'No nation can give itself a government',[109] said de Maistre in 1796. 'We see the wealth of nations increasing, and all the arts of life approaching nearer and nearer to perfection in spite of the grossest corruption on the part of rulers',[110] declared Macaulay a few decades later. The judgement of the individual could not be inferior to the collective reason as Burke sustained, for the individual was endowed with a non-negligible force independent of any natural or divine order. 'We rely on the natural tendency of the human intellect to truth'.[111]

On this thorny question of individual power, Lord Acton was, first and foremost, adamant about distinguishing between human authority and divine authority within religious institutions, the Church and the Papacy. In his essay 'Conflicts with Rome', published a few months before the Syllabus of 1864 and which he devoted almost entirely to challenging the position of Abbé Lamennais, Lord Acton estimated that there was no grosser error than 'to confound religious truth with the voice of ecclesiastical authority', to 'confound the human element with the divine in the Holy See' and to ignore the fundamental distinction that exists between 'sinful agents and the divine institution'.[112] As the theologian Risto Saarinen specified, the notion of the indefectibility of the Church – which Acton returns to here – refers, according to the Nicene Creed, both to the 'sanctity' of the Church and to a *corpus permixtum*, composed, in its concrete reality, of sinful members, a body that constantly needs to be 'reformed'. If for Catholics, more than for Protestants, holiness is an essential part of the Church, determining in relation to sin,[113] the Catholic historian asserts this distinction between the two elements that make up the Church, the human element and the divine element, the heavenly Church, which is by definition of divine origin and the earthly Church which is of human origin. One is fallible since it is human and is only the spokesperson for an authority which is infallible and eternal, since it is divine, an 'authority which transcends all government'. He notes, in this regard, that although the human element in the ecclesiastical administration had endeavoured to conceal itself and to deny its own existence, 'the most severe exposure of the part played by this human element is found in histories which show the undeniable existence of sin, error, or fraud in the high places of the Church'.[114] So that, even infallible doctrinal decisions could not express the entire truth of the supernatural object of faith, and no authority could impose error. 'The voice of the Church' is therefore not necessarily the 'voice of Authority' if the latter proclaims errors rather than the truth of God, as many popes have done, and in particular Pius IX in proclaiming papal infallibility as Church dogma. The confusion between dogma and opinion, on the one hand, and between power and authority, on the other, explained the weakness and illegitimacy of the position adopted by the religious institution as well as the artificiality of the absolute power of the papacy in the nineteenth century according to Acton. Admittedly, if the purpose of the Church's very existence as a manifestation of the 'revealed religion' instituted by Christ was, as Acton put it, 'expressly for the purpose of preserving a definite body of truth', and the Pope its chief guarantor, each decree of this truth 'required a preliminary examination' based on objective rational investigation before the Church and the Pope could proclaim and preserve it'[115] so that, without opposing freedom to authority, Acton defended the temporal and spiritual power of a liberal earthly Church as a human and legitimate authority on condition that it exposed the eternal truth by science, by the constant reaffirmation of knowledge, both historical and ecclesiastical. But, if this knowledge of the past which is 'the safest and the surest emancipation' and historical science 'one of its instruments'[116] is the only one able to access the truth, is it accessible to all individuals?

Since the Renaissance, he ascertained, 'the world has devoted its best energy and treasure to the sovereign purpose of detecting error and vindicating entrusted truth',[117] and even though the historian is superior to any authority in discerning truth, according to him, any reasonable individual could confirm demonstrable truth or condemn falsehood and falsity. And it is in the name of this individual capacity to act in the name of reason that Lord Acton not only pleaded for the constitutional and political work of the French revolutionaries who emancipated French society from the yoke of monarchical and ecclesiastical absolutism but also called on the bishops of the liberal minority to resist the dogma of papal infallibility at the First Vatican Council. For Acton, each man/individual was (potentially) endowed with 'critical' reason which allowed him, through permanent scientific evaluation and research, to pose as an arbiter on a theological dispute and to discern the truth. This is what he claimed for all those who found themselves censored like himself or in contradiction with the Holy See. Everyone had to believe in his conscience that he was in accord with the true faith of the Church and that his freedom of conscience allowed for knowledge to be 'deposited in [one's] mind by study, and transformed by conscience into inviolable convictions'.[118] He thus rejected absolute submission to human authority but bolstered, on the other hand, absolute obedience and submission to God. 'True freedom [...] consists in obeying God.'[119] Passive obedience to God did not however prevent the right of resistance to the human element which represented it (tyrannical popes, a sinful clergy (*Ancien Régime*)) if the latter failed in its temporal functions (fighting the despotism of the modern State) and spiritual ones (custodian of Christian truth), or did not respect either its role (moral and political mediator between men and nations) or its mission (to preserve and propagate divine truth) in civil society. Lord Acton therefore attacked here not only the historical and dogmatic foundations that the Church endorsed in the nineteenth century, but he also applied the liberal theory of the right of resistance to a tyrannical sovereign, to the highest authority of the Church, the Pope. He was very clearly opposed to the idea of a Church representing a *societas perfecta* as Pius IX championed and whose respect would ultimately consist in the 'respect for the See and the papal office' which would necessarily generate an acceptance of the (absolute) sovereignty of the Church.[120] 'I cannot accept your canon that we are to judge Pope and King unlike other men [...] There is no worse heresy than that the office sanctifies the holder of it', he wrote to Bishop Creighton.[121] Because Acton considered the Church and its institutions as a potential significant force in the service of freedom, he vociferated against popes who did not call for respect for freedom of conscience and failed in their mission by becoming absolute tyrants. In the name of freedom of conscience and scientific reasoning, blind submission to authority could not be tolerated and was not tenable for the historian.[122]

In this subtle reconciliation between submission to a legitimate and divine authority and an autonomous individual free to think, act and resist in conscience in his quest for freedom, it is ultimately the search for this divine and infallible truth that represents both the only real check on individual judgement and the only path to freedom. It is 'the knowledge of the truth that sets us free', Acton professed. Therefore, it would seem obvious to all

> how stubborn a phalanx of error blocks the paths of truth; that pure reason is as powerless as custom to solve the problem of free government; that it can only be the fruit of long, manifold, and painful experience; and that the tracing of the methods by which divine wisdom has educated the nations to appreciate and to assume the duties of freedom is not the least part of that true philosophy that studies to 'Assert eternal Providence, And justify the ways of God to men'.[123]

So that the idea of a constraint, of an 'external authority', would be erased in favour of the only 'voice of God' 'who comes down to dwell in our souls, who knows all our thoughts, to whom are owing all the truth we know, and all the good we do; for vice is voluntary, and virtue comes from the grace of the heavenly spirit within'.[124] Natural and divine law thus coincides with individual reason and freedom of conscience. This is why he defended the universality of the *Declaration of the Rights of Man and of the Citizen* since it echoed Christian universality, natural law, which teaches that 'by birth all men are free; they are citizens of that universal commonwealth which embraces all the world, brethren of one family, and children of God'.[125] In this respect, he conjured up the spiritual character of the Declaration which insists on primitive rights, prior to the State and distinct from it, that no human authority could neither confer nor refuse. It was the triumphant proclamation of the doctrine that not all human obligations are assignable to contract, interest or force. The Declaration begins with a call to heaven and defines them in the presence and under the auspices of Almighty God. The preamble implies that man's duties to him constitute man's rights to mankind and indicates the divine origin of the law, without affirming it.[126] The Declaration lists rights that are universal, that come from nature, not from men. These are liberty, property, security and self-defence. 'Authorities are constituted and laws are made so that these original, essential and supreme goods of all humanity are *preserved*'.[127]

Catholic universalism and democratic universalism thus mingle in the defence of freedom and of individual liberties sanctioned by the French Revolution and inscribed in Christianity. If man is indeed subject to the law, to authority and to the divine will, as Burke had maintained, the latter is mistaken in rejecting and condemning the French Revolution as having broken with history since it did, on the contrary, sanction a freedom of divine origin which it was appropriate and necessary to protect by a conscious act of will against tradition. The revolutionaries did not accordingly break the natural and divine order by making a clean sweep of the past but definitively inscribed freedom in the history of humanity as a founding principle, universal and in essence divine.

> It is the first quality of a Liberal to claim the same thing for others and for oneself, to dislike exception and prerogative, to think of all men and all countries, to acknowledge the right of the individual, derived from nature and universal, in preference to the primitive rights of a country or of a clan, obtained by force and not from heaven.[128]

The incompatibility between counter-revolutionary thought (Burke) and the liberal Catholicism of Lord Acton is undoubtedly epitomized in the opposition between the characterization of the Revolution as a civilizational catastrophe, as contingent as it was disastrous, and that of a revolution considered as the syncretism of the whole history of humanity; in the image of the breaking away from time, an invention peculiar to the Revolution, which deprived the people of what constituted them for Burke, while it was part of the philosophy of history, liberalism, for Lord Acton.

Conclusion

Considered in its political, religious, philosophical and moral dimensions and consequences, the French Revolution was effectively for Burke, Macaulay and Acton, the most stupefying event that the world had ever witnessed. In effect, the political thought and philosophy of the three liberals under study, whether conservative or not, Catholic or Protestant (Anglican or not), hinged largely on the interpretation of the Revolution that each of them offered and which permeated their respective works. The tensions between theocentrism and individualism, between heteronomy and autonomy, that is necessarily implied when analysing post-revolutionary liberalism, enlighten the liberal thought and model that each of them proposed in order to preserve freedom and peace in modern post-revolutionary liberal societies. If these three thinkers offer very different solutions to the political, religious and moral problems posed by the French Revolution, their thoughts were all dependent on their (non-)religious convictions. It is in the light of a historical and/or metahistorical conception that their respective works and positions can and must be understood. As Franck Lessay has ascertained, a horizontal and vertical history opposed the sacred and profane conception of the world. For Burke, Anglican theology and divine Providence confirmed the preeminence of a 'world order'. The providential intervention in England did not represent a break but made it possible to save its heritage, unlike revolutionary France which did not know how to conform to the natural and divine order, the actors of the French Revolution freeing themselves and undoing the ties that bonded society at its roots.

Even though Acton shared with Burke the pre-eminence of a divine order, he reversed, along with Macaulay, this Burkean perception of the individual and the world by inscribing the French Revolution in the process of autonomization and emancipation of the individual. But it was the belief in this authority, superior to man, necessarily divine in Acton, secular in Macaulay, which accounts for their divergence as to this process. If they made the founding principle of the French Revolution, the accession to democracy, the end of history and civilization and both embraced a deterministic approach to history, they envisaged this progress of humanity, the progress of the idea of freedom through the centuries differently. Macaulay exposed a political reading of religion and history while Acton's analysis was fundamentally religious. By reconciling Protestant particularism and liberal individualism, Macaulay looked upon Christianity only as a starting point from which it was necessary to depart so that the individual could emancipate himself, progress replacing divine Providence and religion ceasing to be a driving historical force. By reconciling Catholic universalism and liberal individualism, Acton deemed Christianity not only as the starting point but also as the ultimate end of history, by linking progress and religion, religion never ceasing to be *the* driving force of history. Herein lies the full meaning of the expression he took up from the German philosopher Herder, and that he reiterated in his 'Inaugural Lecture', 'history is the true demonstration of Religion'.[129]

Notes

1 Edmund Burke, *Reflections on the Revolution in France*, ed. J.G.A. Pocock (1790; Indianapolis: Hackett Publishing Company, 1987), 9.
2 T.B. Macaulay, 'Southey's Colloquies', in *The Complete Works of Lord Macaulay*, Albany edition (1830; London: Longmans Green and Co, 1898), 479.
3 On Edmund Burke, see notably R. Bourke, *Empire and Revolution. The Political life of Edmund Burke* (Princeton NJ: Princeton University Press, 2017); N. Col, *Burke, le contrat social et les revolutions* (Rennes: PUR, 2001); E. Jones, *Edmund Burke and the Making of Conservatism 1830–1914. An Intellectual History* (Oxford: Oxford University Press, 2017).
4 On T.B. Macaulay, see notably Aude Attuel-Hallade, *Thomas Babington Macaulay et la Révolution française. La pensée libérale whig en débat* (Paris: Michel Houdiard, 2018); J. Clive, *Macaulay: The Shaping of the Historian* (1973; New York: The Belknap Press of Harvard University Press Cambridge, 1987); J. Hamburger, *Macaulay and the Whig Tradition* (Chicago: The University of Chicago Press, 1976).
5 J.G.A. Pocock, 'The Varieties of Whiggism from Exclusion to Reform: A History of Ideology and Discourse', in *Virtue, Commerce and History. Essays in Political Thought and History, Chiefly in the Eighteenth Century* (Cambridge: Cambridge University Press, 1985), 215–330. For an in-depth analysis and comparison between Burke's and Macaulay's political thoughts, thwarting this idea, see Attuel-Hallade, *Thomas Babington Macaulay et la Révolution française. La pensée libérale whig en débat*, 2018.
6 On Lord Acton, see notably R. Pezzimenti, *The Political Thought of Lord Acton. The English Catholics in the Nineteenth Century* (Leominster: Gracewing, 2001); R. Hill, *Lord Acton* (Yale: Yale University Press, 2000); O. Chadwick, *Acton and History* (Cambridge: Cambridge University Press, 1998). Gertrude Himmelfarb, *Lord Acton. A Study in Conscience and Politics* (Chicago: Chicago University Press, 1993).

7   Felix Antoine Philibert Dupanloup (1802–78) was a French Catholic priest. He was among the leaders of Liberal Catholicism in France. He became a representative in the National Assembly in 1871 and a senator between 1875 and 1878.
8   On the link between the French Revolution and the Enlightenment see: *La Révolution française entre Lumières et Romantisme. Actes du colloque de novembre 1989. Cahiers de Philosophie politique et juridique* (Caen: Université de Caen, 1989, n°16).
9   Voltaire was not an atheist, but he was anticlerical and hostile to established Churches. He also questioned the Bible itself.
10 Pocock, 'The Varieties of Whiggism', 310–30; Mark Goldie, 'Priestcraft and the birth of Whiggism', in *Political Discourse in Early Modern Britain*, ed. Q. Skinner and N. Phillipson (Cambridge: Cambridge University Press, 1993), 209–32.
11 Cecil P. Courtney specified that Burke's advocating religious toleration and the belief in truth in every religion would have been considered in France as deism. Cf. 'Burke et les Lumières', in *La Révolution française entre Lumières et Romantisme*, 55–64.
12 He is the brother of the writer Antoine de Rivarol with whom he collaborated on the royalist papers before emigrating in 1790 and becoming an agent of the Princes in Brussels.
13 Edmund Burke, *Letter to the Chevalier de Rivarol*, 1 June 1791.
14 The Brabant revolution (Belgium) had been prompted by the anticlerical policy and religious reforms that his brother Joseph II had undertaken.
15 Burke, *Reflections on the Revolution in France*, 129–30.
16 Ibid., 123.
17 Lord Acton, *Lectures on the French Revolution*, ed. John Neville Figgis and Reginald Vere Laurence (1895–9; London: Macmillan and Co, 1910), 166.
18 Ibid.,167.
19 T.B. Macaulay, 'Gladstone on Church and State (1839)', in *The Complete Works of Lord Macaulay*, 184–5.
20 Stewart Jay Brown, 'The National Churches and the Union in Nineteenth-Century Britain and Ireland', in *Bonds of Union. Practices and Representations of Political Union in the United Kingdom (18th–21st centuries)*, ed. Isabelle Bour and Antoine Mioche (Tours: Presses Universitaires François-Rabelais, 2005), 57.
21 Burke, *Reflections on the Revolution in France*, 87.
22 On this intricate point in Burke's thought, I would like to thank (in alphabetical order) Richard Bourke, Stewart Jay Brown, Norbert Col, and Franck Lessay for their invaluable comments and clarifications.
23 Burke, *Reflections on the Revolution in France*, 137.
24 Macaulay, 'Gladstone on Church and State', 184–5.
25 Burke, *Reflections on the Revolution in France*, 138–9.
26 Acton, *Lectures on the French Revolution*, 165.
27 Ibid., 165.
28 Ibid.
29 T.B. Macaulay, 'Horace Walpole (1833)', in *The Complete Works of Lord Macaulay*, 323–4.
30 T.B. Macaulay, 'The Church of Ireland (1845)', in *The Complete Works of Lord Macaulay*, 153.
31 Lord Acton, Add MSS. 4869, Acton Papers (Cambridge University Library), 20. AEB Owen, *University Library, Cambridge, Summary Guide to Accessions of Manuscripts (other than medieval) since 1867* (Cambridge: for the University Library at the University Press, 1966).
32 Macaulay, 'The Church of Ireland', 151.

33 Lord Acton, 'Mr. Goldwin Smith's *Irish History* (1862)', in *Selected Writings of Lord Acton*, ed. J. Rufus Fears (Indianapolis: Liberty Fund, 1985-8), 90.
34 In that respect, Deane Seamus underpins the fact that for Acton Disestablishment was in effect not only the triumph for freedom but also a necessary preliminary to the successful achievement of Home Rule. Deane Seamus, 'Freedom Betrayed: Acton, Burke and Ireland', *The Irish Review*, no. 30 (2003): 13-35.
35 Macaulay 'The Church of Ireland', 154.
36 Acton, Add Mss 1869, 20.
37 Macaulay, 'Southey's Colloquies', 485.
38 Lord Acton, 'The History of Freedom in Antiquity (1877)', in *Selected Writings of Lord Acton*, vol. 1, 17-18.
39 In Ireland, the tyranny of its institution was perpetuated in the system by which it was upheld, and in the violence with which it was introduced; and this tyranny continues through all its existence. It is the religion of the minority, the church of an alien State, the cause of suffering and of disturbance, an instrument, a creature, and a monument of conquest and of tyranny. Acton, 'Mr. Goldwin Smith's *Irish History*', 91.
40 Roland Minnerath, 'Eglise-Etat', in *Dictionnaire critique de Théologie*, ed. Jean-Yves Lacoste (Paris: PUF, 1998), 383.
41 T.B. Macaulay, 'Burleigh and his Times (1832)', in *The Complete Works of Lord Macaulay*, 190.
42 T.B. Macaulay, *The History of England from the Accession of James II* (1848-1861), vol. I, 57.
43 Lord Acton, 'The Count of Montalembert (1858)', in *Selected Writings of Lord Acton*, 9-17.
44 'T.B. Macaulay to Duncan Mclaren (30 January 1841)', in *The Letters of Lord Macaulay*, ed. Thomas Pinney (Cambridge: Cambridge University Press, 2009), vol. III, 364-5.
45 The *High Churchmen* opposed the appointment of the liberal Anglican Hampden to Oxford in 1836 since, they considered, it was an intrusion by the State into the spiritual affairs of the Church. Macaulay, on the contrary, supported the nomination of Hampden by the State. The controversy in Scotland also revolved around the prerogatives of the State and the Church and opposed lay patrons and local congregations in the appointment of clerics.
46 Lord Acton, 'The Roman Question', *The Rambler* (January 1860).
47 Acton, 'The Count of Montalembert', 9-10.
48 For Lord Acton, it was even in the nature of Protestantism itself 'to confine the Church within the jurisdiction of the State'.
49 Lord Acton, 'Döllinger on the Temporal Power (1861)', in *Selected Writings of Lord Acton*, 86.
50 Hence, his great disappointment and disillusionment at the First Vatican Council.
51 Jean-Louis Gazzaniga and Philippe Ségur, 'Eglise', in *Dictionnaire de philosophie politique* (Paris: PUF, 2005), 217-21.
52 Acton, 'Political Thoughts on the Church (1859)', in *Selected Writings of Lord Acton*, 31; 'History of Freedom in Antiquity', 27.
53 Ibid.
54 'Lord Acton on the Roman Question', in *Selected Writings of Lord Acton*, 359.
55 Ibid.
56 Ibid., 361.
57 Ibid., 86.

58 Lord Acton, 'Dollinger on the Temporal Power', in *Selected Writings of Lord Acton*, ed. J. Rufus Fears (Indianapolis: Liberty Fund, 1985–1988), vol. III, 83. (cf note 49).
59 'Lord Acton on the Roman Question', 361.
60 Acton, 'The Roman Question'.
61 Jean Bauberot, S. Mathieu, 'le Royaume-Uni: l'ébranlement du système de *Church and State*', in *Religion, modernité et culture au Royaume-Uni et en France 1800–1914* (Paris: Editions du Seuil, 2002), 87–91.
62 Burke, *Reflections on the Revolution in France*, 81.
63 Macaulay, 'Southey's Colloquies', 484.
64 Ibid.
65 Macaulay, 'Gladstone on Church and State', 131.
66 The Inquisition, for example (see 'The Protestant Theory of Persecution (1862)' and 'Mr. Goldwin Smith's *Irish History*(1862)'). But later on, he would condemn all forms of persecution and whoever practised it.
67 Michael W.McConnell, 'Establishment and Toleration in Edmund Burke's Constitution of Freedom' in *Supreme Court Review* (Chicago: University of Chicago Law School, 1995, n°393), 393–421.
68 Acton, 'Mr. Goldwin Smith's *Irish history*', 84.
69 Mickael V. Mc Connell, 'Establishment and Toleration in Edmund Burke's "Constitution of Freedom"', *The Supreme Court Review* 1995, (1995), 401.
70 First among them, his mentor, Döllinger. Cf Himmelfarb, *Lord Acton*.
71 Seamus, 'Freedom Betrayed', 32.
72 Acton, *Lectures on the French Revolution*, 172.
73 Ibid., 173.
74 Ibid., 172.
75 Ibid., 173.
76 My translation as for all the quotes taken from original French texts: 'ou bien le parti pris de l'antériorité du monde et de la loi des choses, ou bien le parti pris de l'antériorité des hommes et de leur activité créatrice. Ou bien la soumission à un ordre intégralement reçu, déterminé d'avant et du dehors de notre volonté; ou bien la responsabilité d'un ordre reconnu procéder de la volonté des individus'. Marcel Gauchet, *Le Désenchantement du monde. Une histoire politique de la religion* (Paris: Gallimard, 1985), 26.
77 Lucien Jaume, 'Liberté et souveraineté politique dans le catholicisme', *Cités* 4, no. 12 (2002): 49.
78 Franck Lessay, 'Burke et la nationalisation de la raison' in *La Révolution française entre Lumières et Romantisme*, 67–82.
79 The burkean interpretation of a close relationship between divine providence and the French Revolution had been taken up by Robert Southey, to whom Macaulay replied, worried about the propagation of the ideals and founding principles of the Revolution.
80 'livrée aux aléas et aux souffrances de la vie en expiation de ses fautes'. Lessay, 'Burke et la nationalisation de la raison', 76–7.
81 Norbert Col, *Burke, Le contrat social et les révolutions* (Rennes: PUR, 2001), 237.
82 quoted by Franck Lessay in 'Burke et la nationalisation de la raison', 76–7.
83 Acton, 'The History of freedom in Antiquity', 24.
84 T.B. Macaulay, 'Parliamentary Reform (16 December 1831)', in *The Complete Works of Lord Macaulay*, 491.
85 'la nécessité qui nous entraîne'. Quoted by Marcel Gauchet, in *Le Désenchantement du monde*, 71.

86 Macaulay, 'Parliamentary reform (16 December 1831)', 491.
87 Lord Acton, 'Inaugural Lecture on the Study of History', in *Lectures on Modern History*, ed. John Neville Figgis and Reginald Vere Laurence (1895; London: McMillan and Co, 1906), 14.
88 Acton, Add.Mss.4948, 177.
89 Acton, 'Inaugural Lecture on the Study of History', 10.
90 Ibid., 11.
91 Gauchet, *Le Désenchantement du monde*, 12.
92 'la foi confiante en un avenir plein de promesses est incompréhensible si l'on ne se réfère pas à la foi chrétienne qui faisait de l'avenir l'horizon décisif de notre pensée après le Christ'. Karl Löwith, *Histoire et Salut. Les présupposés théologiques de la philosophie de l'histoire*, translated from German by M.C. Challiol-Gillet, S. Hurstel and J.F. Kervegan (1949/1953 Paris: Gallimard, 2002), 115.
93 'un mal qui semble bon, car l'espérance est toujours en train d'attendre quelque chose de meilleur'. Ibid., 251.
94 'le développement graduel de l'égalité des conditions est un fait providentiel, il en a les principaux caractères; il est universel, durable, il échappe chaque jour à la puissance humaine' (Alexis de Tocqueville, *De la démocratie en Amérique*, 1835–40).
95 Burke, *Reflections on the Revolution in France*, 85.
96 Lessay, 'Burke et la nationalisation de la raison', 77.
97 Massimo Boffa, 'Contre-Révolution', in *Dictionnaire critique de la Révolution française* (1989 Paris: PUF, 2009), 93.
98 Gérard Gengembre, *La Contre-révolution ou l'histoire désespérante* (Paris: Edition Imago, 1989), 28.
99 Lessay, 'Burke et la nationalisation de la raison'.
100 Gengembre, *La Contre-révolution ou l'histoire désespérante*.
101 Ibid.
102 When Butterfield analysed the Whig roots of English liberalism, it was this burkean perception of the individual that he highlighted. The radical criticism of the French Revolution, underlying the whole work, is directed against the liberal individualism of 1789 and the totalitarian state of the Jacobins, the only original thing bequeathed by the Revolution, according to him. The deification of the individual and then of the State were the sources of many of the evils that Europe experienced in the nineteenth and twentieth centuries, for the conservative historian, who distinguished political action inspired by tolerance and Christian humility – reformist, urban, conciliatory – and a typically French revolutionary action from which Irish nationalist would have done better no to have drawn inspiration. Herbert Butterfield, *The Englishman and His History* (1944; Cambridge: Cambridge University Press, 1945), 103–17.
103 Stéphane Rials, *Révolution et Contre-révolution au XIXe siècle* (Paris: Édition Albatros et Duc, 1987), 14.
104 Ibid.
105 Ibid.
106 Lessay, 'Burke et la nationalisation de la raison', 75.
107 Ibid.
108 Col, *Burke, le contrat social et les révolutions*, 238.
109 Joseph de Maistre, *Considérations sur la France* (1796; Paris: Imprimerie Nationale Editions, 1994), 132.
110 Macaulay, 'Southey's Colloquies', 499–500.
111 Ibid., 499.

112 Lord Acton, 'Conflicts with Rome', in *Selected Writings of Lord Acton*, ed. J. Rufus Fears (Indianapolis: Liberty Fund, 1985-1988), vol. III, 235, 249.
113 Risto Saarinen, 'Indéfectibilité de l'Eglise', in *Dictionnaire critique de théologie*, 570-1.
114 Acton, 'Conflicts with Rome', 241.
115 It was one of the crucial elements of the controversy that arose during the First Vatican Council. The use of history-science in theological debate, the application of historical and critical methodology to Sacred Scriptures was particularly evident among German historians and theologians (such as Döllinger). The main problem for Acton and Dollinger was that the theory of infallibility put forward by the pope's supporters was based on 'conclusions transcending evidence and rest[ed] on an unattainable postulate rather than on demonstrable consequences of a system of religious faith'. Only what was not 'decided with dogmatic infallibility [was] for the moment susceptible only to a scientific determination which advance[ed] with the progress of science' and 'bec[ame] absolute when science reache[ed] its definitive results' (Acton, 'Conflicts with Rome', 244).
116 Acton, 'Inaugural Lecture on the Study of History', 29-30.
117 Ibid., 30.
118 Acton, 'Conflicts with Rome', 257.
119 Acton, 'History of Freedom in Antiquity', 24.
120 Bernt T. Oftestad, *The Catholic Church and Liberal Democracy* (London and New York: Routledge, 2019).
121 Acton, Letter to Mandell Creighton, Add.Mss. 6871, 60. It does not however mean that he condemned papal primacy. Primacy and absolutism were not to be confused in his criticism. Papal authority was by definition the most legitimate authority (under the conditions mentioned). Regardless of the human being, the Christian, who implemented it, it was absolutism that he condemned, whether dogmatic, personal and/or institutional. As Gertrude Himmelfarb pointed out, nothing was heretical in this attitude, for Acton, since Catholic theologians had applied to the pope the teaching of Saint Thomas Aquinas on royalty, arguing that it was legitimate to disobey a pope, who ordered the commission of a sin or passed a subversive decree to the Church. (Himmelfarb, *Lord Acton*, 232). See also Acton's 'History of Freedom in Antiquity', 34. In practice, this position applied to the temporal and civil authority, the State, and not to the spiritual one as B.T. Oftestad made clear (Oftestad, *The Catholic Church and Liberal Democracy*).
122 This approach induced him to distance himself from Newmann.
123 Acton, 'The History of Freedom in Antiquity', 19.
124 Ibid., 24.
125 Ibid.
126 Acton, *Lectures on the French Revolution*, 106.
127 Ibid.
128 Acton, Add. Mss 4960, 120.
129 Acton, 'Inaugural Lecture on the Study of History', 12. Yet, Acton's disappointment and disillusionment led him to question religion as the guardian of morals as he grew older, as all religions had promoted persecution, according to him. His morality became therefore essentially and ultimately secular though he could not wholly accept it.

Part Two

Catholicism and liberty(/ies)

4

Liberties before liberalism: Ultramontane political thought in England, c. 1835–50

Colm O'Siochru
Dulwich College, UK

Introduction

The history of Liberal Catholicism in England has been told many times in the form of a bittersweet lament. A 'remarkable attempt to find a *modus vivendi* between the ... Church and the secular principles of the nineteenth century', scientific and political, it was, its first synoptic survey informs us, 'the story of a great hope and a great failure'.[1] The 'foresighted' ideas[2] of a 'tiny band' of scholars[3] – sketched at pace in ephemeral periodicals like *The Rambler* and *The Home and Foreign Review* – caught fire. They articulated sophisticated critiques of modernity's 'irrational' creeds: from 'Kantean conceptualism', Comtean positivism and undogmatic 'neo-Protestantism',[4] to revolutionary liberalism, democratic nationalism, centralizing Caesarism and the 'dismal science' of political economy.[5] They advanced imaginative responses to the Church's myriad problems in this modern age, urging intellectual rigour and freedom, and an end to the anachronistic Constantinian ecclesiology still underpinning Catholic political thought. But incurring suspicion and censure from Rome and its outriders, they were broken on the rack of ecclesiastical authority and left shattered both as men and as a movement. The contemporary arbiters of taste were impressed by their serious-mindedness, charmed by their 'play of mind', and appalled by their suppression.[6] Historians of the movement writing in the midst or aftermath of the Second Vatican Council (1962–5) tend to reach the same partisan judgement from an unapologetically presentist perspective. Mourning the martyrdom of historically minded men, they can 'only admire' those whose 'fate' it was to be 'out of season' – 'prophets reviled in their own time but anticipat[ing] many of the trends of our own century'.[7] But they console the reader with a cheering epilogue: 'failure' was, in fact, but temporary, for the vanquished of Vatican I become the vindicated of Vatican II, spiritual godfathers (alongside J. H. Newman, their sphinx – like fellow-traveller) of a new ecclesiology.[8]

Like every tragedy, this lost cause must have its heroes, flawed but noble. Lord Acton (1834–1902) takes centre stage, grave and gnomic. Scion of a great Catholic house, stepson to a powerful Whig minister and protégé to Ignaz von Döllinger (1799-1890), Catholic Germany's preeminent historian, he arrived in England in 1858 bristling with erudition and bold plans for the galvanization of the Catholic body as it prepared fully to take its place in the life of the nation – plans scuppered by endless conflicts with Rome over the scope of ecclesiastical authority and the nature of Catholic politics.[9] At Acton's right-hand, 'flicking his whip at Bishops ... throwing stones at Sacred Congregations, and ... discharging pea-shooters at Cardinals',[10] stood the Shakespeare scholar, philosopher and prolific polemicist, Richard Simpson (1820-76), whose 'impish' style infuriated the hierarchy almost as much as his 'pugnacious' assertion of the rights of free thought on all things not touched by dogma.[11] To be sure, Acton was also flanked by men more circumspect, like the Irish Liberal MPs, William Monsell (1812-94) and Thomas O'Hagan (1812-85), and the War Office clerk, T. F. Wetherell (1830-1908), who sought by pragmatic reformism on matters like the Irish economy, and principled constitutionalism on matters like the Roman Question, to give this circle an enduring voice in ecclesiastical and national affairs.[12] But trenchant views and waspish tempers lent liberal Catholics' conflicts with Rome a provocative quality that would ultimately prove ruinous. H. N. Oxenham (1829-88), for example – like Simpson, an Oxford convert who lost his living and found a role as a lay controversialist – articulated a vision of Catholic education so de-clericalizing, and a theory of the Church's temporal power so minimizing, that Newman felt obliged publicly to rebuke him, and even Acton balked at his incorrigibly 'disputatious' manner.[13]

But if these men were awkward, historians suggest, they were also tragically misunderstood: they not only sought the good of the Church by placing her on a surer footing in modernity's treacherous terrain, but unlike exponents of earlier, very different species of liberal Catholicism, like Félicité de Lamennais, remained loyally within her communion across decades of deepening division and in spite of Rome's highhandedness, from the condemnations implicit in the *Syllabus Errorum* (1864) of the congresses of Malines and Munich – Montalembert's call for a 'free Church in a free State'; Döllinger's demand for a free Catholic *Wissenschaft* – to the declaration of papal infallibility (1870) and the brute assertion of force by which it was realized.[14] That loyalism, of course, diminishes neither the struggle nor its scars. These mavericks thundered against the emergence of a 'gigantic tyranny', which sought 'to force on us not only the dogmas and laws of the Church, but ... its own "instincts" and "tones" and "old womanisms"';[15] they fought tooth-and-nail with Döllinger during the Council's proceedings,[16] and guided W. E. Gladstone's hand as that inexhaustible volcano erupted in 1874 with a moral crusade against 'Vaticanism' and what he claimed to be its corrosive effects on British Catholics' civic loyalties;[17] Acton even came to describe the papacy as 'the fiend skulking behind the crucifix' and drifted towards an 'intellectual agnosticism'.[18] Some few were driven further still: the *Rambler*'s first editor, J. M. Capes (1813-89), grew so exasperated with the 'Papal autocracy['s]' reign of 'terror', so depressed by its 'suicidal' war against the 'critical faculty', that he fled Rome for the freedom of positivism's 'historical Jesus'.[19] But this was the exception that proved the rule: the same profound belief that had drawn them to or anchored them in the Catholic faith of their youth – incarnational mystery and dogma; the unity and universality of a Church grounded on the same[20] – meant that most liberal Catholics would not risk the taint of neo-Jansenism by following Döllinger into schism.²¹ 'Communion with Rome', Acton cried, 'is dearer to me than life'²² – even as he was being interrogated by Cardinal Manning on suspicion of heresy and denounced by the Catholic press as '*ipso facto* excommunciate'.²³ And so on those matters that had animated them for some twenty years, the liberal Catholics fell silent, or ceased, at least, to speak as Catholics.

Thus conveyed, the tragedy appears multifaceted. Lay men of faith and goodwill were lost to the Church or alienated from it. With them was suffocated a stimulating voice that might have saved Newman from marginalization; built a vibrant ecumenical movement of mind with Anglo-Catholic thinkers and social reformers; and steered the Church in a very different, 'progressive', direction – one that broke free from the intellectual sterility, cultural claustrophobia and political reaction of the decades that followed, and leaped boldly into the sunlit uplands of *aggiornamento*. Here the story finally names its villain triumphant: ultramontanism. This was 'the siege structure and mentality behind which the Catholic Church had barricaded herself ever since the Tridentine Counter-Reformation';²⁴ a tradition constantly renewed across the long nineteenth century by anti-Gallicans like Bishop John Milner, counter-revolutionaries like Joseph de Maistre, culture warriors like Louis Veuillot, neoscholastic philosophers like Matteo Liberatore and radical anti-liberals like Hilaire Belloc. And just as 'the people of God'²⁵ finally broke out of this 'fortress Church'²⁶ in the 1960s, and set about canonizing those who a century before had lit the path to liberty, so their ultramontane gaolers were made to atone for the 'perduring' 'trauma' they had inflicted.²⁷ Historians savaged the ignorant ascendancy that had too long stood athwart history shouting '*non possumus*'. They depicted a party of overgrown schoolboys, selfish, bullying, fat and fatuous, turbulently emotional and psychologically 'insecure'; a party of intellectually 'sterile' bureaucrats, their imaginations stunted by 'stiff-necked scholasticism', their egos titillated by Inquisition role-play; a party of 'ineffective dreamers' with authoritarian – even 'demonic' – tendencies, bent on 'war against the secular State'.²⁸ Ultramontanism often merited little more than the self-evident description as the process by which Rome's ecclesiastical and aesthetic-devotional domination was secured.²⁹ Where it did, it was pathologized as a toxic 'ecclesial ideology':³⁰ the synthesis of a 'fanatical', 'autocratic' clericalism in ecclesiastical government and culture;³¹ a 'tyrannous Transcendentalism' in theology, seeking escape from 'infinite doubt' in the infallible fortress on the Tiber;³² and an irrational, reactionary politics, so fixated on a Christendom resurrected and an 'anti-christian' liberalism cast down, that it could find few meaningful projects for its energies beyond frustrated anti-Garibaldianism;³³ 'aggressive' campaigns for sectarian education;³⁴ 'hopelessly irrelevant' schemes for social reform,³⁵ frothed mutterings about masonic conspiracies and a proto-fascist flirtation with 'cultural and political revolution'.³⁶ Thus, tragically, were Catholics ghettoized from the modern world – English Catholics, perhaps, even more than most.³⁷

Clearly, Acton's injunction that the historian was to be 'hanging-judge' is one his vindicators took to heart. In the mouths of professed admirers and practitioners of historical scholarship, the anachronism and presentist partisanship with which much of the literature treats ultramontanism is as egregious as it is ironic. Problematic, too, is the undiscriminating way in which it swallows and regurgitates the definition of ultramontanism by its contemporary critics. It implicitly accepts the kind of judgements found in Acton's polemical 1863 survey of its intellectual history, in which he denounced the theology of this 'extreme' party as 'recklessly' anti-historical – confusing the 'substance' of dogmas like 'the existence of God' with the contingent 'accidents' of Roman devotions – and its politics as irreducibly Maistrean, an apology for '[t]yranny, poverty, and slavery'.[38] It further fails to historicize the ways in which such judgements developed during the debates over Modernism and filtered into the foundational texts of 'Second Spring' historiography – like those of Wilfrid Ward, who warned that if the 'rigidity of Rome', so indispensable to meeting the Reformation 'emergency', could not now respond to the new 'exigencies of the times' by re-engaging with the liberal ultramontane tradition of orthodox Mennaisians, like Jean-Baptiste Henri Lacordaire, a 'false conservatism' would condemn the Church to 'fossilism'.[39]

At its most unself-conscious, much of this literature is even indebted to tropes deployed by ultramontanism's avowed non-Catholic enemies. In its common characterization as the closing of the Catholic mind and the ghettoization of Catholic society, we hear uncanny echoes of those ultra-Protestants, Whigs, Liberal Anglicans and positivists, who denounced ultramontanism as an abominable, backward-looking desire for a 'hierocracy' founded on 'moral and mental slavery':[40] a would-be 'temporal ... [and] spiritual despotism', a 'fortress' and 'prison-house' of 'superstition and fraud'.[41] Such ritual denunciations became integral to the liturgy of British liberalism. Sitting through the performance, decade after decade, Catholics gradually felt fury subside into boredom.

W. H. Kent OSC bemoaned the fact that, even at the end of the nineteenth century, admirable theologians like A. M. Fairbairn could locate Catholicism's 'ultimate source in ... despair of the reason'; born of an unwillingness seriously to engage with Catholic thought, this kind of superficiality, he moaned, was 'painful' to observe in intelligent minds.[42] Yet – some outstanding individual studies of ultramontane intellectual history notwithstanding[43] – Kent's sense of frustration in 1899 would not be entirely misplaced today, in the second decade of the twenty-first century.

Developments in adjacent fields now render that paradigm not only problematic but untenable. In Britain, Mary Heimann has shown that Second-Spring revivalism was no Roman imposition; the identity of the emerging community was primarily negotiated in old devotional forms long-shared by both English and Irish Catholics, with women and 'ordinary souls' shaping it just as much as the Curia's foot soldiers.[44] Scholars of German Catholicism have urged historians of religion to discard a lens crafted by teleologically minded secularization theorists, and take the ultramontane revival seriously on its own terms, charting the formation of a modern Catholic identity in forms of ritual representation and symbolic 'resacralization'; in cultures of 'clericalism' and 'feminization'; in the ascendancy gained by Ligorian ethics and neo-Thomist philosophy; in a paradoxical politics that was populist, nationally minded, and lay-led, but also papalist, internationalist and anti-Erastian.[45] And the historiography of France, Italy, Spain and Austria, where Ultramontanism was far from a minority occupation, offers a stimulating example of how this can be realized. Historians like Dale Van Kley, Philippe Boutry and Marina Caffiero have contextualized the ultramontanism that emerged in the late-eighteenth century as a self-consciously 'orthodox' political theology – but one that cannot straightforwardly be characterized as reactionary, or even conservative, for what it sought, in theology as in politics, was the world's sacramental regeneration.⁴⁶

Indeed, as the remainder of this chapter argues, that ultramontanism was developed by its advocates in England in decidedly liberal ways, long before the missionaries of the *Rambler* emerged to inform, educate and entertain. It focuses on the years before the great transformations wrought to the Catholic body by the waves of Tractarian conversions and Irish migration (1845–50), the revolutions of 1848 and their aftermaths, and the restoration of the hierarchy in 1850. It explores the body of ultramontane political argument articulated in the *Dublin Review*, a quarterly journal founded by Rome's 'man on the spot', Nicholas Wiseman (in collaboration with the Irish hero of Emancipation, Daniel O'Connell), which quickly became the most influential organ of Catholic thought in Britain and Ireland.⁴⁷ In its pages, we can trace the development of a distinct epistemology and ecclesiology, and a radical critique of Malthusian social thought and political economy. But I wish to focus specifically on the party's constitutional discourse: on the conceptualization of 'Christendom' by Wiseman and some of his allies. I suggest in conclusion that no nuanced understanding of 'liberal Catholicism' – at least in its British context – can be grounded in a false juxtaposition with the 'liberal conservatism' propounded by these ultramontanes.

I Wiseman's campaign in context: Preaching liberty to the counter-culture

Born in Seville in 1802 – in a land where, as one biographer put it, 'the mysteries of religion … entwine[d] themselves round the daily lives of the people'⁴⁸ – Wiseman was first educated at Ushaw College, Durham, where he might in time have become a disciple of the historian, John Lingard, exponent *par excellence* of England's moderate form of Catholic enlightenment.⁴⁹ But the Tridentine world soon summoned him home; a 'new era' dawned when, as a wide-eyed sixteen-year-old, he heard the words 'Ecco Roma' and set foot in 'the queen of cities'.⁵⁰

In restoration Rome, Wiseman fell under the spell of the *intransigenti* (or *zelanti*), whose anti-Jansenim, as Pelletier has meticulously demonstrated, had become the Curia's 'dominant mode of evaluating the ecclesiology of the Revolution'.⁵¹ The '*scuola antigiansenistica*' remobilized seventeenth- and eighteenth-century theories casting Jansenists as an ecclesiastical fifth column, bent on subverting incarnational faith, enslaving the pope, ending the Church's *potestas indirecta* and erecting a 'monstrous civil theocracy' directed by an enlightened elite.⁵² It ascribed to the Jansenist-Gallican synthesis, and its other, local iterations – like Febronianism – causal significance in ushering in the Revolution. Conspiring with Protestants, *philosophes* and masons, the enemy within had weakened the Church's doctrine and discipline as prelude to a wider attack on Christendom and the sovereignty of the incarnate God.⁵³ The ultramontane answer to this challenge was a robust reassertion of Tridentine Catholicism. This is not, however, to be confused with the reactionary politics of Europe's restored rulers, nor conflated with the Traditionalism of Maistre and Bonald. Remaining firmly rooted in Thomist thinking, Roman ultramontane philosophy built on the work of orthodox *lumi*, who had called for a critical but eirenic engagement with both Newtonian natural philosophy and the language of natural rights and intra-mundane progress.[54] Its *ressourcement* theology drew on the best 'liberal' scholarship in history, archaeology, patristics, symbology and oriental languages. Its ecclesiology balanced a Suarezian, juridical model of the Church as a *societas perfecta* (a self-sufficient body politic, independent of the state but supreme in matters religious) with a vision of the Church as Christ's mystical body, the means of the world's sacramental regeneration.[55] And its political theology saw the mission of that Church in the revolutionary world as obvious: the defence of the supernatural economy of the incarnation (sacraments, saints, stigmatics, miracles, popular devotions)[56] against those bent on toppling Christ from his throne – the 'jansenistical' elites of every land, who, in a vast conspiracy, attempted to control the Church by expropriating its property and hollowing out its religious life. This species of liberalism, they argued, was merely the continuation of revolution by other means. But this struggle against liberalism did not pit the Church against 'the people'. To the contrary: the Church was the natural ally and guardian of the people, who loved the easy yoke of Christ, and who were coming gradually to realize that 'liberalism' did not mean democracy so much as it meant exploitative, oligarchic rule.[57]

When Wiseman returned to England in the early 1830s – a biblical scholar of international repute, a correspondent with leading lights of the Catholic revival, like Montalembert and the Schlegels, and the pope's appointed man for the conversion of a country where Protestantism seemed in crisis and the ramparts of the confessional state seemed to be crumbling[58] – he brought this populist ultramontanism with him. He set about 'Romanizing' the recently emancipated Catholic community, rebuking recusants for a lingering 'Cisalpine' sentiment that tainted them with Gallicanism and Jansenism; and he taunted High Churchmen and Tractarians that schism and eucharistic heresy had left them little more than crypto-Calvinists in fine vestments. But if much of his campaign thus centred on the rhetorical battle to identify Catholicism with its ultramontane iteration, just as significant were Wiseman's more eirenic efforts to persuade his hostile audiences that ultramontanism offered solutions to the politico-theological problems of modernity. In the 'hungry forties', many of these were social and economic; and here, he was assisted by the professoriate of Maynooth, a generation of young scholars shaped by anti-Jansenist theology and O'Connellite politics, and shepherded by the formidable theologian, C. W. Russell. They played an important role in formulating a critique of Malthusianism, one further developed in appeals to incarnational anthropology and natural-law ethics by Lacordaire and other Mennaisian economists at the Catholic University of Louvain, like Charles de Coux (1787–1864).[59] But Wiseman was also keen to emphasize ultramontanism's answer to the constitutional crisis of Christendom – thrown up by the French Revolution but, in an age of restive liberalism and paranoid reaction, unresolved by the restoration settlement. In this, he drew support from Thomas Chisholm Anstey (1816–73), who had recently moved from Tasmania to the Middle Temple, and, under Wiseman's direction, from a flirtation with Tractarianism to an obsession with Belgian guilds and German metaphysics.[60] He also relied heavily on John Burton Robertson (1800–77), who, after a schooling at Ware, studied for several years at La Chênaie, Lamennais' Breton base, becoming a disciple of the eucharistic symbologist, Olympe-Philippe Gerbet, and then moved to Germany, where at Bonn, the poet, A. W. Schlegel, and canonist, Friedrich Windischmann, drew him into the world of German ultramontanism and its preoccupation with 'the coming Middle Ages'.[61]

Wiseman and his band saw in the present state of Christendom a paradox. There were certainly grounds for optimism. As the *zelanti* observed, 'the people' was not necessarily a revolutionary category: they had risen against the Church's enemies both with the armalite (from the Tuscan revolts against Josephism in 1787 to the campaign of 1830 against Orangeist tyranny in Flanders) and with the ballot box (most notably under the prophetic leadership of O'Connell, against the Irish species of Orangeist despotism). Indeed, although Lamennais' divinization of the demos stood condemned by Gregory XVI – his attempt 'to engraft on Catholicism revolutionary principles', Robertson lamented, caused 'the most … eloquent apologist … since Bossuet' to plunge into an 'apostasy' [*sic*] 'the most melancholy … since that of Tertullian'[62] – the Liberator's loyalty proved that a Catholic politics, popular and orthodox, remained possible. But ultramontanes also saw reasons to be fearful. Restoration had promised to set the Church free, but everywhere the old chains were reforged: Mennaisians felt stifled by the dead hand of Bourbon Gallicanism; German ultramontanes like Josef Görres raged against the Church's oppression by Protestant and neo-Febronian princes; even the pope's patrons propped up the Temporal Power in troublingly transactional terms.[63] In this moment of uncertainty, ultramontanes felt torn, and began to contemplate the necessity of a third way: if it proved too compromising to seek by political means (radical or restorationist) the world's '"regeneration"', then perhaps it would be necessary to defend 'purity of doctrine' by severing ties with the political order, thus saving the Church from either democratic or neo-Josephist 'bondage'.[64]

As Wiseman well knew, these were questions that haunted Anglicans, too. Tractarians like John Keble and Hurrell Froude feared that in the UK, as on the continent, Erastian forces laid hands on the Established Church's temporalities and promoted latitudinarian divines to dissolve its doctrines; those like E. B. Pusey worried about a knee-jerk anti-Establishmentarianism that would renounce the Christendom ideal and return the Church to the catacombs.[65] Wiseman's wager across the 1830s and 1840s was that Tractarians could be convinced that Rome had an answer to the crisis of Christendom, where Anglicanism did not. He would show them that political ultramontanism was, in the words of Maistre, not only 'a *contrary* revolution, but *the contrary of* revolution';[66] that it had found imaginative new ways to rescue what 'the Revolution' sought hungrily to devour.[67] But drawing more directly on the future-oriented liberal ultramontanism of Mennaisians like Frédéric Ozanam (1815–53) and pluralist romantics like Friedrich Schlegel (1772–1829), Wiseman's cohort argued that the victim in Revolution's maw was not an abstract quality – 'sovereignty' or 'tradition' – but something more historically specific (and likelier to resonate in English minds): the 'liberty consecrated' of Christendom. Displaying Tocquevillian optimism, they suggested that this liberty could be *re*-consecrated in an alliance of those faithful to the incarnation: the papacy and the peoples.[68]

The *Dublin* circle thus sought to situate ultramontanism in Britain's romantic-conservative 'counter-culture'.⁶⁹ That culture was vibrant, radical, Christian and cantankerous. In a sea of contrarians, the ultramontanes were at odds with all their would-be allies, and thus very much at home. They were wedded in principle to the Constantinian ideal of Church-State union; to the rights and duties of property; to the notion that a nation's welfare lay in the alliance of crown, Church, corporations and people against the factionalism of a venal elite; and to the belief that a nation's constitution was a delicate organism that developed in imperceptible, almost mystical, ways, and did not admit of abstract reinvention.⁷⁰ But ultramontanes could not accept that these were *English* truths, yielding 'English liberties' and an English moral character fit to hold them: they were the common inheritance of Christendom; English exceptionalism had not cultivated these principles so much as it had exposed them to peril by planting them in poisoned Protestant soil. High Tories upheld the constitution in Church and State, but their Establishment was Rome's enemy and needed to be destroyed. Liberal Tories upheld property, but their Malthusianism made it the tool of oligarchic capitalism. Paternalists – whether of a Young England, Tractarian or Carlylean persuasion – sought to 'prescribe' a spiritual 'medicine' for an ailing 'body ... politic', but they did so vainly, outside the 'COMMUNION OF CHRIST'S CHURCH CATHOLIC'.⁷¹ Nor did the chasm separating ultramontanes from English conservatism bespeak an affinity for legitimism; they feared the oblivion to which it would condemn them and felt excitement at the prospects of a democratic age. Thus, in a time of socio-economic dislocation and political tumult, this first generation of ultramontanes ploughed their own furrow in a crowded field, seeking to convince England's liberals and conservatives, alike, that the temporal power of the Catholic Church meant ordered liberty for Europe and that the pope was the ultimate guarantor of both gothic freedoms and international peace.

II Ultramontane history

They sought to persuade on the ecumenical basis of 'scientific' historical argument; their narratives were thus framed in ways that emphasized the relationship between Church and state, while seeking to preserve the integrity of the spiritual and temporal orders. In the mediaeval 'Ages of Faith', they claimed, the Church which had once 'formed a community set apart from a corrupt world' now baptized that world, so that it 'bec[ame] Christian'. In the consecrated polity of Christendom, the relations between sovereign and subject were 'settled'; 'paternal' values underpinned an authority never vicious, an obedience never grudging. There flourished in the 'mixed monarchy' of each Christian polity a true political liberty. The monarch was no mere 'pensioner' of parliament, but a guardian of fundamental laws. Aristocratic dominance did not preclude popular influence but guarded against outbreaks of wild democracy. Municipal institutions checked centralizing trends that fed the ambitions of degenerate metropolitan elites, preserving the rich plurality of the commonwealth. And the Church's unfettered freedom – and its temporal power, which allowed it to exercise 'considerable influence in matters of state' – served to guarantee this complex system of overlapping 'liberties'.[72]

As Robertson sought to show, this was not simply a vision of the past, but a manifesto for the future. Influenced by Catholic canonists like Windischmann and George Phillips (1804–72), he drew deeply on Görres and Friedrich Schlegel, 'supreme oracles of that illustrious school of liberal Conservatives', whose voices seemed to him like 'Burke thundering from his tomb', and whose teachings contained the 'seeds of the future political regeneration of Europe'.[73] Both men had been scarred by Bonapartism, which had imposed on Europe the 'political materialism' of the French Revolution: its 'dead, mechanical absolutism', its cosmopolitan rationality and law, its bureaucratic 'centralization' and its promotion of 'blood-suck[ing]' speculative finance. Both Schlegel and Görres shared with Savigny and his disciples a desire to see Roman law revived, and with it an appreciation of the polity as a single but irreducibly plural organism. The Christian commonwealth of the future would recognize in law the five 'eternal corporations in human society – the family – the church – the state – the guild – and the school'; it would defend the integrity of their corporate lives and safeguard their 'organic cooperation'. Thus would it obviate the 'military despotism' of bloody-handed revolutionaries and bloody-minded reactionaries and forestall the kind of anarchic democracy that might facilitate their emergence, the 'loose, shifting mass of disunited atoms, ready to receive any form or impress'.[74]

The belief – 'organic and counterrevolutionary, … [that] infinitesimal interactions between individuals and the institutions that formed them' could bring about 'moral progress' – was one propagated by the early Maistre.[75] But the *Dublin* reviewers clearly believed that the ideal would resonate in England. Germany's Burkeans would remind England's that the constitution their common master so valorized was rooted in '"Germanic freedoms"', which had evolved from '"participation in the Wittenagemots"' to the assertion, in Magna Carta, of an '"eternal"' 'popular freedom'; and that, for all her 'Protestant zeal', England's constitution had 'preserved more of what be called *political Catholicism*, than almost any other country'.[76] And English scholars like Sir Francis Palgrave (1788–1861) and S. R. Maitland (1792–1866), building on a tradition dating back to Tudor jurists like Sir Edward Coke (1552–1634), would convince them of the spiritual, symbolical and legal continuities between the empire of Rome and the Gothic nations.[77]

It was only at this point that Ultramontanes turned to the papacy. They cast its role in this history as the guardian of Christendom's liberties: a task 'too great for the feebleness of humanity'.[78] That Tractarians, neurotic about Erastianism, might pay careful attention to such an argument, did not pass unobserved. The unanimous chorus of European scholarship, they were informed, testified to the indispensability of the papacy's 'political supremacy' in disciplining 'regal tyranny' and standing for the reign of Christ and the rights of the *pauperes christi*; against that, who cared for the croakings of provincial Anglican divines, like Henry Soames?[79]

Such arguments were eloquently advanced by Felix Papencordt (1811?–41). He had grown up in Westphalia and, before studying under A. W. Schlegel and Leopold von Ranke, attended the Grammar School in Paderborn, the Jesuit ethos of which was then being challenged by Westphalia's post-Napoleonic rulers: the enlightened Prussian bureaucracy.[80] It seems likely that it was when working in Roman archives (c. 1836–40) on barbarism and populism,[81] that Papencordt met Wiseman and won his admiration. Although he was not uncritical of the mediaeval papacy, his background – and very likely the radicalization of Catholic Germany by the Athansius dispute – seems to have moulded a temperament fit for the ultramontanism of the Munich circle's *Historisch-politische Blätter*. He judged the Hildebrandine model the only true defence of the Church's political, and thus doctrinal, liberty; for the forces of worldliness – secular princes, compromising prelates – were ever at work to bring Christ's mystical body into 'bondage'. But this model was also the groundwork of Christendom's ordered liberty. Erastians thwarted and her supremacy acknowledged, the papal Church kept strictly to her proper sphere, serving as the '"guardian"' of doctrinal purity and as instigator of worldly '"regeneration"'.[82]

Among the most impressive fruits of this regeneration, ultramontanes argued – seeking to appeal to those liberal Tories wedded to Castlereagh's Concert system – was the medieval Church's 'paternal umpirage' of international affairs. Here, Wiseman brandished the work of German Protestants who, in the welter of Revolution, had come to admire Rome (or even to convert). The Savigny-school jurist, K. F. Eichorn, the philosopher-poet, Novalis, and the economist, Adam Müller, were all marshalled to support the claim that papal supremacy had made possible a 'marvellous scheme of international jurisprudence'. Papal Christendom had faced criticism; but as 'the moderns' looked about them for principles that would once more bring 'order and progress' to Europe, would they not look with 'envy' on the 'glory' of Christendom?[83]

Honesty would surely cause them to regard with shame the era that followed. The Reformation exploded the architecture of international political order, 'extinguish[ing] the relations of several states with the rest of Christendom, and introduc[ing] distrust and division into the whole community'. With the peoples cut off from their papal protector, nothing could stop the rise of national despotisms, like that of the Tudors.[84] The pattern was everywhere identical: a greed-driven Reformation engorged the Crown, suborned the ancient corporations, drove Christ from the public sphere and lured men into 'profane' private lives. (Ultramontanes found consolation in the 'avenging ministers' sent by heaven to punish such royal sacrilege: hereditary madness and other forms of 'family misfortune'.)[85] Protestant 'absolutism', appealing to 'noxious' court Jansenists, then gradually seduced Habsburgs, Wittlesbachs and Bourbons. Thus, in rebellion and conspiracy, was all Christendom protestantized. In time, the legislation of 'despotic bureaucrats' tormented the people and guaranteed that the '"Church was ... not merely despoiled, but fettered, ... secularised, and incorporated with the abstract state"'.[86] And across all the realms of post-Reformation Europe, where the citizen was 'mummified', the ancient corporations 'dissolved' and the Church enslaved, there brewed Revolution and its 'procession of ... furies': 'universal anarchy', 'savage' wars, 'plunder' and 'terrorism'.[87]

By such a process, Ultramontanes averred, had Christendom been deconsecrated and destroyed. But it would be wrong to suggest that they were fantasists, who thought Eden could simply be restored. The 'Ages of Faith' were certainly idealized by Wiseman's circle, and their successors demonized, but that does not mean that they were guilty of the kind of sinister *naïveté* later ascribed to them by liberal Catholics, like Acton. They well understood that the eleventh-century states of Christendom were plagued within by 'infidelity', 'ignorance' and proto-Erastianism and that their borders were menaced by internal strife and 'Asiatic Mahometanism'.[88] In fact, not only were these days far from halcyon, they were also irretrievably lost. Anstey and Robertson employed the metaphor of 'childhood' in describing the middle ages, accepting that its 'innocent ... aspirings' belonged to the past. In the centuries of 'adolescence' (Reformation to Revolution), Protestants and Catholics, *alike*, had 'grievously offended against their mother'.[89] The 'glowing fragments' of Kenelm Digby's romantic-mediaeval *oeuvre* were haunting, one of Wiseman's converts insisted, precisely because they were gone.[90]

III The modern middle ages

In their own minds, then, these ultramontanes did not seek to weave infantilizing stories for the faithful, nor think themselves literary Jacobites, clinging to a long-vanished ideal. They sought to speak to a world in its 'manhood', disenchanted of childhood's 'generous sentiments', but prepared, as a prodigal son, to 'recall to mind' youth's 'heroic achievements'. The more truthfully Catholics made that age of childhood known, the keener would be their compatriots' understanding of its 'contradistinction' to modernity's maladies.[91] Hildebrandine Christendom would never – should never – be restored, Anstey insisted, sensitive to English criticism of papal tyranny and popish plots:[92] the kind of temporal power wielded by the popes in the twelfth century did not need to be claimed or exercised in the nineteenth. But in 'rending justice to the past', modernity's political contours could be reimagined. Churchmen might be brought to recognize that, at a time of growing civil tyranny, the mediaeval Church had wielded her *plenitudo potestatis* in defence of liberty; and that modernity was a regression from Christendom's liberties to antiquity's 'sorceresses' of power and 'state-idolatry'.[93] Every Tractarian shrieking about 'national apostasy' might be made to see that such a Protestant – and Jansenist-inspired 'Caesarism' had become intrinsic to 'the code of political liberalism' – as was evident in attacks on the Church from London to Lisbon and Madrid to Mexico City.[94]

The present-mindedness of this historiography should not distract us from its future-oriented utopianism. Like their brethren in Munich, Wiseman's party held out to 'Catholicly inclined minds' the prospect of a different kind of liberalism: one that did not serve the interests of plutocrats and radicals, but guaranteed the interlocking liberties of a plural body politic. And if the goal was a neo-mediaeval organism, the means, Wiseman suggested, would be modern and democratic, realized in a new alliance of those faithful to the incarnation: the papacy and the peoples. As in the days of Hildebrand, so now again, Christ's Vicar heard the 'louder peal of that popular opinion, which all along had ... [repudiated liberal] tyranny' and yearned for God and liberty. Together, they could reimagine and remake Christendom.[95] This sanguine approach to democracy and its re-sacralizing potential was carefully positioned so as to avoid conflation with Lamennais' political theology. Instead, Wiseman drew on the French diplomat and historian, Alexis de Tocqueville (1805–59), whose *De la*

Démocratie en Amérique (2 vols. 1835–40) acknowledged that democracies – prone to Caesarism and individualism – were always dangerous and often wicked, but also demonstrated that the Church, in moulding their public spirit, could flourish in democratic lands.⁹⁶ Wiseman's bullishness about this prospect – made clear in his article on South America – was reinforced in a striking way, with the radical, H. S. Chapman, commissioned to write a series of articles on Catholicism's progress in the new world.⁹⁷ This editor of Bentham had seen in Montreal the power of mobilized Irish and French Catholics in pursuit of an elected legislative council; he had come to the Tocquevillian conclusion that, far from 'the "natural enemy of democracy"', Catholicism could be its champion and beneficiary.⁹⁸ Clearly, Wiseman believed that the good news of that reconciliation needed to be preached by Catholic papers – even if the author was more at home in the anti-clerical *Westminster* than in the explicitly – clerical *Dublin*.⁹⁹

Conclusion

The historiography of liberal Catholicism buried this brand of liberal-conservative ultramontanism. In this, it followed Acton, who, in the midst of the poisonous controversies of the 1860s, traced the genealogy of his opponents and conveniently found that men like Liberatore, Veuillot and Manning emerged from a toxic Maistrean gene-pool. Acton was not so much contextualizing as he was de-historicizing ultramontanism in order to demonize it. One contingent manifestation of the tradition – one which, under intellectual pressure from positivism and historicism, and under political attack from the forces of Risorgimento and Kulturkampf, had radicalized into something apocalyptically cranky¹⁰⁰ – was taken to represent its very essence; the hanging judge saw to it that the crimes of the sons were visited on their fathers.

But ultramontane political thought was more varied and dynamic than this. In the 1830s and 1840s, as we have seen, there flourished in England an ultramontane political discourse that was consciously orthodox but also consciously 'liberal' in its methods and goals: positioning itself as eirenic and scientific, it sought to speak to Britain's 'respectable public opinion' in the 'liberal conservative' language of Catholic Italy, France and Germany, denouncing the antichristian liberalism begun in Reformation apostasy and culminating in revolutionary tyranny, and holding out the prospect of a modern middle ages, where liberty was not idolized but consecrated. It may be tempting to again follow Acton and imagine that this was a discourse of sentimental rather than principled liberalism; that it was little more than a convenient pose in the heady days of the 1830s, when a Catholic populism seemed plausible – but that when populist push came to democratic shove, the mask slipped and Bonald lurked behind. But the evidence does not bear this out. Even before the storm over 'Vaticanism' had abated, ultramontanes like W. G. Ward could concede that the Church's 'right of command' had fallen into abeyance; that 'Liberal principles' allowed, however inadequately, 'the social influence of religion'; and that Catholicism had 'come to … terms with the [modern] State'.¹⁰¹ Despite its manifold faults, England's constitution approximated to the optimum political system for the Church – and argument still being rehearsed to Catholic undergraduates at Oxford and Cambridge twenty years later by Jesuits of unimpeachable ultramontane credentials.[102] And key to the strength of that constitution, they insisted – enlisting the disciples of Schlegel and Görres to do battle with the 'Caesarism' of the new political monisms: liberal, positivist, nationalist or socialist – was its rootedness in a Catholic pluralism.[103] Acton cannot alone claim paternity of that tradition, nor should Otto von Gierke be seen as its sole German inspiration in England;[104] for ultramontanes, too, sought a model of modern liberty in imagined mediaeval plurality. In fact, ultramontanism was in many respects far closer to liberal Catholicism than contemporary partisans might have liked to admit. If historians are to escape the legacy of that partisanship, they might begin by exploring the ways in which ultramontanes spoke a language of liberty, and liberal Catholicism was but a species of ultramontanism.

Notes

1   Josef Altholz, *The Liberal Catholic Movement in England: The 'Rambler' and Its Contributors, 1848–1864* (London: Burns & Oates, 1962), vii. [In the notes that follow, the place of publication is London, unless otherwise stated.]
2   Damian McElrath, *Richard Simpson, 1820–1876. A Study in XIXth Century Liberal Catholicism* (Louvain: Publications universitaires de Louvain, 1972), xvii.
3   R.J. Schiefen, 'Review [of McElrath, *Richard Simpson*]', *Catholic Historical Review* 62, no. 4 (October, 1976): 626.
4   See, e.g., Charles Meynell, 'The Philosophy of the Absolute', *Rambler* 22 (September, 1858): 173–90; Richard Simpson, 'Mr Buckle's thesis and method', *Rambler* 22 (July, 1858): 27–42; H.N. Oxenham, 'The Neo-Protestantism of Oxford', *Rambler* 4 (March, 1861): 287–314.
5   See, e.g., Sir John Acton, 'Cavour', *Rambler* 5 (July, 1861): 141–65; Acton, 'Nationality', *Home and Foreign Review* [*HFR*] 1 (July, 1862): 1–25; Simpson, 'Bureaucracy', *Rambler* (February, 1859): 113–25; J.M. Capes, 'Communism', *Rambler* 5 (February 1850): 109–24; Thomas O'Hagan, 'Ireland in 1853 – Hopes of Progress', in *Occasional Papers and Addresses* (1884), 271–312.
6   Matthew Arnold, 'The Function of Criticism at the Present Time', *National Review* 19 (1864): 241.
7   W.M. O'Sullivan, 'Henry Nutcombe Oxenham: "Enfant Terrible" of the Liberal Catholic Movement in Mid – Victorian England', *Catholic Historical Review* 82, no. 4 (October, 1996): 660. Cf. Gertrude Himmelfarb, *Lord Acton: A Study in Conscience and Politics* (Chicago: The University of Chicago Press, 1962), vii.
8   Altholz, *Liberal Catholic Movement*, vii; McElrath, *Simpson*, xviii; C.W. Hutton, 'Roman Catholic Social and Economic Thought in England c.1880–c.1914. Some Tentative Steps Towards a "Third Spring"?', Oxford D.Phil Thesis (2012), 239–43; Meriol Trevor, *Newman. Light in Winter* (London: Macmillan, 1962); J.D. Holmes, *More Roman than Rome: English Catholicism in the Nineteenth Century* (London: Burns & Oates, 1978), 111–49.
9   Himmelfarb, *Acton*, 35ff; Roland Hill, *Lord Acton* (New Haven: Yale University Press, 2000), 108ff.

10 J.H. Newman to Acton, 5 July 1861, quoted in Ian Ker, *John Henry Newman: A Biography* (Oxford: Oxford University Press, 2009), 500.
11 McElrath, *Simpson*, xii.
12 See, e.g., Monsell, *A Lecture on the Roman Question, delivered at Limerick December 1st, 1859* (1860); Wetherell, 'Thoughts on the causes of the present war', *Rambler* (July, 1859), 186–98.
13 Acton to Simpson, 6 February 1863, in Josef Altholz, Damian McElrath, J.C. Holland, *The Correspondence of Lord Acton and Richard Simpson*, 3 vols. (Cambridge: Cambridge University Press, 1971–5), III, 261–3. For Oxenham's spats with Newman and Acton: O'Sullivan, '"Enfant Terrible"', 647–55, 641–6.
14 T.A. Howard, *The Pope and the Professor: Pius IX, Ignaz von Döllinger and the Quandry of the Modern Age* (Oxford: Oxford University Press, 2017), chapters 2–3.
15 Simpson to Acton, 3 September 1863, in *Correspondence*, III, 15.
16 See, e.g., Victor Conzemius, 'Lord Acton and the First Vatican Council', *Journal of Ecclesiastical History* 20 (October, 1969): 247–94; O'Sullivan, '"Enfant Terrible"', 658–9.
17 Josef Altholz and John Powell, 'Gladstone, Lord Ripon, and the Vatican Decrees, 1874', *Albion* 22, no. 3 (Autumn, 1990): 451.
18 Acton to Lady Blennerhassett, (February, 1879), quoted in J.N. Figgis and R.V. Laurence, eds., *Selections from the Correspondence of the First Lord Acton* (London: Longmans Green, 1917), I, 56; Owen Chadwick, *Acton and History* (Cambridge: CUP, 1998), 199.
19 *Reasons for returning to the Church of England* (1871), 4–5, 87–8; 96–102; *To Rome and Back* (1873), 'Preface', 349–52; *What Can Be Certainly Known of God and of Jesus of Nazareth?* (1880), x.
20 McElrath, *Simpson*, 28–43; O'Sullivan, 'Enfant Terrible', 639–40.
21 See [Oxenham's] criticisms of the 'inopportunists': 'The Rival Bishops on the New Dogma', *Saturday Review*, 28 (28 May 1870): 700; Acton, 'Contemporary Literature', *HFR*, 2 (January, 1863): 278; 'Quirinus Nepos', *Tablet*, 19 November, 1921: 664–5.
22 Acton to the *Times*, 21 November 1874, repr in *Selections from Correspondence*, 125.
23 Hill, *Acton*, 260–7; 261 quoting from *The Tablet*, 28 November 1874: 674.
24 McElrath, *Simpson*, 48–9.
25 Chapter II of the Dogmatic Constitution of the Church, *Lumen gentium* (1964), speaks of the Church as 'the People of God'.
26 For the development of this concept in the historiography of English Catholicism: John Bossy, *The English Catholic Community, 1570–1850* (Darton: Longman and Todd, 1975), 385; Kester Aspden, *Fortress Church: The English Roman Catholic Bishops and Politics 1903–63* (Hertfordshire: Gracewing, 2002).
27 McElrath, *Simpson*, 49.
28 Trevor, *Newman: Pillar of the Cloud* (London and Oxford: Macmillan, 1962), 3, 350–2, 634–6; *Light in Winter*, 4–19; Himmelfarb, *Acton*, 17–29, 36. For the continuation of the trope in the literature on modernism's integralist enemies, see Ellen Leonard, 'English Catholicism and Modernism', in *Catholicism Contending with Modernity: Roman Catholic Modernism and Anti-Modernism in Historical Context*, ed. Darrell Jodock (Cambridge: CUP, 2000), 248–74.
29 E.g., Holmes, *More Roman*.
30 Lawrence Barmann, 'The Pope and the English Modernists', *US Catholic Historian*, 25 (Winter, 2007): 31–4, 50.
31 Holmes, *More Roman*, esp. 55–9, 72–87, 100, 111, 149, 192, 249–54.

32 Gabriel Daly, *Transcendence and Immanence: A Study in Catholic Modernism and Integralism* (Oxford: Clarendon Press, 1980), 120; C.D. Cashdollar, *The Transformation of Theology, 1830–1890: Positivism and Protestant Thought in Britain and America* (Princeton, NJ: Princeton University Press, 1989), 444–5, 16.
33 Dermot Quinn, *Patronage and Piety: The Politics of English Roman Catholicism, 1850–1900* (Basingstoke: Macmillan, 1993), xii–xv, 10–12, 48, 55.
34 Eric Tenbus, *English Catholics and the Education of the Poor, 1847–1902* (London: Pickering & Chatto, 2010), 1–9.
35 Aspden, *Fortress Church*, 1–9, 63.
36 J.R. Lothian, *The Making and Unmaking of the English Catholic Intellectual Community, 1910–1950* (Notre Dame, Indiana: University of Notre Dame Press, 2009), xxii–xxiii; Tom Villis, *Reaction and the Avant-Garde: The Revolt against Liberal Democracy in Early Twentieth-Century Britain* (London: Tauris Academic Studies, 2006), 1–14.
37 Contrast Martin Conway, *Catholic Politics in Europe, 1918–1945* (Oxfordshire: Routledge, 1997), 3–5, 20–4, 99–100, with Lothian, *Intellectual Community*, 369.
38 Acton, 'Ultramontanism', *HFR*, 3 (July, 1863), 187, 204, 168–70, 175–85; Acton, letter to the *Times*, 21 November 1874, repr in J. Rufus Fears, ed., *Selected writings of Lord Acton*, 3 vols. (Indianapolis: Liberty Classics, 1988), III, 368.
39 *Problems and Persons* (1903), xiii, 66–90; *William George Ward and the Catholic Revival*, (1912 [1893]), 82–129, vii–xi; *Men and Matters* (1914), v–ix, 304–7.
40 W.C. Cartwright, 'The Italian question', *Westminster Review* 71 (April, 1859): 444–5, 460–1; Gladstone, *The Vatican Decrees in Their Bearing on Civil Allegiance: A Political Expostulation.* (1874), 12.
41 Robert Southey, *Book of the Church*, 2 vols. (1824), II, 528; Frederic Harrison, 'Rome Revisited', *Fortnightly Review* 53, no. 317 (May, 1893): 713, 703, 716–7.
42 'Dr. Fairbairn on "Catholicism"', *Dublin Review* [*DR*] 124 (April, 1899): 391–7, 406.
43 See, e.g., Sheridan Gilley: 'Heretic London, holy poverty and the Irish poor, 1830–1870', *Downside Review* 89 (1971): 64–89; K.T. Hoppen, 'Church, State, and Ultramontanism in Mid-Victorian England: The Case of William George Ward', *Journal of Church and State* 18 (1976): 289–309; James Pereiro, *Cardinal Manning: From Anglican Archdeacon to Council Father at Vatican I* (Leominster: Gracewing, 2008 [1998]); Cadoc Leighton, 'Finding Antichrist: Apocalypticism in Nineteenth-Century Catholic England and the Writings of Frederick Faber', *Journal of Religious History* 37, no. 1 (March, 2013): 80–97; P.C. Erb, 'Introduction', in *The Correspondence of Henry Edward Manning and William Ewart Gladstone. The Complete Correspondence 1833–91*, ed. P.C. Erb, 4 vols. (Oxford: Oxford University Press, 2013), I, xiii–cxx.
44 *Catholic Devotion in Victorian England* (Oxford: Clarendon Press, 1995); 'St Francis and Modern English Sentiment', in *Christianity and Community in the West: Essays for John Bossy*, ed. Simon Ditchfield (Aldershot: Taylor & Francis, 2001), 278–93.
45 Anderson, 'The Limits of Secularization: On the Problem of the Catholic Revival in Nineteenth-Century Germany', *Historical Journal* 38 (September, 1995): 647–50; 'Piety and Politics: Recent Work on German Catholicism', *Journal of Modern History* 63, no. 4 (December 1991): 686–90, 704.
46 See, e.g., Van Kley, 'Christianity as Casualty and Chrysalis of Modernity: The Problem of the French Revolution', *American Historical Review* 108, no. 4 (October 2003): 1081–104; Philippe Boutry, 'Une théologie de la visibilité: le projet *zelante* de resacralisation de Rome e son échec (1832–1829)', in *Cérémonial et rituel à Rome*

(XVIe-XIXe siécle), ed. M. Visceglia and C. Brice (Rome: Ecole française de Rome, 1997), 343f; Marina Caffiero, 'La maestà del papa. Trasformazioni dei rituali del potere a roma tra XVII e XIX secolo', in *Ibid.*, 281–316.

47 For the *Dublin*'s foundation in context: P.A. Richardson, 'Serial Struggles: English Catholics and Their Periodicals, 1648–1844', University of Durham Ph.D. Thesis (2003), 201ff.

48 *Records and Recollections of St. Cuthbert's College, Ushaw* (Preston, 1889), 106.

49 J.P. Chinnici, *The English Catholic Enlightenment: John Lingard and the Cisalpine Movement* (Shepherdstown: Patmos Press, 1980). On this contested term: Michael Printy, 'History and Church History in the Catholic Enlightenment', *Modern Intellectual History* 18 (2021): 248–60.

50 Wiseman, *Recollections of the Last Four Popes and of Rome in their Times* (1858), 4–5.

51 Gerard Pelletier, *Rome et la Révolution française. La théologie et la politique du Saint-Siège pendant la Révolution française (1789–1799)* (Rome: Ecole française de Rome, 2004).

52 S.H. de Franceschi 'L'autorité pontificale paceau legs de l'antiromanisme catholique et régaliste des lumières: Réminiscences doctrinales de Bellarmin et de Suàrez dans la théologie politique et l'ecclésiologie catholiques de la mi-XVIIIe siècle', *Archivum Historiae Pontificiae* 38 (2000): 146–58.

53 Giuseppe Pignatelli, 'Le origini settecentesche del cattolicesimo reazionario: La polemica antigiansenista del *Giornale ecclesiastico di Roma*', *Studi Storici* 11, no. 4 (October-December, 1970): 755–82.

54 Van Kley, 'From the Catholic Enlightenment to the Risorgimento: The Exchange between Nicola Spedalieri and Pietro Tamburini, 1791–97', *Past & Present* 224 (2014): 109–62.

55 M.C. Shea, 'Ressourcement in the Age of Migne: The Jesuit Theologians of the Collegio Romano and the Shape of Modern Catholic Thought', *Nova et Vetera* 15, no. 2 (2017): esp. 585–7.

56 Marina Caffiero, *La politica della santità. Nascità di un culto nell-età dei Lumi* (Rome: Laterza, 1996).

57 Van Kley, 'Spedalieri and Tamburini', §III.

58 For the context of Wiseman's arrival: Ward, *The Life and Times of Cardinal Wiseman*, 2 vols. (1912 [1897]), I, chapter 3.

59 On the pre-iteration of the 'devotional revolution' at Maynooth: Dónal Kerr, 'Dr Patrick Murray (1811–1882)', *Irish Theological Quarterly* 49 (1982): 229–50. On Russell: Ambrose Macaulay, *Dr Russell of Maynooth* (Darton: Longman and Todd, 1983). On political economy at Louvain: Gilbert Faccarello, 'From the Foundation of Liberal Political Economy to Its Critique. Theology and Economics in France in the Eighteenth and Nineteenth Centuries', in *The Oxford Handbook to Christianity and Economics*, ed. Paul Oslington (Oxford: OUP, 2014), 87–9.

60 On Anstey: Edward Lucas, *The Life of Frederick Lucas*, 2 vols. (2nd edn. 1887), I, 10–36; Richardson, 'Serial Struggles', 210–12.

61 Robertson, 'Gerbet on the Eucharist', *DR* 1 (May, 1836): 200–21; *The Philosophy of History; in a Course of Lectures delivered by Frederick von Schlegel, with a Memoir of the Author*, ed., trans. Robertson, 2 vols. (6th edn. 1848 [1835]), I, v-vi. On the 'utopian reactionism' of Schlegel's concept of the 'coming Middle Age': Paul Gottfried, *Conservative Millenarians: the Romantic Experience in Bavaria* (New York: Fordham University Press, 1979), 18–21, 110–14.

62 Robertson, 'Religious and Social Condition of France', *DR* 16 (March, 1844): 5; 'Joseph de Maistre', *DR* 33 (December, 1852): 423–4.
63 Emile Perreau-Saussine, *Catholicism and Democracy: An Essay in the History of Political Thought* (Oxford: Princeton University Press, 2012), 47–9; Gottfried, *Millenarians*, chapter 6; Owen Chadwick, *A History of the Popes, 1830–1914* (Oxford: OUP, 2003), 9–12.
64 Felix Papencordt, 'Sylvester II and Gregory VII', *DR* 6 (May, 1839): 315–7, quoting Johannes Voigt, *Hildebrand als Papst Gregor VII und sein Zeitalter* (Weimar, 1815); Wiseman, 'Authority of the Holy See in South America', *DR* 5 (July, 1838): 237, 248–9.
65 Simon Skinner, *Tractarians and the 'Condition of England': The Social and Political Thought of the Oxford Movement* (Oxford: Clarendon Press, 2004), 90–3.
66 Maistre, *Considérations sur la France* (1797), ed. P. Manent (Bruxelles: Editions Complexe, 1988), 166.
67 Bee Wilson, 'Counter-Revolutionary Thought', in *The Cambridge History of Nineteenth-Century Political Thought*, ed. Gareth Stedman Jones and Gregory Claeys (Cambridge: CUP, 2011), 9.
68 For the 'future-oriented' quality of these varieties of ultramontanism: John Morrow, 'Romanticism and Political Thought in the Early Nineteenth Century', in *Ibid.*, 39–76; Jon Vanden Heuvel, *A German Life in the Age of Revolution. Joseph Görres, 1776–1848* (Washington, DC: Catholic University of America Press, 2001), 250–303; C. Harrison, *Romantic Catholic: France's Postrevolutionary Generation in Search of a Modern Faith* (Ithaca: Cornell University Press, 2014).
69 For an overview of this 'counter-culture' and its historiography: Skinner, *Tractarians*, 18–23.
70 For this acute summary of English conservatism: Emily Jones, *Edmund Burke and the Making of Modern Conservatism, 1830–1914. An Intellectual History* (Oxford: OUP, 2017), 18, 18n11, 21–4.
71 Wiseman, 'National Holydays', *DR* 14 (May 1843): 481–505.
72 Robertson, 'Hurter on the Institutions, Manners, and Customs of the Middle Age', *DR* 28 (March, 1850): 50–5; Anstey, 'Ozanam's *English Chancellors*', *DR* 3 (October 1837): 305–9; Wiseman, *Lectures on the Principal Doctrines and Practices of the Catholic Church, delivered at St. Mary's, Moorfields, during the Lent of 1836*, 2 vols. (1836), I, 95.
73 Robertson, 'The Life and Writings of Görres', *DR* 6 (January, 1839): 44; *The Philosophy of History* (1st edn. 1835), lv. On their 'Burkeanism': Gottfried, *Conservative Millenarians*, 13, 246–7.
74 *Philosophy of History*, xxvii-xlix; 'Görres', 36–8. This paragraph draws on: Martin O'Malley, 'Currents in Nineteenth-Century German Law, and Subsidiarity's Emergence as a Social Principle in the Writings of Wilhelm Ketteler', *Journal of Law, Philosophy and Culture* 3, no. 1 (2008): 26–30; J.Q. Whitman, *The Legacy of Roman Law in the German Romantic Era: Historical Vision and Legal Change* (Princeton, NJ: Princeton University Press, 2014 [1990]), 8; Michael Dreyer, 'German Roots of the Theory of Pluralism', *Constitutional Political Economy* 4, no. 1 (1997): 12–16; John Inglis, *Spheres of Philosophical Inquiry and the Historiography of Medieval Philosophy* (Leiden: Brill, 1998), 41–7.
75 Carolina Armenteros, *The French Idea of History: Joseph de Maistre and His Heirs, 1794–1854* (Ithaca, NY: Cornell University Press, 2011), 312–13.
76 'Görres', 46–51, quoting *Germany and the Revolution*, trans John Black (1820); *Philosophy of History*, xlix-lii; 'Chancellors', 305–9.

77 Robertson, 'Summary of German Literature', *DR* 6 (January, 1839): 282; 'Görres', 36–7. For favourable references to Palgrave: 'W. F.' [Finlason], 'Robberies of Religion, Ancient and Modern', *Rambler* 10 (November 1852): 390–3; to Coke: 'Chancellors', 321.

78 'Chancellors', 310.

79 Thomas Flanagan, 'The Anglo-Saxon and Ancient British Churches', *DR* 18 (March, 1845): 128–30, 132–6, 149–55; 'Chancellors', 319–21; 'Hurter', 53–5; Flanagan, 'The Church and Empire in the Thirteenth Century', *DR* 17 (December, 1844): 492–4.

80 Friedrich Hohmann, 'Von der Jesuitenschule zum staatlichen Gymnasium Theodorianum', in Klemens Honselmann, *Von der Domschule zum Gymnasium Theodorianum in Paderborn* (Paderborn: Verein für Geschichte und Altertumskunde Westfalens, 1962).

81 *Geschichte der vandalischen Herrschaft in Afrika* (Berlin, 1837); *Cola di Rienzo und seine Zeit* (Hamburg, 1841).

82 'Gregory VII', 302–7, 315–17 (quoting Voigt).

83 'Hurter', 51–4; 'Chancellors', 319–20. Anstey's references to Wiseman in these pages relate to his essay 'La vita ed il Pontificato di Gregorio VII, pubblicata da Sir R. Greisley, Baronetto', *Annali della Scienze Religiose* 1, no. 2 (settembre – ottobre, 1835): 267–77; 1.3 (novembre-dicembre, 1835), 374–84.

84 'Chancellors', 321; Flanagan, 'Mary, Queen of Scots', *DR* 19 (September, 1845): 195–229.

85 Dominick Murphy, 'The Reformation in Sweden. – Gustavus Wasa', *DR* 19 (September, 1845): 262–5.

86 Robertson, 'Moral and Intellectual Condition of Catholic Germany', *DR* 11 (August 1841): 57, 78–9, 91–2, 104; quotation at 57 from Görres, *Athanasius* (1837).

87 'Görres', 38–45; *Philosophy of History*, xviii-xx, xxxvii.

88 'Gregory VII', 268.

89 'Hurter', 51; 'Chancellors', 309.

90 Capes 'Short Notices', *Rambler*, 3 (November, 1848), 211.

91 'Hurter', 51; 'Chancellors', 321, 311.

92 Bernard Ward, *The Dawn of the Catholic Revival in England, 1781–1803*, 2 vols. (1909), II, 62–3.

93 'Chancellors', 321, 307–11. For Anstey's crusades against anti-Catholic legislation: Bernard Ward, *The Sequel to Catholic Emancipation: The Story of English Catholics Continued Down to the Re-establishment of the Hierarchy in 1850*, 2 vols. (1915), I, 76–8; II, 72–82.

94 Wiseman, 'South America', 237, 248–9. Cf. Wiseman, *Essays on Various Subjects*, 3 vols. (1853), II, 1–26; 27–72; 73–102.

95 Wiseman, 'South America', 248–9, 251–2.

96 Perreau-Saussine, *Catholicism and Democracy*, 51–8; Jeremy Jennings, 'Constitutional Liberalism in France', in *Cambridge History of Nineteenth-Century Political Thought*, 365–9.

97 See [Chapman] in the *DR*: 'The Canadian Question', 3 (July, 1837), 79–113; 'The Irish in America', 3 (October, 1837), 452–68; 'Principles of Colonization: New Zealand', 4 (January, 1838), 67–96.

98 [Chapman], quoting Tocqueville, 'Transatlantic Travelling', *DR* 7 (November, 1839): 428.

99 R.S. Neale, 'Chapman, Henry Samuel', *Australian Dictionary of Biography* (1969), accessed 6 February 2017, https://adb.anu.edu.au/biography/chapman-henry-samuel-3193.

100 See, e.g., W.F. Finlason, 'Jansenism, Gallicanism and Jacobinism', *DR* 37 (September, 1854): 96–189; Manning, *The Temporal Power of the Vicar of Jesus Christ* (1861) London: Burns and Oates, 1880; William Barry, 'Modern Society and the Sacred Heart', *DR* 25 (July, 1875): 1–38.

101 Ward, 'Hergenröther on Church and State', *DR* 20 (October, 1877): 317–25; Henry Coleridge?, 'The Liberalism of Lacordaire', *The Month* (June, 1870), 653–5.

102 Ward, 'Church and State', *DR* 26 (April, 1876): 365–70; Joseph Rickaby, *Political and Moral Essays* (Chicago: Benziger, 1902), 67–71.

103 See, e.g., Josef Hergenröther, *Catholic Church and Christian State. A Series of Essays on the Relation of the Church to the Civil Power*, trans. C.S. Devas, 2 vols. (1876); C.S. Devas, *Studies of Family Life. A Contribution to Social Science* (1886).

104 See, e.g., Jacob T. Levy, 'From liberal constitutionalism to pluralism', in *Modern Pluralism: Anglo-American Debates since 1880*, ed. Mark Bevir (Cambridge: CUP, 2012), 26–33.

5

Historical and ecclesiological foundations of Spanish Catholic liberalism. From the Jansenist imprint to the Constitution of Cádiz of 1812

Bernard Callebat
Institut Catholique d'Etudes Supérieures (ICES) Institut Catholique and Université de Toulouse
Text translated from the French by Aude Attuel-Hallade and Cynthia Attuel

Introduction

The concept of Catholic Liberalism does not designate a political philosophy, but rather a wide range of intellectual attitudes of theological, ecclesiological and pastoral conduct, difficult to determine as a whole. The plurality of critical and methodological positions adds to the difficulties in identifying and defining it. Epistemologists, political scientists, historians of religious thought have always had difficulty in giving its origin or meaning: Catholic Liberalism[1] '[...](if it really exists) presupposes the general matrix of liberalism, regardless of the divergences between liberal currents: the rule of law, the limitation of power, individual liberties founded in 1789, civil equality, human rights, public liberties, freedom of conscience and religion without a monopoly imposed by the state.'[2] Relating its meaning to the history of Spain adds to the complexity of the enterprise.[3] A biased vision of the Spanish *Ancien Régime*, on the French historicist model, would tend to understand this history as a confrontation between, on the one hand, liberals, modernizers, and on the other hand, Catholics, reactionaries. This perception is inaccurate: from the militant, explicit and convinced Catholicism of modern-day regalists to the authors of the Constitution of Cádiz, it can be certified that the vast majority of liberal theologians and public men were imbued with Catholic culture.[4] Those who built the Spanish state of law, its stable legal framework, were mostly Catholics and liberals. Moreover, among those who defended a consensual separation of Church and State, or freedom of conscience, there were liberal Catholic meanings.[5]

If the notion of Catholic Liberalism may have varied under the auspices of the Madrid powers, it is difficult to deny the existence of a convergent epistemological base, essential to define its substance. Despite obvious differences, the figures of Spanish Catholic Liberalism share several positions of principle, involving the rationality of an independent state, the quest for knowledge in the face of ignorance, the expression of a jansenizing faith and the desire for reforming a Catholic Church weakened by Protestant quarrels. Behind these ambitions, there was the desire to claim, against Roman authority, a detachment from religious consciences and sometimes a real secession from ecclesial doctrine, even if it paradoxically relied on patristic Tradition.[6]

In eighteenth-century Spain, all Spaniards accepted the Catholic faith. This for the people was an indisputable and immutable fact, since it was the '*fe de los antiguos*'. In fact, the Enlightenment, the crucible of Spanish Catholic Liberalism, did not initially want to be irreligious or enemies of the faith.[7] The *ilustrados*, like the rest of the Spaniards, did not question dogmas, that is, the content of the act of believing[8]; they did, on the other hand, challenge the way of believing.[9] At times, they did not find sufficient meaning in the traditional faith and sought a new form of religiosity. Thus, a vast spiritual concern was born that merged into a social and religious problem. A defining element of Enlightenment, religiosity was the rejection of all forms of religion that did not conform to rational assumptions. It was the external cult, the popular piety, so magnified in the Baroque period and so hated in the Age of Enlightenment.[10] The tendency opposed to the baroque religiosity of the predominance of external signs was the ideal of the Enlightenment, as it had been for Renaissance humanism.[11] The return to the origins of Christianity, an era idealized by humanists and scholars of the Enlightenment, was the great aspiration, reinforced in the seventeenth century by the enormous success of the Jansenist mentality, inspiring liberal and Catholic sociabilities (Part I).

The Spanish elites, who were familiar with the ideas of the seventeenth century, were fully convinced by the new ideas. Over time, a new mentality emerged among them which, alongside the moral rigour and ideal of the Apostolic Church characteristic of Jansenism, was inspired by the episcopal principles of French Gallicanism, at the same time as they were advocated by the European movement known as *Aufklärung*.[12] After the *Guerra de Independencia*, this view necessarily implied a change in the status of the Catholic Church in Spain, and its affinity with the Synod of Pistoia along with the Civil Constitution of the Clergy of 1790 in France was considered to be translated into the Constitution of Cádiz of 1812 (Part II).

I The sources of Catholic Liberalism in the eighteenth century: Spanish late Jansenism

1 The prodromes of Spanish Catholic liberalism

The existence of Spanish Jansenism as the primary form of Catholic Liberalism has been a controversial fact in Spanish historiography. In an aside significantly titled *The Ghost of Spanish Jansenism*, Teófanes Egido wanted to question the rigour of the term by placing Jansenism on the same level as Freemasonry, Philosophism or Atheism, some of the various labels with which the Spanish Enlightenment has been adorned in classical literature.¹³ The fact remains that Jansenism was a social, religious, political and European reality. In Spain, things were partially different,¹⁴ but there were common marked characteristics with the rest of Europe:

> [W]hen we refer to eighteenth-century Jansenism, it is not the original Jansenism put forward by Jansenius in his doctrine of grace. Alongside it, there is another Jansenism, which is the ideology of the enemies of the Jesuits, which the Jansenists opposed, defending a form of spirituality opposed to theirs and which was reflected above all in the field of morality (…). It is necessary to add other aspects still present in the history of the Church, such as Episcopalism and conciliarism, which claim to be based on a return to the true origins of Christianity as it was practiced in the first centuries.¹⁵

And this is not surprising, given that, on the one hand, foreign influence on eighteenth-century thinkers had been constant, and on the other hand, Spanish Jansenism had been the latest of all the European expressions to emerge, taking up multiple elements that had already been developed by them.¹⁶

2 Spanish 'sui generis' Jansenism or the first inflection of Catholic liberalism

Jansenism had first been a French reality, especially after the consequences of the condemnation of Jansénius' proposals, followed by those of Pasquier Quesnel (1634–1719). The first extensions of the religious crisis affected the Spanish Netherlands, from which the controversy had emerged.¹⁷ The other regions of Europe marked by the Port-Royalist quarrel were the Italian peninsula and Austria. The rest of Europe was reached sporadically. But the least that can be said of Spanish Jansenism is that it was a *sui generis* Jansenism, devoid of a common doctrine and strategy, mixed with external elements and internal conditioning, more difficult to circumscribe than others, because it often manifested itself via various ideological conceptions, on the occasion of circumstantial events, generally polemical, or even existed with a certain clarity only in the spirit of its opponents.

What can be affirmed, in fact, is that there existed in Spain a politico-religious movement, which many contemporaries called *Jansenism*, although it did not emerge from it, and whose ill-defined characteristics could not be separated from the vast spiritual process of the Enlightenment throughout Europe. Nor was there any pure Jansenism, but rather a composite of diverse and even disparate elements whose relevance varied according to the circumstances. And finally, that the possible internal cohesion of this movement did not come so much from a systematized doctrine as from a common spirit and a spirit of renewal, shared, to a large extent, by the majority of its protagonists.

Some of the basic ideas of this movement, fixed on the return to the origins, had been disseminated from France, where the works of the Benedictines of Saint-Maur had fertilized the renewal in the field of ecclesiastical history.¹⁸ The works of Noël Alexandre (1639–1724), Claude Fleury (1640–1723) and others were very well received in Spain; they aroused an interest in the knowledge of the Holy Scriptures, the early Church and the Fathers. But the influence of works from abroad was also linked to the Spanish tradition itself and its rediscovery. It is enough to recall the work of Benito Jeronimo Feijóo (1676-1764),[19] Enrique Flórez (1702-73) or Gregorio Mayans y Siscar (1699-1781)[20] and their collaborators, who tried by all means to correct historical errors and falsehoods.[21]

Another important element of Spanish Jansenism, which intervened with varying intensity and in multiple forms, was the struggle against Molinism, which was constantly virulent and widespread in Spain.[22] During the eighteenth century, punctuated by events such as the publication of the bull *Unigenitus* of Clement XI and the brief *Demissas preces* of Benedict XIV,[23] the polemics were numerous, aroused by Pedro Manso de Tapia (1669-1736)[24] or Cayetano Benítez de Lugo (1676-1739) or by the scandal caused by the untimely condemnation of the works of Cardinal Enrico Noris (1631-1704).[25] The Augustinians were considered close to the Jansenists and frequently confused with them. It was not uncommon for misunderstandings to be aimed at both. Thus, the partisans of a stricter morality appeared for their opponents as the disciples of asceticism and spirituality of Port-Royal.

The regalist current, which had always had many followers in Spain and had flourished since the Middle Ages,[26] was to have a greater impact on the events of the end of the century:

Menéndez Pelayo pointed out that Spanish Jansenism had more to do with Gallicanism than with the theological ideas of Jansenism.[27]

In Spain, therefore, the picture needs to be nuanced. Both the Catholic Enlightenment and Regalism, and the reformist spirit in ecclesial order and spirituality, had their roots in the Spanish tradition of the sixteenth and seventeenth centuries. However, whatever the influence of this tradition, there is no doubt that currents from outside played a major role in the movement of Spanish Jansenism. The French publisher Antoine Boudet,[28] on a trip to Spain in 1763, noted the wide distribution of foreign books, especially those devoted to theology and law, from France, Italy and Switzerland.[29] Among the various works were the writings of Antoine Arnauld, Pierre Nicole, Jean Racine, Claude Fleury, Zeger Bernard Van Espen, Justinus Febronius, François-Philippe Mésenguy, Julio Lorenzo Selvaggio and Pietro Tamburini.[30]

Though the French contribution was important, the other areas of influence on Spanish Jansenism, with Zeger Bernard Van Espen, Justinus Febronius and especially Antonio Pereira de Figueiredo (1725-97), a figure of Portuguese regalism were also significant.[31] Zeger Bernard Van Espen can be considered the most influential author on Spanish canonists and Enlightenment reformers. In the same vein, the work of his disciple, Justinus Febronius, *De statu ecclesiae et legitima potestate romani pontificis liber singularis, ad reuniendos dissidentes in religione christianos compositus*, circulated freely in Spain and enjoyed great prestige. If it deserved to be refuted by a personality like Francisco Fabián y Fuero,[32] it was considered by others as a basic work to justify the desired ecclesiastical reforms. The Attorney General Pedro Rodríguez de Campomanes (1723-1802)[33] used it extensively in the *Tratado de la regalia y de amortización* and the *Juicio imparcial*.[34]

3 The shadow of the Pistoia Synod on Spanish Catholic liberalism

In addition to works of French and Central European origin, those from Italy also played an important role in Castilian mentalities.[35] Despite their local differences, Italian Jansenism is probably the closest to some Latin characteristics of Spain of the time, and it can even be added that the games of influences were mediated by Italian authors.[36]

In Spain, the works of Carlo Sebastiano Berardi (1719-68)[37] or Alessandro Pompeo Berti (1686-1752),[38] and, with the events in Tuscany, Giuseppe Zola (1739-1806),[39] Pedro Tamburini (1737-1827),[40] some writings of the Bishop of Pistoia, Scipio of Ricci (1741-1810),[41] and the Acts of Pistoia,[42] exerted a real influence. Some clerics and laity had also engaged in pastoral work, advocating certain ecclesiastical reforms. The bishop of Barcelona, José Climent (1766-75),[43] had relations with the *Appellants* and had shown himself to be a prudent defender of the Church of Utrecht, for which he was sued.[44] But he was not alone: even the members of the commission charged with judging his writings were not unfavourable to what was happening in the Netherlands.[45] The polemics and multiple writings reached several prelates and Father Francisco Javier Vásquez,[46] general of the Augustinians, who was also in contact with Father Jean-Charles Augustin Clément (1717-1804)[47] and Gabriel Dupac de Bellegarde.[48]

These Jansenists, even without forming a coherent and organized group, as could be the ultramontanes and the more indefinite mass of the 'third party', were very active and exercised a significant influence in the faculties of theology and law, in some seminaries and also in a part of the high clergy. The correspondence of the Spanish elites with Abbot Henri Grégoire (1750-1831),[49] or the chronicles of Spain inserted in the *Nouvelles ecclésiastiques* and the *Annales de la religion*, would suffice to note these affinities, and above all a similarity of feelings between the authors, considered as defenders of the truth, at the head of which, in the last years of the century, the illustrious bishop of Pistoia. In many respects, the Synod of Pistoia[50] was revolutionary: it claimed to take up practices of the first centuries of the Church and reformist ideas already present at the Council of Trent. It intended to reinterpret all the ordinances supposedly truncated by the Counter-Reformation.[51]

Rome may have astonished by its silence, which seemed excessive, even perjury, but it had not been silent. Pope Pius VI appointed two commissions to examine the Acts of Pistoia before proceeding with a condemnation that occurred on 28 August 1794, in the bull *Auctorem fidei*[52]. The accusation of Jansenism that was levelled against it was not a surprise in Spain. The inquisitors were very sensitive to the problem of the traffic of Italian books circulating everywhere. Thus, in 1790, a professor from Salamanca, Veremundio Arias, wrote to the Inquisition of Valladolid to denounce the public sale of Jansenist works in the city's bookstores.[53] The Spanish Jansenists of the late eighteenth century agreed on certain points with the regalists because they saw in civil power the only possible check on the papal absolutism of the time.[54]

II The efficiency of Spanish Catholic liberalism in the Constitution of Cádiz of 1812

1 The slow exit from traditional Catholicism

At the end of the eighteenth century, religious and ecclesiastical questions played a paramount role in Hispanic mentalities. The Spaniards of the time were believers; the Church and its ministers were such a palpable reality that it was difficult to find an area in it that was not connected with their institutions.[55] The society of the eighteenth century was a society sacralized around the clergy and the family model. However, some elements of transformation appeared progressively in the transition from this century to the next. This was the case of Episcopalism, which was not new in Spain, but which emerged with notable force and became the ideology or pretext to bring change to the ecclesiastical world, especially after the coming to power of Manuel Godoy (1767–1851) as Secretary of State, at the head of the Spanish government:

> Godoy's aggressive ecclesiastical policy gave him the support of the royal bureaucracy, that wished to eliminate the remaining control of the pope over the Spanish Church and strengthen the power of the bishops. The new regalism of the nineties reflects the growing influence in official circles of the program of ecclesiastical reform elaborated at the Synod of Pistoia in 1786.[56]

Italian reformism as well as the French revolutionary wave aroused sympathies, reinforcing a certain anticlericalism at the same time as it led to a public criticism of the role played by the clergy in Spanish society. Under the *Ancien Régime*, the clergy was a political issue of the first order. The general confusion between Church and State did not contribute to clarifying the situation, so that it was problematic to differentiate the two institutions, although at the theoretical level, the principle of the subordination of temporal power to supernatural power was maintained.[57] The special legal status of the clergy, a large body endowed with special privileges (the *fuero eclesiástico*) had ended up creating political confusion to the point of making it one of the main political activities of the Bourbons.[58]

The economic question of the Church was another subject of debate.[59] The clergy in general felt burdened by the heavy state taxation, so that the rejection of absolutism was a frequent attitude among the clergy. Moreover, the extraordinary tax burdens had exacerbated the existing economic inequality among the Spanish clergy between, on the one hand, parish and village priests whose incomes in normal times were insufficient and, on the other hand, the wealthy cathedral clergy, as well as religious communities, that managed to circumvent the difficulties with greater success. The *ilustrados* had become accustomed to rejecting irrational forms of faith, including classical devotional practices. Even though opportunities were scarce, the apparatus of enlightened despotism was responsible for curbing them, most often by ignoring them. The fact remains that religious conflicts, quite virulent under the reign of Carlos IV, were more often confrontations between ruling minorities, between supporters and opponents of the Enlightenment. Reform proposals, in most cases, remained at the stage of debate.

As the century drew to a close in Spain, the atmosphere in favour of a profound reform of the Church was most favourable. The Enlightenment, with all its possible contradictions, had succeeded in creating a new mentality, increasingly distant from traditional religion. The following years would attest to this fact with the abdication of Fernando VII (1784–1833) and the new Constitution of Bayonne.[60]

2 The 'Estatuto of Bayona' and the Bonapartist constitutional order

The *Estatuto of Bayona* of 1808, also called the *Charter of Bayonne* or the *Statute of Bayonne*, and officially designated in French as the *Constitutional Act of Spain*, was promulgated on 6 July 1808 by Joseph Bonaparte, as King of Spain.[61] This monument was obviously inspired by the Bonapartist model of the rule of law, with the aim of introducing an autocratic regime, including an elementary system of freedoms, like the *Napoleonic constitutionalism*.[62] Completed on 7 July 1808, this *Magna Carta* was characterized, among other things, by the fact that it was a granted Charter and not a Constitution strictly speaking, since, on the one hand, the people had not participated in its drafting, and on the other hand, it emanated directly from a royal decision.

Above all, this text determined that Spain was a confessional state, so that the only religion allowed was the Catholic, apostolic and Roman religion; Article 1 of Title 1 on the *Religión* – which already indicated its importance from a statutory point of view – was explicit: 'La religión Católica, Apostólica y Romana, en España y en todas las posesiones españolas, será la religión del Rey y de la Nación, y no se permitirá ninguna otra'.[63] With regard to its promoters, three groups of influence can be distinguished: the *conformists*, the *assimilationists* and the *reformers*. The first group, generally unversed in political issues, accepted everything Napoleon proposed in his constitutional project, thus supporting – albeit through inactivity – the initial constitutional challenge, which had clear French connotations.[64] The second group were more in line with French constitutionalism. This was advocated, for example, by Juan Soler, who complained that the draft statute recognized too many Spanish elements. He called for the abolition of the pre-eminence of the Catholic religion as the first constitutional article in order to replace it, as a matter of priority, with the principle that 'Spain is a constitutional monarchy established by law'.[65] As for the reformers, they disagreed with the project on certain points and tried to ensure that it included elements of the *Ancien Régime* (absolutists and conservatives) as well as new institutions, to which the Enlightenment and the liberals aspired. From the summer of 1808, historical events unfolded with extraordinary dynamism, marked by the great Spanish victory of Bailén, the hasty flight of Joseph Bonaparte from his Madrid court and the peninsular campaign of Napoleon himself. However, from the first weeks of 1809, the Bonapartist state could begin to develop in Spain,[66] and thus apply a constitutional model which, only in the sphere closest to Joseph's centres of political decision-making, had a character of minimal inspiration.[67] The reality of the war, intensified and internationalized by the landing of a British expeditionary contingent, minimized the possibilities of the

Bayonne constitutional text in the political and ideological configuration of a Spain that had never been independent.

Insurgent Spain had configured itself in an active exercise of sovereignty that was institutionally expressed in the *Juntas Supremas de defensa*, headed by a *Junta Central*, which acted as depositories of national sovereignty, but under the presidency of personalities totally identified with the *Ancien Régime*, or under the political direction of reformist figures such as José Moñino y Redondo, Count of Floridablanca (1728–1808)[68] or José de Jovellanos.

3 Liberal Catholic tolerantism and the Constitution of Cádiz

At the beginning of the nineteenth century, the constitution of 1812 was the most important text emanating from the Cortes de Cádiz. Its doctrinal content and scope have made it a point of reference not only for Spanish Catholic liberalism but also for all European religious currents.[69] The place assigned to the Catholic Church in the new political order determined the importance it has had, because of its temporal implications and its relations with social institutions. This exhibition of faith is illustrated by the importance of the number of clerics, members of the Cortes: they made up about a third of the representatives (their number varied between 90 and 97)[70] while the lawyers were only about 60, the civil servants, 55 and the military, with only 37 deputies, struggled to gather 10 per cent of them. Landowners, academics, merchants, doctors and nobles made up the negligible 3 per cent of the representatives.[71]

In this assembly, there were three constitutional tendencies: first, the *realist deputies*, whose doctrinal affiliation was based on a mixture of scholastic tradition and national historicism, which was reflected in particular in the defence of Francisco Suárez's doctrine of *translatio imperii*[72] and the sovereignty shared between the king and the Cortes. These representatives criticize both French revolutionary thought and absolutist doctrines: neither revolution nor reaction.[73] The second tendency was formed by the Liberal deputies, whose constitutional principles were basically the same as those defended by the French *patriots* in the Assembly of 1789, including national sovereignty and a conception of the division of powers aimed at making the unicameral Cortes the centre of the new state. Philosophical references linked them to the commonplaces of *rationalist jusnaturalism* and were not lacking among some Liberal MPs. Most of them preferred to justify their theses – including national sovereignty and the division of powers by referring to a supposed medieval Spanish liberalism.[74] The American deputies formed the third constitutional tendency present in the Cortes. The French invasion of 1808 had given rise, in the vast territories of Spanish America, to the beginnings of a process of emancipation that culminated ninety years later with the independence of Cuba, Puerto Rico and the Philippines.[75] Their constitutional projects mixed principles from Spanish neo-scholasticism and Indian law with revolutionary principles, especially those of Rousseau, to which must be added the influence of certain Dutch and German naturalists, notably Grotius and Pufendorf.[76]

It is in the preamble of the constitution that the first reference to religion can be found. The text presented by the commission began by invoking the Trinity in the strictest dogmatic formulation: 'In the name of God, Almighty, Father, Son and Holy Spirit, Author and supreme legislator of society.'[77] The importance of the Catholic religion was obvious. The preamble to the Constitution merely extended the ordinance that had previously set the ceremonial approved by the Regency Council for the installation of the Cortes. It was representative of the Catholic sentiment which, in the conception of its organizers, prevailed among the representatives of the Spanish nation.[78]

For their part, the Liberal MPs adopted a moderate position, and finally conciliated. For them, the Constitution was fundamentally a political document aimed at ordering social coexistence, and in fact, it was not for them to teach religion in it. The Constitution of Cádiz certainly proclaimed the confessionality of the State, but, in substance, it did not differ much from other modern constitutions, whether the American Constitution of 1787 or the French Constitution of 1791. It responded to the same principles and characteristics that corresponded to the liberal state. However, the Spanish Constitution of 1812 contained a detailed statement of individual rights and freedoms. Article 12 of the Constitution, by emphasizing the fundamental character of religion and maintaining the link with the idea of the historic Constitution of Spain, based on the firmness of religious law, effectively avoids any absolutization by leaving the final formula ambiguous:[79] 'The religion of the Spanish nation is and will perpetually be the Catholic religion, apostolic, Roman and the only true one. The Nation protects it by wise and just laws and forbids the exercise of any other.'[80] In 1813, during the debate on the Inquisition, the deputies returned to this final point: how to interpret the protection that the State had to provide to religion?

For the liberal camp, the issue had become serious because of the intolerance that this pre-eminence could create, but at the same time, it was difficult for them to reject a conception already sanctified by society. It was a time of tension, uncertainty and hope when the Liberals relished moments of glory, but also drank from the chalice of bitterness and disappointment. Foremost among them was Joaquín Lorenzo Villanueva y Astengo (1757–1837), a Spanish clergyman, historian and liberal writer of the Enlightenment. He is the great defender of Spanish ecclesiastical regalism.[81] In particular, he participated in the most committed gatherings of a Jansenist and anti-Jesuit nature, such as that of the Countess of Montijo, and even maintained relations with Father Gregory. Much of the[82] religious policy of the Cortes was inspired by this deputy, who was particularly hated by conservatives. Joaquín Lorenzo Villanueva y Astengo was unquestionably a Liberal Catholic. Subject, like any open-minded person, to the changes that the time brought, he nevertheless held fast to his religious convictions and to the defence of the established order of divine origin. He was not a revolutionary, far from it. In fact, he was more anxious than others that the Catholic religion be enshrined in the constitution as the only possible religion, protected by power and by law. One could not doubt his religious sentiments, even if they were in favour of ecclesiastical reform, in particular, the division between the spiritual power of the pope and the civil power of the king in matters of external ecclesiastical discipline. For the same reason, he was a supporter of bishops as successors of the apostles and opposed religious orders which were not necessary to the Church and which, dependent on Rome, undermined royal authority.[83]

Conclusion

Many of the measures proclaimed by the Cortes must historically be seen as late regalism, which sought to superimpose state authority on the Catholic hierarchy and diminish the Vatican's influence over the Spanish Church. In the same vein, the vow of Santiago was suppressed, an old claim of many Spanish cities that paid this homage to the Cathedral of Santiago de Compostela. It was the liberal deputy José Alonso López y Noball (1763–1824) who was at the root of this measure which gave rise to a clash between conservatives and liberals. It was especially with the abolition of the Tribunal of the Inquisition that the Liberals left their mark on constitutional change.[84,85] The debate was one of the most difficult in the history of the Cortes, giving rise to many tensions. The result of the vote, ninety votes in favour and sixty against, shows how bitter the debate was between Liberals and Conservatives.[86] It was decree CCXXIII of 22 February 1813 that abolished the Inquisition, putting an end in Spain to an institution that had been promulgated on 1 November 1478 by Sixtus IV, in the bull *Exigit sincerae devotionis affectus,* and which for a long time was considered a state within a state.[87] If the argument was reminiscent of some debates of the Legislative Assembly of 1791 and of the Convention in 1793,[88] it differed because of the Iberian particularisms. Spanish Catholic liberalism was the result of a multiple product, at the confluence of the philosophy of the Enlightenment, of religious sentiments and of the relevance of the reforms initiated by the Cortes de Cádiz. This deployment of the concepts of national sovereignty, separation of powers, freedom of the press, individual freedom and denomination of the State were the hallmarks of the relationship between modernity and Hispanity. It explained both the tolerantism of Spanish Catholic liberalism and the slow and gradual process of secularity introduced by the Constitution of 1812.

Notes

1. Contemporary historiography has often reported that liberalism, at least since the Enlightenment, has been religion's rival warring brothers, pitting itself against each other for the control of the modern world. This ideological standardization must be qualified, by integrating the status of liberal neutrality that broadens the scope of the relations of subordination and police between religion and the State. At first glance, it seems that religion defies liberal values. Religious interests are often inaccessible to non-believers, and therefore difficult to justify reasonably, especially if one argues that religions, as overarching moral doctrines, often encroach on the autonomy of its own members (by morally compelling them to act in a certain way). By breaking down religion into different normative dimensions, Laborde attests that these tensions are not as troubling. On the one hand, many other non-religious ideologies and practices may also be inaccessible by challenging autonomy. On the other hand, liberalism can accommodate a background of religiosity, in the name of moderation. On this point, read Cécile Laborde, *Liberalims's religion* (Cambridge: Harvard University Press, 2017), 124–67.
2. Lucien Jaume, 'La Place du catholicisme libéral dans la culture politique française', in *Charles de Montalembert.*

3   P. Cezero Galan, *Religión y laicismo en la España contemporánea. Un análisis ideológico* in *Religión y sociedad en España (siglos XIX y XX), Actas reunidas y presentadas por Paul Aubert* (Madrid: Casa de Velázquez, 2002), 128.
4   The work of Félicité de Lamennais (1782–1854) played a significant role in the history of Spanish Catholic liberalism; it was translated in Spain by Mariano José de Larra in 1836, under the title *El dogma de los hombres libres,* and in 1854, the politician Joaquín María López wrote a *Glosa a las palabras de un creyente, by Mr. Lamennais,* which remained unpublished until the posthumous publication of a collection of the author's works. Cf. E. La Parra, 'El eco de Lamennais en el progresismo español: Larra y Joaquín María López', in *Libéralisme chrétien et catholicisme libéral en Espagne France et Italie dans la première moitié du XIXe siècle* (Aix en Provence: Université de Provence, 1989), 323–42.
5   Jean Bauderot, 'Sécularisation et Laïcisation. Une trame décisive', in *L'Histoire religieuse en France et en Espagne,* ed. B. Pellistrandi (Madrid: Collection de la Casa de Velázquez, 2004), 17–38.
6   George Rudé, *Europa en el siglo XVIII: La aristocracia y el desafío burgués* (Madrid: Alianza Editorial, 1978), 95.
7   J. Pamparacuatro Martin, 'Lenguaje y moral en el siglo XVII: la controversia entre Jansenistas y Jesuitas', *Pensamiento* 76, no. 289 (2020): 408.
8   G.A. Franco Rubio, 'El ejercicio del poder en la España del siglo XVIII. Entre las prácticas culturales y las prácticas políticas', *Mélanges de la Casa de Velasquez* 35 (2005): 51–77.
9   A. Miranda Alvarez, 'Siglo ilustrado y siglo de las luces, dos denominaciones a caballo entre dos siglos', in *Actas del Congreso 'Enter Siglos. Cultura y literatura en España desde finales del siglo XVIII a principios del XIX'', Bordighera,* ed. E. Caldera and R. Frodli (Roma: Bulzoni, 1993), 39–53.
10 J.L. Abellan, 'Del Barroco a la Ilustración (siglos XVII y XVIII)', in *Historia crítica del pensamiento español* (Madrid: Espasa Calpe, 1988).
11 The fact remains that, and F.-A. Isambert has made it very clear, the 'popular religion' was not opposed to the 'official religion'; on the contrary, it corresponded rather to an intuitive and non-intellectual way of living the religious fact and it was thus opposed to a 'scholarly' religion. Read F.A. Isambert, *Le Sens du sacré, fête et religion populaire* (Paris: Ed. de Minuit, 1982), 118.
12 It is true that the crisis of Catholic theology had the effect of valuing the social dimension of Christianity in apologetics at the expense of university theology. This is why the theology of the *ilustrados* reversed the situation by seizing Cartesianism, less to study its intrinsic content than to use it as a means to reconnect with St. Augustine, to whom the theology of the *Aufklärung* referred to. J. Critstobal de Gregorio, 'Los ilustrados y la Ilustración. Implicaciones ético-jurídicas', *Boletín de la Facultad de Derecho de la UNED* 8-9 (1995): 125–46.
13 T. Egido, 'La religiosidad de los ilustrados', in *La época de la Ilustración. El Estado y la cultura (1759-1808),* ed. Mr Batllori (Madrid: Espasa Calpe, 1987), vol. I, 418–26.
14 G. Dufour, *Lumières et Ilustración en Espagne sous les règnes de Charles III et de Charles IV (1759–1788)* (Paris: Ellipses, 2006), 119.
15 A. Morales, 'El jansenismo en España y su carácter de ideología revolucionaria', in *A Revolução francesa e a Península ibérica* (Coimbra: Instituto de Historia e Teoria das Ideas, Faculdade de Letras, 1988), 349. Unless otherwise indicated, translations from Spanish to French are the author's.

16 Conversely, Parisian Port-royalist circles were influenced by Spanish spirituality, in particular that of Louis de Grenade who was one of the first to implement the Counter-Reformation in Spain: 'More spiritual and closer to the intimate religiosity that had so seduced the French since the seventeenth century, the work of Louis de Grenade was very much in tune with the mentality of several Parisian booksellers of the eighteenth century, close to Jansenism' in N. Blas Martin, 'Un país más extranjero que la China: libros españoles en las librerías parisinas del siglo XVIII', *Cuadernos de Ilustración y Romanticismo* 24 (2018): 388.

17 F. Hildesheimer, *Le Jansénisme. L'histoire et l'héritage* (Paris: Desclée de Brouwer, 1992), 56: 'Although the Netherlands were the cradle of the doctrine and a land of refuge for its persecuted cultists, it welcomed it in a different way according to the split between the Catholic Spanish Netherlands and the reformed United Provinces. In the first case, Jansenism developed around the home of Leuven (…). On the other hand, although a priori unfavorable to the Catholics, the United Provinces offered their refuge to the Jansenists.'

18 H. Daniel-Odon, 'Les Bénédictines de Saint-Maur et l'histoire au XVIIe siècle', *Littératures classiques* 30 (1997): 33–50.

19 Mr. Rosso, 'Feijóo et les frontières du savoir', in *Soglie e interazioni. I linguaggi espanici nella tradizione e nella contemporaneità*, Atti del XXVI Convegno dell'AISPI (Trento: Università degli Studi di Trento, 2013), 473–86.

20 J. Salas Alvarez, 'La antigüedad clásica en la España Sagrada del Padre Henrique Flórez de Setién y Huidobro', *Gerión* 27 (2009): 57–78.

21 The author displayed clearly regalist positions, about the denunciation of Roman pre-eminence, joining the Jansenist postures of the time. See A. Mestre Sanchis, *Mayans y Siscar y el pensamiento ilustrado español contra el absolutismo* (León: Universidad de León, 2007), 128. 'It must not be forgotten that, both for Mayans and Campomanes, the king represented the people in the election of bishops and, fundamentally, in ecclesiastical affairs with temporal implications. Therefore, the kings, representatives of the Christian people, and the bishops, representatives of the Spanish hierarchy, had to curb the absolute power of the papacy, which had shown enormous greed for centralism and the accumulation of power.'

22 S. Hermann de Francheshi, 'Agustinismo y molinismo del uso que los "Salamnticenses" (1631) hicieron de las enseñanzas de San Agustín contra las tesis de Luis de Molina', *Criticón* 118 (2013): 81–97.

23 S. Hermann de Francheshi, 'Les Derniers feux de la querelle de la grâce. Le jansénisme français et la question thomiste à la fin du XVIIe siècle', *Ephemerides Theologicae Lovanienses* 8, no. 1 (2010): 27–81.

24 The philosophical-theological thought of Pedro Manso de Tapia is part of the current of the scholastic renewal of the eighteenth century, and more particularly in what is called the Augustinian School. In the theological field, his work was important because of his ardent revival of the theological theses of St. Augustine. Pedro Manso, known to his contemporaries as *Doctor fundatissimus*, contributed to the restoration and dissemination of the Augustinian School in Spain, Europe (Italy and Germany, mainly), America and the Philippines. His name is still associated with the famous and harsh controversy *Sanctus Augustinus de virtutibus infidelium* in Salamanca, published in Valladolid in 1721 and prohibited in 1723. See 'Inquisición', in *Diccionario de la Compañia de Jesús. Biográfico-Temático, III, Infanta of Santiago-Piatkiewicz*, ed. C.E. O'Neill and J. Ma Dominguez (Roma; Madrid: Institutum Historicum and Universidad Pontifica Comillas, 2001), col. 2035.

25   In the lively doctrinal debates that agitated the pontificate of Benedict XIV, especially on the relationship between grace and nature, on the constitution *Unigenitus* and the publications that spread everywhere, including in Spain, Pope Lambertini wanted to give himself the greatest possible freedom. The Roman condemnations of works that were both the expression of rigorist and more violently anti-Jesuit circles must be seen in the difficult attempt to find the right balance. It is in this context that two works by Cardinal Enrico Noris, *Historia pelagiana* and *Dissertatio de synodo V œcumenica*, subsequently denounced by the Spanish Inquisition, were relieved of their condemnation by Benedict XIV, who forcefully defended one of the principal representatives of the Augustinian School of Theology, reaffirming not only the full orthodoxy of Noris, but thereby claiming a certain freedom in areas not dogmatically defined. See P.D. Giovannoni, 'Il contesto italiano ed europeo', in *Prospero Lambertini. Pastore della sua città, pontefice della cristianità*ed. A. Zanotti (Argelato: Minerva Edizione, 2004), 15–33.

26   Since the beginning of the thirteenth century, royal and Roman authorities maintained permanent quarrels, pushing some pontiffs to fulminate censorship against monarchical encroachments. It denounced *'persecutions, insults, oppressions and hostile incursions'* about the control of the vacancies of cathedral churches and monasteries, of the detention of clerics before secular courts, the intervention in electoral procedures, the fraudulent use of the rights of the Holy See, of the limitation of the 'Privilegia and libertates' of the Church. King Alfonso X's claim to legally enshrine the principles of interventionism in ecclesiastical life set a founding precedent for Spanish regalism. Cf. C. Ayala Martinez, 'Política eclesiàstica de Alfonso X. El Rey y sus obispos', *Alicante* IX (2014–2015): 41–105.

27   M. Menendez Pelayo, *Historia de los heterodoxos españoles* (Alicante: Biblioteca Miguel de Cervantes, 2003), 1050.

28   Antoine Boudet had previously been arrested and imprisoned in 1747 for having printed and distributed forbidden works, in particular, the *Nouvelles ecclésiastiques* See M. Menuet, 'The "*Nouvelles ecclésiastiques*" (1728–1750) face à leurs opposants: quelques polémiques autour du prêt à l'intérêt', *Oeconomia* 8, no. 1 (2018): 29–44.

29   L. Sanchez Espinosa, 'Los libreros Ángel Corradi y Antoine Boudet y la importación de libros franceses para la Academia de San Fernando', *Bulletin hispanique* 114, no. 1 (2012): 195–216. See also R. Mathis, 'Diffuser le jansénisme au risque de la prison ? Les imprimeurs "jansénistes" et le pouvoir royal (1643–1712)', in *Port-Royal et la prison*ed. J. Lesaulnier, (Paris; Nolin: Université Port-Royal, 2011), 197–211.

30   The fact was still proven in the early nineteenth century. The case of Mariano Lucas Garrido (1775–1831), a Jansenist priest, is quite characteristic of this progressive, perfectly trained and erudite clergy, with an abundant library including the classical works of French and Italian Jansenism. See A. Astorgano Abajo, 'La biblioteca jansenista del canónigo Mariano Lucas Garrido (1831), secretario de Meléndez Valdés', *Dieciocho* 43 (2020): 103–36.

31   'Catálogo das Obras de António Pereira de Figueiredo mandado fazer por ele mesmo a 28 de Junho de 1780. Torre do Tombo, manuscript da Livraria, b. 1938', in *Padre António Pereira de Figueiredo. Erudição e polémica na segunda metade do século XVIII* (Roma: Roma Editora, 2005), 373–7.

32   V. Leon Navarro, 'Conflictos ideológicos durante los primeros años de don Francisco Fabián y Fuero en la mitra valenciana', in *La catedral ilustrada. Iglesia, sociedad y cultura en la Valencia del siglo XVIII*, ed. E. Callado Estella (València: Institucio Alfons el Magnanim, 2015), vol. 3, 137–85.

33 It was he who dealt directly with the expulsion of French Jesuits who had taken refuge in Spain in 1764. The question was brought before the Royal Council to determine whether asylum should be granted to these exiles. Attorney General Campomanes issued a decidedly negative opinion on 20 July 1764, in which he exaggerated the dangers that the arrival of large numbers of emigrants would entail. The main reasons for the refusal of asylum were based on the arguments that the French parliaments had used against the Company, considering it an ungovernable body, and whose constitutions were totally incompatible with the State. Campomanes' opinion on the French exiles of July 1764 contains the seeds of the attacks that he exposed two years later in a famous opinion of 31 December 1766, on which the expulsion of the Spanish Jesuits by Carlos III was based. Read M. Revuelta Gonzalez, 'Negación de asilo a Jesuitas franceses refugiados en España en el dictamen del fiscal Campomanes en 1764', *Miscelànea Comillas* 65, no. 126 (2007): 101–24.

34 F. Garcia de Cortazar and J.M. Gonzalez Vesga, *Breve historia de España* (Madrid: Alianza Editorial, 2016), 348.

35 J. Perez-Magallon, 'Jansenio, agustinismo y la batalla propagandística entre Francia y el imperio hispánico', *Criticón* 118 (2013): 137–49.

36 *Le Jansénisme et l'Europe. Actes du colloque international organisé à l'Université du Luxembourg les 8, 9 et 10 novembre 2007*, ed. R. Baustert (Tübingen: Narr, 2010). See also W. Doyle, *Jansenism: Catholic Resistance to Authority from the Reformation to the French Revolution (Studies in European History)* (London: Palgrave Macmillan, 2000).

37 A. Lupano, 'Le Traité inédit "*Della povertà religiosa*" (1759): L'antiromanisme universitaire turinois selon Angelo Paolo Carena et son maître Carlo Sebastiano Berardi', in *Droits antiromains XVIe-XXIe siècles. Juridictionnalisme catholique et romanité ecclésiale*, ed. S. de Franceschi and B. Hours (Lyon: LAHRA, 2017), 149–68.

38 M. Rosa, 'Jesuitisme et antijésuitisme dans l'Italie du XVIIe siècle', in *Les antijésuites. Discours, figures et lieux de l'antijésuitisme à l'époque moderne*, ed. P.A. Fabre and C. Maire (Rennes: Presses Universitaires de Rennes, 2010), 587–619.

39 Mr. Rochini, 'Teologia politica ed ecclesiologia del piccolo numero: l'idea del martirio nel giansenismo italiano settecentesco', *Rivista di Storia del christianesimo* 15 (2018): 359–76.

40 G. Schettini, 'Confessional Modernity: Nicola Spedalieri. The Catholic Church and the French Revolution', *Modern Intellectual History* 17, no. 3 (2020): 677–705; G. Grasso, 'Pietro Tamburini difensore della Chiesa di Utrecht. Ruolo dell'edizione belga del "de tolerantia", Ghent, 1784', *Revue d'Histoire ecclésiastique* 1–2, no. 114 (2019): 265–88; D.K. Van Kley, 'From the Catholic Enlightenment to the Risorgimento: The Exchange between Nicola Spedalieri and Pietro Tamburini, 1791–1797', *Past & Present* 224 (2014): 109–62.

41 C. Gori, *Scipione de' Ricci. Vescovo di Pistoia* in *Il Covile* XV, no. 862 (2015): 13–15.

42 *Atti e decreti del concilio diocesano di Pistoia dell'anno 1786* (Vol. I: Ristampa dell'edizione Bracali. Indici a cura di P. Stella; Vol. II: Introduzione storica e documenti inediti. A cura di Pietro Stella, Firenze, Olschki, Biblioteca storica toscana), Series II, vol. 9 (1986), vol. I: XII-XII: 256–144–32, con 2 tavv. F.T.; vol. II: VI–698 con 4 tavv. F.T.

43 A.J. Smidt, 'Piedad e ilustración en relación armónica. Josep Climent i Avinent, obispo de Barcelona, 1766–1775', *Manuscrits* 20 (2002): 91–109.

44 R. Corts I Blay, 'La figura episcopal y pública by Josep Climent en Barcelona (1766–1775)', *Pedralbes* 26 (2006): 81–103.

45 J. Viejo Yharrassarry, 'El caso climent ¿ Ilustración católica o catolicismo ilustrado ?', *Hispania. Revista española de historia* LXXXI, no. 269 (2021): 651–81.
46 A. Astorgano Abajo, 'Poesía y jansenismo en el Convento de los agustinos calzados de Salamanca en tiempos de Meléndez Valdés', *Revista de Estudios Extremeños* LXXII, no. 1 (2016): 147–208.
47 J.P. Chantin, 'À la recherche des évêques constitutionnels jansénistes', in *Gouverner une Eglise en Révolution. Histoire et mémoires de l'épiscopat constitutionnel*, ed. P. Chopelin (Paris, Lyon: LAHRA, 2017), 219 et seq.
48 Bellegarde (1717–89) had a remarkable network of correspondents from the principal countries of Europe, such as Italy, Spain, Germany, Portugal, France, etc., with whom he maintained epistolary relations on Jansenist subjects and publications. The spread of Jansenist ideas in Austria and Portugal is attributed to his truly prodigious activity. His work is largely inspired by the anti-ultramontane current which, in Portugal, continued to spread throughout the second half of the eighteenth century and even in the nineteenth century. See C. Dos Santos, *O Jansenismo em Portugal* (Porto: Faculdade de Letras da Universidade do Porto, Departamento de História e de Estudos Políticos e Internacionais, 2007), 13.
49 V. Sciutti Russi, 'Abolir l'Inquisition d'Espagne: une lettre de l'Abbé Grégoire', *Annales de la Révolution française* 333 (2003): 121–32.
50 On the extension of networks and international propaganda, see R. Taverneaux, *La vie quotidienne des Jansénistes* (Paris: Hachette, 1985), 246–7: 'The press and the networks for the transmission of thought were not only the instruments of the Jansenist dynamic: they gave rise to new sociological or spiritual combinations, fostered the resurgence of apparently disappeared feelings, developed polarizations around ideological foci (…)'.
51 The synod of Pistoia took place from 18 to 28 September 1786 with three aims, politico-ecclesiastical Jansenism, which put forward the relegation of the pontiff, liturgical and sacramental reform and moral rigorism. The epilogue of this assembly was the failure of the National Council of Tuscany which met from April to June 1787, a prelude to the accession of Peter Leopold to the imperial throne in 1790. His death two years later confirmed the failure of the reform. Cf. J.-A. Saranyana, 'La eclesología de la Revolución en el Sínodo de Pistoya (1786)', *Anuario de Historia de la Iglesia* 19, (2010): 61.
52 *Du Jansénisme au modernisme: la Bulle Auctorem fidei, 1794, pivot du magistère romain magisterium*, ed. J.B. Amadieu and S. Icard (Paris: Beauchesne, coll. 'Théologie historique', 2020).
53 F.J. Fernandez de la Cigona, *El liberalismo y la Iglesia española. Historia de una persecución. Antecedentes* (Madrid: Speiro, 1989), 1278.
54 J. Perez, *Brève histoire de l'Inquisition en Espagne* (Paris: Fayard, 2002), 174.
55 A. de la Hera Perez-Cuesta, 'The "Monarchia Catholica" española', *Anuario de Historia del Derecho español* 67 (1997): 661–75.
56 J.M. Santana Perez, 'Carlos IV ¿ El último gobierno del despotismo ilustrado y el primer fracaso del liberalismo en España ?', *Presente & Pasado* 9, no. 18 (2004): 105.
57 The Concordat of 1753 placed all appointments in the hands of the king, but he did not have the power to give them instructions, although many behaved as officials and collaborators of reformism in public and civil affairs. The reformers, described as Jansenists by their opponents, weren't able to counter these attacks with a coordinated propaganda. See O. Rey Castelao, 'Las relaciones entre la Monarquía y la Iglesia en el siglo XVIII ¿ La evolución de un modelo europeo ?' in *Las monarquías*

española y francesa (siglos XVI-XVIII) ¿ Dos modelos políticos ? ed. A. Dubet and J.J. Ruiz Ibáñez (Madrid: Casa de Velázquez, 2010), 201–11.

58 M. Calvio Tojo, 'Reconocimiento de la jurisdicción eclesiástica por el Estado español', *Almogaren* 36 (2005): 350 et seq.

59 A. Garcia-Baquero and L.C. Alvarez Santalo, '*Riqueza y pobreza del clero secular en la Sevilla del Antiguo Régimen (1700–1834)*', *Trocadero, Revista de Historia Moderna y Contemporanea* 8–9 (1996–1997): 11–46.

60 The conflictual situation experienced by Spain at the beginning of the nineteenth century led to a very particular configuration. There were three distinct Spains. That of Joseph Bonaparte, imposed by Napoleon and to which a part of the nobility and the liberal bourgeoisie rallied. Opposite, we find insurrectionary Spain or Spain of the *Juntas*, which defended the nullity of the abdications of Fernando VII – who had reigned between March and May 1818 – and, consequently, the principle that the legitimate kings of Spain were always the Bourbons. Finally, the chaos that reigned on the Spanish continent gave birth to a 'third' Spain, that of the American territories, which knew their own convulsive reality at the beginning of the nineteenth century. Cf. M. Rodriguez Fernandez, 'Las tres España of 1808', *Revista Aequitas* 11, (2018): 50 et seq.

61 I. Fernandez Sarasola, 'La responsabilidad del Gobierno en los orígenes del constitucionalismo español: el Estatuto de Bayona', *Revista de Derecho Político* 41 (1996): 177–214.

62 H. Dippel, 'Constitucionalismo moderno. Introducción a una historia que necesita ser escrita', *Historia constitucional* 6 (2005): 181–99.

63 In the first version, Napoleon had tried to strike a balance between the concordat system and the importance of the Catholic Church in the monarchy. That is why, while recognizing the monopoly of the Catholic religion and the intolerance of all other religions, the draft limited itself to tolerating only the Catholic cult, and not religion. Read J.B. Busaall, *Le spectre du jacobinisme. L'expérience constitutionnelle française et le premier libéralisme espagnol* (Madrid: Collection of the Casa de Velázquez (56), 2012), 33–90.

64 As such, they supported, more than the other two groups, the unenvied title of 'Famosos Traidores' and the idea that this constitution was a foreign text, imposed and supported because of their collaboration. Read J. Lopez Tabar, *Los famosos traidores. Los afrancesados durante la crisis del Antiguo Régimen (1808–1833)* (Madrid: Biblioteca Nueva, 2001), 23–102.

65 I. Fernandez Sarasola, 'La forma de gobierno en la Constitutión de Bayona', *Historia Constitucional* 9 (2008): 64.

66 One of the first projects was to convene the Cortes in Madrid, because both Napoleon and his opponents knew that without the support of the Spanish parliament, it was impossible to prolong the planned reforms. Joseph Bonaparte ignored this summons by creating new institutions that were not provided for by the *Statuto de Bayona* as the *Council of State*, the *Ministry of the Interior*. Read J.M. Puyol Montero, 'Los proyectos de Napoleón y de José Bonaparte para la convocatoria de unas Cortes en Madrid (1808–1812)', *Anuario de Historia del Derecho español* 85 (2015): 203 et seq.

67 At the beginning of his reign, Joseph Bonaparte received many supporters, because his measures represented progress and modernity as opposed to the structures of the *Ancien Régime*. First among these supporters was the highest Spanish aristocracy, who had participated in the Assembly of Notables of Bayonne. Consult A.M.

Moral Roncal, 'La nobleza española en la política y diplomacia durante la edad contemporánea', *Doors* 89, no. 30 (2015): 83–5. However, the Spanish nobility soon became aware of the indignation that the arrival of a new king provoked in a large part of the Spanish population. After the French defeat at the Battle of Bailén, as was the case for many members of the army, some of these aristocrats began to abandon the Bonapartist regime. Read J. Mercader Riba, *José Bonaparte Rey de España (1808-1813). Estructura del estado español bonapartista* (Madrid: Consejo Superior de Investigaciones Científicas, 1983), 316.

68   J. Hernandez Franco, 'Pasado y presente de Floridablanca como objeto de la Historia', *Mixtures of Casa Velásquez* 39 (2009): 163–86.

69   M. Suarez Cortina, 'Liberalismo, política y constitución en la España contemporánea (una miranda desde la historia constitucional', *Historia y Política* 19 (2008): 292.

70   M. Moran, 'Los diputados eclesiásticos en las Cortes de Cádiz: revisión crítica', *Hispania Sacra* 42 (1990): 35–60. By the same author, 'Conciencia y revolución liberal. Actitudes políticas de los eclesiásticos en las Cortes de Cádiz', *Hispania Sacra* 42 (1990): 485–92.

71   F. Andujar Castillo, 'La Corte y los militares en el siglo XVIII', *Estudios: Revista de Historia Moderna* 27 (2001): 91–120; *Military poder elites: las guardias reales en el siglo XVIII* in *La pluma, la mitra y la espada. Estudios de Historia institucional en la Edad Moderna*, ed. J.L. Castellano & ly. (Madrid: Universidad de Burdeos, 2000), 65–94.

72   S.R. Castano, 'La teoría de la traslación del poder en Suárez, entre tradición y ruptura', *Mediaevalia. Revista de pensamiento medieval* 8, no. 2 (2015): 93–114.

73   Realists did not believe in written laws as much as liberals and tended to place institutions at the centre of the political system: Crown, Courts, States, Universities. Political debates soon revealed their differences with the Liberals. Read J.V. Suanzes-Carpegna, 'Las Cortes de Cádiz y la Constitución de 1812 (una visión de conjunto)', *Anuario by Derecho Parlamentario* 26 (2012): 193.

74   The liberal tendency – in which Agustín Argüelles (1766-1844), José María Queipo de Llano, conde de Toreno (1786-1843) or Diego Francisco Muñoz Torrero (1761-1829) distinguished themselves – refers to the concept of national sovereignty, understanding the nation as an ideal and abstract entity, different from the simple sum of individuals or provinces. The nation is sovereign, not because of the vacancy of the throne, but because it was its natural and inalienable condition. Although the rationale is not always clear, this design is rooted in the *iusrationalist*, based on the theories of the State, nature and the social pact: individuals, free and equal by nature, must renounce part of their freedoms to constitute a State and in another movement, society, by the social pact, confers the ownership of sovereignty on the community or nation. Cf. R. de Blanca Torres, 'El fundamento ideológico de la Constuitución de Cádiz de 1812. Ilustración y romanticismo. El sentido de la presencia de los textos jurídicos medievales en la Constitución de cádiz de 1812', *Revista de la Facultad de Ciencias Sociales y Jurídicas de Elche* 1, (2009): 158–67.

75   C. Barney, 'La Nueva España in the crisis of 1808', *Cuadernos de Historia del Derecho* 19 (2012): 49–63.

76   It was the crisis of the Spanish monarchy that inaugurated much of the conceptual references that the American republics would use to establish their political principles. Citizenship will take on a particular nuance among the indigenous populations of South America, especially in Peru. See F. Nunez, 'La imagen del "indio" en los debates de las Cortes de Cádiz (1810-1812)', *Historia* 1 (2018): 16–23.

77 We will use the edition *La Constitución de 1812: Edición conmemorativa del segundo centenario*, introdución de L. Lopez Guerra (Madrid: Edición Tecnos, 2012).
78 El Rey, nuestro Señor Don Fernando VII, y en su nombre el Supremo Consejo de Regencia de España e Indias, en el día en que debe verificarse la apertura e instalación de las Cortes generales del Reino, considerando que esta extraordinaria y tan deseada congregación, la más solemne y general de toda la Nación española, y de que no hay ejemplo en los siglos anteriores, es por el número, universalidad y modo de elección de sus representantes un Congreso, en que unidos por el amor y común interés, y más aún por la cristiana caridad los españoles de los dos mundos, tratan en primer lugar de defender, conservar y ampliar en ellos la verdadera Religión Católica Apostólica Romana, los derechos del legítimo Monarca, que Dios ha concedido a las Españas (…). See E. de Diego Garcia, 'The "Orgánica" of las Cortes 1810–1813', *Cuadernos de Historia Contemporánea* 24 (2002): 31.
79 J.M. Laboa, 'La libertad religiosa en la historia constitucional española', *Revista de Estudios políticos* 30 (1982): 157–74.
80 Article 12: 'La religión de la Nación española es y será perpetuamente la católica, apostólica, romana, única verdadera. La Nación la protege por leyes sabias y justas, y prohíbe el ejercicio de cualquiera otra.'
81 V.L. Navarro, 'El grupo valenciano y el reformismo de Joaquin Lorenzo Villanueva anterior a las Cortes de Cádiz', *Anales de la Universidad de Alicante. Historia Contemporánea*, 1983, 9–33.
82 L. Ramirez Aledon, 'Joaquín Lorenzo Villanueva y la polémica sobre la carta del obispo Gregoire contra la Inquisicíon española in 1798', *Cuadernos de Ilustración y Romanticismo* 13 (2005): 13–54.
83 He will be forced into exile, like many Catholic liberals, at the time of the return of Fernando VII and the policy of repression carried out from 1823. Read E. Solez Pascula, 'Ocios de espanoles emigrados: Una revista del exilio londinense', in *Disidencias y exilios en la espara moderna, Actas de la IV Reunión Científica de la Asociación Española de Historia Moderna, Alicante, 27–30 de mayo de 1996*, ed. A. Mestre-Sanchís and E. Gimenez-Lopez (Alicante: Caja de Ahorros del Mediterráneo, Universidad de Alicante, 1997), 833–48.
84 This measure was introduced by Decree CCIII of 14 October 1812, which had been preceded by an order of 1 September 1812 on the extinction of Santiago's vow: 'That, in accordance with the same Constitution, the privilege of the vow of Santiago is extinguished, and that, consequently, the judges of first instance must hear it.'
85 J. Lasarte, 'Nota sobre José Alonso y López, diputado en las Cortes de Cádiz y del Trienio Liberal', *Revista de Estudios Regionales* 98 (2013): 234–5.
86 G. Dufour, '¿ Cuándo fue abolida la Inquisición en España ?', *Cuadernos de Ilustración y Romanticismo* 13 (2005): 99–106.
87 J. Martinez Millan, *La Inquisición española* (Madrid: Alianza Editorial, 2021), 58 ff.
88 J.J. Clere, 'L'aboliton des droits féodaux en France', *Cahiers d'Histoire* 94–5 (2005): 135–57.

6

Between Sinai and Calvary: Spanish Catholicism in the face of freedom of worship in 1869

Francisco Javier Ramon Solans
Universidad de Zaragoza

Introduction

The goal of this chapter is to analyse Catholic opposition to religious freedom in Spain in 1869 from a new perspective. The convergence between Legitimist and Catholic sectors during this initial offensive against the revolutionary regime has led to identifying the former as anti-liberal. However, a large part of Spanish Catholicism after 1848 had accepted the principles of the liberal system – restricted suffrage and a limited framework of freedoms – but not the democratic principle or an assumption of the plural nature of societies. In order to analyse these issues, I will focus on the arguments used by these Catholic sectors both in the Spanish Congress and in Catholic associations and the press.

'Great is God in the Sinai ... but there is a greater God, greater still, which is not the majestic God of the Sinai, but the humble God of Calvary.' In this way, the republican member of congress, Emilio Castelar, was leading up to the conclusion of his brilliant intervention in the Constituent Assembly of 12 April 1869 in favour of religious freedom: 'Great is the religion of power, but greater is the religion of love; great is the religion of implacable justice, but greater is the religion of merciful forgiveness; and I, in the name of the Gospel, come here to ask you to write religious freedom into your fundamental Code, in other words, liberty, fraternity, equality amongst all men.'[1]

Castelar's words did not just represent arguably one of the greatest landmarks in Spanish parliamentary oratory, but also tangible proof that the 1868 Revolution was neither antireligious nor violent towards the clergy.[2] The historiography has shown that many prominent revolutionaries were liberal Catholics or, while they may have broken with the Catholic Church, still defined themselves as Christian.[3] Besides overthrowing the Bourbon dynasty and establishing universal suffrage, the revolutionaries coincided in the need to reform relations between church and state. The aim was not just to secularize the state, but also to neutralize the church as a political force and, in order to do so, they tried to limit its associative development and undermine its economic capacity and social influence.

It is within this context that the first set of measures introduced by the Minister of Grace and Justice, Antonio Romero Ortiz, in the provisional government of 1868 must be understood: the suppression of the Society of Jesus and all monasteries established since 1837, the ban on religious communities from acquiring property and the closure of the conferences of the Society of Saint Vincent de Paul. The speed with which they were passed, their scope and the form in which they were carried out through revolutionary councils generated widespread discontent among many Catholics. Indeed, measures such as the abolition of the Society of Saint Vincent de Paul called into question the initial commitment of some liberal Catholics to the 1868 Revolution. Such was the reaction in the press that the government had to back down and authorize the establishment of the women's branch of the conferences. The Catholic feminist *avant-la-lettre* and social reformer Concepción Arenal had written a harsh article against the government, the publication of which she postponed for two years in the hope that it would reverse its decision. Therein, she pointed out that the ban did not reflect public opinion, or freedom of association or even the interests of the revolutionary party.[4] Vicente de la Fuente, one of the founders of the Society of Saint Vincent de Paul in Spain in 1850 and the *Asociación de Católicos Españoles* (Association of Spanish Catholics) in 1868, wrote to his friend and fellow driving force behind these two associations, José María Quadrado, pointing out that

> The falsifiers of Spanish democracy have been and continue to be hopeless and disheartened beyond measure. Instead of attracting Catholics to democracy, something easy and feasible, considering the circumstances in the northern provinces of Spain and the courtly rot within the palace of Charles IV and his son and granddaughter, they have had the singular ability to become antipathetic to all Catholics and all good men. It is impossible to be clumsier than such people: they come to clean off mud with their hands already muddied; they seek to clean the mud of hypocrisy with the mud of impiety.[5]

Nevertheless, the issue that would most stir up Catholic public opinion was that of the debate around and passing of freedom of worship. By means of studying the mobilization against this measure, I will offer a more nuanced interpretation of what is typically considered its antiliberal nature in order to demonstrate how many of its leading figures came from a moderate liberal background, had embraced the principles of a parliamentary system and possessed extensive associative experience which they put at the service of their cause. Indeed, this position was perfectly compatible with the experience of nineteenth-century Spanish parliamentary regimes which maintained a strict confessional framework with a Catholic definition of citizenship, religious intolerance and state financing of the Catholic creed. In order to address these issues, I will initially concentrate on the social mobilization against these measures through Catholic associationism, and then analyse the parliamentary opposition organized by two prelates who were elected as members of the constituent *Cortes* (Spanish parliament).

I Mobilization of civil society

Recently, the historiography has demonstrated the importance of religious organizations in mobilizing and politicizing the population during the first half of the nineteenth century. Both on account of the techniques employed and the figures they achieved, it can be argued that they played a decisive role in shaping civil society. A good example of this would be the Irish Catholic Association, which by 1828 had amassed 3 million associate members and, thanks to the support of the Catholic Church structure, carried out very original protest activities such as simultaneous meetings to demand equal rights for Catholics.[6] Likewise, these associative movements enjoyed a strongly transnational dimension and the same Irish Catholic Association became a global point of reference as in the case of the *Piusvereine* (pious associations) which were founded in the Germanic cultural sphere from 1848 onwards in order to defend church rights.[7]

These campaigns against freedom of worship demonstrated how in Spain, in the same way as in other European countries like the UK, France, Belgium and Germany, Catholics had assimilated the use of strategies of mobilizing civil society.

Although on occasion they were presented as weapons of the enemy, the truth is that Catholics were pioneers in the use of such mobilization strategies and they managed to achieve record numbers in terms of participation.[8] The debate over freedom of worship served as a stimulus for an unprecedented mobilization within Spanish Catholicism with the collection of more than 3 million signatures and the establishment of an associative network throughout the peninsula, the creation of the *Asociación de Católicos Españoles* (Catholic Association of Spaniards) and, later and independently, the *Asociación de la JuventudCatólica* (Association of Catholic Youth) and the *Asociación Católica de Señoras* (Catholic Association of Women).[9]

The first revolutionary measures, such as suppressing the Jesuits and curbing the number of monasteries, provoked the establishment of an opposition which was expressed (among other ways) in the collection of signatures. On 15 October, women in Seville handed in the first petition to the government to call for the repeal of these measures. This was followed by petitions on behalf of women in Madrid, Écija, Segovia, Toledo and Valladolid, as well as residents of Astorga, Pamplona, Salamanca and Mendigorría and members of the Progressive Party in Orihuela.[10] The Bishop of Jaén also took the protest to the Minister of Grace and Justice and appealed to the 'right of petition' and 'citizens' rights' in order to substantiate his positions.[11]

Once this first set of measures had been passed, on 25 October 1868 the provisional government took a further step and stated in its manifesto to the nation that the 'most important [reform] of all, due to the essential alteration that it introduces into the secular organisation of Spain, is that related to the approach to religious freedom'.[12] Once more, it would be Catholic women who took the initiative. In November 1868, the Countess of Montijo and the Marchioness of Santiago were the driving forces behind the collection of twelve thousand signatures by women in Seville. For her part, the president of Sunday schools in Madrid sent out a circular to similar societies throughout the country, and that had been federated since 1857 in a royal association, in order to gather signatures against freedom of worship.[13] On 1 December 1868, the nuncio Alessandro Franchi informed Secretary of State Antonelli that 'a healthy reaction on healthy principles is demonstrated with true solace in all good people. The example of the ladies in Seville and Madrid was the cry of alarm sent out to all Catholic Spain.'[14]

In this latter missive, the nuncio already mentioned a meeting, held at the home of the Marquis of Viluma, of several Catholic notables to establish a lay association with the goal of capitalizing on and coordinating the mobilization against the secularizing legislation. From the outset, they sought the backing of prelates and the blessing of the Holy See, but maintained an independent lay dimension in order to compliment ecclesiastical activity.

The association defined itself as apolitical, yet in reality it could be said that it sought to be non-partisan in order to avoid, on the one hand, any exclusive association with Carlism and, on the other, to distance itself from parties which had been front and centre on the political stage during the Isabelline period. Although there were Neo-Catholics, Carlists and moderates within its ranks, the idea prevailed that, as opposed to 'a gathering of Catholic notables, but spent in political struggles, a Council of non-political Catholics, detached from commitments and willing to work rather than make speeches, [would be] preferable'.[15] The goal of choosing the moderate Marquis of Viluma, who had unsuccessfully pushed for a dynastic union between Isabel II and the Carlist branch, was for him to mediate within an association with different political sensibilities. The marquis himself insinuated in various letters to José María Quadrado that his appointment had been a compromise choice and that his work was compromised by this difficult balance.[16]

The progress of this association was followed closely from the Holy See thanks to the correspondence between the nuncio and the secretary of state. In December, they published a manifesto and instructions so that this petition to maintain the status quo of the concordat signed in 1853 – namely that of Catholic unity and religious intolerance – would be adhered to uniformly. From the outset, an improvised yet successful mechanism was implemented that, with the support of the nunciature, the ecclesiastical hierarchy, the press and the associative framework, would manage to collect 3,448,396 signatures (plus another half a million late signatures as well as spoilt or blank papers that remained to be submitted) in 10,110 towns in just four months. On 3 April 1869, they were presented to congress in a spectacular ceremony in which they were transported in five luxury coaches and deposited by the Bishop of Jaén.[17] In the petition that was handed in to the *Cortes*, the *Asociación de Católicos Españoles* demanded its rights and condemned the difficulties, pressure and coercion which had hindered the free exercise of these rights:

> The right to petition has always been a sacred right in Spain. Monarchs have never attempted to limit or impede it; and although now no law has been passed to refute it, nevertheless, for Catholics it does not exist; for the first time, respectfully addressing the authorities has been forbidden; it has been considered an offence, and presenting the wishes of the peoples to the public authorities has

been persecuted and punished ... We have been able to ascertain that freedoms which are proclaimed will never be for Catholics, that they will never enjoy that of association, nor of assembly, nor of the press, nor of petition.[18]

There were constant complaints in both public forums and the press. The organizers were aware of the fact that although the mobilization was spectacular, something that had never been seen before in Spanish society, it was clearly insufficient to convince a chamber controlled by the revolutionary coalition. Those 3.5 million people did not even make up a quarter of a total population that had risen to 15.5 million people. Nonetheless, nor was the figure sufficiently low to be ignored and the press which supported freedom of worship took charge of questioning it, accusing the clergy and the organizers of falsification, invention and forcing entire families and minors to sign. Be that as it may, the driving forces behind collecting and organizing the signatures also acknowledged some difficulties, as the Marquis of Viluma confessed to José María Quadrado:

[W]hat he does not know is that there were very few who sent back the counted signatures and as well arranged statements as those of this province. There were a lot who stopped including copies, many who neglected to express to which province they belonged, quite a few who kept the originals, sending us a simple copy without authorisation of any kind ... You will respond by making up for and amending all these defects, it is really irritating and annoying but not of such importance that it can excuse the inaction or indolence with which the Council proceeds; laziness or negligence which perturbs all of us and makes us fear for the life of the Association.[19]

Although irregular signatures were discounted, this was still an unprecedented level of mobilization within Catholicism and Spanish civil society. In the face of such spectacular activity, the question arises of how such a powerful organization was capable of emerging and taking shape in such a short space of time. Frequently, the analysis of this mobilization has been reduced to an explanation of the origins of social Catholicism and Catholic Action, either as a brief successful parenthesis in the history of a failure or as proof of the vitality of secular Catholicism on the eve of the creation of Catholic Action.[20] However, the success of the association should not just be analysed as a starting point for subsequent mobilizations, but also as the result of a learning and socialization process.

In the first place, it is clear that the success of the association can be explained by the immediate circumstances in which it emerged, by the possibilities which were unleashed by the new freedom of revolutionary association and by the radical nature of certain measures which incited many Catholics into taking action. The suppression of the Society of Saint Vincent de Paul also led to a lot of energy being expended in this spirited mobilization against the new secular measures. However, the scope of this mobilization would not have been possible if not for a prior associative experience, especially within the very conferences of Saint Vincent de Paul. In this sense, it is worth recalling that some members of the *Asociación de Católicos Españoles* like Vicente de la Fuente and José María Quadrado had contributed to the establishment and remarkable development of the Society of Saint Vincent de Paul in Spain between 1849 and 1868. Still, this does not mean that the new association was a simple replica of the society, since some members of the latter secretly continued with their aid activities, as was the case of its founder, Santiago Masarnau, or continued to operate as part of both groups, like Vicente de la Fuente himself.[21]

Moreover, their associative experience was inspired by reference points in other parts of Europe, especially those of the Catholic movement in Germany, Belgium and Ireland. Actors like Vicente de la Fuente had travelled throughout Europe and had attended events as important as the Second Malines Congress in 1864. Furthermore, the leading figures themselves were aware of the similarities between the Saint Vincent de Paul conferences and the new *Asociación de Católicos Españoles*. As José María Quadrado, a driving force behind both groups, pointed out:

> There was a notable analogy, I am not afraid to proclaim it, between the conferences of Saint Vincent and the nascent Catholic associations. Both, although obedient to the voice of prelates and respectful and deferential to the priesthood even in what did not strictly concern the spiritual ministry, constituted a kind of secular militia with their own set of rules and organisation, in accordance with ecclesiastics in objectives, but different in nature. Deriving all their vigour and effectiveness from the Church, receiving from it their sanction, anointing it with all their efforts, while they marched to a separate beat from that of the clergy, it was not because of a strategic ruse or shameful dissimulation, not due to fear of or flattery towards modern precautions, not because of reckless rivalry or presumptuous competition, but in order to assist it with the best results and with the greater freedom of action in the different spheres that its situation distances it from or which close it off to unjust suspicion. In the domestic home and in public life, in the university and in the press, in property and in industry, in the exercise of their respective profession or work, under great spotlights and in the furthest reaches, at all hours and in a thousand different explicit or indirect but always dignified ways, heads and members of the family can exercise their influence without any distinction of rank or condition, and united and linked to one another form a great electric chain whose exhilarating jolt extends to all corners of the land.[22]

The creation of the *Asociación de Católicos Españoles* generated tension with the Carlist movement, which aspired to capitalize on Catholic discontent during the *Sexenio democrático*. Vicente de la Fuente wrote to José María Quadrado, underlining that

> There is great danger for the association in Carlism. Fervent Carlists look askance at it. You see what nonsense that idiot Vildósola said and how many invectives he launched against it in his untimely pamphlet about dynastic fusion. The governing Council, animated by the spirit of Saint Vincent de Paul, has not wished to respond and has requested that there shall be no answer. How that pleases me![23]

The letter referred to Antonio Vildósola, a Carlist parliamentarian and journalist, and his work titled '*Las' apariencias y la realidad de la fusión dinástica* (*The outward appearance and reality of dynastic fusion*, 1869). Therein, he accused the *Asociación de Católicos Españoles* of disassociating the Catholic reaction from Carlism and positioning itself in favour of the deposed monarch, Isabel II.[24] Once again, in a letter, Vicente de la Fuente distanced himself from any political party and denounced the fact that Carlism sought to subordinate the cause of Catholicism to that of the pretender to the throne:

> Here the fervent Carlists look askance at the *Asociación Católica* just as, back in the day, they did not look favourably on the Society of Saint Vincent de Paul. For them, it's a question of all or nothing.
>
> I'm not for that. They take it for granted that Don Carlos is coming. I ask them, and if he doesn't come? Truth be told, even if he should come, I don't want to see the cause of Catholicism linked to that of Carlism. I'm just Catholic, not Carlist, or Isabelline, or royalist, or moderate, or progressive, or republican; and that's taking account of the fact that I'd be the latter, as I said in my work on the diversity of worship, if European Democracy were not so coarse and ungodly.[25]

Vicente de la Fuente represented a generation of Spanish Catholics that had accepted a moderate liberal system and did not yearn for the *Ancien Régime*. Yet they condemned, in the same way as much of the political spectrum of that time, democratic positions and deplored freedom of worship: 'I'm not an absolutist either, but I'm even less of a democrat, and even so, for my part, I would be a democrat, very much a democrat, if democracy in Europe and the Americas were not so brutal, coarse and ungodly.'[26] It is hardly surprising that his attendance at the Second Malines Congress in 1864 left him with mixed feelings. On the one hand, he strongly disagreed with the Count of Montalembert in regard to freedom of worship, its bases and its suitability, but he did concur with him in the need to adapt to the new political language:

> *We are not theologians: we are politicians.* We respect the judgment of Popes and Councils, of Fathers and Doctors, but we see the world, we see its progress and its ideas, and for those reasons we judge. We appeal to experience, and we do not seek to be guided by brilliant utopias, and an already unrealisable optimism. We are not in the Middle Ages; we are living in the middle of the nineteenth century, in the century of liberty. Nowadays, issues are no longer resolved by repression, but by freedom.[27]

II Catholic unity in parliament

Ecclesiastics also exerted pressure through elections to the Constituent Assembly in January 1869. In the first place, as had been happening throughout the nineteenth century, the pulpit played a central role in the electoral campaign, promoting candidates and parties which were favourable to its own interests.[28] Furthermore, although it may seem paradoxical, the new electoral legislation promoted by the provisional revolutionary government in 1869 eliminated restrictions on candidates coming from the clergy. We should remember that ecclesiastics had occupied a very important place in the first Spanish representative congresses while the 1812 Constitution was in place and that this charter reserved a special place for the church in the ceremonies and rituals associated with the electoral process. However, such active participation declined as a consequence of the tension stirred up by Mendizábal's seizure and sale of religious order's property and the breaking off of diplomatic relations with the Holy See in 1837. The electoral law of 18 March 1846 excluded *de iure* ecclesiastics from parliament and only left the door of the upper chamber, the senate, open to prelates who, after being chosen by the monarch, would serve for life.[29]

In the face of future elections, the nuncio Franchi expressed his doubts to Secretary of State Antonelli: 'Taking into account the immense influence of the clergy among the population' and if the elections were free from violence or coercion, he pointed out that he would not hesitate to recommend the participation of the clergy as 'useful and positive'.

However, believing that they were not going to run their normal course, he would prefer that 'the clergy abstain from participating personally in the elections' and that it would limit itself to 'affecting an indirect salutary influence on the people, reminding the faithful on this occasion that they cannot participate in any evil and that they are obliged to promote good'.[30] His words already reveal a mistrust of democracy or the integrity of future elections. The nuncio believed that the direct participation of the clergy could have had very negative consequences in the face of an electoral result which pointed to a victory of the revolutionary coalition.

In spite of the nuncio's advice, ecclesiastics took part in the January 1869 elections for the first time since 1822. The elections were followed closely by the nunciature in Madrid and the Holy See. In total, four ecclesiastics were elected: the Canon of Vitoria, Vicente Manterola, the Bishop of Jaén, Antolín Monescillo, the archbishop of Santiago de Compostela, Miguel García Cuesta, and the Chaplain of Córdoba, Luis Alcalá Zamora Caracuel. Faced with a lack of recent precedents, the prelates consulted the Holy See through the nuncio about whether it was appropriate or not to consent to taking up parliamentary representation. The final reply was that, faced with the complexity of the issue, they were free to take whatever decision they wanted.[31] Whatever the case, neither the presence of ecclesiastics as elected representatives in parliament nor their participation in electoral campaigns constituted an Iberian exception and there were other European examples throughout the nineteenth century.[32]

With the exception of Luis Alcalá Zamora, a revolutionary close to Prim who voted in favour of freedom of worship, they were all elected on traditionalist tickets. However, only Canon Vicente Manterola had any explicit commitment to the Carlist cause.[33] The rest followed an intransigent direction, in line with that of the Vatican, yet as we will see, they were flexible when it came to distinguishing between thesis and hypothesis and they knew how to adjust their discourse to the new political context. Both prelates supported the mobilization of civil society through the creation of the *Asociación Católica de Españoles*, the *Asociación Católica de Señoras* and the *Asociación de la Juventud Católica*.[34]

In the session of 13 April 1869 at which freedom of worship was debated, Antolín Monescillo used the key points of liberal discourse to defend his positions. In order to do so, he first of all appealed to the notion of citizens through a well-known quote in which Saint Paul defended his status as a Roman citizen so as not to be flogged before being tried:

> The gentlemen of the commission are sufficiently independent, and I respect the independence of all men, because I too am independent, and this reminds me of what Saint Paul said: *Civis romanus sum*. [Demonstration of approval]. I too am a Roman citizen; I, who pride myself on being a Spanish citizen, recognise this independence, this noble, this holy, this glorious independence in the gentlemen of the commission.[35]

After appealing to his status as a citizen in order to defend his right to intervene in parliamentary debates, Monescillo demonstrated his agreement with the principles of justice and equity which guided the constituent commission with the aim of turning them around and defending his own positions. The Bishop of Jaén then went on to defend his commitment to freedom and did so based on his vast experience as a columnist in newspapers like *El Católico*, *El Pensamiento Español* and *La Cruz*:

> Will you want to believe that I also come from the field of freedom? You will say: and how does this Bishop come from the field of freedom? How? Forty years he does so debating, forty years he does so defining, forty years he does so arguing in newspapers, because I too have been a journalist, a poor journalist, a wretched journalist; I have come from the field of freedom, fighting endlessly in newspapers, in books, in pamphlets, in arguments ... I come, then, from the field of freedom and I do not fear freedom; I want the recognition of freedoms, but I do not want impunity of guilt or sin; and I say *sin*, because, equally in criminal and in moral matters, sin, like crime and misdemeanour, is transgression, it is a departure from the law: so that, when speaking of any transgression, whether crime or misdemeanour, I can call it by the generic name of *sin*.[36]

He was outlining, then, an interpretation of freedom in moderate conservative terms, in which the limits of freedom of expression were clearly established on the basis of crime and sin. In this sense, his thinking resembled the press laws which had prevailed during liberal regimes in the nineteenth century and the 1848 Spanish penal code itself which condemned blasphemy and proselytizing. In other words, the Bishop of Jaén defended the status quo which had prevailed until that time within liberal systems: Catholic unity and religious intolerance, both of which had been reflected in the 1851 Concordat.

The prelate concluded his speech on April 13 by questioning the moral relativism which religious freedom implied, given that '*Pluralitas Deorum nulitas Deorum*: to a plurality of Gods, a nullity of Gods; to a plurality of religions, a nullity of religions. See, then, why I come to support religious unity, because I believe that if all religions are false, there is no true morality: morality is based on religion.'[37] On 14 April, he continued with his speech in which he defended de facto tolerance of other faiths, but always on the basis of their errors: 'tolerance does not frighten us in the concept it implies; on the contrary, we preach it according to the traditional precept: *diligite homines: interficite errores*: love all men but detest errors.'[38] For him, the issue was clear: freedom of worship was not the goal, but 'freedom of attack' with which to challenge Catholic dogmas.[39]

For that reason, together with other representatives, he introduced an amendment which sought to eliminate the idea of freedom of worship and leave the text thus: 'being the Religion of the Spanish nation the Roman Catholic Apostolic one, the State undertakes to protect it and to support, by way of compensation, the faith and its ministers.' On this occasion, it was Cardinal Miguel García Cuesta, the Archbishop of Santiago, who was in charge of advocating the idea. In his speech of 27 April, he defended positions which resembled closely those of the Bishop of Jaén:

> I want things to remain in the status quo: we already have a practical tolerance which should satisfy all foreigners and I believe that if this is sufficient, we are in no position to break our unity, envied by foreign nations; all of them tend towards such unity: it is well known that one of the great statesman of our times said that he would lose an arm to have the religious unity in England that we have in Spain.[40]

Thus, according to the Cardinal of Santiago, 'we already have a practical tolerance, which is sufficient for foreigners of different religions to come without fear of any kind to our Spain, nobody will pick on them, nobody will tell them anything.'[41] In contrast to those who resorted to Montalembert's theses in order to demand freedom of worship, Cardinal García Cuesta did not openly condemn their positions and limited them to the context of France, concluding by contemplating freedom of worship there: 'in France, I would accept freedom or tolerance of faiths because it is the case that it has it; but Spain is not France. We Spaniards know no other religion than the Roman Apostolic Catholic one, which almost everyone follows.'[42] Although it was a rhetorical device, the Archbishop of Santiago de Compostela's position extended to the limits of Catholic orthodoxy.

In regard to allusions to the Vatican position, he pointed out that the pope had not spoken out against freedom, but against liberalism because 'it is a very vague word: it has a good meaning, and another meaning which is not so good.'[43] The pope had condemned certain errors. It was a similar case with modern civilization, in the face of which the church, he stated, 'has added to its rituals formulas to bless those things which did not previously exist. The Church has done this: far from condemning such things, the Pope has constructed telegraphs and railways in his states.' Once again, he was not opposed to modern civilization as a whole, but instead to some of its aspects: 'rationalism, anti-Christianity, doctrines which aspire to abolish Christianity in the world'.[44]

Finally, on 5 June 1869, the wording proposed by the commission was passed with 163 votes in favour and only 40 against. The wording of the article which was passed is truly confusing. It is based on the regalist principle that the nation is obliged to maintain the Catholic faith, but later recognizes freedom of worship for foreign residents in

Spain 'without any more limitations than those universal rules on morality and rights' and adds a third paragraph in which it is stated that 'if any Spaniards should profess a religion other than the Catholic one, everything stipulated in the previous paragraph is applicable to them'. With that, the principle of Spanish Catholic citizenship that had prevailed in previous constitutional texts was broken; that is, one could be Spanish without being Catholic, but it did so by affirming that this was not a normal option and it maintained the principle of financing one particular denomination.

III After the storm

The passing of the 1869 Constitution did not put an end to the tension which had developed around the subject of religion in the public sphere, and further confrontations emerged over civil marriage and the separation of church and state in the *non nata* constitution of the First Spanish Republic. Uprisings in the summer of 1869 in defence of religion and, above all, the creation of the Carlist *Sociedad católico monárquica* (Monarchical Catholic Society) implied a burden for the association, especially following the outbreak of the civil war in 1872. Nevertheless, its situation during this period was still a long way from the paralysis and collapse that is usually depicted. Indeed, it was precisely in 1870 when the *Asociación de Católicos Españoles* grew stronger territorially with the establishment of a dense network of provincial, district and parish councils. Moreover, the association laid the groundwork for the first Catholic university – *Estudios católicos* (Catholic Studies) – which remained active until 1875, developed a vast network of Catholic primary schools for boys and girls and financed a diverse range of publications in order to propagate Catholicism and counteract growing Protestant propaganda.[45] Among these initiatives, one should highlight the publication by the *Asociación de Católicos Españoles* of the *Catecismo acerca del protestantismo* (Catechism on Protestantism, 1869) by Cardinal García Cuesta, a work which would go through twenty editions and sell more than 300,000 copies. In the same way as Monsecillos, García Cuesta maintained several heated discussions in the media and, between 1868 and 1869, wrote several letters to the editors of *La Iberia* and *Pensamiento español* in order to counteract texts published by Protestant pastors.[46] Towards the end of 1869, the associative network would be completed with the founding of the active *Asociación católica de Señoras* in Madrid and the creation of other sister associations in the principal Spanish cities in the years that followed.

The *Asociación de Católicos Españoles* continued to organize demonstrations, like that of 18 June 1871 in the San Isidro district of Madrid in defence of the papacy on the twenty-fifth anniversary of the accession of Pius IX to the pontifical throne. Its members also took part in, although did not lead, the campaign against passing a limited form of freedom of worship in the private sphere in the 1876 Constitution. The main impediment to the development of the association would be precisely the division of energies between the central council and the provincial council in Madrid which was created in 1870. The former was virtually dissolved in 1883 with the death of its president, the Marquis of Mirabel, while the different provincial councils survived, albeit in an isolated and uncoordinated form, until 1889.[47]

The experience of the *Sexenio democrático* was essential for the creation of the first confessional party in Spain, *Unión católica* (Catholic Union), which was founded by Alejandro Pidal y Mon in 1881. A member of *Juventud Católica* in Madrid, Pidal y Mon sought to create a political party that would unite Catholics and in which the defence of their religion would not be subordinate to other interests. Old members of the governing council of the *Asociación de Católicos*, like León Carbonero y Sol, the Count of Orgaz and the Marquis of Mirabel, joined the new party.[48] The party also counted on the support of the then Archbishop of Valencia, Antolín Monescillo, who backed the party and openly criticized the positions of the Carlists.

While there had been some prior brief experiences of Catholic political parties, it was during the last third of the nineteenth century when they expanded as a reaction to the secularizing measures promoted in what were known as the cultural wars, that is, a growing tension with other faiths and the emergence of socialist and anarchist working-class movements. In this regard, the founding of the *Zentrum* (Centre) political party in Germany in 1870 would mark a new stage in the organization of political Catholicism. In elections to the *Reichstag* in 1874, this party achieved 28 per cent of the general vote and 83 per cent of the Catholic vote. The success of this organization would serve, in turn, as inspiration for other political parties. Based on the same conservative confessional line would be groups like the *Parti catholique* (Catholic Party), founded in Belgium in 1884, and the *Katholisch- Konservative Partei der Schwitzerland* (Catholic Conservative party of Switzerland), established in Switzerland in 1912. Following the *Rerum novarum* (1891), some confessional parties would commit to a more democratic vision and more social outlook. Along such lines would be the *Christene Volkspartij* (Christian People's Party), which was founded in Belgium in 1891 by the priest Adolf Daens, and the *Christlichsoziale Partei* (Christian Social Party), created in Austria in 1891.[49]

The political experience of the *Unión católica* was somewhat brief and it dissolved in 1884, with many of its membership being absorbed by the *Partido Conservador* (Conservative Party). From the outset, the former had encountered numerous difficulties in establishing itself on account of the violent campaign it suffered in the press by Carlist and intransigent media. In Spain, the Catholic political spectrum was quite fractured between the *Partido Conservador* and the more radical options of Carlism and intransigentism. It seemed, then, that there was no space for a purely Catholic party, given that all catholic parties on the political right in Spain presented themselves as Catholic.

Conclusion

On the night of 18 June 1871, the Catholic media had encouraged placing lanterns and decorations on building facades to celebrate the twenty-fifth anniversary of the papacy of Pius IX. During the night, several balconies were stoned and lanterns and banners destroyed in Madrid and other Spanish cities. The legitimist newspaper *El Pensamiento español* questioned:

Where are our individual rights? Where is the freedom that the Constitution guarantees us? Where is the Government? If the demonstration yesterday had been undertaken by Protestants or any religion other than the Catholic one, which is the only true one and that of the immense majority of Spaniards, would not the Government have taken great pains to protect it?

The anticlerical republican writer Roberto Robert, who had enjoyed that night in Madrid, responded to this question they had been 'condemned in the Syllabus'.[50] Both *El Pensamiento español* and Roberto Robert's reaction allow us to observe two forms of exclusionary rhetoric. The former deprived non-Catholics of citizenship, while the latter limited the rights of Catholics in the public sphere. Be that as it may, the newspaper's questions illustrate how some Catholics had embraced the language and practice of rights, freedoms and parliamentary representation, although this was a restrictive and strategic interpretation which did not accept the principle of plurality.

The case of the Spanish *Sexenio democrático* demonstrates how the Catholic Church, while it officially maintained an openly antiliberal discourse, had integrated perfectly democratic practices like petitions, made use of the freedom of association to develop a dense associative network and freedom of the press and parliament to defend its positions and appeal to the constitution and its freedoms to defend its positions. In the end, the political experience acquired during this period would be crucial in putting together the first Catholic political party in Spain, *Unión católica,* one more step in embracing parliamentary practices, especially when these took on a conservative nature and guaranteed what were termed the 'rights of God'. Nevertheless, the full acceptance of the Rights of Man would be a much longer and more tortuous story, the outcome of which would have to wait until the Second Vatican Council.[51]

Notes

1   *Discursos parlamentarios de Emilio Castelar en la Asamblea Constituyente* (Madrid: Editores A. De San Martin y Agustín Jubera, 1877), vol. I, 278–9.
2   Gregorio de la Fuente Monge, 'El enfrentamiento entre clericales y revolucionarios en torno a 1869', *Ayer* 44 (2001): 127–50.
3   Gonzalo Capellán de Miguel, 'Más allá de la nación: religión, filosofía de la historia y humanidad en la España del siglo XIX', *Rubrica contemporanea* 9, no. 17 (2020): 31–55; Gonzalo Capellán de Miguel, 'El problema religioso en la España contemporánea. Krausismo y catolicismo liberal', *Ayer* 39 (2000): 207–41; Francisco Martínez Hoyos, 'Cristianos liberales en la España decimonónica: el mito de la irrelevancia', *Aportes* 98, no. 3 (2018): 115–47; Ester García Moscardó, 'La cruz como dogma del progreso: Democracia y religiónen Roque Barcia Martí', in *Dimensiones religiosas de la Europa del Sur: (1800–1875),* ed. Rafael Serrano García, Ángel de Prado Moura and Elisabel Larriba (Valladolid: Universidad de Valladolid, 2018), 147–63.
4   Concepción Arenal, 'La Sociedad de San Vicente de Paúl y la Revolución', *La Voz de la Caridad,* 15 January and 1 February 1871. She would be even harsher in her criticism of the abolition of the Sisters of Charity, arguing that 'freedom of worship'

should not be interpreted as the 'absence of worship'. Concepción Arenal, 'La libertad de cultos en las casas de beneficencia', *La Voz de la Caridad*, 1 September 1871. On the conferences of the Society of Saint Vincent de Paul, see Federico Suárez, *Santiago Masarnau y las Conferencias deSan Vicente de Paúl* (Madrid: Rialp, 1994), 190–4.

5   Quoted in Miguel Duran Pastor, *Cartas de Vicente de la Fuente a Jose Mª Quadrado* (Palma de Mallorca: Obradors, 1981), 110–13.
6   Maartje Janse, '"Association Is a Mighty Engine": Mass Organization and the Machine Metaphor, 1825–1840)', in *Organizing Democracy: Reflections on the Rise of Political Organizations in the Nineteenth Century*, ed. Henk teVelde and Maartje Janse (Basingstoke: Palgrave Macmillan, 2022), 55–76; Maartje Janse, 'A Dangerous Type of Politics? Politics and Religion in Early Mass Organizations: The Anglo-American World, c. 1830', in *Political Religion beyond Totalitarianism: The Sacralization of Politics in the Age of Democracy*, ed. Joost Augusteijn, Patrick Dassen and Maartje Janse (Basingstoke: Palgrave Macmillan, 2013), 55–76.
7   Bernhard Schneider, 'Reform of Piety in German Catholicism, 1780–1920', in *Piety and Modernity*, ed. Jarlert Anders (Leuven: Leuven University Press, 2012), 193–224 and Bernhard Schneider, 'Insel der Märtyrer oder ein Volk von Rebellen? Deutschlands Katholiken und die irische Nationalbewegung in der Ära Daniel O'Connells (ca. 1820–1847)', *Historisches Jahrbuch* 128 (2008): 225–75.
8   Diego Palacio Cerezales, 'Forjadas por los adversarios. Movilización católica en la era del liberalismo (1812–1874)', *Historia y Política* 46 (2021): 175–206.
9   Vicente Cárcel Ortí, *Iglesia y revolución en España (1868–1874). Estudio histórico-jurídico desde la documentación vaticana inédita* (Pamplona: Eunsa, 1979), 537–81 and Gregorio Alonso, *La nación en capilla. Ciudadanía católica y cuestión religiosa en España, 1793–1874* (Granada: Comares, 2014), 278–9.
10 *La Cruz*, vol. II, 1868, 383–96 and 408–18.
11 *La Cruz*, vol. II, 1868, 371–9, 372.
12 *La Cruz*, vol. II, 1868, 357.
13 Palacios Cerezales, 'Forjadas por los adversarios', 175–206.
14 'Letter from the nuncio Franchi to Secretary of State Antonelli (Madrid, 1 December 1868)', Vatican Apostolic Archive (VAA), Nunciature in Madrid, box 463, title III, 23.
15 Vicente de la Fuente, 'Origen, desenvolvimiento, beneficios y estado actual de la Asociación de Católicos', in *Crónica del Primer Congreso Católico Nacional Español. Discursos y trabajos presentados* (Madrid: Tipografía de los Huérfanos, 1889), vol. II, 398–401, 398. See also *La Asociación de católicos en España. Noticia de su origen, organización, estado actual y gracias que le ha otorgado la Santa Sede, publicada por la Junta Superior de la misma* (Madrid: Imprenta de la Compañía de Impresores y Libreros, 1878). On the diverse nature of the association, see Begoña Urigüen, *Orígenes y evolución de la derecha española: el neocatolicismo* (Madrid: CSIS, 1986), 331.
16 Miguel Durán Pastor, 'De "El Conciliador" a la "Unidad Católica"', *Bolletí de la Societat Arqueòlogica Lul·liana: revista d'estudis històrics* 42 (1986): 131–51.
17 Palacios Cerezales, 'Forjadas por los adversarios', 200.
18 *Petición dirigida a las Cortes constituyentes a favor de la Unidad católica en España* (Madrid: Imprenta de 'La Esperanza', 1869), 6.
19 Letter from the Marquis of Viluma to José María Quadrado, dated 14 April 1868 and reproduced in Durán Pastor, 'De "El Conciliador"', 150.
20 For some authors, the mobilization during the *Sexenio democrático* (six democratic years) was intense but ultimately interrupted by the Carlist uprising. Thus, one

would have to wait until 1889 for the full organization of a Catholic movement in Spain and it would be marked by a weak experience of social Catholicism in Spain. Feliciano Montero García, *El primer catolicismo social y la Rerum Novarum en España (1889-1902)* (Madrid: CSIC, 1983); Feliciano Montero García, *El movimiento católico en España, 1889-1936* (Alcalá de Henares: Editorial Universidad de Alcalá, 2017). Other interpretations have highlighted the importance of this experience in shaping Catholic Action in Spain. José Andrés Gállego, 'Génesis de la acción católica española, 1868-1926', *Ius canonicu* 13, no. 26 (1973): 369-404. More recent interpretations have argued for integrating Catholic mobilization during the *Sexenio democrático* within the frame of a long Spanish cultural war between 1868 and 1931. Joseba Louzao Villar, 'Catholicism Versus Laicism: Culture Wars and the Making of Catholic National Identity in Spain, 1898-1931', *European History Quarterly* 43, no. 4 (2013): 657-80 and Francisco Javier Ramón Solans, '"El catolicismo tiene masas". Nación, política y movilización en España, 1868-1931', *Historia contemporánea* 51 (2015): 427-54.

21 Fuente, 'Origen, desenvolvimiento', 399.
22 José María Quadrado, 'Naturaleza de estas asociaciones', *La Unidad católica*, no. 2 (14 March 1869). Reproduced in José María Quadrado, *Ensayos religiosos, políticos y literarios* (Palma de Mallorca: Tipografía de Amengual y Muntaner, 1896), vol. IV, 22-3.
23 Reproduced in Duran Pastor, *Cartas de Vicente de la Fuente*, 104-5, 105.
24 Antonio Vildósola, '*Las' apariencias y la realidad de la fusión dinástica* (Madrid: Pérez Dubrull, 1869), 8-9.
25 Reproduced in Duran Pastor, *Cartas de Vicente de la Fuente*, 107-8.
26 Vicente de la Fuente, *La pluralidad de cultos y sus inconvenientes* (Madrid: Imp. De La Esperanza, 1865), 373.
27 Ibid., 159.
28 Carmelo Romero Salvador, *Caciques y caciquismo en España (1834-2020)* (Madrid: Catarata, 2021), 156-60 and Juan Antonio Inarejos Muñoz, 'Sotanas, escaños y sufragios. Práctica política y soportes sociales del neo – catolicismo en las provincias castellano-manchegas (1854-1868)', *Hispania sacra* 60, no. 121 (2008): 297-329.
29 Francisco Javier Ramón Solans and Raúl Alberto Mayoral Trigo, 'Sociología de los diputados por Aragón en las Cortes de Cádiz', *Revista de historia Jerónimo Zurita* 87 (2012): 259-79 and Pedro Víctor Rújula López and Francisco Javier Ramón Solans, 'Representantes y representación: los diputados aragoneses en las Cortes de Cádiz', *Trienio: Ilustración y liberalismo* 61 (2013): 7-28.
30 'Draft of the letter from nuncio Franchi to Secretary of State Antonelli (Madrid, 16 November 1868)', VAA, Nunciature in Madrid, box 463, title II, 17.
31 'Letter from Secretary of State Antonelli to the nuncio Franchi (Rome, 10 February 1869)', VAA, Nunciature in Madrid, box 463, title II, 17.
32 Timothy Tackett, *Par la volonté du peuple. Comment les députés de 1789 sont devenus révolutionnaires* (Paris: Albin Michel, 1997); Yves Déloye, *Les voix de dieu. Pour une autre histoire du suffrage electoral: le clergé catholique français et le vote XIXe-XXe siècle* (Paris: Fayard, 2006).
33 Carlo Verri, *Controrivoluzione in Spagna. I carlisti nell'assemblea costituente (1869-1871)* (Rome: Viella, 2021), 37.
34 For Cardinal Monescillo, see Rafael Sanz de Diego, *Medio siglo de relaciones Iglesia-Estado: el Cardenal Antolín Monescillo y Viso (1811-1897)* (Madrid: Universidad Pontificia Comillas, 1979) and Francisco Alía Mirandaand Antonio de Juan García,

ed., *Centenario del Cardenal Monescillo (1897–1997)* (Cuenca: Ediciones de la Universidad de Castilla La Mancha, 1997), vol. I. For Cardinal García Cuesta, see Carlos García Cortés, *El Cardenal García Cuesta (1803–1873). Un eminente arzobispo compostelano en la España liberal* (Santiago de Compostela: Cabildo Catedral de Santiago, 2006).

35 *Petición dirigida a las Cortes constituyentes a favor de la Unidad católica en España*, 290.
36 Ibid., 292–3.
37 Ibid., 293.
38 Ibid., 300.
39 Ibid., 305.
40 Ibid., 324.
41 Ibid., 345.
42 Ibid., 346.
43 Ibid., 351.
44 Ibid., 351.
45 Fuente, 'Origen, desenvolvimiento' and *La Asociación de católicos en España. Noticia de su origen*.
46 García Cortés, *El Cardenal García Cuesta*.
47 Fuente, 'Origen, desenvolvimiento' and *La Asociación de católicos en España. Noticia de su origen*.
48 Urigüen, *Orígenes*, 369.
49 On the rise of Catholic parties, see Wolfram Kaiser, *Christian Democracy and the Origins of European Union* (Cambridge: Cambridge University Press, 2007) and *The Cross and the Ballot: Catholic Political Parties in Germany, Switzerland, Austria, Belgium and the Netherlands, 1785–1985* (Boston: Humanities Press, 1999). On the culture wars, see Wolfram Kaiser, 'Introduction: The European Culture Wars', in *Culture Wars: Secular-Catholic Conflict in Nineteenth-Century Europe*, ed. Christopher Clark and Wolfram Kaiser (Cambridge: Cambridge University Press, 2003), 1–11.
50 Quoted in Fuente Monge, 'El enfrentamiento', 150.
51 Daniele Menozzi, *Chiesa e diritti umani. Legge naturale e modernità politica dalla Rivoluzione Francese ai nostri giorni* (Bologne: Il Mulino, 2012).

Part Three

Temporal and spiritual power and education

7

Sin, grace and secular history: Pierre Paul Royer-Collard's criticism of the anti-sacrilege law of 1825

Daniele Giuseppe Palmer
King's College, Cambridge

The aim of this edited volume is to shed historical light on the term 'Liberal Catholicism'. Its origins lie in nineteenth-century Britain and France, and those who came to deploy it – at times as a self-assigned term, but also by others as a means of criticism – did so by thinking about the relation between the Catholic creed and the French Revolution. In what way, if any, could an adherent to the Roman Church offer a favourable appraisal of 1789 and its effects?

Given the copious writings and seemingly numerous figures who have over time come under the 'Liberal Catholic' rubric, the task of this volume is an arduous one. The term itself arose as a means to demarcate those members of Catholicism keen to give a positive response to at least some revolutionary consequences from those for whom 1789, and everything that came after, was to be rejected.[1] In effect, the *liberal catholique* figure and their *Catholicisme liberal* – within the case of France, the remit of the present chapter – was posited in opposition to those seeking to turn back the political and social clock. To account for Liberal Catholicism, not only must its opposite be understood but one must also account for the exceptions and oddities that belay too strong a definition. This chapter proposes to look at these latter items.

In 1857, Charles de Rémusat authored a two-part essay, titled 'Du Traditionalisme', for *Revue des Deux Mondes*. The core contention of the piece was to define, flesh out and inevitably keep separate those forms of Catholicism that either looked positively to the French Revolution or sought to condemn it, politically, theologically and even spiritually. Both the putative liberals and their ostensible foes, the traditionalists, were engaged in the same 'cause of truth': Christianity was unendingly 'immutable in its substance'.[2] Yet while both sides may have shared the same understanding of the Church's sources, they differed, Rémusat believed, in how its truth ought to be defended, and from what. For the traditionalists, among whose ranks one found Joseph de Maistre and Louis de Bonald – the two figures Rémusat based his essay on – it was the 'ideas of the old regime' which best guarded the Gospel's veracity from dilution and corruption, and it could only ever be considered valid if allowed to take root and flourish 'in the manner of the Middle Ages'.[3] Then there are the others, such as the publicist Felicité de La Mennais and the poet Alphonse de Lamartine, for whom the 'principles of 1789' could be melded with the Christianity of the 'seventeenth century': a variant which was 'still enlightened, still enlarged by the supreme ideas of the rights of the human conscience'.[4]

Underpinning Rémusat's diagnosis of traditionalism – and thus, even if in the negative, of a more liberal implementation of Catholicism – there was a sense of the relationship between humanity's secular, historical condition and whatever eternal and universal contents could be attributed to Christianity's temporal presence. Said differently, Rémusat's core concern, which he assesses and documents with the distance of a mere observer, pertained to how various Catholic positions afforded humanity a role in its own history. For the traditionalist, at least in Rémusat's eyes, the human person, and more significantly human rationality, was barred from any participation. As a term, traditionalism designates the 'whole body of ideas and arguments which … tends to exclude the free intervention of reason', it denies 'human intelligence any legitimate share in the work of science, beliefs, and institutions'.[5] And thus it decouples the individual person, or the emancipated community from that which forms 'the heritage of every civilised society'.[6]

What traditionalists looked to, unsurprisingly, was tradition. Those customary means by which society develops and, more significantly, remains stable are the locus of Christianity's providential mission in history. For Maistre, whose own seemingly eschatological diagnosis of the French Revolution scared liberals and royalists alike, traditions were to be considered the soteriological and institutional bedrock of society. As he wrote in his brief tract *De l'état de nature*, in which he took aim at Jean-Jacques Rousseau and the entire Enlightenment tradition of contractualism, the 'general character' of traditions is forever 'unalterable and necessarily based on truth'.[7] That polities are to be monarchical, that politics and the law derive from the ancient model of the *paterfamilias*, and that thought always be subjugated to the criterion of revealed religion are but the outward manifestations of an initiatory truth that traditions preserve.[8] To deviate from what has been handed down, and thus to operate outside the remit of those ancient structures of sociability, would not only be hazardous but would be in direct violation of the truth – the truth of both human nature and the truth of God's plan for secular history, all tied together by the 'supple chain' that links Man to God.[9]

Maistre made the implication of this position clear in *Considérations sur la France* (1797), his general commentary and condemnation of the French Revolution. 'In the workings of man,' Maistre wrote, 'all is as poor as its author; the sights are restricted, the means rigid, the springs inflexible, the movements painful, and the results monotone.'[10] And when humanity does manage to intervene, the 'irregularities produced' – when human action deviates from the divine plan – 'the operation of the free agents, are tidied up in the general order'.[11] With an image whose brutality lent it pride of place in the annals of political philosophy, Maistre then compares God's action with that of an able gardener: in an effort to allow the fruits to flourish, all weeds and needless leaves are pruned. Much like scissors to tree branches, human death and social chaos allow God to shore up his own plan for history. Humanity needs merely to stick to that initiatory truth handed down to it and stored in tradition.[12]

It was in large measure as a reaction to this style of argument that the liberal Catholics mounted their position. A good exemplary case, as gestured at above, would be Lamennais. In his *Des progrès de la révolution et de la guerre contre l'Eglise* published in 1829, the claim put forward was that both abject rationalism – where the individual is wholly separated from the community – and the politicized Church of the *Ancien Régime* failed to do service to Christianity's eternal and universal truth. Looking to 1789, which the text sought to make sense of, Lamennais contended that Christ's message inheres in history through an ever-present and ever-working providential order.[13]

Yet unlike Maistre, what Lamennais saw was not a customary order that required maintenance but one which was sensitive to the oscillating winds of divine intervention. The political change and the subsequent social effects brought on by 1789 were themselves in line with God's plan. For since Christianity's 'dogmas … contain all truth, [and] its precepts and counsels … contain all virtue', it cannot but 'incessantly develop … the feeling of moral perfection'.[14] '[F]or the true progress of enlightenment,' Lamennais wrote, is coterminous with the ever stronger, and ever more redemptive, 'Christian traditions', whose 'universality and perpetuity, the two great characteristics of all that is divine, are becoming more and more manifest'.[15] And thus even in the tumults of the French Revolution not only was God's hand discernible but his redemptive, emancipatory plan was coming ever more to fruition.

At the heart of both positions there is a sense, if not a belief, that humanity's salvific, sacred history – the subject of bygone universal histories – was mixed in with the workings of the secular world. For Maistre as well as for Lamennais, it cannot be denied that the priority given to providence and to a providential order affords humanity, whether passively or actively, the means to immediately at least witness God's hand in history. Translated in different, albeit still useful terms: both Lamennais and Maistre believed human perfectibility, firstly, to be achievable on earth and, secondly, that the stage or degree of one's 'perfectioning' corresponded to the divine plan. Yet while for Lamennais, human perfection corresponded with ever greater progression, for Maistre it correlated with sticking to the traditional, *Ancien Régime* model of social and moral organization. Presented in these terms, Rémusat's insistence on the demarcation between liberals and traditionalists, at least in the context of Catholicism, is shored up: to understand where one lies it is necessary to take into account their understanding of tradition. The static nature of customs, or of their content, provides a sketch of a plan to be followed. And to hold to this means to reject any change that threatens the established order. Rémusat in fact contended that, at heart, the dividing line between liberal Catholics and traditionalists is that of 'the new' against 'the old': a war between those for whom Francis Bacon's statement that *veritas filia temporis, non auctoritatis*, was to be either assented to or despised.[16]

But Rémusat's claim, much as the sense animating the present volume, is a contentious one. Liberal Catholics rejected immutable traditions, often to the extent of emptying from within the very creed they held to. Yet they held to the belief that God directly acted on history. This can be seen in Lamennais. By the 1830s, the onetime priest began preaching a Catholicism that had more in common with Henri de Saint-Simon's wholly godless *Nouveau Christianisme* (1825) than with what he himself once described as the infallible and indefectible tradition of the Chair of Saint Peter. Despite this, there did exist a way of thinking about Catholicism that, while employable by the liberal adherents to the Church, nevertheless rejected an all too human account as well as one which prisoned God's providence in the confines of ancient traditions.

Pierre-Paul Royer-Collard, a figure who only more recently has come back to the attention of scholars, was among Restoration France's first detractors of the royalist cause. A staunch supporter of the Charter that had been *octroyée* by Louis XVIII in 1815 (after a botched attempt in 1814), he believed it necessary to integrate into France's institutional and political structures the more salutary effects of the Revolution: a representative system, a clear constitutional order, the right to a free press. Having said this, Royer-Collard did believe in the necessity of a monarchy, as well as a strong sense of tradition, as the only effective means to guarantee stability. Royer-Collard's core political concern was to keep in delicate balance the requirements of society and social order, on the one hand, and the political principles of a freer, more open and more representative society, on the other. The social, as Pierre Rosanvallon has noted, was for him the font of fact; the political, by extension, was the remit of the practicable.[17] But save for some exceptions, and an all too few number of them, Royer-Collard's religion has received lacklustre attention.[18]

The way Royer-Collard came to formulate his Catholic belief, as well as how he argued for its implementation, sheds useful light on the liberal/traditionalist divide. Like both Lamennais and Maistre, he was a great observer of custom and traditions, those *mœurs* which constituted France's historical identity and which furnished the basis of its then-current social order. Yet unlike them, he did not believe traditions in any way manifested some divinely mandated, providential order. Neither in the static sense Maistre held to, nor of the developmentalist kind Lamennais put forward. For Royer-Collard, the cities of Man and God could not be more distant, and whatever is done or is attempted down on Earth has no immediate bearing on humanity's heavenly condition. Traditions, much as history itself, stood in stark opposition to the divine.

In what follows I can only offer a sketch of Royer-Collard's answer to the question of the Christian truth's relation to history. And even less will I be able to provide a comprehensive account of his religiosity, his political thought and the interconnections between the two. But what can be provided is a closer look at one instance in Royer-Collard's political life where his own religious proclivities burst into the foreground: during the debate over the Law on Anti-Sacrilege in 1825. To quote one of Royer-Collard's first biographers, Eugène Spuller:

> It is said that, of all his speeches, Royer-Collard preferred the speech on the law of sacrilege; it is indeed perhaps the most beautiful that he delivered; what is more certain is that this speech is the greatest service that he rendered to the cause of common sense, political reason, freedom of conscience and general civilisation. It is only seventy years ago that it was necessary to bring these strong words to the rostrum and to recall these great principles, these necessary truths. We must not forget that the world is constantly being tossed from progress to reaction and from

reaction to progress. Royer-Collard has pronounced the separation of religion and politics, and has decided this question with such authority that there is no need to return to it; that if, however, there were still to be a struggle against this confusion, which is as absurd as it is criminal, it would be in the speech on sacrilege that the best weapons would still be found.[19]

And yet his intervention has garnered scant interest, and in the case of the few exceptions, those studies that have been written are limited in their conceptual explication. It is the contention of this chapter that, when looked at for its immediate content, Royer-Collard's words offer a world of arguments and traditions of thought that not only problematize the liberal/traditionalist dichotomy, but opens up research to, at times renewed, avenues of enquiry.[20]

The anti-sacrilege law that was passed on 20 April 1825 has been signalled to have been an 'emblematic' moment in the Restoration's religious history: the struggling *ecclesia militans* gave way to an ever more triumphant incarnation. The *projet de loi* that was at first proposed by Louis XVIII and Joseph de Villèle in 1824 was intended to re-Christianize France, to reel it back from the pagan paths it had taken ever since 1789. Though it failed to pass through the Chamber of Deputies in the first instance, it later became law under Charles X: all affronts to God and Church were punishable by death. But it did not pass without obstinate opposition. Lamennais described it, and all attempts to defend it, as a hotchpotch of contradictory and incoherent ideas, whose falsity could not be more dangerous to the social, political and also spiritual health of the country. And while Charles X's time as monarch was filled with numerous attempts to re-Christianize, and de-revolutionize, France, the law on anti-sacrilege represented a singularly important moment in French history: never, not even in Gallicanism's heyday, did crimes committed against God – under which blasphemy falls – enter the remit of what a temporal sovereign could chastise.

This was Royer-Collard's core concern. And it was on these grounds that he mounted his attack on the proposed law in his intervention of 12 April 1825. 'Not only does it introduce into legislation a new crime,' he argued, 'but, what is more extraordinary, it creates a new principle of criminality, an order of crimes that is, so to speak, supernatural.'[21] It cannot be stressed enough how central to Royer-Collard the distinction between the temporal and eternal was. However simple and however bland it may appear – it was, after all, a central tenet of what could be considered the moderate contributions of seventeenth- and eighteenth-century political philosophy – it was the violation of the instrumental, if not inherently true distinction that most troubled Royer-Collard.

The concern was not moral or political, it was theological. And this was so only because the law itself, and what it sought to deal with, was by Royer-Collard defined as 'theological'.[22] Whatever may be considered supernatural does not fall under the auspices of human reason, as the mind does not have the means to 'either discover or comprehend it'.[23] All that can be said to belong to the City of God, and all that is attributable to the plans and actions of the divine, can only ever be 'made manifest by a religious faith that is illuminated by revelation'.[24] The monarch, his ministers and even France itself could not pretend to share in the process which brings to light the truth of Christianity. To speak ill of God, to besmirch his countenance, to sully through worldly ways and deeds what is sacred is to be condemned. But the act of sacrilege is one committed against God alone; it is a rejection of, and maybe also an affront to, the divine source of truth and the divine person himself. No one, no institution and thus no law could speak on God's behalf.

To Royer-Collard's mind, sacrilege could only be directed towards God alone. And much as no institution could speak on God's behalf, no other temporal body could feign offence in his stead. The anti-sacrilege law, in making itself the arbiter of religion, cast itself also as the victim of blasphemy. 'But an insult against God and an insult against man,' Royer-Collard emphasized, 'are two things so prodigiously different that they always remain distinct.' And so, Royer-Collard continued:

> What is the crime that is defined and punished? Is it the offence to society that is found in the insult to God, that is to say, in sacrilege, or is it the sacrilege itself? It is sacrilege alone, simple sacrilege. Is it possible for society to be included with God in sacrilege? No; God alone is holy and sacred. Would it be necessary to use the stratagem of legal proof to give substance to the offences of society? No.[25]

Taken literally, this was Royer-Collard's assessment of the law, and his criticism of it: to keep distinct the two spheres, and to do so while chastising the overreaches of the temporal.

To criticize, if not outwardly ridicule, Charles X's attempts to employ an ever more politicized Catholicism had become widespread. The reactionary push had begun with Villèle in 1820, a year whose political significance culminated in the assassination of Bourbon duke of Berry, Charles-Ferdinand of Artois, at the hands of the Bonapartist Louis Pierre Louvel. Some in fact saw in Villèle's and Charles X's co-opting of religion the resurgence of Gallicanism. The claim was that the eternal truths of Christianity – more specifically Catholicism – were being subsumed into the French state. This was a position central to those identifiable as 'liberal Catholics', for whom the royalist reaction to the French Revolution led to a reawakening of Gallican sentiments. Lamennais, so far often appealed to as an exemplary case of the liberal Catholic cause, believed this, and said so. In his *Des progrès de la révolution et de la guerre contre l'Église*, Gallicanism constituted one of the principal threats to human liberty to have emerged from the French Revolution.[26]

But the charge against Gallicanism had broader ramifications than merely that of strengthening liberal claims. Maistre also believed Gallicanism to threaten the internal cogency of Catholicism. In *Du Pape* he laid all theological authority at the feet of the Roman Church, contending that only a truly ultramontane sense of Christianity's earthly presence could preserve it from dilution and corruption. Ultramontanism existed in the background of many attacks on this resurgent Gallicanism. Pierre-Simon Ballanche, a onetime follower of Maistre who would later support, albeit at a distance, the Saint-Simonians, kept in an awkward balance a varyingly ultramontane sense of Christianity's earthly incarnation and a positive appraisal of the French Revolution's effects. In keeping the Christian *culte* far from the mundane interests of national politics, Christianity's truly emancipatory vocation could be reconciled with the ever more liberal push of human history. Ballanche put it directly, or at least apparently so: only a universal Church could encourage unfettered and disinterested neighbourly love.[27]

But here the concern was ethical. The truths of Christianity, however universal and eternal, were moral truths which manifested themselves in social institutions. While Gallicanism may have been the object of criticism, its opposite – ultramontanism – often remained lingering in the background. Lamennais himself began his career as a publicist among the ultramontane ranks, as did Ballanche. And in some sense, the liberal Catholicism that sought to place distance between Crown and Creed nevertheless fell back on some other earthly witness to Christianity. By claiming that the core of Christianity was an ethical truth – a truth which manifested itself socially – it was almost necessary to connect the spiritual realm with the temporal. This was a position that Scholastic political theory, with its interest in natural laws, extensively explicated, and which many Catholic thinkers throughout the seventeenth and eighteenth centuries clung to. But it was something Royer-Collard sought to avoid, and his intervention in the debate around the law on sacrilege attests to this.

By making his criticism theological, what Royer-Collard was relying on was a sense of Christianity that did not prioritize the ethical as did Ballanche and the others. This is not to say that ethics or morality did not figure in Royer-Collard's thought, and in particular how he saw religion to contribute to society. As he would later write to Alexis de Tocqueville, 'politics without morality is only a game of dupes and knaves, or the oppression of the weak by the strong.'[28] Religion impeded this from happening. But this did not require Christianity's ethics to be its principal truth. Nor is morality the metric by which the Church's role in history is to be evaluated. There existed a reach to religion's existence that could not be accounted for purely through the behavioural prescriptions it provided. But this was not specific to religion alone, or rather religion was one of many phenomena which pointed to the inherent limitations of an overwhelmingly temporal view of existence. 'Human societies,' Royer-Collard told the Chamber of Deputies, 'are born, live and die on earth.'[29] And as though speaking from beyond the pale of this plain of reality, he added: 'There their destinies are fulfilled.'[30]

And all this, for Royer-Collard, does 'not contain the whole of man'.[31] The theological truth which he believed Christianity contained, and which impeded him from making too strong an ethical description of its contents, was one which pertained to humanity itself. And thus the reticence to side with those for whom Christianity could be ascribed a moral definition was the fruit of a disagreement in anthropology. And, in part too, in psychology. In committing oneself to God, Royer-Collard contended, one is giving oneself to an 'invisible world' that is entirely beyond the remit of worldly occurrences – the anthropology – and 'human faculties' – the psychology.[32] But in saying this, it was clear that Royer-Collard's intervention was balanced on a knife edge. On the one side, there lay his criticism of Charles X's stringent, reactionary measures; yet on the other, there is a sense that Royer-Collard was further underlining the differences between his positions and those of figures many may have considered his allies. But the very language Royer-Collard spoke in was not one all that amenable to the liberal Catholic case. Manifestly denying the state's hold over things religious, Royer-Collard was keen to underline humanity's impotence with regard to what Christianity preached.

'Relegated forever to the things of the earth, the human race has no share in religious beliefs,' adding: 'in its temporal capacity, it neither knows nor understands them.'[33]

The frailty or inherent limitation in humanity Royer-Collard spoke of carried distinctive baggage. Catholic writers of all stripes – and even those not professing the faith – saw the human person to be limited, and wrote about them as such. In many senses this was a staple of eighteenth-century anthropology, ranging from scepticism to rationalism. And even more specifically to those traditions Royer-Collard was not only aware of but had engaged with as a philosopher – principally when he taught at Paris' Imperial Faculty of Letters under Napoleon – the very language of *perfectibilité* and *perfectionnement* saw amelioration as the correction of flaws, the filling of *lacunae* that arose with humanity itself. But that human limitations were coterminous with its existence did not impede thinkers from aspiring to nevertheless eviscerate them. And this was not only the case for the likes of Rousseau. The traditionalist Louis de Bonald genuinely held to perfection's earthly practicability, and he earnestly preached and wrote about how it could come about. His *Théorie du pouvoir politique et religieux* (1796), equal to Maistre's *Considérations* in its vitriol if only tempered in its register by an impulse to systematize, was intended to demonstrate how 'perfection in all forms [is], in religious and political societies, the *necessary fruit of its constitution*.'[34] Yet what constituted Bonald's ideal polity was a system untouched by the prerogatives of reason, wholly 'old' and unenlightened to use Rémusat's language. 'The state which is in accordance with the nature of God is perfection, since God is perfection itself', Bonald wrote, '[t]he state which is in accordance with the nature of intelligent man is also perfection, since intelligent man is like God.'[35] Notwithstanding this perfection was possible, and it was attainable within the arc of human history. For Royer-Collard, contrarily, humanity could never be rid of its frailty, at least not during its time on earth.

Royer-Collard's understanding of the human self, seen in these terms, touches on what has often been considered his Jansenism. Most scholars, and even coeval commentators, have been quick to mention his vicinity to Port Royal, to that system of ideas – and, I would say, sentiments – that gave substance to a Jansenist stake. But to say that Royer-Collard was a follower of Cornelius Jansen is not alone sufficient.[36] By the end of the eighteenth century, Jansenism had lost a significant amount of its overtly religious contents. The onetime heretical confession, whose apparent strict adherence to Augustinianism fashioned it into a French kind of Protestantism, was no longer considered by France's ecclesial and political institutions that significant a threat. Jansenism's wariness of papal authority – and for good reason, it was Rome which was among the first to dismiss them as more than mere heterodoxy – led it to find allies among the Gallicans. It was without doubt an odd, and at times contentious, allegiance, but one which did facilitate its sanitization in France. And the repugnance they were met with by the Jesuits, early-modern Europe's most vociferous proponents of a seemingly secularized natural law approach to thinking about history, and thus too about humanity, did not fail to win them approval among the Society of Jesus' enemies. In the context of French history, there is a more than strong correlation between the Jesuit's fall into disrepute and Jansenism's acceptance into society.

Put simply, the creed to which Jansenists held was of a simplified church, a purer rite, a closer relationship between God and Man. But not so close as to elevate the human to the divine. One of Jansen's core tenets, which he believed to have derived directly from Augustine, was the centrality of original sin in explaining the human condition, both on earth and with regard to its salvific end. Against the Molinism of the Jesuits, whose views Jansen and his followers considered so pagan they were Pelagian, there could be no universal salvation that would automatically extract the human person from their earthly lot. People are born sinful and remain so; here in history, in the *saeculum*, nothing can be done to avoid this. From this followed the second proposition: in so far as original sin could only be atoned directly, God's irresistible grace was to be considered the sole means of salvation. The way Jansenism had it, this excluded any active participation in one's salvation, and notoriously – hence the diatribe against the Jesuits – free will was not given any soteriological relevance. Humanity can be saved through, and only exclusively because of, God's direct intervention in history through the Incarnation.

Taken as a theological position, its stakes are quite clear. Jansenism proposes a strict Augustinianism that has no time for casuistry, probabilism, natural law or even providential salvation. God's *gratia gratis data* is both sufficient and exclusive. Its anthropology, which is of use in explaining Royer-Collard's own positions, is even starker. By making original sin a defining attribute for humanity – which a sizeable part of Medieval Catholic theology had gone great lengths to dilute – the human person emerges as frail, flawed and inherently fallen. Nothing, and thus no one, can bridge the divide between this state, that of mundane existence and that of eternal salvation. The two worlds are divided by an unsurmountable gap.

This, in broad strokes, is the baggage with which Royer-Collard spoke in April 1825. The beauties of the Catholic religion, when taken sincerely and purely, see in humanity's 'weakness' and 'sickness' not the means to found a renewed Zion, but those with which to work with the ruins of a dilapidated, yet entirely human and truthful Jerusalem.[37] In the midst of his criticism of the proposed law, Royer-Collard even took aim at the Church itself, albeit with greater tact than most of his Jansenist coreligionists. When one realizes that '[t]hese two worlds touch each other [but] must never be confused', all that can be afforded humanity in its earthly existence is guidance towards amelioration.[38] Yet this signifies neither perfection nor redemption, as a human institution, however much it may be of divine origin, cannot extend into the heavens. And much as the institutions and prelates of the Church cannot offer atonement, they also cannot chastise. The 'Church's vocation' is to stave away damnation, to be a witness to salvation; it cannot devour humanity 'with the flames of the heavens'.[39] And in quoting Augustine, Royer-Collard added that for all its 'medicinal' value, the Church can only ever 'preserve the sinner from those eternal sentences which are without remedy'.[40] In a truly Augustinian fashion, Royer-Collard affirmed the ecclesial mission to bring about contrition, and not forgiveness.

But by proposing a law in a domain where not even the Church had a voice – 'sacrilege is theological', Royer-Collard at one point exclaimed – the French state was taking on the role of arbiter of things spiritual.[41] But an inherently human, and purposefully temporal, body could not even offer the pretence of assisting in the eternal, and least of all could it provide a sense of its contents. The French state, much like the men whose ministries it populated and the citizens over whom they have dominion, is flawed. Human societies, Royer-Collard decried, can never but offer 'imperfect and faulty justice'.[42] From its very sources, the state, much as the person, is unable to be privy to a pure sense of the divine truth. If even the earthly witness to Christ – the See of Saint Peter – is unable to extol or lambast sin itself, how can a machine geared exclusively to the arbitration of things civil believe itself even amenable to sensing God's call? The state, as will all bodies intended to aid in the governance and administration of humanity's temporal condition, can never go beyond the sense of self-preservation as 'the need and the right' of their existence.[43] Royer-Collard maintained no illusions about the body politic and its corruptibility, and so considered only immediate, earthly sustenance a suitable ambition. And much as its sources or roots were sullied by the dirt of the earth, its ends too could not be all that pure. The state, as with politics taken in its broadest possible sense, was concerned with the mitigation of interests with the aim of arriving at a seemingly acceptable end.[44] But the flaws and inadequacies of human justice render that which is acceptable to humanity not even a chimaera of its divine counterpart.

And much as his intentions are limited, so too is his mind: Man's sinfulness curtails even the reaches of thought. Royer-Collard premised his discussion of the anti-sacrilege law on the distinction between the realm of the temporal and that of the eternal, and what he found to threaten the integrity of both society and religion – understood as Christianity's temporal manifestation – was the law's confusion of the two spheres. When this relationship, that between 'Man and God', is confused, what was generated was theocracy:

> I wanted to mark, by breaking a long silence, a strong opposition to the theocratic principle which threatens both religion and society, all the more odious because it is not, as in the days of barbarism and ignorance, the sincere fury of a too ardent zeal which rekindles this torch ... The theocracy of our time is not so much religious as political; it is part of this system of universal reaction which is sweeping us along.[45]

What is being done 'consists of confounding [...] an insult against God with an insult against society'.[46] And in so doing, what is placed under the remit of the penal code is not only inaccessible to it, but it is beyond the remit of 'human justice'.[47] The sense of 'human grandeur', itself a product of the feebleness inherent to the historical person, leads one to think that it is possible to bring under secular auspices what ought to remain exclusive to the invisible world – whose invisibility, for Royer-Collard, was caused by how stunted the vision on earth is and how inadequate imagination is in compensating for it.[48] And as thus as with all errors, which sin allows, frailty is its source, and Royer-Collard's diagnosis of the law's initial causes did not steer far from these: 'it is stricken with ignorance and impotence'.[49]

Yet while inadequacy may have generated the initial error, Royer-Collard made clear that what was being attempted went beyond mere human confusion and limitations. He likely would have agreed with Seneca in saying *errare humanum est, sed in errare perseverare diabolicum*. Around the law on anti-sacrilege, the reactionary forces which both proposed it and pushed for its approval had constructed a veritable political ploy, 'an art that has never failed'.[50] It was that stratagem that the theological question of blasphemy provided the French state: the capacity to act with the full force of an indisputable justification. As has been mentioned above, Royer-Collard saw politics to be a sullied affair, one where interests and strength dictate both tone and substance of how governance is executed. What Charles X and his ministers were attempting was mere strategy, it was a politics that spoke with the force of spiritual justification in the interest of securing unencumbered dominion.

And here too Royer-Collard's intervention in the Chamber of Deputies ought to be read within a consciously Jansenist framework of thought. However, unlike in the case of his theology – or, better, his soteriology – and the implications this had for his sense of human nature, the overtly political applications, or even simply inspirations, of Royer-Collard's Jansenism require a few prefatory remarks. It has often been mentioned by scholars that Jansen's theological commentaries lost their sting when the movement got closer to Gallicanism.[51] The seventeenth century is thus to be seen as a moment when Jansenist theology was dulled. What lingered was a vague ecclesiological sense, in part derived from Jansen's writings but greatly expanded upon by later followers. In looking at the hierarchies of the Church, both in Rome and in France, a set of Jansenist texts and ideas emerged that explicitly drew out their theology's, and its anthropology's, implications. This is what the scholarship considers Jansenism's second life, when the concern with justification moved from pertaining (exclusively) to salvation to being interested (primarily) in political structures.[52]

For Royer-Collard, the anti-sacrilege law had 'vaguely invoked' religion, and yet it aided 'marvellously' in providing the terms by which the state could 'justify' its use of political coercion.[53] This general formulation of the relationship between justification, politics – understood as coercion or force – and theological ignorance or imprecision was a tenet of what can be broadly construed as eighteenth-century Jansenist political theory. Yet leaving vagaries and generalities aside, one text offered a strikingly similar account of the abuses of secular sovereign power: Gabriel-Nicolas Maultrot's *Origine et étendue de la puissance royale, suivant les livres saints et la tradition*, which was published in 1789. Maultrot offered an extensive application and explication of Jansenism's concerns about when politics finds religion, with the distinction which one ought to maintain between the two acting as the premise. 'If we go through all the functions dependent on the monarch,' Maultrot wrote, 'we find none relating to the soul: they are all exercised over the body, over goods, over external and temporal objects.'[54] With this, Maultrot gave what he saw to be a description of what 'Providence has left to the power of men', and thus the body of concerns which delimited the remit of earthly governance.[55] But having outlined what the monarch and his ministers can do on earth, Maultrot then chastises the religious justification they often provide themselves. 'Why should we thus tighten the rights which the Creator has attached to mankind?', Maultrot asked, 'Why seek in Heaven a power enclosed in the freedom of man, and multiply miracles without necessity?'[56]

Maultrot's tract was concerned with disentangling the right to governance that is, by necessity, afforded to humanity from those abuses of religion that often provide it moral legitimation. By reaffirming the distinction between the temporal and the spiritual, what surfaced were those capacities secular existence produced by the very logic of temporal existence: maintenance of goods, the defence or representation of interests, the protection of individuals. But Maultrot was more than merely attempting to make an analytical observation. By asserting that humanity naturally had the right to govern, he attempted to obviate the need to make recourse to God as the source of sovereign power. While 'the power of the Bishops is incontestably divine', Maultrot wrote, 'men have no share in it'.[57] The belief that 'civil Power' has its origin in the same place as 'spiritual Power' is both theologically incoherent and politically harmful: 'it is impossible for men ... to confer the power to remit sins and to administer the Baptism.'[58]

And what allows God to provide atonement, and his Church to facilitate contrition, is the absolute truth that lies at the heart of the spiritual realm. The certainty that came with Christianity's eternal veracity is one untouched by the frailties of sin. Yet '[i]f one pretends that Sovereigns receive their power directly from God, this is to conclude that they can never be stripped of it'.[59] For Maultrot, the conflation of the secular sovereign's prerogatives with those of God inhibited resistance. Taken theologically, this implied no means to defend oneself from those frailties and that brokenness that, as a fallen man, even a governor was sullied by. But for a Jansenist, to give oneself blindly to a sovereign unenlightened by their sense of cosmic order was unthinkable. This is an instance where the absolutes of theology are finely accommodated by the necessities of politics.

Maultrot's political theory, as ought to be clear, was one which fitted rather neatly into that kind of republicanism that late-eighteenth-century French thought was giving light to. Yet that he did so as a Jansenist, uninterested in earthly perfectibility but geared towards the betterment of humanity's secular lot, made his thought pliable even to a position that did not wholly discredit a monarchical arrangement. Political Jansenism, like Maultrot himself, was not as overtly aligned with the kind of republicanism Calvinism seemed to necessitate. What they had to say stemmed from observations of ecclesial structure: of what the Church itself could offer, and what those other institutions of human origin could do to compensate. When governance was targeted, the two prongs of Maultrot's case – the inherently secular sources of government and the right to resist illegitimate sovereigns – were merely an outworking of this.

One finds the same in Royer-Collard. And, I believe, reading his intervention during the anti-sacrilege debates alongside Maultrot offers a useful insight into the reaches of Jansenist political arguments. Leaving to one side the theological and anthropological proclivities a Jansenist mindset brings, Royer-Collard can be found to entertain the same concerns that inebriated Maultrot's *Origine et étendue de la puissance royale*. In a brief section dedicated to divvying up the secular and the eternal, Royer-Collard argued that a subject must maintain the 'inviolable recourse against the tyrannies of this world'.[60] And they must do so precisely because of the excesses 'the charm of weakness and sickness' can bring about. The anti-sacrilege law would have allowed Charles X to find refuge in religious legitimation, inhibiting civic resistance on the grounds that it would be in defiance of a divine will. '[I]t is not of its own authority, of its own inspiration and by its own energy that the law declares sacrilege,' Royer-Collard argued, 'but by that received by the Catholic Church.'[61] And much like civil power may avoid resistance, the tyrannical imposition of Charles X and his ministers further 'usurped' religion and the manifestation of spiritual power – wholly ecclesial, and never human.[62] What France would then witness was 'religious power that dictates civil law', and Royer-Collard added:

> Thus the law has a religious belief, and as it is its work, it must be obeyed; the truth, in matters of faith, is its domain; sovereignty decides on it; it regulates it with a power as absolute as the other interests of society; it sanctions it, if necessary, by torture.[63]

The separation of the spiritual from the temporal thus lent itself to various tenets of Royer-Collard intervention. While it may be illegitimate to trace the entirety of his central argument back to Jansenism, both this movement's theology and its politics – as exemplified by Maultrot – do offer a means to identify the stakes Royer-Collard believed were involved: it was a veritable corruption of the very relationship between Man and God. Yet while Maultrot's treatise was at pains to show how religion could only ever find a public life in the Church, Royer-Collard did deviate ever so slightly from this line. But in doing so, it should not be thought that he was somehow violating his own religious principles. As was mentioned above, Jansenism, especially when considered for its contributions to political discussion, can never be reified into a unitary doctrine.

According to Royer-Collard, however much as the French state risked exceeding its role as a figure in humanity's salvific history, there is one realm of action where the secular world, and thus earthly society, cannot prescind entirely from a religious explanation. 'Man is a religious being,' Royer Collard exclaimed, and this 'is a fact that falls under the faculties, and I dare say, under the sense of the law.'[64] However much the spiritual could never touch the temporal, the desire to live in accordance with the Christian creed, and thus to place as one's objective the outward manifestation of one's (supposed) eternal lot, does have earthly consequences. And entire societies, much as their institutions, bear witness to it.

Eighteenth-century French Jansenists like Maultrot may have come close to arguing for the near total neutrality of the state, even if their onetime allegiance with Gallicans made this often awkward. But Royer-Collard's own position, at least as he expressed it in 1825, did not strictly adhere to these earlier claims, yet it was not a total reversal of their arguments. In his intervention Royer-Collard underscored the need for France's constitution to recognize a plurality of religions: 'Would anyone dare to claim that States have the right, among the various religions that are professed on earth, to decide which is the true one? This would be blasphemy.'[65] Yet he was also keen to underline the 'preeminence' of Catholicism: even the 'Charter is not indifferent, it is not neutral', and as with France's 'public and private mores', all of society 'received the ineffable imprint' from the Church.[66]

One possible explanation does not require one to look far. Royer-Collard was writing in the wake of a series of texts that pitted Christianity against those forces which had ostensibly torn up society.[67] François-René de Chateaubriand's famed *Génie du christianisme* was written with this in mind – a text which Rémusat, in his essay on fundamentalism, described as 'ingenious' and 'beyond all works suspect of reactionary politics'.⁶⁸ A language emerged, and one which Royer-Collard deployed, that saw in postrevolutionary France the drive towards social disaggregation. There was a sense that the Jacobinism of the later years of the French Revolution, in all its anarchy and gratuitous violence, had foregrounded what one critic called 'individuellisme, l'universel égoïsme'.⁶⁹ The *liens sociales*, the argument ran, that had been broken by the revolution had in part been religious in origin, formed from the institutions of the Church as well as those social virtues the *culte* and the *rite* inculcated. And in response, it was believed necessary to retrace France's Christian roots, to show how its most fundamental mores – those practices which most kept the country united – extended from the Church. In a speech Royer-Collard gave several years prior to 1825, he observed a society that had been made into 'dust' by the death of those traditional forms of sociability that religion brought about.⁷⁰ (As a sidenote, it is striking to find Royer-Collard explicitly speak in the language of society turning into dust, *en pussière*, as it reminds one of Edmund Burke's own pronouncements on the death of religion and its effects in his *Reflections on the French Revolution*: 'the commonwealth itself would, in a few generations, crumble away, be disconnected into the dust and powder of individuality'.⁷¹)

But this only gives a general sense of the vocabulary on offer to Royer-Collard, while what has been attempted aims at providing an understanding of the concerns and arguments that animated his more intimate religiosity. For mores to bear the countenance of Christianity, the relationship between God and history is tightened, at least at first glance. But this is a position that is hard to reconcile with the abject dualism that structured Royer-Collard's sense of religion. Yet it would also be disingenuous to find his religion, or at the very least his own formulation of it, wanting. One of the driving concerns of his intervention during the anti-sacrilege debates was to free up the spiritual from the temporal, and vice versa. But in arguing for a secular society free from the obstreperous attempts to wrestle away from the heavens what does not belong on earth, Royer-Collard was scaling back even further on politics' hold on religion. What he did believe possible, if not theologically sanctioned, was to ask not what religion could provide the sovereign, but what it could supply the faithful. That is, by locating religion at the plain of morality and custom, religion's earthly vocation to aid faith is reinforced. Mores, morality and customs do not in themselves contain some divine scintilla; they remain realities that are all too human. And thus the use of religion's 'external and visible' attributes to governments is understandable, Royer-Collard claimed, as they contribute 'powerfully to the order, peace and happiness of societies'; but 'the truth does not enter into it: it falls neither into the power nor under the protection of men'.⁷² So even religion's earthly mission is not concerned with pronouncements on the veridical, but rather with providing what aids in leading the life of a sinner who has come to faith. Royer-Collard was in fact often keen to highlight how Christianity's most useful social virtue is prudence. His understanding of it was very much anchored in the Augustinian and Jansenist traditions. He defined it as that which allows a person 'prévoyance', a capacity for being 'vigilant' and capable of discerning or revealing what to do 'in a moment of danger'.⁷³ The language he adopts is reminiscent of Augustine's use of Cicero's formulation of prudence as 'the practical knowledge of things to be sought for and things to be avoided'.[74] It is an experiential or pragmatic aid; and however much it originated in a witness to something divine – prudence is considered intimately tied to the person of Christ – it itself does not contain that divine truth. As with all things earthly, Christian virtues and the Church's secular presence are instrumentally, not ontically, tied to God.

Those who thought otherwise were mere 'materialists'.[75] For Royer-Collard, postrevolutionary France was 'pressed between theocracy and atheism', but both forces equally sought to flatten the divine: the latter intentionally, the former by consequence.[76] The sense of religion to which he clung, like Jansen, Maultrot and his Jansenist coreligionists, was of an historical faith, a sense that to be Christian exclusively meant one assenting to the incorruptible, immutable and wholly ineffable belief in the singular earthly instantiation of God's spiritual realm through the incarnation. Everything that came before it, and everything that followed, was either expectation or promise. Like all those who looked to grace alone, to the inherently Christological centrality of the Catholic creed, both profane and sacred history could not offer anything but a simple human account of otherworldly salvation. Nothing in time, nothing that is mundane could help humanity get closer to its salvific end. And all that could be hoped for was the richness of an inner life that desired, however prudentially, to return to God when the spirit finds liberation in death.

What Royer-Collard brings to light is the roles providence and grace play in delimiting an ostensibly Catholic response to political society. When providence is foregrounded, as was done by Maistre and Lamennais, the distance between this world and the other is shortened. And salvation, by consequence, becomes all the more obtainable in the *saeculum*, allowing history to be the theatre where the eternal fate of humanity is decided on. (This is also why actions and enacted religion – *culte, rite, traditions sociales* – are prioritized over faith and promise.) Where instead grace is found to retain its sole place in the salvific equation, it is thought that the world of Man and that of God requires differing, and distinct, concerns and behaviours. For as faith alone links humanity to the divine, and does so only when history comes to its end, the secular, temporal existence of society ought not to pretend to be in any way pertinent to the real history of salvation. All that can be done on earth is reinforce the otherness of the heavenly realm and of our heavenly state, and in so doing prop up a political reality which merely attenuates malign compulsions and encourages the flourishing of those considered salutary.

The arguments Royer-Collard put forward, as is evident, were inherently liberal: they sought to reconcile liberty with religion. Yet unlike those others whom the scholarship considers liberal Catholics, Royer-Collard did not seek to humanize religion. And maybe here an even stronger form of liberal Christian religiosity can be had. When humanity's earthly life is considered to be beyond the pale of the spiritual, when sin is its defining feature and salvation is its – temporally – unreachable cure, the worldly becomes the sole mode of social and political existence. It would make little sense to see in this a push towards secularization, for the secular is both its beginning and end. But it is worth seeing in Royer-Collard's sense of religion, his Jansenism that was heavily indebted to Augustinianism, the sources of this position. It may even strike one as unsurprising that his closest political ally, François Guizot, was a somewhat lapsed Calvinist, another form of Christianity directly rooted in Augustine, in the sole value of grace, and one that profoundly disdained any human attempt to touch God. It is about time that scholars take seriously the religious worlds these figures inhabited. Even if foggy, a set of terms and assumptions littered their speeches, structured their writings, and formed their minds. And unless an effort is made, a mindset antithetical to religion is less than ill-equipped to understand what was being said.

Notes

1 The scholarship on liberal Catholicism is patchy, and it is not this chapter's duty to enumerate it. But some useful sources, even if only as guides, are: Anatole Leroy-Beaulieu's, *Les Catholiques libéraux: l'Église et le libéralisme de 1830 à nos jours* (Paris, 1885) is among the first studies of this group of figures, and in many respects deals in terms that contemporary scholarship maintains. Marcel Prélot's, *Le libéralisme catholique: textes choisis et présentés* (Paris, 1969) largely enumerated the figures, as did Geroges Weill's, *Histoire du catholicisme libéral en France, 1828*-1908 (Paris, 1979). John K. Huckaby's 'Liberal Catholicism in France' (The Ohio State University) is, despite having remained an unpublished doctoral thesis, a priceless resource in English. For more recent examples, see: Julien Barroche, 'Maurice Hauriou, juriste catholique ou libéral?, *Revue française des idées politiques* 28, no. 2 (2008): 307–35; Sylvain Millbach, 'Les catholiques libéraux et la presse entre 1831 et 1855', *Le mouvement social* 215, no. 2 (2010): 9–34 and 'Les catholiques libéraux et la Révolution française autour de 1848.«Elle est toujours vivante: elle nous entoure, elle domine', *Annales historique de la Révolution française* 362 (2010): 55–78.
2 Charles de Rémusat, 'Du Traditionalisme', Revue des Deux Mondes 9 (1857): 44. All translations, unless otherwise stated, are my own.
3 Ibid.
4 Ibid.'[À] celle de notre XVIIe siècle, encore éclairée, encore élargie par l'idée suprême des droits de la conscience humaine.'
5 Ibid., 48. 'Ce dernier mot, que nous n'avons pas créé et qui est passé dans la controverse contemporaine, pourrait servir à désigner en général tout l'ensemble d'idées et d'argumens qui, dans la philosophie, la politique, la religion, tend à exclure l'intervention libre de la raison, car il ne peut être pris comme un système et combattu à ce titre qu'autant qu'il est exclusif.'
6 Ibid.
7 Joseph de Maistre, *Examen d'un écrit de J.-J. Rousseau sur l'inégalité des conditions* (Lyon: Not known, 1884), 547. '[L]eur caractère général est Inaltérable et nécessairement fondé sur la vérité'.
8 Ibid., 538.
9 Joseph de Maistre, *Considérations sur la France* (London: not known, 1797), 1.
10 Ibid., 2. 'Dans les ouvrages de l'homme, tout est pauvre comme l'auteur; les vues sont restreintes, les moyens roides, les ressorts inflexibles, les mouvements pénibles, et les résultats monotones.'
11 Ibid. 'Dans les ouvrages divins, les richesses de l'infini se montrent à découvert jusque dans les moindres éléments: sa puissance opère en se jouant; dans ses mains tout est souple, rien ne lui résiste; pour elle tout est moyen, même l'obstacle; et les irrégularités produits par l'opération des agents libres, viennent se ranger dans l'ordre général.'

12 Ibid., 49.
13 Félicité de La Mennais, *Des progrès de la révolution et de la guerre contre l'Eglise* (Paris: De Belin, Mandar et Devaux, 1829), 15.
14 Ibid., 4. 'Par ses dogmes qui contiennent toute vérité, par ses précepts et ses conseils qui renferment toute vertu, il tend incessamment à développer l'intelligence et le sentiment de la perfection morale.'
15 Ibid., 279. '[L]es traditions chrétiennes, fournissent de nouveaux appuis à la foi, dont l'universalité, la perpétuité, ces deux grands caractères de tout ce qui est divin, deviennent chaque jour plus manifestes.'
16 Rémusat, 48.
17 Pierre Rosanvallon, *La démocratie inachevée* (Paris: Gallimard, 2000), 112–18.
18 The only two studies which have come close to offering a look at the role of religion in Royer-Collard's thought are Jean-François Jacouty, 'Tradition et modernité dans la pensée politique de Royer-Collard', *Revue française des idées politiques* 27, no. 1 (2008): 75–109 and Corrine Doria's, *Pierre Paul Royer-Collard (1763–1845): un philosophe entre deux revolutions* (Rennes: Presses Universitaires de Rennes (PUR), 2018). While both are indispensable in recentring Royer-Collard in accounts of Restoration politics, both do barely mention his religion and his interest in theology. Neither, in fact, looks to his religious sources or the theological assumptions of his arguments.
19 Eugène Spuller, *Royer-Collard* (Paris, 1895), 182. 'On assure que, de tous ses discours, Royer-Collard préférait le discours sur la loi du sacrilège;c'est en effet le plus beau peut-être qu'il ait prononcé;ce qui est plus certain, c'est que ce discours est le plus grand service qu'il ait rendu à la cause du bon sens, de la raison politique, de la liberté de conscience et de la civilisation générale. Il n'y a que soixante-dix ans à peine qu'il a été nécessaire de porter ces fortes paroles à la tribune et de rappeler ces grands principes, ces vérités nécessaires. Il ne faut pas oublier que le monde est incessamment ballotté de progrès en réaction et de réaction en progrès. Royer-Collard a prononcé la séparation de la religion et de la politique, et tranché cette question avec une telle autorité, qu'il n'y a plus à y revenir. Que si, cependant, il y avait à lutter encore contre cette confusion aussi absurde que criminelle, ce serait dans le discours sur le sacrilège que l'on trouverait encore les meilleures armes.'
20 Corinne Doria has written briefly about Royer-Collard opposition to the law on sacrilege: 'Le « juste milieu » entre le trône et l'autel. Pierre Paul Royer-Collard et la loi sur le sacrilège de 1825', *Revue d'histoire ecclesiastique* 110, no. 1–2 (2015): 135–53. Though she offers a comprehensive account of the general reactions, looking at journals and other 'doctrinaire' figures, she does not provide an in-depth study of what his Catholicism provided his political thought.
21 Paul Dupont, ed., *Archives parlementaires* (Paris, 1880), XLIV, 575. '[C]e qui est bien plus extraordinaire, il crée un nouveau principe de criminilaité, un ordre de crimes pour ainsi dire surnaturels, qui ne tombent pas sous nos sens, que la raison humaine ne saurait decouvrir ni comprendre, et qui ne se manifestent qu'à la foi religieuse éclairée par la révélation.'
22 Ibid., 578.
23 Ibid., 576.
24 Ibid., 575.
25 Ibid.,'Est-ce l'offense à la société qui se rencontre dans l'outrage à Dieu, c'est-à-dire, dans le sacrilége, ou bien est-ce le sacrilége lui-même? C'est le sacrilége seul, le sacrilège simple. Est-il possible que la société soit comprise avec Dieu dans le sacrilége? Non; Dieu seul est saint et sacré. Serait-il besoin du stratagème de la preuve légale pour donner un corps aux offenses de la société?'

26 Lamennais, 29.
27 Pierre-Simon Ballanche, *Ville des Expiations* (Paris: H. Falque, 1907), 13.
28 Alexis de Tocqueville, *Oeuvres complètes*, ed. J.P. Mayer (Paris, 1970), vol. XI, 27.
29 Dupont, 576.
30 Ibid.
31 Ibid.
32 Ibid., 578.
33 Ibid., 576. 'Releguée à jamais aux choses de la terre, la loi humaine ne participe point aux croyances religieuses: dans sa capacité temporelle, elle ne les connaît ne les comprend; au delà des intérêts de cette vie, elle est frappée d'ignorance et d'impuissance.'
34 Louis de Bonald, *Théorie du pouvoir politique et religieux* (Paris, 1848), I, 217. '[L]a perfection, ou ce qui est la même chose, la constitution politique de la société devroit se trouver toujours avec la perfection de la religion ou la constitution religieuse.'
35 Ibid., 32. 'L'état conformeà la nature de l'homme intelligent est aussi la perfection puisque l'homme intelligent est semblable à Dieu.'
36 Gemma Simmonds', 'Jansenism (1640–1713): An historico-theological account with special reference to one twentieth-century response' (University of Cambridge: Doctoral Dissertation) remains, till this day, one of the best English-language studies of Jansenism.
37 Dupont, 576.
38 Ibid.
39 Ibid., 579.
40 Ibid. 'Voilà, Messieurs, la vocation de l'Eglise; elle a été appelée par Jésus-Christ à sauver les hommes, et non à les dévorer par le feu du ciel, ce qui explique le système admirable de son Code pénitientiel, tout médicinal, dit saint Augustin, et tout occupé de détruire, non l'homme, mais le péché, afin de préserver le pécheur des peines éternelles, qui sont sans remède.'
41 Ibid., 578.
42 Ibid., 576.
43 Ibid.
44 Ibid.
45 *Ibid.*, 579. 'J'ai voulu marquer, en rompant un long silence, ma vive opposition au principe théocratique qui menace à la fois la religion et la société, d'autant plus odieux, que ce ne sont pas, comme aux jours de la barbarie et de l'ignorance, les fureurs sincères d'un zèle trop ardent qui rallument cette torche ... La théocratie de notre temps est moins religieuse que politique; elle fait partie de ce système de réaction universelle qui nous emporte.'
46 Ibid., 576. 'J'ose avancer que toute l'habileté qui a été déployée dans la défense du projet de loi devant l'autre Chambre a consisté à confondre, avec un art qui n'a jamais été en défaut, l'outrage à Dieu avec l'outrage à la société.'
47 Ibid.
48 Ibid., 575.
49 Ibid., 576.
50 Ibid., 578.
51 Dale K. Van Kley, *The Religious Origins of the French Revolution, 1560–1791* (New Haven, CT, 1996), 35–8.

52   Arnaud Orain makes this case in the essay 'The Second Jansenism and the Rise of French Eighteenth-Century Political Economy, *History of Political Economy* 46, no. 3 (2014): 464–90.
53   Dupont, 579.
54   Gabriel-Nicolas Maultrot, *Origine et étendue de la puissance royale, suivant les livres saints et la tradition* (Paris, 1789), 10. 'Qu'on parcoure toutes les fonctions dépendantes de la royauté, on n'en trouvera aucune relative à l'ame: elles s'exercent toutes sur le corps, sur les biens, sur des objets extérieurs & temporels'.
55   Ibid.
56   Ibid.
57   Ibid., 7.
58   Ibid., 7. '[Q]u'il est aussi impossible aux hommes de conférer le pouvoir temporel, que de conférer celui de remettre les péchés, & d'administrer le Baptême, & qu'il faut également dans les deux cas, que le Ciel s'ouvre, & qu'il en descende un pouvoir divin.'
59   Ibid., 7. 'Quand le pouvoir civil viendroit du Ciel, aussi immédiatement aussi certainement que celui des Evêques & du Pape, on en conclurroit donc sans fondement, qu'il ne peut pas être enlevé par les hommes.'
60   Dupont, 576.
61   Ibid.
62   Ibid.
63   Ibid. 'Ainsi, la loi a une croyance religieuse, et comme elle est souveraine, sa croyance doit être obéie. La vérité en matière de foi est de son domaine; la souveraineté en decide, elle la règle avec un pouvoir aussi absolu que les autres intérêts de la société; elle la sanctionne, s'il en est besoin, par des supplices.'
64   Ibid., 578. 'L'homme est un être religieux: c'est un fait qui tombe sous tes facultés et, si je t'ose dire, sous les sens de la loi.'
65   Ibid., 577. 'Ce serait une absurdité toute l'immortalité de Rome et d'Athènes est dans l'histoire. Est-ce qu'on oserait prétendre que les Etats ont le droit, entre tes diverses religions qui se professent sur la terre, de décider laquelle est la vraie? Ce serait un blasphème.'
66   Ibid., 578.
67   For a study on the various linguistic formulations used so describe social disaggregation, see Marie-France Piguet, 'Individualisme. Du Producteur à Tocqueville', *Mots, Les langages du politique* 96 (2011).
68   Rémusat, 47.
69   François-Auguste Fauveau de Frénilly, *Considération sur une année de l'histoire* (London, 1815), 27.
70   Quoted in Propser de Barante, *La vie politique de M. Royer-Collard. Ses discours et ses écrits* (Paris, 1864), 131.
71   Edmund Burke, *Reflections on the Revolution in France* (New Haven, CT, 2003), 81–2.
72   Dupont, 576. 'Mais cette alliance sauroit comprendre de la religion que ce qu'elle a d'extérieur et visible, son culte et la condition de ses ministres dans l'Etat. La vérité n'y entre pas; elle ne tombe ni au pouvoir ni sous la protection des hommes.'
73   Royer-Collard, 'Discours de la Chambre des Pairs', in Barante, *La vie politique de M. Royer-Collard*, I, 457.
74   Cicero, *De Officiis*, ed. and trans. Walter Miller (Cambridge, MA: Harvard University Press in 1913, 1975), 1.43.153. Also, Royer-Collard's overtly Jansenist sense of

prudence maintains Augustine's own Neo-Platonic re-reading of Cicero; this is opposed to the Scholastic interpretation of prudence originating in Aquinas' use of Aristotle formulation: 'right reason applied to action', Aristotle, *Nicomachean Ethics*, ed. Roger Crisp (Cambridge: Cambridge University Press, 2000), 1143a.

75   Dupont, 579.
76   Ibid., 577.

8

'A free Church in a free state'. The relationship between Church and State in the thought of Charles de Montalembert

Arthur Hérisson
École française de Rome, Italy

Introduction

French Catholicism in the mid-nineteenth century was marked by a split between intransigent and liberal Catholics, which divided both the clergy and the laity.[1] The intransigent Catholics, whose major figure was the journalist Louis Veuillot,[2] considered that the Church could not compromise with 'modern civilization', whose liberalism they considered contrary to its message. Their ideas tended to prevail at this time, not least of all because of the doctrinal stiffening that marked the pontificate of Pius IX after the European revolutions of 1848–9.[3] Faced with them, liberal Catholics considered a conciliation between the Church and modern society not only possible but desirable.

The main advocate of liberal Catholic ideas in early-nineteenth-century France was Abbé Félicité de Lamennais. Hostile to the old Gallicanism and the forms of State control of the Church that it legitimized, he defended a liberal programme and the separation of Church and State in his newspaper *L'Avenir*.[4] In 1832, however, Pope Gregory XVI condemned the theses of the Breton priest in the encyclical *Mirari vos*.[5] Lamennais having subsequently broken with the Church, from the July Monarchy until the Vatican Council, it was one of his former disciples, Count Charles de Montalembert, who became the principal representative of liberal Catholicism in France.[6]

Born in London in 1810 to an emigrant aristocrat father and a mother from an old Scottish family, Montalembert was educated by his maternal grandfather in England before continuing his studies in France. From his English youth he retained a lifelong interest in the British political system and in liberal ideas. In the early 1830s he met Lamennais and took part in the writing of *L'Avenir*. When the ideas promoted by the paper were condemned by the papacy, the Count submitted to Rome's judgement. He became a peer of France in 1835 and defended the cause of the Church in the upper house, leading the Catholic mobilization for freedom of education in the 1840s.[7] From then on, and for thirty years, he became one of the main figures of French Catholicism, defending a liberal Catholicism concerned with reconciling the Church and modern society.

One of the main issues Montalembert had to deal with in these years was the relationship between Church and State. Such a question was indeed particularly important in France at that time. After the fall of the Bourbons in 1830, Catholicism had lost its status as the religion of the State, but the relationship between Church and State was still governed by the Concordat concluded by the first consul Napoleon Bonaparte and Pope Pius VII in 1801. I would like to analyse Montalembert's thinking on this subject. I will follow a chronological plan in order to better highlight the influence of contemporary events on Montalembert's writings on this subject. The essay will thus be articulated around the analysis of three texts, which represent the three main moments of Montalembert's thinking.

It was not until the 1840s that Montalembert really began to write about the relationship between Church and State.[8] He then considered this question mainly through the prism of freedom of education, which was the major battle he was waging at the time. A second step in his thinking was marked by the publication of *Des intérêts catholiques au XIXe siècle* in 1852.

The question of the relationship between Church and State was considered in relation to a double context: the strengthening of the authoritarian regime of Louis-Napoleon Bonaparte and the support that the prince-president received from intransigent Catholics. Montalembert thus had to take a stand not only in relation to the State, as in the 1840s, but also in relation to other Catholics. Finally, under the Second Empire, the Count's thinking deepened. In a context marked by the rise of intransigent Catholicism, the Count deepened his reflection in the two major speeches he gave in the Belgian city of Mechelen in 1863.

I An analysis of the relationship between Church and State through the lens of the struggle for freedom of education (1840s)

1 The denunciation of the state's monopoly on education

During the 1840s, Montalembert became the main leader of the 'Catholic party' which was mobilizing to obtain freedom of secondary education, against the monopoly held since Napoleon by the University, i.e. the administration in charge of education in France. In 1843, the Count published a pamphlet entitled *Du devoir des catholiques dans la question de la liberté d'enseignement*. The booklet explored the issue by linking it to the broader theme of the secularization of French society,[9] which was one of the most important concerns of Catholic opinion at the time. Montalembert analysed the importance of irreligion in France as a consequence of the State's monopoly on secondary education:

> The main and permanent reason for public irreligion in France is to be found in the present education of youth, such as the State has constituted a monopoly of

it. The whole of the institutions of public instruction, which form the University of France, and outside of which a usurped despotism does not allow anything to arise, is the hearth in which is formed and maintained this public spirit which, in the matter of religion, is nothing and believes in nothing.[10]

According to the Count, the consequences of the University monopoly were all the more important because, since the revision of the Charter in 1830 following the installation of the July Monarchy, the French State no longer recognized Catholicism as its religion. However, Montalembert considered that it was an illusion to want to turn France into a Catholic State, as it had been from Clovis to Louis XIV, and he acknowledged that Catholics did not run the State and probably would not do so for a long time.[11]

Because of this situation and the threats it posed to Catholicism, Catholics had to seek first and foremost to 'strengthen by all legitimate means the purely moral empire of Religion over the individuals and families who still profess it'.[12] To achieve this, they had to set themselves the goal of ending the monopoly of the University. Thus, Montalembert did not call for the destruction of the University, nor for its Christianization, which he considered impossible since even the Restoration had not been able to achieve this.[13] He only demanded the end of the University monopoly, i.e. the possibility for Catholics to open their own educational institutions alongside those of the State.

This destruction of the university monopoly was not demanded on the basis of any special right of the Church in education, but in the name of common liberties. It was thus a purely liberal argument that the Count put forward. In this way he justified the end of the university monopoly by the Constitutional Charter, which guarantees the respect of religious freedom in its article 5:

> The State has no right, on pain of violating the constitution which is the very condition of its existence, to impose on all citizens a system of education which compromises the maintenance of religious belief within their families. The fact that the State has no religion does not mean that it can prevent citizens from having one. Far from it, the Charter not only promises freedom of education, but it solemnly guarantees religious freedom: this freedom, as far as a positive religion like Catholicism is concerned, is nothing but a mockery if, by virtue of a series of extralegal dispositions ... the executive power finds itself invested with the exclusive right to shape the beliefs and morals of childhood.[14]

Montalembert's thinking was marked by an anti-State sensibility that was fairly widespread among Catholics of the time. Influenced in particular by the memory of the revolutionary period, various Catholics, like certain liberal thinkers, denounced the threats posed to public liberties by the contemporary strengthening of the powers of the State.[15] Montalembert thus presented the monopoly of education as something unprecedented in history and unparalleled in the Europe of his time, 'because even under the most despotic governments, there are Universities supervised by the State; but nowhere are they the State itself; nowhere has the State made itself the schoolmaster directly'.[16] The University monopoly was described as a formidable weapon in the hands of State despotism:

> The University ... represents above all and serves marvellously this tendency of the State to bend everything to the implacable level of a sterile uniformity. It is through it that this new despotism, which threatens the world, tends to replace the Church and the family, those two sacred centres of the moral freedom of the human race.[17]

Montalembert thus made the University one of the central cogs in the control of individuals by the contemporary State. In this perspective, the decline of Catholicism was presented as the condition for the possibility of a despotism without equal in history. As Sylvain Milbach has noted, the Count was thus outlining a very particular kind of liberalism, where 'the individual, the family, has for protection against temporal forces only the religious convictions which imply independence and resistance'. The Church was described as a bulwark, guaranteeing citizens against the abuses of the State.[18] Although he did not quote him in his pamphlet, Montalembert was here clearly influenced by the thought of Joseph de Maistre who, in *Du Pape*, had presented the papacy as a power capable of protecting the people from the abuses of despotism.[19]

2 The abandonment of the Ancien Régime ideal of the alliance of the Throne and the Altar

As a counterpoint to the French situation, Montalembert praised the 'Belgian system which saves religion through freedom'.[20] For the French liberal Catholics of the July Monarchy, Belgium was indeed a model.[21] After gaining independence from the Netherlands in 1830, the country had enacted a liberal constitution in 1831, which guaranteed freedom of conscience, press, assembly and association as well as freedom of education. In the course of their struggle for national independence, Belgian Catholics had formed an alliance with the liberals and had taken advantage of the common freedoms to strengthen the position of the Church in society.[22] Montalembert was all the more sensitive to this Belgian model because he knew it personally: his wife was the daughter of one of the architects of the country's independence, Count Félix de Mérode, and he had also established personal relations with some of the country's leading politicians.[23]

Following the Belgian example, Montalembert called for a reciprocal independence of Church and State, which would allow the Church to escape the interference of the State by benefiting from common freedoms, and in particular the freedoms of éducation and association. His 1843 pamphlet thus already reflected a major feature of his thinking, which he would develop during the decades of the 1850s and 1860s: the abandonment of the ideal of collaboration between State and Church that had marked the *Ancien Régime*, where the two powers supported each other and where the Church could prosper thanks to the privileges granted to it by political power. According to the Count, in modern society as it existed in the nineteenth century, privileges were not only useless but harmful to Catholicism and it was only by benefiting from common liberties that the Church could prosper. Montalembert said, moreover, that he did not regret the old days when the State and the Church had been closely associated, because this association had often been made to the detriment of the Church's independence[24] – the remark reflected his rejection of Gallicanism, which he had inherited from Lamennais.

3 Mobilizing Catholics for the Church's cause

In practical terms, the abandonment of the old system of collaboration between Church and State had an important consequence. Since the Church could no longer count on the protection of the State, Catholics had to mobilize to defend the interests of religion in society. To this end, Montalembert put forward several possible means of action: the electoral struggle, the press, but also petitions.[25] The importance given to this last mode of action was linked to the impact in France of the victories achieved by British Catholics in the previous decades.[26] Daniel O'Connell's action was held up as an example in this respect.[27] In doing so, Montalembert paved the way for the strategy of structuring the Catholic movement that would be followed by the Church in most European countries in the second half of the nineteenth century. The mobilization in favour of freedom of education can be seen as a kind of French prodrome of such a strategy.

Rejecting the alliance of the Throne and the Altar, Montalembert was not, however, in favour of an absolute separation of Church and State. He only wanted a separation that could be described, using Jacqueline Lalouette's term, as 'moderate',[28] the main objective being to obtain an end to the surveillance exercised by the State over the Church. For this reason, the Count did not question the Concordat concluded in 1801 between the First Consul Napoleon Bonaparte and the Papacy, which served as a framework for relations between the State and the Catholic Church. He distinguished it, however, from the Organic Articles, a sort of implementing decree that Bonaparte had added unilaterally and subsequently and which hindered the freedom of the Church. Montalembert thus denounced in particular the jurisdiction of the State Council in religious matters, which allowed the State to watch over the clergy.[29]

The mobilization of Catholics in favour of freedom of education proved on the whole to be fruitful, since it led to the passing of the Falloux law in 1850. Although Montalembert had already begun to reflect on the question of the relationship between the Church and the State in the 1840s, this reflection had remained relatively undeveloped. A few years later, however, Louis-Napoleon Bonaparte's coup d'état and the establishment of an authoritarian regime, which had been widely welcomed by French Catholics, led the Count to deepen his thinking on this point.

II Faced with the establishment of an authoritarian regime supported by the Church: *Des intérêts catholiques au XIXe siècle* (1852)

1 The divisions of French Catholics regarding the New Regime

In October 1852, Montalembert published *Des intérêts catholiques au XIXe siècle*. The book was written in reaction to the events that had marked French political life during the previous year. On 2 December 1851, Louis-Napoleon Bonaparte had carried out his coup d'état and on 14 January 1852 a new constitution had consolidated the power of the prince-president. Although Montalembert had initially been reticent about the conditions under which the coup had been carried out and had signed a protest against the dissolution of the Assembly, the armed insurrections that had broken out in Paris and the provinces had subsequently led him to give his public support to the president. These insurrections had indeed seemed to manifest the fears spread in conservative circles at the end of 1851 about a possible socialist takeover in 1852.[30] Montalembert was from then on, together with Veuillot, one of the pillars of the rallying of Catholics to power.[31]

Quite quickly, however, offended in particular by the confiscation of the possessions of the Orléans and perhaps also disappointed at not having succeeded in getting some of the measures he had hoped for adopted (freedom of higher education, freedom of association), the Count distanced himself from the head of State.[32] In contrast to him, at the same time, a large proportion of Catholics supported the new government. Louis Veuillot and his newspaper *L'Univers*, but also influential members of the episcopate such as Mgr Parisis, were panegyrists of the regime that was set up in 1852. The split between liberal and intransigent Catholics, which had already been noticeable in the final years of the struggle for freedom of education, became more pronounced. The intransigents supported the restrictions on liberties decided by the regime and welcomed the benefits it bestowed on the Church – very symbolically, one of the first measures taken by the prince-president after the coup d'état had been to return the Pantheon to Catholic worship. Montalembert, for his part, defended a diametrically opposed position in *Des intérêts catholiques au XIXe siècle*.

2 The observation of a religious revival during the first nineteenth century made possible not by government support but by freedom

The book opens with the historical observation that Catholicism had undergone a revival throughout Europe in the first nineteenth century, to the extent that its situation had changed completely between 1800 and 1852. At the beginning of 1800, when Pius VI had died in exile in Valence and his successor had not yet been elected, 'Catholicism must have seemed to the wise men of the world a corpse that had only to be buried.'[33] However, 'half a century passed, and everything was transformed. Everywhere religion has regained its place in the front rank; everywhere the Church is recognised as a power of the first order.'[34] For Montalembert, the cause of such a change was not to be found in the benevolence of governments towards the Church. In France, during the Restoration, the Bourbons had thus surrounded the Church with their solicitude without it really benefiting, and in 1830, the revolution that had driven out the Bourbons had also turned against the Church.[35] By contrast, the Church had emerged stronger from the July Monarchy and the Second Republic, which had not been favourable to it:

> Let us compare her situation in 1830 with that which she took without effort in 1848, at the end of a reign to which she had almost always been condemned to resist; let us compare it with that which she retained in 1852, after four years of continuous struggle against the perils of anarchy.

It was not, therefore, the Empire or the Restoration; it was neither the protection nor the sympathy of the authorities that gave her the strength she possesses today, the relative improvement that everyone feels, the manifest progress that is revealed every day.

What is it then? It must be said: it is freedom, nothing but freedom, and the struggle made possible by freedom.

The same cause has produced the same effect everywhere. Suffice it to mention England and O'Connell, Belgium and its constitution, Holland and the whole of Germany.[36]

For Montalembert, it was thus to freedom alone that Catholicism owed its revival. However, this thesis was far from being shared by all Catholics of his time. Cautiously, the Count took care to specify that he was not seeking to enunciate absolute and timeless principles, but only to highlight the conditions in which the Church could prosper within nineteenth-century societies:

I do not intend to profess here any absolute, universal theory, exclusively applicable to all centuries and to all peoples. I only claim that among most Christian peoples, and in the present state of the world, freedom is a good, a relative good, not an absolute one.[37]

This precision was important. It enabled the Count to avoid the risk of censure from the Papacy, which was then little convinced of the benefits of liberalism and whose ideal was still largely that of collaboration between political power and the Church. On the one hand, by placing himself in the practical domain and not at the level of absolute theory, Montalembert was able to avoid appearing to condemn the past periods when Church and State had worked hand in hand. On the other hand, he avoided entering into frontal opposition with the teachings of the encyclical *Mirari Vos* of 1832, in which Gregory XVI had condemned the ideas of *L'Avenir*.[38] Montalembert's prudence on this point was all the more important because no one had forgotten the important role he had played in the newspaper.

3 Freedom according to Montalembert

It is necessary to clarify what Montalembert meant by 'freedom'. The Count gave this notion an aristocratic definition, both conservative and antidemocratic, insisting in particular on the opposition between freedom and equality. It was not, he said, 'the infallibility of human reason', nor 'the foolish heresy of the indefinite perfectibility of man', nor 'the consecration of envy under the name of equality', nor 'the idolatry of numbers under the name of universal suffrage and sovereignty of the people', nor 'unlimited, absolute freedom', but 'regulated, contained, ordered, tempered freedom, honest and moderate freedom …; freedom which, far from being hostile to authority, can only coexist with it, but whose disappearance immediately turns authority into despotism'.[39]

Montalembert's conception of freedom was notably nourished by references to the Middle Ages,[40] which was then the object of a re-evaluation by Catholics.[41] According to the Count, the Middle Ages had been characterized by the alliance between the Church and freedom, and this alliance had unfortunately been broken for two and a half centuries, first by the establishment of the absolute monarchy and then by the Revolution. The Count thus condemned not only the work of the revolutionaries but also that of the *Ancien Régime*. In particular, he described Louis XIV as 'that great leveller, that all-powerful precursor of democracy, ... the most formidable opponent of the authority of the Holy See and of the independence of the Church'.[42] This criticism of the absolute monarchy was linked in particular to a rejection of Gallicanism, by which the royal power had imposed its authority on the clergy of France. Like many Catholics of his time, Montalembert had been marked by what a bishop of Amiens, Mgr Salinis, had called the 'movement towards Rome', i.e. the process of strengthening the place of the papacy in the Church. On this point, as on others, the Count's thinking was particularly influenced by the writings of Joseph de Maistre and Félicité de Lamennais.

Montalembert's definition of freedom, vague as it was, provided a kind of middle way between two perils: that embodied by democrats and that embodied by despotism. Freedom was what made it possible to avoid the abuses of 'the unlimited power of man over man, whether this power is exercised by one or by the multitude, in the name of an irremovable dynasty or in the name of the sovereign people'.[43] Contemporaries could not be mistaken in interpreting these words: Montalembert was aiming at the French 'democ-soc' as much as at Louis-Napoleon Bonaparte, at the advocates of a democratic and social republic as much as at the man around whom an authoritarian regime was being built. An entire chapter of the book is devoted to drawing a parallel between the error of the Catholics who had rallied to democracy in 1848 and those who rallied to Louis-Napoléon Bonaparte in 1852.[44]

Faced with the former, Montalembert was careful to distinguish what he considered true freedom from freedom as claimed in the name of democracy and revolution:

> There is nothing in common but the name between this freedom demanded by Catholics and that which serves as a mask for democracy and revolution. I have said elsewhere how incompatible freedom is with the democratic and revolutionary spirit. ... As soon as democracy prevails, we can announce with certainty that freedom is done for. ... Basically, democracy is incompatible with freedom, because it is based on envy under the name of equality, whereas freedom, by its very nature, constantly protests against the tyrannical and brutal level of equality. In order to maintain itself, democracy condemns all that want to live and act to abdicate all personal values, and to plunge into servile adoration before the phantom of reason and virtue of the masses. It thus logically and gradually destroys not only all traditions, all ancient and hereditary rights, but also all independence, all dignity and all resistance.[45]

Faced with Louis-Napoleon Bonaparte's supporters, the Count invoked the authority of Fénelon against that of Bossuet, theorist of a close alliance of the Church with absolute power.⁴⁶ He called on Catholics not to side with the prince-president at the risk of losing all that they had gained through freedom in the previous decades.⁴⁷ According to him, the temptation to look for a protector in the prince-president was dangerous, because the latter could one day turn against them:

> Of all governments, the one that has always exposed the Church to the greatest dangers has been absolute government. It does not matter whether it is the absolutism of the crowd or the absolutism of one. A power without restraint, without control, that is to say an omnipotent power, is necessarily formidable to the Church, because it can do anything; because omnipotence is too strong a temptation for human infirmity; because the one who can do anything wants to do anything ....
>
> Even by allying itself with the Church before the inevitable struggle begins, absolute power can only give it favors and rest, honors and privileges; but it will never give it either rights or strength.⁴⁸

Rejecting absolute power, Montalembert thus equated freedom with 'representative, constitutional and parliamentary government', which he considered, 'in the present state of morals and institutions of Europe, [as] the only possible form of political liberty':⁴⁹

> Wherever the servitude of the Church exists or has existed, it has been the work of absolute power. Nowhere, in our century, has it been produced by parliamentary government. This last regime has not broken the chains of the Church everywhere, indeed it has not. It has broken them, however, in France, in England and in Belgium; that is already something. And everywhere else it has provided Catholics with the means ... to prepare their future emancipation.
>
> Under parliamentary government, the Church does not dominate in the political order, and I think that this domination is neither in her wishes nor in her interest; but she has what is worth a thousand times more than power, she has rights. Under absolute power, she has nothing, except what is conceded to her by the good pleasure of the moment. She has for support only the secular arm, which most often withdraws at the moment when she counts on it most, or rises only to strike her. All modern history is there to demonstrate this.'⁵⁰

Such a conception of freedom led the Count to consider that the Church should claim for itself only the common liberties and not the privileges granted by an absolute power which always risked taking them away.

Montalembert's work had an important impact. Louis Veuillot, a fervent supporter of Louis Napoleon Bonaparte, responded to it in his newspaper *L'Univers* with four articles, the last two of which were eloquently entitled 'De la liberté sous l'absolutisme'.⁵¹ In contrast to Montalembert, the journalist defended the idea that the church needed to prosper a strong political power, giving her privileges. Overall, Montalembert's ideas remained a minority within French Catholicism in the following years.

III Facing the Second Empire and the progress of intransigent Catholicism in the Church (1852–70)

1 A limit to Montalembert's liberalism: The defence of the Papal States

Throughout the Second Empire, Montalembert never ceased to denounce the position of intransigent Catholics and to point out the precarious nature of the situation from which the Church benefited. Only a liberal regime, in which the Church enjoyed the freedoms common to all, was in his opinion able to guarantee her against arbitrariness. Such an idea led him to relativize the interest of the concordats. Thus, when a Concordat was signed in 1855 between Austria and the Holy See, the terms of which were very favourable to the Church, Montalembert wrote on this subject to the Italian man of letters Cesare Cantù:

> I think it is too much forgotten that all the liberties guaranteed to the Church by this treaty, and others much more extensive, were assured to Catholicism, twenty-five years ago, by the Belgian Constitution. I fear that the censorship exercised by the ecclesiastics and the monopoly of education entrusted to the bishops will provoke a formidable reaction against religion, even in the German States of Austria.[52]

The liberal convictions of Montalembert were not however without limits. He rejected in Rome, in the Papal States, the moderate separation of the Church and the State which he wished elsewhere. He was therefore a fervent defender of the temporal power of the papacy, which was threatened by Italian unification.[53] The Count justified his position by the singular nature of the Papal States: it was indeed intended to guarantee the spiritual independence of the Pope, which required that the Pontiff not be subject to any political power. In 1863, Montalembert summarized his opinion on the subject as follows:

> The separation of the two powers would be a trap for the spiritual power, which is always disarmed, and whose freedom rests only on the faith of a word that can change and under the hand of a force that can strike, if the supreme head of this spiritual power were not absolutely and fully independent. And the highest degree of independence here on earth is sovereignty. The wisdom of men, the experience of the times and the hand of God have united for a thousand years to assure the first Pontiff of the true Church the rank of king, and in his domain these two powers are confused, so that they can be divided everywhere else …. Pontifical sovereignty, a unique exception and distinct on this point alone from the other powers of the earth, is the consequence of the separation of powers, far from being its contradiction.[54]

It is known that Cavour, the great architect of Italian unity, took advantage of the tension that existed in Montalembert's thought between Catholic and liberal ideals. In particular, he took from the Frenchman the famous formula 'A free Church in a free State'. Montalembert had coined it in 1860 in an open letter to the same Cavour to denounce his policy in Italy,⁵⁵ the Italian president of the Council used the expression in 1861 to summarize the program by which he wished to make Rome the capital of the new kingdom of Italy while guaranteeing the pope the freedom necessary for his spiritual magisterium.⁵⁶ Cavour's adoption of this slogan did considerable harm to liberal Catholic ideas.

The brutal deterioration of relations between the imperial regime and the papacy that followed the Italian War of 1859 was interpreted by Montalembert as a confirmation of the validity of his liberal theses. Because the intervention of France in Italy had as a consequence the weakening of the papacy, the French Catholics largely switched to the opposition.⁵⁷ In response, the laws that restricted freedom in the Empire were now applied to them. The Catholic press, in particular, was closely monitored and the country's main religious newspaper, *L'Univers*, was suppressed.

2 The first speech of Mechelen (20 August 1863)

In 1863, on the occasion of the Congress of Belgian Catholics organized in the city of Mechelen, Montalembert gave two great speeches, which were the occasion for him to reaffirm his liberal theses.⁵⁸ He defended his formula 'A Free Church in a Free State', which he explained as a demand for 'the freedom of the Church based on public liberties'.⁵⁹ He also reiterated the vain character of the hope nourished by some Catholics to see the *Ancien Régime* resurrected. According to him, any alliance between the Church and the State, between the throne and the altar, which presupposed for the State the obligation to protect the Church and to use coactive power against its enemies, was henceforth impossible.⁶⁰ Thus, he wrote:

> There is no longer a single country in the world where the Church can rely on the exclusive protection of any power. All attempts to consolidate or renew the ancient alliance of altar and throne on the basis of the use of coactive power against the opponents of the Church have failed miserably.⁶¹

The system of privilege being, according to him, definitively dead, Montalembert again called upon Catholics to accept modern society with sincerity. The desire to return to the *Ancien Régime* was judged not only illusory but also dangerous for religion because, in modern societies, 'the mere appearance of a too intimate alliance of the Church with the throne is enough to compromise and weaken her'.⁶²

The main difference between the Mechelen speeches and the work *Des intérêts catholiques au XIXᵉ siècle* was the way in which Montalembert now considered democracy. The term had indeed lost the clearly pejorative connotation it had under his pen in 1852. The Count now defined democracy simply as 'political equality' and 'the abolition of all privileges and constraints with regard to religion, that is, the freedom of worship'.⁶³ If he accepted it as inevitable, Montalembert nevertheless pointed out the dangers that accompanied the consolidation of democracy. According to him, only Catholicism could help to overcome them:

> The natural affinities of democracy, on the one hand, with despotism,⁶⁴ on the other, with the revolutionary spirit, is the great lesson of history and the great threat

of the future. Constantly tossed between these two abysses, modern democracy is painfully seeking its footing and its moral balance. It will only succeed with the help of religion.[65]

Montalembert denounced in particular the growing centralization which offered to the State a power and new spaces of intervention, like education and charity.[66] This situation was analysed as a threat to the future, because the strengthening of the State risked leading to a tyranny much stronger than those of the past. Taking his inspiration from the German theologian Ignaz von Döllinger – who himself took up an idea already expressed by the Spaniard Juan Donoso Cortes in his *Speech on Dictatorship* (1849)[67] –, he said:

> The unitary despotism of the Roman Empire was much less threatening to the freedom of the soul and of the Christian faith than would be the absolutism of the modern State: these first Caesars knew neither censorship, nor police, nor official education, nor bureaucracy, nor telegraphy, nor railroads, nor gendarmerie, nor any of the infinite resources that civilization puts at the service of tyranny.[68]

According to Montalembert, this situation made the existence of a Church independent of the State all the more necessary. Catholicism was presented as a counterweight to the dangers engendered by the strengthening of the powers of the State. Drawing partial inspiration from Tocqueville, whom he quoted elsewhere, he thus affirmed:

> The more one is a democrat, the more one should be a Christian; for the fervent and practical worship of God made man is the indispensable counterweight to this perpetual tendency of democracy to constitute the worship of man believing himself God.[69]

Religion was thus presented as a means of counterbalancing the overwhelming force of the State, by inspiring moral strength in the citizen.

3 The second speech of Mechelen (21 August 1863)

In his second speech, Montalembert dealt more particularly with the freedom of worship. Carefully, he made sure distinguish on this subject 'dogmatic intolerance' and 'civil tolerance'. The freedom of worship was thus above all described as a means for the Church to free itself a little more from the political power. It was thus turned not against the pretensions of the Church but against those of the State.

The count specified moreover his conception of the relations between Church and State, which was not that of an absolute separation:

> The reciprocal independence of Church and State, which is the great law of modern societies, in no way entails their absolute separation, still less their reciprocal hostility. (Assent.) This absolute separation is not at all an essential condition of religious or public freedom. On the contrary, it can very well be combined with

an appalling oppression. We saw this clearly during the French Revolution. ... The Church and the State can and even must agree to reconcile their respective interests, to give to society as well as to the individual such advantages, such rights as this agreement alone can guarantee. There is a possible, legitimate, often necessary alliance between the two, which can and must be serious and lasting, but for which their mutual independence, their autonomy is the sovereign condition. ... This alliance can include concessions as well as reciprocal commitments.[70]

Clarifying his thoughts a few weeks after his speeches, he would also say that his formula 'A free church in a free state' had already been applied in England, in the United States, but also in Austria, since the country had experienced a liberal regeneration.[71]

The speeches of Mechelen were the last great interventions of Montalembert in public life. His opponents reported them to Rome, hoping a condemnation by the papacy. A consultor of the Holy Office, the barnabite Bilio, was thus charged to give his opinion on these speeches.[72] His highly critical work can be seen as a reflection of the position of the Curia and the Pope on the issue of freedom of conscience.[73] Bilio pointed out that the two main errors that Catholics should guard against with regard to the relationship between Church and State were the subordination of the Church to the State and their separation. He noted that Montalembert had distinguished himself by fighting the first of these errors, both in the past and in his two speeches at Mechelen. But, according to the Roman prelate, the count did not distance himself frankly enough from the second.

If no official condemnation was carried against the speeches of Mechelen, Pius IX charged his secretary of State, the cardinal Antonelli, to write a private letter to the count to make known his disapproval[74] and, one year later, in December 1864, the publication of the *Syllabus* could be interpreted as an implicit condemnation of the Mechelen speeches. Disavowed by the papacy, the Count chose to remain silent. From 1865 onwards, he was afflicted by illness, which led him to withdraw from public debate until his death in 1870[75].

Conclusion

Regarding the relations between Church and State, Montalembert's ideal was thus that of a 'reciprocal independence'. He never called for an absolute separation, such as would exist in France after 1905 – and for good reason: this perspective was hardly defensible for a Catholic in the middle of the nineteenth century since it had been condemned by the papacy in 1832. Montalembert thus never questioned the Concordat of 1801: like the Papacy, he only denounced the Organic Articles, which Napoleon Bonaparte had added unilaterally and which allowed the State to exercise increased surveillance over the Church.

Montalembert's conception of the relationship between the Church and the State was based on a historical imagination which, paradoxically, he shared in good part with intransigent Catholics, but to draw opposite conclusions. In the tradition of Joseph de Maistre, he described the Middle Ages as a kind of golden age of the Church, allowed by freedom. Conversely, the *Ancien Régime* was denounced as the era of Gallicanism, during which the absolute monarchy had tried to subjugate the Church of France by distancing it from the papacy.

From this vision of history, Montalembert drew the idea that, in the nineteenth century, only common liberties could allow the Church to prosper, while a regime of privileges made it dependent on the arbitrariness of the rulers, in addition to distancing it from the people. The Count was reinforced in this idea by his analysis of the revolutions of the first part of the century: anticlerical in 1830, whereas the Restoration had surrounded the Church with its benefits, favourable to religion in 1848, whereas the July monarchy had been suspicious of the Church. Montalembert thus rejected as dangerous the will of his intransigent Catholic adversaries to see established in France an authoritarian regime which, while having suppressed the common liberties, would grant the Church a certain number of privileges. On the whole, his ideas, which ran counter to the intransigent stiffening of European Catholicism at that time, remained largely in the minority during his lifetime. However, they had a substantial influence in the following century.[76]

Notes

1 Sylvain Milbach, 'Catholicisme intransigeant et catholicisme libéral au XIXe siècle', in *Histoire du christianisme en France*, ed. Alain Tallon and Catherine Vincent (Paris: A. Colin, 2014), 341–60.

2 Eugène Veuillot and François Veuillot, *Louis Veuillot*, 4 vols. (Paris: V. Retaux and Lethielleux, 1899–1913); Pierre Pierrard, *Louis Veuillot* (Paris: Beauchesne, 1998); Arthur Hérisson, 'Louis Veuillot, *L'Univers* et l'intervention des laïcs dans les affaires de l'Église de France au milieu du XIXe siècle', *Revue d'histoire de l'Église de France* 100, no. 245 (2014): 333–54. In English: James F. McMillan, 'Rediscovering Louis Veuillot: The Politics of Religious Identity in Nineteenth-Century France', in *Visions/Revisions: Essays on Nineteenth-Century French Culture*, ed. Nigel Harkness (Oxford: Peter Lang, 2004), 305–22.

3 On the pontificate of Pius IX: Roger Aubert, *Le Pontificat de Pie IX (1846–1878)* (Paris: Bloud & Gay, 1952); Giacomo Martina, *Pio IX*, 3 vols. (Roma: Pontificia università gregoriana, 1974–90).

4 Sylvain Milbach, *Lamennais (1782–1854)* (Rennes: Presses universitaires de Rennes, 2021). In English, reference can be made to: Richard Allen Lebrun and Sylvain Milbach, eds., *Lamennais, a Believer's Revolutionary Politics* (Leiden: Brill, 2018).

5 Marie-Joseph Le Guillou and Louis Le Guillou, eds., *La Condamnation de Lamennais* (Paris: Beauchesne, 1982).

6 On Montalembert, the most important works are: Édouard Lecanuet, *Montalembert*, 3 vols. (Paris: C. Poussielgue, 1895–1902); Antoine de Meaux and Eugène de Montalembert, eds., *Charles de Montalembert. L'Église, la politique, la liberté* (Paris: CNRS Éditions, 2012); *Montalembert et ses contemporains* (Paris: les Éd. du Cerf, 2012); Manuela Ceretta and Mario Tesini, eds., *Montalembert pensatore europeo* (Rome: Studium, 2013).

7 Sylvain Milbach, *Les chaires ennemies. L'Église, l'État et la liberté d'enseignement secondaire dans la France des notables (1830–1850)* (Paris: Honoré Champion, 2015).

8   Within *L'Avenir*, it was Lacordaire and Lamennais rather than Montalembert who dealt with the question of the relationship between Church and State. The Count was much more interested in external issues, and in particular the fate of oppressed Catholic nations.
9   Milbach, *Les chaires ennemies*, 272.
10 'La raison principale et permanente de l'irréligion publique en France, se trouve dans l'éducation actuelle de la jeunesse, telle que l'État en a constitué le monopole. L'ensemble des institutions d'instruction publique, qui forme l'Université de France, et au dehors duquel un despotisme usurpé ne laisse rien surgir, voilà le foyer où se forme et s'entretient cet esprit public qui en fait de religion n'est rien et ne croit à rien'. The translations from the French are the author's. Charles Forbes de Montalembert, *Du devoir des catholiques dans la question de la liberté d'enseignement* (Paris: l'Univers, 1843), 14–15.
11 Montalembert, *Du devoir des catholiques*, 24.
12 'fortifier par tous les moyens légitimes l'empire purement moral de la Religion sur les individus et sur les familles qui la professent encore'. Montalembert, *Du devoir des catholiques*, 17–18.
13 Montalembert, *Du devoir des catholiques*, 18.
14 'L'Etat n'a pas le droit, sous peine de violer la constitution qui est la condition même de son existence, d'imposer à tous les citoyens un système d'éducation qui compromet le maintien de la croyance religieuse au sein de leurs familles. De ce que l'État n'a point de religion, il n'en résulte point pour lui la faculté d'empêcher les citoyens d'en avoir. Bien loin de là, la Charte non-seulement promet la liberté d'enseignement, mais elle garantit solennellement la liberté religieuse: cette liberté en ce qui touche à une religion positive comme le catholicisme, n'est plus qu'une dérision, si en vertu d'une série de dispositions extralégales [...] le pouvoir exécutif se trouve investi du droit exclusif de façonner les croyances et les moeurs de l'enfance'. Montalembert, *Du devoir des catholiques*, 19.
15 Emiel Lamberts, *The Struggle with Leviathan. Social Responses to the Omnipotence of the State, 1815–1965* (Leuven: Leuven University Press, 2016).
16 'car même sous les gouvernements les plus despotiques, il y a des Universités surveillées par l'État; mais nulle part elles ne sont l'État même; nulle part l'État ne s'est fait directement maître d'école'. Montalembert, *Du devoir des catholiques*, 24.
17 'L'Université [...] représente surtout et elle sert merveilleusement cette tendance de l'Etat à tout ployer sous l'implacable niveau d'une stérile uniformité. C'est par elle que ce nouveau despotisme, qui menace le monde, tend à se substituer à l'Eglise et à la famille, ces deux foyers sacrés de la liberté morale du genre humain'. Montalembert, *Du devoir des catholiques*, 32.
18 Milbach, *Les chaires ennemies*, 276.
19 Carolina Armenteros, *The French Idea of History: Joseph de Maistre and His Heirs, 1794–1854* (Ithaca: Cornell University Press, 2011).
20 'système belge qui sauve la religion par la liberté'. Montalembert, *Du devoir des catholiques*, 75.
21 Jean-Marie Mayeur, 'Quelques rencontres entre les catholiques français et les catholiques belges', *Le Mouvement Social*, no. 178 (1997): 27–35.
22 Vincent Viaene, *Belgium and the Holy See from Gregory XVI to Pius IX (1831–1859). Catholic Revival, Society and Politics in 19th Century Europe* (Leuven: Leuven University Press, 2001).

23 Roger Aubert, 'Montalembert et Adolphe Dechamps. Contribution à l'histoire des relations de Montalembert avec la Belgique', *Revue d'histoire de l'Église de France* 56, no. 156 (1970): 91–113.
24 Montalembert, *Du devoir des catholiques*, 38.
25 Montalembert, *Du devoir des catholiques*, 70.
26 Benoît Agnès, *L'appel au pouvoir. Les pétitions aux parlements en France et au Royaume-Uni (1814–1848)* (Rennes: Presses universitaires de Rennes, 2018).
27 Laurent Colantonio, 'Daniel O'Connell. Un Irlandais au cœur du débat politique français, des dernières années de la Restauration à la Deuxième République' (Doctoral thesis, France, Université de Paris VIII, 2001).
28 Jacqueline Lalouette, 'Les catholiques libéraux français et l'idée de séparation des Églises et de l'État au XIXe siècle', in *Charles de Montalembert. L'Église, la politique, la liberté*, ed. Antoine de Meaux and Eugène de Montalembert (Paris: CNRS Éditions, 2019), 115–43.
29 Charles Forbes de Montalembert, *Discours sur la question de la liberté de l'Église dans la discussion du projet de loi sur les fonds secrets* (Paris: Sagnier et Bray, 1844), 29–31.
30 Guillaume Cuchet and Sylvain Milbach, 'The Great Fear of 1852', *French History* 26, no. 3 (2012): 297–324.
31 Luca Sandoni, '"Un coup d'État de Dieu". Approches catholiques du 2 décembre 1851, entre théologie et politique', *Revue d'histoire de l'Église de France* 103, no. 2 (2017): 247–70.
32 Édouard Lecanuet, *Montalembert*, III: 46–51.
33 'le catholicisme devait paraître aux sages du monde un cadavre qu'il ne restait plus qu'à enterrer'. Charles Forbes de Montalembert, *Des Intérêts catholiques au XIXe siècle* (Paris: J. Lecoffre, 1852), 9.
34 'un demi-siècle s'écoule, et tout est transformé. Partout la religion a repris sa place, au premier rang; partout l'Église est reconnue comme une puissance du premier ordre'. Montalembert, *Des intérêts catholiques*, 10.
35 Montalembert, *Des intérêts catholiques*, 66–8.
36 'Que l'on compare sa situation en 1830 avec celle qu'elle a prise sans effort en 1848, au sortir d'un règne auquel elle avait été presque toujours condamnée à résister; qu'on la compare avec celle qu'elle a gardée en 1852, après quatre années de luttes continuelles contre les périls de l'anarchie. Ce n'est donc ni l'empire, ni la restauration; ce n'est ni la protection, ni la sympathie du pouvoir qui lui ont valu la force qu'elle possède aujourd'hui, le mieux relatif que chacun ressent, le progrès manifeste qui chaque jour se révèle. Qu'est-ce donc? Il faut le dire: c'est la liberté, rien que la liberté, et la lutte rendue possible par la liberté. La même cause a produit partout le même effet. Il suffit de citer l'Angleterre et O'Connell, la Belgique et sa constitution, la Hollande et l'Allemagne tout entière'. Montalembert, *Des intérêts catholiques*, 68.
37 'Je n'entends professer ici aucune théorie absolue, universelle, exclusivement applicable à tous les siècles et à tous les peuples. Je prétends seulement que, chez la plupart des peuples chrétiens, et dans l'état actuel du monde, la liberté est un bien, un bien relatif, non absolu'. Montalembert, *Des intérêts catholiques*, 70.
38 Among other things, the encyclical condemned several modern freedoms, including the 'pestilential error' (*pestilentissimo errori*) that everyone should be guaranteed freedom of conscience. It also called on princes to support the Church.
39 'la liberté réglée, contenue, ordonnée, tempérée, la liberté *honnête et modérée* [...]; la liberté qui, bien loin d'être hostile à l'autorité, ne peut coexister qu'avec elle, mais dont la disparition fait aussitôt dégénérer l'autorité en despotisme'. Montalembert, *Des intérêts catholiques*, 70.

40 Montalembert, *Des intérêts catholiques*, 74.
41 About the myth of medieval *cristianitas*: Giovanni Miccoli, 'Chiesa e società in Italia fra Ottocento e Novecento: il mito della cristianità', in *Fra mito della cristianità e secolarizzazione. Studi sul rapporto chiesa – società nell'età contemporanea* (Casale Monferrato: Marietti, 1985), 21–92; Daniele Menozzi, 'Tra riforma e restaurazione. Dalla crisi della società cristiana al mito della cristianità medievale (1758–1848)', in *Storia d'Italia, Annali 9, La Chiesa e il potere politico dal Medioevo all'età contemporanea*, ed. Giorgio Chittolini and Giovanni Miccoli (Turin: Giulio Einaudi Editore, 1986), 767–806.
42 'ce grand niveleur, ce précurseur tout-puissant de la démocratie, [...] le plus redoutable adversaire de l'autorité du saint-siège et de l'indépendance de l'Église'. Montalembert, *Des intérêts catholiques*, 139–40.
43 'pouvoir illimité de l'homme sur l'homme, que ce pouvoir soit exercé par un seul ou par la multitude, au nom d'une dynastie inamovible ou au nom du peuple souverain'. Montalembert, *Des intérêts catholiques*, 71–2.
44 Montalembert, *Des intérêts catholiques*, 82–3.
45 'Il n'y a rien de commun que le nom entre cette liberté réclamée par les catholiques et celle qui sert de masque à la démocratie et à la révolution. J'ai dit ailleurs combien la liberté était incompatible avec l'esprit démocratique et révolutionnaire. [...] Dès que la démocratie l'emporte, on peut l'annoncer avec certitude, c'en est fait de la liberté. [...] Au fond, la démocratie est incompatible avec la liberté, parce qu'elle a pour base l'envie sous le nom d'égalité, tandis que la liberté, par sa nature même, proteste sans cesse contre le niveau tyrannique et brutal de l'égalité. Pour se maintenir, la démocratie condamne tout ce qui veut vivre et agir à abdiquer toute valeur personnelle, et à se plonger en adoration servile devant le fantôme de la raison et de la vertu des masses. Elle détruit ainsi logiquement et graduellement, non-seulement toutes les traditions, tous les droits anciens et héréditaires, mais encore toute indépendance, toute dignité et toute résistance'. Montalembert, *Des intérêts catholiques*, 77–9.
46 Montalembert, *Des intérêts catholiques*, 72.
47 Montalembert, *Des intérêts catholiques*, 80–1.
48 'De tous les gouvernements, celui qui a toujours exposé l'Église aux plus grands dangers a été le gouvernement absolu. Peu importe que ce soit l'absolutisme de la foule ou l'absolutisme d'un seul. Un pouvoir sans frein, sans contrôle, c'est-à-dire un pouvoir omnipotent, est nécessairement redoutable à l'Église, par cela seul qu'il peut tout; parce que l'omnipotence constitue une tentation trop forte pour l'infirmité humaine; parce que celui qui peut tout, veut tout [...]. Même en s'alliant à l'Église avant de commencer la lutte inévitable, le pouvoir absolu ne peut lui donner que des faveurs et du repos, des honneurs et des privilèges; mais il ne lui donnera jamais ni droits ni forces.' Montalembert, *Des intérêts catholiques*, 91–2.
49 'dans l'état actuel des moeurs et des institutions de l'Europe, [comme] la seule forme possible de la liberté politique'. Montalembert, *Des intérêts catholiques*, 110.
50 'Partout où la servitude de l'Eglise existe ou a existé, elle a été l'oeuvre du pouvoir absolu. Nulle part, dans notre siècle, elle n'a été produite par le gouvernement parlementaire. Ce dernier régime n'a pas brisé partout les chaînes de l'Église, il s'en faut. Il les a brisées toutefois en France, en Angleterre et en Belgique; c'est déjà quelque chose. Et partout ailleurs il a fourni aux catholiques les moyens [...] de préparer leur émancipation future. Sous le gouvernement parlementaire, l'Eglise ne domine pas dans l'ordre politique, et je pense que cette domination n'est ni dans ses voeux ni dans

son intérêt; mais elle a ce qui vaut mille fois mieux que le pouvoir, elle a des droits. Sous le pouvoir absolu, elle n'a rien, hormis ce qui lui est concédé par le bon plaisir du moment. Elle n'a pour appui que le bras séculier, qui le plus souvent se retire au moment où elle y compte le plus, ou ne se lève que pour la frapper. Toute l'histoire moderne est là pour le démontrer'. Montalembert, *Des intérêts catholiques*, 149–50.

51   *L'Univers*, 6, 13, 18 et 19 November 1852.

52   'Je trouve qu'on oublie beaucoup trop que toutes les libertés garanties à l'Église par ce traité, et d'autres beaucoup plus étendues ont été assurées au Catholicisme, il y a vingt-cinq ans, par la Constitution Belge. Je crains que la censure exercée par les ecclésiastiques et le monopole de l'enseignement confié aux évêques ne provoque contre la religion une formidable réaction, même dans les États Allemands de l'Autriche'. Letter to Cesare Cantù, reproduced in: Francesca Kaucisvili Melzi d'Eril, ed., *Carteggio Montalembert-Cantù (1842–1868)* (Milan: Editrice Vita e Pensiero, 1969), 127.

53   Like Montalembert, a large proportion of French liberal Catholics were sympathetic to the cause of the temporal power of the papacy. Cf. Arthur Hérisson, 'Défendre Pie IX mais s'opposer à Veuillot. Les catholiques libéraux face à la question romaine', in *Les forces de la modération. Ligne politique ou accommodements raisonnés dans les crises politico-religieuses européennes (XVIᵉ–XIXᵉ siècles)*, ed. Olivier Andurand and Albane Pialoux (Bruxelles: Peter Lang, 2020), 293–310.

54   'La séparation des deux pouvoirs serait un piège pour le pouvoir spirituel, toujours désarmé, et dont la liberté ne repose que sur la foi d'une parole qui peut changer et sous la main d'une force qui peut frapper, si le chef suprême de ce pouvoir spirituel n'était pas absolument et pleinement indépendant. Or, le plus haut degré de l'indépendance ici-bas, c'est la souveraineté. La sagesse des hommes, l'expérience des temps et la main de Dieu se sont unies depuis mille ans pour assurer au premier Pontife de la véritable Église le rang de roi, et, dans son domaine, ces deux pouvoirs sont confondus, afin qu'ils puissent être divisés partout ailleurs [...]. La souveraineté pontificale, exception unique et distincte sur ce seul point des autres pouvoirs de la terre, est la conséquence de la séparation des pouvoirs, bien loin d'en être la contradiction'. Charles Forbes de Montalembert, *L'Église libre dans l'État libre. Discours prononcés au Congrès catholique de Malines* (Paris: Ch. Douniol et Didier et Cie, 1863), 102–3.

55   Charles Forbes de Montalembert, *Lettre à M. le Comte de Cavour* (Paris: C. Douniol, 1860).

56   Speech of 27 March 1861 before the Chamber of Deputies.

57   On this issue: Arthur Hérisson, 'Les catholiques français face à l'unification italienne (1856–1871). Une mobilisation internationale de masse entre politique et religion' (Doctoral thesis, Paris, Université Paris 1 Panthéon-Sorbonne, 2018). A publication of this doctoral thesis is planned for spring 2022 by the Publications de l'École française de Rome.

58   Roger Aubert, 'L'intervention de Montalembert au Congrès de Malines en 1863', *Collectanea Mechliniensia* 35 (1950): 525–51.

59   Montalembert, *L'Église libre dans l'État libre*, 6.

60   Montalembert, *L'Église libre dans l'État libre*, 130–1.

61   'Il n'existe plus un seul pays au monde, où l'Eglise puisse faire fond sur la protection exclusive d'un pouvoir quelconque. Toutes les tentatives faites pour consolider ou renouer l'antique alliance de l'autel et du trône sur la base de l'emploi du pouvoir

coactif contre les adversaires de l'Eglise, ont misérablement échoué'. Montalembert, *L'Église libre dans l'État libre*, 26.
62 'la simple apparence d'une alliance trop intime de l'Eglise avec le trône suffit pour la compromettre et l'affaiblir'. Montalembert, *L'Église libre dans l'État libre*, 29.
63 Montalembert, *L'Église libre dans l'État libre*, 22.
64 It was Napoleon III in particular that Montalembert was aiming at.
65 'Les affinités naturelles de la démocratie, d'un côté, avec le despotisme, de l'autre, avec l'esprit révolutionnaire, sont la grande leçon de l'histoire et la grande menace de l'avenir. Sans cesse ballottée entre ces deux abîmes, la démocratie moderne cherche péniblement son assiette et son équilibre moral. Elle n'y arrivera qu'avec le concours de la religion'. Montalembert, *L'Église libre dans l'État libre*, 18.
66 Montalembert, *L'Église libre dans l'État libre*, 41–2.
67 Arthur Hérisson, 'Catholicisme intransigeant, progrès technique et modernité politique au milieu du XIXe siècle. La dystopie d'un "monde sans le pape" chez Juan Donoso Cortès et Louis Veuillot', *Le XIXe siècle au futur. Penser, représenter, rêver l'avenir au XIXe siècle. Actes du VIIe Congrès de la SERD*(2018) (online publication, https://serd.hypotheses.org/files/2018/08/He%CC%81risson_Congres-SERD_XIXe-siecle-au-futur.pdf). It may be thought that Montalembert quoted Döllinger in Mechelen rather than Donoso Cortès, whose writings he was familiar with, because the latter had been closer to Veuillot's ideas at the end of his life than to his own, and that it would therefore have been awkward to refer to him in a speech defending a liberal programme.
68 'Le despotisme unitaire de l'empire romain était bien moins menaçant pour la liberté de l'âme et de la foi chrétienne que ne le serait l'absolutisme de l'Etat moderne: ces premiers Césars ne connaissaient ni la censure, ni la police, ni l'enseignement officiel, ni la bureaucratie, ni la télégraphie, ni les chemins de fer, ni la gendarmerie, ni aucune des ressources infinies que la civilisation met au service de la tyrannie'. Montalembert, *L'Église libre dans l'État libre*, 50.
69 'Plus on est démocrate, plus il faudrait être chrétien; car le culte fervent et pratique du Dieu fait homme est le contrepoids indispensable de cette tendance perpétuelle de la démocratie à constituer le culte de l'homme se croyant Dieu.' Montalembert, *L'Église libre dans l'État libre*, 55.
70 'L'indépendance réciproque de l'Église et de l'État, qui est la grande loi des sociétés modernes, n'entraîne nullement leur séparation absolue, encore moins leur hostilité réciproque. (Assentiment.) Cette séparation absolue n'est pas du tout une condition essentielle de la liberté religieuse ou publique. Tout au contraire, elle peut très-bien se combiner avec une effroyable oppression. On l'a bien vu sous la Révolution française. [...] L'Eglise et l'État peuvent et même doivent s'entendre pour concilier leurs intérêts respectifs, pour donner à la société comme à l'individu tels avantages, tels droits que cette entente peut seule garantir. Il y a entre l'une et l'autre une alliance possible, légitime, souvent nécessaire, qui peut et doit être sérieuse et durable, mais dont leur indépendance mutuelle, leur autonomie est la condition souveraine. [...] Cette alliance peut comporter des concessions comme des engagements réciproques'. Montalembert, *L'Église libre dans l'État libre*, 142–4.
71 Montalembert, *L'Église libre dans l'État libre*, 187. Contrary to what he had written to Cesare Cantù eight years earlier, Montalembert said that he saw in the Austrian concordat an admirable act, which, with the exception of two or three clauses which had not been applied, contained nothing incompatible with freedom of worship.

72 Giacomo Martina, 'Verso il *Sillabo*. Il parere del barnabita Bilio sul discorso di Montalembert a Malines nell'agosto 1863', *Archivum Historiae Pontificiae* 36 (1998): 137–81.
73 Giacomo Martina, *Pio IX (1851–1866)* (Rome: Pontificia università gregoriana, 1985), 322.
74 Lecanuet, *Montalembert*, III: 373–4.
75 André Latreille, 'Les dernières années de Montalembert', *Revue d'histoire de l'Église de France* 54, no. 153 (1968): 281–314.
76 On the influence of Montalembert's thought in France and Italy in the twentieth century: Ceretta and Tesini, *Montalembert pensatore europeo*.

J. H. Newman facing the spirit of the day: A focus on the idea of education in the Victorian context

Maud Besnard
Institut Catholique de Rennes

Introduction

Even though the English liberal spirit may go back to the Reformation which challenged clerical authority and promoted free thinking in sciences, the European liberal movement truly started with the French Revolution with a new credo defending popular sovereignty, equality of man and freedom of thought. Liberalism found its roots in the respect for dignity and worth of the individual and even went so far as to recognize private judgement or opinion as a fundamental right. By 1831, John Stuart Mill[1] stated that from now on, the common man was free to rely on his own method of thinking, reasoning and judging facts. He was to become his own authority. Of course, this new paradigm which put man at the centre of any intellectual, philosophical and political considerations had dramatic consequences on the questioning of traditional institutional issues such as law, education, morals in society. In the field of education, historical and political forces were at work to offer a new set of values remoulding the relation between knowledge and man.

I Education and moral virtue

One of the most edifying examples of this new paradigm was Robert Peel's *Inaugural Address to the New Library and Reading Room in Tamworth on 19 January 1841*. As soon as the 1820s, libraries were spreading out in England as a means to support popular education. They were often associated with the Mechanics' Institutes founded mostly in main industrial cities such as Glasgow, London or Manchester. By 1850, there were 600 Institutes in England, most of them included libraries. The development of libraries, both public and private, was part of a main political objective: the spreading of knowledge and the intellectual improvement of the population. Peel, the deputy of Tamworth and President of the newly founded library, was convinced that offering 'rational recreation' (i.e. the reading of books) to the male and female population of his district would be a source of intellectual pleasure and comfort. In the 1840s, Robert Peel was more of a liberal conservative who made his own the theory that the diffusion of knowledge moderated human passions which otherwise may lead to deviant behaviour such as alcoholism, gambling, domestic violence or criminal offences, the main evils of Victorian society.

The chief figure who worked towards the extension of knowledge in society was Lord Henry Brougham, the Whig political man. As soon as 1825, Lord Brougham in his 'Practical Observations Upon the Education of the People' championed the democratization of knowledge in society especially among the working classes. In 1826, his Society for the Diffusion of Useful Knowledge founded in London followed the same educational pursuit by publishing cheap scientific books and periodicals for those who did not get formal school teaching. His educational doctrine rested upon three main arguments – the fact that acquiring knowledge would help people improve their working skills, encourage them to make scientific discoveries by themselves and offer them peaceful recreation and relaxing intellectual leisure.

If Peel was supportive of this egalitarian approach of education, he was also convinced that the diffusion of knowledge would arouse the moral conduct of each individual. In fact, the main argument Peel defended in his speech rested on the idea that the more knowledge and information the common man would get the more virtuous he would become. The inherent relation between profane knowledge and moral progress was a major cornerstone of Peel's liberal conception of education when he declared to his audience that being 'accustomed to such contemplations' (i.e. profane knowledge), the common man 'would feel the moral dignity of his nature exalted'[2] as though only intellectual nourishment would logically maintain and emphasize the innate goodness in human nature. The exercise of reason itself would necessarily engender a higher spiritual life. Peel was indeed convinced that secular knowledge (i.e. mainly physical science) was to become a new form of religion, a leading principle which would directly connect man to God.[3] Thus Peel stated that the study of science would lead to 'more enlarged conceptions of God's providence and a higher reverence for His name'.[4] Peel was obviously a man of his time, ready to challenge Christian religion as a source of true knowledge. Lord Brougham himself as Rector of Glasgow University (1825) had earlier declared in his inaugural speech that religion was similar to mere idiosyncrasies and individual accidents, hence it should be ranked as a mere sentiment. Religious liberalism was indeed the doctrine sustaining that all religious creeds were only matters of private opinion or personal sentiments therefore escaping any form of rational knowledge.

Most of the Christian world was more and more receptive to the liberal spirit of the age. In the mid-nineteenth century, the Broad Church movement was representative of the religious liberalism which impregnated a part of Victorian society. Broad Churchmen challenged religious dogma and accepted that religious matters be an object of investigation. The spirit of tolerance they were showing was contrasting with the more conservative Anglo-Catholicism of the High Church, the other branch of Anglicanism. The High Churchmen firmly relied on the ecclesiastical and apostolic tradition and were hostile to any form of liberalism in religion, hence defending the Scriptures as the exclusive moral guidance of human conduct.

John Henry Newman, the High Church Anglican priest who converted to Catholicism in 1845, had already denounced in his Anglican sermons (1825–43) what he considered the great evil of the time, that is to say, the doctrine making believe that the growth of moral virtue was inherently linked to the intellectual improvement, then marginalizing or desacralizing the Scriptures as a mere pleasant reading activity. 'The religion of the day'[5] as he defined it in one of his *Parochial and Plain Sermons* was a quest for novelty and change eventually bringing endless dissatisfaction to the human mind and soul. Newman accused the 'religion of the day' or what he also called the 'religion of civilization' of being a mere imitation of true Christianism that suited a civilized and refined period of time like the nineteenth century. To him, liberal education[6] was favouring this new type of false religion producing refined and well-taught men he would describe as being 'polished in their manners, kind from natural disposition or a feeling of propriety. Thus their religion is based upon self and the world, a mere *civilization*'.[7] He even went so far as to herald the 'gentleman' as the archetype of the civilized world in his treaty of education, *The Idea of a University* (1873). The Newmanian gentleman[8] was a refined cultivated mind who mixed up the wiseness of knowledge with the virtue of religious duty by considering that virtue was nothing more than the graceful in conduct that literature and poetry brought to him. Therefore, Newman insisted on the fact that liberal education made not the Christian nor the Catholic but the gentleman, a mere civilized man. He rightly denounced the common idea that education would be the *organon* of moral and religious virtue, criticizing at the same time the tendency to replace Christian conscience with a moral sense detached from divine authority. Hence, the 'religion of civilization' would be a mere humanist form of religion based on human reasoning and not on Christian dogma. For Newman, the churchman, the only true agent of an internal moral transformation of the self – a true moral conversion – was Christianism experienced in sacred places, not at school nor even in libraries.

The Newman/Peel doctrinal differences lie in the finality they granted to education. Newman sustained that intellectual improvement by the exercise of reasoning faculties leads each individual to progressive advances to the fullness of his original destiny. If the cultivation of the mind is a necessary help towards the realization of the self, it has not the power to elevate one's moral virtuousness. The moral improvement of society will be effective by the spiritual cultivation of the individuals: their obedience to divine authority, their practice of ecclesiastical rituals, their reverence towards the Bible. As for Peel, he was truly convinced that popular education focusing on exclusive logical reasoning thanks to the promotion of scientific books would necessarily lead to the elevation of the moral standards of society and eventually lead to its spiritual wellbeing.

II Education: a mechanistic vs organic conception of knowledge

By the 1830s, many acute observers warned on the slow breaking down of the traditional order. John Stuart Mill in his essay 'The Spirit of the Age' had already questioned the new liberal paradigm in process, putting forward the idea that the Victorian period was first and foremost a period of transition between an old decaying society based on a medieval structure and a new regenerating present and future hence stating that

> Mankind are [sic] divided into those who are still what they were and those who have changed: into men of the present age, and the men of the past. To the former, the spirit of the age is a subject of exultation; to the latter, of terror. [...] The nineteenth century will be known to posterity as the era of one of the greatest revolutions of which history has preserved the remembrance, in the human mind, and in the whole constitution of human society.⁹

Mill took over the German *Zeitgeist* or 'spirit of the day' in English language to describe the new system of ideas and values deeply modifying the political discourse and the societal and cultural practice. The Victorians had indeed a clear conscience of the transitional era which occurred between a past which was almost forgotten and a future which remained to be defined: 'Mankind have [sic] outgrown old institutions and old doctrines, and have not yet acquired new ones.'¹⁰ In his essay 'Sartor Resartus', Thomas Carlyle announced that the period was favourable to a true reconstruction of thought, letting behind the old beliefs and welcoming the new ones. Doubtless John Stuart Mill, Thomas Carlyle, Thomas Macaulay and others all felt the radical change which was already in the atmosphere and which had already been theorized by the pioneer of the usefulness, Jeremy Bentham, in *An Introduction to the Principles of Morals and Legislation* (1780).

The concept of Utilitarianism would become the new philosophical and moral paradigm in trend in the Victorian bourgeoisie. We may underline two main radical changes in the mode of thinking over the individual and society in Benthamite theory: first the reification or rationalization of the individual in society hence the following predominant issue of being useful (human functionality) which would lead to the rationalization of the modes of instruction: the Mechanics' Institutes for manual workers; the workhouses for people with disabilities, orphans and poor people; or the civic universities for scientific and technical workforces in industrial cities. The real-world skills taught in these types of institutions were becoming prevalent over the traditional liberal arts medieval universities (Oxford and Cambridge) taught to the aristocratic gentlemen. The rationalization of instruction partook of a common aim, that is to say, giving a useful meaning to life as though religion was no longer sufficient to give people a meaning to their own existence. The second radical change that Utilitarianism brought was the arithmetic/quantitative relation between the general interest and the moral principle of pleasure. In his 'Tamworth Speech', Peel clearly stated that knowledge that books were offering in the various facilities established in the country (libraries, reading room, clubs, ...) would be a source of appeasement for the mind and soul as though the educational process was above all an external process based on a mechanistic reaction of human behaviour (the reaction of desire and pleasure) when facing a certain amount of knowledge. By removing from the equation the individual conscience, man's very nature as a human being in quest for his well-being and personal development was progressively denied.

When John Walter, the chief editor of *The Times*, invited Newman to reply to Peel's Tamworth speech, the latter published a series of seven letters under the pseudonym 'Catholicus' one month later, in February 1841. In doing so, he highlighted and strengthened the sharp division between the traditional God-centred vision of society and the anthropo-centred paradigm in process. In his letters, Newman reasserted that the cultivation of the mind required a long-time effort which would eventually lead to a deep internal change of the self, hence deploring the corruption of its true meaning at the time:

> What in one form or other is the chief error of the day, in very distinct schools of opinion, – that our true excellence comes not from within, but from without; not wrought out through personal struggles and sufferings, but following upon a passive exposure to influences over which we have no control. They will countenance the theory that diversion is the instrument of improvement, and excitement the condition of right action.[11]

In his works and more particularly in *The Idea of a University*, J. H. Newman had the opportunity to denounce the mechanistic philosophical habit of mind and relied on the traditional arguments which had always prevailed in society, that is to say, a Christian conception of man as a whole and complex person who could not be reduced to a mere reasoning animal or a mere receptacle of information. According to Newman, the law of progress was grounded on the implementation of our incomplete and imperfect nature by means of the acquisition of knowledge and he was convinced that a true liberal education or the teaching of liberal arts should have no other finality than to cultivate the mind and to be a means for the man to achieve full development. 'True culture' as he said was the process of developing our natural dispositions or character. The cultivation of the mind was a mental development, an enlargement of the intellect. It was the living process of connecting all knowledge in order for the man to have a connected view of things and of the world.

> True enlargement of the mind is the power of viewing many things at once as one whole, of referring them severally to their true place in the universal system, of understanding their respective values, and determining their mutual dependence.[12]

Newman's organic conception of culture was in contradiction with the mechanistic view of knowledge which mostly spread out over the period of the Enlightenment and throughout the nineteenth century. Culture was then conceived as a quantitative and passive acquirement of knowledge. In his discourse 6, 'Knowledge viewed in Relation to Knowledge', Newman deplored that

> All things now are to be learned at once, not first one thing, then another, not one well, but many badly. Learning is to be without exertion, without attention, without toil; without grounding, without advance, without finishing. There is to be nothing individual in it; and this, forsooth, is the wonder of the age. What

the steam engine does with matter, the printing press is to do with mind; it is to act mechanically, and the population is to be passively, almost unconsciously enlightened, by the mere multiplication and dissemination of volumes.[13]

Newman strongly condemned the idea which would consist in believing that knowledge would exist independently from the human mind and be digested and assimilated without the active part of the individual. The transmission of facts is only the first step of the process of acquisition: the human intellect has to sieve through knowledge in order to hold possession of it wholly. Thus it implies that the cultivation of the mind is an inward faculty which should be trained through the teaching of Humanities. To Newman, liberal education granted the full training of the intellect since it stimulated all our intellectual faculties (reasoning, contemplation, imagination and creativity) and in doing so knowledge 'exerts a subtle influence in throwing us back on ourselves, and making us our own center, and our minds the measure of all things'.[14]

But Newman also warned that this inward movement must not be reduced to a mere contemplation of the self with the danger of leaning towards selfishness and egoism; it must rather be a transitional step towards an outward movement of the self in order to be connected with the Other, i.e. our Creator. This twofold movement (the inward and outward movement) was part of what Newman defined as the realization of the self. In Newman's terminology, 'to realize oneself' is to take into account the individuality of the man as an intelligible substance; it is to know oneself better and go deep into one's own interiority. In his work *An Essay on Aid of a Grammar of Assent*, Newman said about the process of realization that

> Man begins with nothing realized (to use the word), and he has to make capital for himself by the exercise of those faculties which are his natural inheritance. Thus he gradually advances to the fullness of his original destiny. Nor is this progress mechanical, nor is it of necessity; it is committed to the personal efforts of each individual of the species; each of us has the prerogative of completing his inchoate and rudimental nature, and of developing his own perfection out of the living elements with which his mind began to be. It is his gift to be the creator of his own sufficiency; and to be emphatically self-made. This is the law of his being, which he cannot escape; and whatever is involved in that law he is bound, or rather he is carried on, to fulfil.[15]

III Mixed education or the process of secularization in society: a case study

Peel's liberal spirit was equal to his search for social cohesion and unity by means of popular education and self-education. Indeed, he was truly convinced that secular knowledge, i.e. scientific knowledge, would become the new founding principle of society thanks to its diffusion in various institutional and non-institutional places. Meanwhile he considered that 'religion' was necessarily a factor of social divisions and inequality hence the trend towards the invisibility of all religious doctrines from places of education. In England, the University College London was the most representative of this liberality in education. Its cofounder, Henry Brougham, argued that religious instruction weakened the faculty of reasoning and imbued the mind with superstitious ideas. Peel was convinced that the removal of any dogmatic religious knowledge would go with the removal of diverging doctrinal opinions and would eventually lead to social harmony since there would be no longer room for any divergence or debate over the subject of religion what he called 'partisanship' in his Tamworth speech. Before his audience, he promised that 'in the selection of subjects for public lectures everything calculated to excite religious or political animosity shall be excluded' and he concluded by saying that he has 'laid the foundation of an edifice in which men of all political opinions and of all religious feelings may unite in furtherance of Knowledge, without the asperities of "party feeling"'.[16]

The quest for social unity was partly built on the unwillingness to offend any particular religious denominations and on the excessive confidence and exaltation in human knowledge to the point of weakening in the minds of men that reverence for the authority of divine truth. Profane knowledge was becoming a substitute for Christianism as a social bond. If educational reformers such as Lord Brougham supported this ideological trend, it was mainly because they regarded religion as a mere private opinion or personal feeling and certainly not as a branch of universal knowledge. Under Peel's government from 1841 to 1846, the exclusion of theology from the educational system was clearly acknowledged as a means to warrant religious equality.

Indeed, when he became prime minister, he took on the university education issue in Ireland where the catholic community was reluctant to study at Trinity College, the protestant university college founded by Elisabeth 1st in Dublin. On the 22nd of November 1844, he decided with his government to create non-confessional university colleges called the *Queen's Colleges* in the three major Irish cities: Cork, Galway and Belfast. Their main purpose was to welcome the Irish youth of any religious confession. As Colin Barr underlined: 'The idea was that students from all religious backgrounds would be educated together and religion itself would play no role in either the running of the college or its curriculum.'[17]

The removal of theology was then the condition of mixed education in the *Queen's Colleges*; religious instruction was optional and was taught outside the Colleges. The very day the bill on *Queen's Colleges* was introduced in the House of Commons in May 1845 by James Graham, the then State Secretary, Sir Robert Inglis, the conservative representative of Oxford University and a staunch defender of High Church views, declared before the Assembly the following: 'Nothing (...) was more calculated to promote such a Godless scheme of education, than the measure now before the House.'[18] In Ireland, Daniel O'Connell, in the name of the catholic clergy, denounced with strength the 'atheism' of the British government.

The catholic hierarchy itself was also divided on the issue of mixed education. At the time the British government was on relatively good terms with Rome and the moderate fringe of the Irish catholic hierarchy. Peel thought indeed that some of the Irish catholic bishops would support his plan of non-confessional establishments.

In fact, on the 21st of May 1845, the majority of the Irish bishops voted against the setting of mixed education in Ireland on the basis that it was 'dangerous to the faith and morals of the Catholic pupils'.[19] Nevertheless the unity of the Irish catholic hierarchy did not last very long. In June, Dr Murray, Archbishop of Dublin, was ready to make a couple of concessions with Peel's government. After a compromise was set between the government and Dr Murray, *The Queen's Colleges Act* was passed on the 31st of July 1845 in Parliament. The three *Queen's Colleges* were then gathered under the name *Queen's University of Ireland* by a royal charter on the 3rd of September 1850, allowing their students to graduate in art, medicine and law.

As the secularization of Western thinking was underway in Europe, the Roman Catholic Church counterattacked and defended Christianism as a founding principle of all European nations. On the 3rd of October 1846, Pius IX officially condemned the non-confessional establishments (*The Queen's Colleges*). The Rescripts of the Propaganda Congregation, published on the 9th of October 1847 and on the 11th of October 1848, confirmed this condemnation and recommended that a catholic university be built in Ireland.

The protection of the Roman Catholic ethos was indeed the main finality that Pius IX and his representative in Ireland, Dr Cullen, wished to assign to this new university. At stake was the protection of the catholic faith and values from the flourishing anti-Christian philosophies spreading over Europe as Pius IX had clearly stated it a few years before in his Encyclical *Qui Pluribus*[20] on faith and religion. It was obvious that the new Catholic University of Ireland which would open in Dublin in 1854 was held as the paragon of catholic moral values and a welcoming educational place not only for the Catholics of Ireland but also for the Catholics of Europe.

It is worth underlining that the *Queen's Colleges* and the Catholic University of Ireland both founded on the Irish soil were the paragon of the tensions between two conceptions of society respectively defended by two institutions: the State and the Church. On the one hand, education became a political object under Peel's government and as such was submitted to the influence of public opinion and thinkers. The spirit of the day was obviously oriented towards social concerns, how to reduce social differences in society and enhance people's well-being Developing new models of education was part of a seeming egalitarian process mainly based on the attempt to erase or at least to soften conflicting opinions in society in order to guarantee social unity and cohesion. Religion was no longer considered as a social moderator but rather as a conflict accelerator according to liberal thinkers and as such the invisibility of the religious matter in the field of education started with the foundation of non-confessional establishments whose priority was to answer the social and economic needs of industrialization. On the other hand, the Church had always assigned a moral purpose to education, that is to say, the obedience to Christian values and their implementation in society as a way to maintain social order. When Pius IX officially launched the creation of the Catholic University in Dublin in 1851, he wished that it would become the representative of the Holy Sea in the British Empire by welcoming the Catholic English-speaking gentry and middle class and at the same time by responding to the movement of secularization which had already started to impregnate Western thought.

IV The gentleman: the archetype of the culture of imagination

Throughout the nineteenth century, liberal thought tended to consider classical education as belonging to the ancient world. The measure of all branches of knowledge was their level of utility in the industrial society and many Victorian figures did not hesitate to repudiate the liberal arts publicly. For instance, James Anthony Froude, the newly appointed rector of St Andrews in Scotland, deplored the devotion granted to subjects which had no practical end in life:

> History, poetry, logic, moral philosophy, classical literature, are excellent as ornament. If you care for such things, they may be the amusement of your leisure hereafter, but they will not help you to stand on your feet and walk alone (...). You cannot learn everything (...), and the only reasonable guide to choice in such matters is utility.[21]

Beyond their criticism of the teaching of Greek and Latin, those in favour of a more practical and professional education put into question the status of the liberal arts. The seven liberal arts which took root in the Greek Antiquity were classified into two distinct groups of studies. The *Trivium* included the literary studies: grammar/rhetoric and dialectic and the *Quadrivium* included the scientific studies: arithmetic/astronomy/geometry/music. Both the *Trivium* and *Quadrivium* constituted the fundamental knowledge taught in the medieval universities throughout Europe.

For those in favour of the culture of action, the liberal arts only helped people get good manners and erudition whereas vocational and practical education was at the service of a true economic and political finality. Practical education was promoted to diminish social inequalities in the Victorian society and to endow a fairer treatment between all people. On the contrary, the Humanities or liberal arts mostly taught in Oxford and Cambridge were associated with the privileges of the gentlemen issued from the English aristocracy.

However other major thinkers and observers of Victorian society were eager to defend the culture of imagination or the culture of humanism which was according to them the true culture necessary to form the mind properly.

In his manifesto against Victorian anti-intellectualism *Culture and Anarchy. An Essay in Political and Social Criticism*, Matthew Arnold restored the important status of the culture of the mind in contrast with what he called the 'philistinism' of the bourgeois society or middle class who depreciate the intelligence of both the artist and the philosopher. The Philistine embodies thoughtless action and business spirit in Arnold's thought. For him, true culture means the study of perfection:

> The whole scope of the essay is to recommend culture as the great help out of our present difficulties; culture being a pursuit of our total perfection by means of getting to know, on all the matters which most concern us, the best which has been thought and said in the world, and, through this knowledge, turning a stream of fresh and free thought upon our stock notions and habits, which we now follow staunchly but mechanically.[22]

Beyond his idealist vision of culture, Arnold contributed to defend what David J. DeLaura called 'a humanist conscience of history'.[23] It is precisely a Hellenistic type of humanism that Arnold celebrated in his successive works. Hellenism was not only a fundamental element of the intellectual life, it was also a cultural standard which Europe followed from Antiquity onwards. For Matthew Arnold, the Greek culture was the best shield against the outrageous and dehumanizing industrialization of his time. The aristocracy, the middle class and the lower classes which he called respectively the Barbarians, the Philistines and the Populace in *Culture and Anarchy* promoted the culture of trade and business or what he called 'Hebraism'. The humanist function of society could be restored on the condition that Hellenist culture be promoted for it embodied the culture of sentiment and thought which had the power according to Arnold to teach: 'dignity, the love of the things of the mind, the flexibility, the spiritual moderation'.[24]

In *The Idea of a University*, Newman also defended the Greek and Roman heritage, that is to say, liberal knowledge embodied in the figure of the 'gentleman' he depicted in his treaty on education. The 'gentleman' in Newman's conception of culture is a refined man possessing a large knowledge on every field of study: 'A habit of mind is formed which lasts through life, of which the attributes are, freedom, equitableness, calmness, moderation, and wisdom.'[25] The gentleman is the fruit of a long tradition of humanism. The 'gentleman' in Newman's terminology is the heir of the *kalos kagathos* of the Greek Antiquity. In her work entitled *J.H. Newman on the Nature of the Mind. Reason in Religion, Science, and the Humanities*, Jane Rupert makes an analogy between the Newmanian gentleman and the Greek archetype of liberal education:

> Newman refers to the Greek model of the gentleman represented in the term *kalos*, beautiful, and *agathos*, noble or good. (…) *kalokagathia*, or gentleman, had come to refer not to social rank but to the ranks of the speculative and imaginative minds that were to make the Athenians the educators and 'civilizers' not of Greece only, but of the European world.[26]

But the culture of humanism Newman defended was also a culture of language. In a way, his idea of culture was close to the romantic anthropology whose dogma was based on the idea that man was essentially formed by language. Newman viewed human culture as a historical development of the *logos* which not only grew within man but also constituted the genius of a people, the spirit of a nation. Newman emphasized this twofold articulation of culture thanks to what seemed to him the most emblematic, the science of words. The science of words (literature, poetry, grammar, translation) offers a large panel of expressions, phrases, aphorisms which crystallize a specific mode of thought and way of life and are witness to the complexity and the richness of the language and culture of humanity. Faced with the culture of facts whose language was deprived of any imagery substance and which led to a sterilization of any human significations, Newman wished to focus on the humanist dimension of culture by defending the idea that all forms of knowledge communicated and were in communion altogether thanks to the reciprocity of their significations. Such was the case for literature, poetry or the fine arts. Newman dedicated a large part of his thought to the literary culture and to its influence on human development. Literature is indeed both personal since it is the expression of a personal thinking, and public since it sounds out the opinion of the day in view of uniting people together. Literature conveys a certain idea of man for its aim is to translate and express the truth about the self.[27] If Western literary works contribute to convey a model of humanity since they tend to depict the psychology of the European peoples, their authors/writers themselves tend to mould the language thanks to their personal style of writing. In short, literature moulds as much as it interprets humanity according to the defenders of a humanist culture.

Conclusion

Facing the liberal intellectual forces at work in the Victorian era, J. H. Newman staunchly defended both the Christian heritage and the medieval culture of humanity which had been the pillar of Western thought. As the traditional institutional authority was breaking down, Newman's *Idea of a University* was reasserting the legitimacy of Christian fundamental thinking in education by defending the teaching of universal knowledge, both profane and religious, against the progressive specialization of the sciences which may lead to exaggerating the rationalization of human reason. But at the same time he refused to confound education and religion, intellectual training and moral formation while the frontier between Christian culture and the culture of civilization was becoming porous. It is finally worth noting that *The Idea* has been the object of acute studies by twentieth- and twenty-first-century critical thinkers in an attempt to reassess Newman's thought and its influence in the Christian and post-Christian world.

Notes

1   John Stuart Mill, *Mill: The Spirit of the Age* (1831), *On Liberty* (1859), *The Subjection of Women* (1869), Selected and Edited by Alan Ryan (Oxford: A Norton Critical Edition, 1997).
2   Robert Peel, *Inaugural Address, Delivered by the Righ Hon. Sir Robert Peel, Bart.MP., President of the Tamworth Library and Reading Room, on Tuesday, 19 January 1841*, 2nd edn (London: James Bain, 1841), 26.
3   On this issue, Robert Peel made reference to Davy Humphry's reflections in his speech: 'His mind should always be awake to devotional feeling; and in contemplating the variety and the beauty of the external world, and developing its scientific wonders, he will always refer to that infinite wisdom, through whose beneficence he is permitted to enjoy knowledge; in becoming wiser, he will become better; he will rise at once in the scale of intellectual and moral existence – his increased sagacity will be subservient to a more exalted faith, and in proportion as the veil becomes thinner, through which he sees the causes of things, he will admire more the brightness of the Divine light, by which they are rendered visible.' Peel, *Inaugural Address*, 28.

4   Ibid., 26.
5   'What is the world's religion now? It has taken the brighter side of the Gospel, – its tidings of comfort, its precepts of love; all darker, deeper views of man's condition and prospects being comparatively forgotten. This is the religion *natural* to a civilized age, and well has Satan dressed and completed it into an idol of the Truth. As the reason is cultivated, the taste formed, the affections and sentiments refined, a general decency and grace will of course spread over the face of society, quite independently of the influence of Revelation. That beauty and delicacy of thought, which is so attractive in books, then extends to the conduct of life, to all we have, all we do, all we are. Our manners are courteous; we avoid giving pain or offence; our words become correct; our relative duties are carefully performed. Our sense of propriety shows itself even in our domestic arrangements, in the embellishments of our houses, in our amusements, and so also in our religions profession. Vice now becomes unseemly and hideous to the imagination, or, as it is sometimes familiarly said, "out of taste." Thus elegance is gradually made the test and standard of virtue, which is no longer thought to possess an intrinsic claim on our hearts, or to exist, *further than* it leads to the quiet and comfort of others. Conscience is no longer recognized as an independent arbiter of actions, its authority is explained away; partly it is superseded in the minds of men by the so-called moral sense, which is regarded merely as the love of the beautiful; partly by the rule of expediency, which is forthwith substituted for it in the details of conduct. Now conscience is a stern, gloomy principle; it tells us of guilt and of prospective punishment. Accordingly, when its terrors disappear, then disappear also, in the creed of the day, those fearful images of Divine wrath with which the Scriptures abound. They are explained away. Every thing is bright and cheerful. Religion is pleasant and easy; benevolence is the chief virtue; intolerance, bigotry, excess of zeal, are the first of sins. Austerity is an absurdity; – even firmness is looked on with an unfriendly, suspicious eye. On the other hand, all open profligacy is discountenanced; drunkenness is accounted a disgrace; cursing and swearing are vulgarities. Moreover, to a cultivated mind, which recreates itself in the varieties of literature and knowledge, and is interested in the ever-accumulating discoveries of science, and the ever-fresh accessions of information, political or otherwise, from foreign countries, religion will commonly seem to be dull, from want of novelty. Hence excitements are eagerly sought out and rewarded. New objects in religion, new systems and plans, new doctrines, new preachers, are necessary to satisfy that craving which the so-called spread of knowledge has created. The mind becomes morbidly sensitive and fastidious; dissatisfied with things as they are, desirous of a change *as such*, as if alteration must of itself be a relief.' John Henry Newman, 'The Religion of the Day', in *Parochial and Plain Sermons*, vol.1, sermon 24 (London: Rivingtons, [1834] 1870), 311–12.
6   A liberal education refers to the teaching of the seven liberal arts dating back to the Antiquity and Medieval Ages. The liberal arts comprise three literary subjects: rhetoric, grammar and dialectic and four scientific subjects: arithmetic, geometry, astronomy and music.
7   Newman, *Paroch. Sermons*, vol. 1, sermon 3, 'Knowledge of God's Will'.
8   'The true gentleman in like manner carefully avoids whatever may cause a jar or a jolt in the minds of those with whom he is cast; – all clashing of opinion, or collision of feeling, all restraint, or suspicion, or gloom, or resentment […]. He respects piety and devotion; he even supports institutions as venerable, beautiful, or useful, to which he does not assent; he honours the ministers of religion, and it contents him to

decline its mysteries without assailing or denouncing them. He is a friend of religious toleration, and that not only because his philosophy has taught him to look on all forms of faith with an impartial eye, but also from the gentleness and effeminacy of feeling, which is the attendant on civilization.' John Henry Newman, *The Idea of a University* (Oxford: Clarendon Press, [1873]1976), 179-80.

9 John Stuart Mill, *Mill: The Spirit of the Age, On Liberty, The Subjection of Women*, Selected and Edited by Alan Ryan (Oxford: A Norton Critical Edition,1997), 3.
10 Ibid., 5.
11 John Henry Newman, *Discussions and Arguments on Various Subjects* (London: Basil Montagu Pickering, 1872), 266.
12 Newman, *The Idea*, 122-3.
13 Ibid., 127.
14 Ibid., 186.
15 John Henry Newman, *An Essay on Aid of a Grammar of Assent* (London: Longmans, Green and Co., [1870] 1917), 349.
16 Newman, *Discussions*, 283.
17 Colin Barr, *Paul Cullen, John Henry Newman, and the Catholic University of Ireland 1845-1865* (Notre Dame: University of Notre Dame Press, 2003), 30.
18 'Academical Institutions in Ireland', Hansard, 9 May 1845, vol. 80.
19 Barr, *Paul Cullen*, 31.
20 'Each of you has noticed, venerable brothers, that a very bitter and fearsome war against the Catholic commonwealth is being stirred up by men bound together in a lawless alliance. These men do not preserve sound doctrine, but turn their hearing from the truth. They eagerly attempt to produce from their darkness all sorts of prodigious beliefs, and then to magnify them with all their strength, and to publish them and spread them among ordinary people ... In order to easily mislead the people into making errors, deceiving particularly the imprudent and the inexperienced, they pretend that they alone know the ways to prosperity. They claim for themselves without hesitation the name "philosophers". They feel as if philosophy, which is wholly concerned with the search for truth in nature, ought to reject those truths which God Himself, the supreme and merciful creator of nature, has deigned to make plain to men a special gift ... these enemies never stop invoking the power and excellence of human reason; they raise it up against the most holy faith of Christ, and they blather with great foolhardiness that this faith is opposed to human reason.' Pie IX, *Qui Pluribus*, 9 November 1846.
21 James Anthony Froude, *Inaugural Address Delivered to the University of St Andrews*, 19 March 1869.
22 Matthew Arnold, *Culture and Anarchy. An Essay in Political and Social Criticism* (London: Smith, Elder and Co., 1869), 5.
23 David J. DeLaura, 'Pater and Newman: The Road to the Nineties', *Victorian Studies* 10, no. 1 (1966): 40.
24 Matthew Arnold, *Schools and Universities on the Continent* (London: MacMillan and Co., 1868), 265.
25 Newman, *The Idea*, 96.
26 Jane Rupert, *J.H. Newman on the Nature of the Mind. Reason in Religion, Science, and the Humanities* (Lanham: Lexington Books, 2011), 73.
27 Jean Honoré, *La Pensée de J.H. Newman. Une Introduction* (Paris: Ad Solem, 2010).

Conclusion: Contested faith or contested liberty? – Contexts and strategies of liberal Catholicism

Peter Schröder
University College London (UCL), UK

The existing scholarship on Liberal Catholicism is far from coherent and consistent.[1] This is presumably not that surprising, given that the term itself was contested from its very inception in the nineteenth century. It emerged during the controversial thinking about the relation between the Catholic creed and the French Revolution. Coined by those who used Liberal Catholicism as a self-referential concept to denote the positive relationship between Catholicism and emerging bourgeois liberal thinking, Liberal Catholicism was equally used in a derogatory fashion by those who intended to turn back the results of the post-revolutionary period. Liberal Catholicism is thus not a neutral concept but a contested combat term in the political field. The general perception of Catholicism, in particular in the political domain of the nineteenth century, is not that nuanced. Catholicism is often simply perceived as traditional and conservative, if not as reactionary and counter-revolutionary.[2] It is the considerable merit of this volume to provide a much more discerning picture, and to open the debate about Liberal Catholicism beyond the specialized scholarly studies and to put it on the research agenda of nineteenth-century political thought.[3]

During his long service as Pope from 1846 to 1878, Pius IX was in charge of formulating the Catholic position and response to the various challenges to the Catholic Church. The stiffening of the doctrinal position of the Holy See – most notoriously in the doctrine of papal infallibility[4] – was motivated by internal theological disputes *and* the perceived external threat to the Catholic Church. The looming unification of Italy was a concrete menace to the political power and independence of the Papacy, but the moral and political change throughout Europe and beyond was eventually of a much more far-reaching impact on the Catholic Church. In 1846, Pius IX pronounced his views of the social order in the encyclical letters *Qui Pluribus*, which give a taste of the increasingly intransigent Papal position:

> [A] very bitter and fearsome war against the Catholic commonwealth is being stirred up by men bound together in a lawless alliance. These men do not preserve sound doctrine, but turn their hearing from the truth. They eagerly attempt to produce from their darkness all sorts of prodigious beliefs, and then to magnify

them with all their strength, and to publish them and spread them among ordinary people.[5] Do we see here the Catholic defence against secularisation? Liberal Catholics needed to take the Papal position into account. However, was such a battle for or against secularisation and disenchantment of religious believes actually waged in the nineteenth century?

The very concept of secularization was invented in the nineteenth century as a polemical political term to push back on the influence of the church within society and politics.[6] What this term entails, however, is not particularly clear. This is because the

> various accounts of a process of secularisation are not themselves histories in the empirical sense. Rather, they constitute an array of competing theological and philosophical programs, each advancing what purports to be a history of secularisation, but only as a means of prosecuting various factional cultural-political agendas, some dedicated to secularism, others to sacralism.[7]

It is, therefore, crucial that we pay particular attention when and how we refer to the idea of secularization. Awareness of the conflicting and polemical use of the term is also key to appreciate the positioning of liberal Catholicism in the theological and political debates of the nineteenth century.[8] Moreover, even for a self-declared secular thinker[9] as, for instance, John Stuart Mill, religion remained an important component and moral basis for society in his theory of utilitarianism.[10]

Liberty and liberalism[11] were as contested as Catholicism in the nineteenth century and the different contexts and strategies of liberal Catholicism need to be unearthed to understand their original intention and position. As this volume demonstrates, it is equally important, not to perceive liberal Catholicism as one homogenous camp or movement. Indeed, there are competing strands. As, for instance, one of the chapters shows, the nineteenth-century historiography of liberal Catholicism deliberately repressed the brand of liberal-conservative ultramontanes[12] 'in the midst of the poisonous controversies of the 1860s'.[13] Many of the *dramatis personae* we encounter in this volume are not necessarily known to the non-specialist. As the studies in this volume demonstrate, many of them are situated in an important relationship to the various presumably more familiar main currents of nineteenth-century political thought. Benjamin Constant, John Stuart Mill, Matthew Arnold, Alexis de Tocqueville or Joseph de Maistre, to name but a few of the well-known political thinkers, are discussed in relation to the proponents of liberal Catholicism. The nine chapters in this volume thus offer new insights and discussion of the relationship between liberal Catholicism and 'classical' liberal and social thought, on the one hand, and liberal Catholicism with conservative political and social thought, on the other.[14]

The volume opens with a reassessment of the very notion of and relationship between Christianity and modernity by Bernard Bourdin. The understanding and evaluation of liberal Catholicism depend on understanding this relationship. Bourdin offers a revisionist interpretation of our understanding of modernity, which he does not simply want to juxtapose to Christianity. Relying on Hans Blumenberg's *Die Legitimität der Neuzeit*, and in particular, his interpretation of Ockham's nominalism,

Bourdin argues that the widely held interpretation that modernity is the fruit of the secularization of Christianity is a fundamental misunderstanding. On the contrary, he asserts that we should recognize that modernity is the fruit of a work of Christianity on itself.[15] The individual and the notion of individual freedom and equality, as well as the formation of the State and hence the relationship between individual and the State, are interpreted as a genesis of modernity which depends on its Christian heritage. Bourdin's interpretation briefly touches upon the seventeenth century, during which these criteria of individuality 'entered fully into their philosophical meaning to implement the autonomy of modern political rationality'.[16] Drawing briefly on Constant, he shows implicitly that liberal Catholicism was only a phase within this development and concludes instead with an explanation how the totalitarian regimes of National Socialism and Communism shook normative political modernity. However, Bourdin's wide-ranging analysis also situates liberal Catholicism within the wider European history of political thought.

Frédéric Libaud discusses the thought of John Henry Newman, a High Church Anglican priest who converted to Catholicism in 1845. He scrutinizes Newman's concern of religious relativism. This is the reason why Newman claimed that he 'resisted to the best of [his] powers the spirit of liberalism in religion'.[17] Libaud shows the limits liberalism necessarily had for a Catholic like Newman, as faith in God's revelation could not and should not be assessed by human reason. But should he be considered as an anti-liberal? Liberalism in religion denied the existence of absolute truth and in consequence thus denied the Catholic faith. The realm of Christian spirituality depended on the belief in God's revelation and Newman was not prepared to compromise this aspect of his faith in view of the secular political claims of liberalism. The ensuing tensions between the sphere of the political and the sacral can hardly be reconciled. Newman's writings reveal this tension. With Newman, we can see again, how in the nineteenth century the struggle for a new society was shaped by a dispute about the underlying fundamental values and the role religion should play in defining these.

The chapter by Aude Attuel-Hallade 'Edmund Burke, T.B. Macaulay, Lord Acton and the French Revolution: The Church, the State and the Individual' discusses these major political thinkers. The context-sensitive interpretation shows the influence of Burke on Macaulay and Acton and she highlights the similarities and differences between their positions. Attuel-Hallade's analysis demonstrates that Macaulay and Acton took different positions regarding the relationship between Church and State, despite their shared persuasion, that toleration of religious minorities was an essential principle and prerequisite for peaceful order and liberty alike. While Macaulay opted for an Erastian solution to the problem posed by the religious tensions and conflicts, Acton took the opposite direction. The former perceived the control of the Church by the State as the only solution and a precondition for peace and stability, whereas the latter held that the Church was the only force that could prevent abuse of the – potentially despotic – power of the modern state. At the heart of their concern in the political landscape of post-revolutionary modern societies was – once more – the exploration of the potential for reconciliation between Liberalism and Catholicism. However, Attuel-Hallade shows that there is another aspect to this debate. The perception of the individual changed profoundly with the French Revolution. The place and the role of the individual in civil society and history needed to be reassessed and redefined. Attuel-Hallade depicts the ensuing political tension and epistemological challenge, which arose from this new understanding of individual agency and independence. Most thinkers found it at best problematic to reduce their worldview to 'individual sovereignty'. If there was still acceptance that there existed a power above humans, what was the consequence on the place and role of the individual in civil society and history? Acton turned to this question. He thought that liberalism should be understood in a much wider framework. For him liberalism was more than a principle of government. It was also as a philosophy of history. Attuel-Hallade considers how Acton constructed this deliberation as a history of progress which provided a subtle reconciliation between the idea of an autonomous individual and his submission to a legitimate and divine authority. She analyses how this reconciliation between the individual and 'a world beyond' was taken up and redefined by Macaulay.

With a revisionist approach, Colm O'Siochru in the chapter, 'Liberties before Liberalism', studies the ultramontane political thought in England. O'Siochru demonstrates how in a troubled period of political turmoil and socio-economic upheaval, the first generation of ultramontanes advanced their position with the aim 'to convince England's liberals and conservatives alike, that the temporal power of the Catholic Church meant ordered liberty for Europe, and that the pope was the ultimate guarantor of both gothic freedoms and international peace'.[18] The challenges of modernity were not only felt by conservatives, and it would be misleading to subscribe to a Whig history of linear progress which had to overcome the impediment of backward-looking forces. The world of the nineteenth century, as much as our own, was and is much more complex than that. The example of the ultramontanes amply demonstrates how their critique of the challenges of modernity put the Catholic Church under considerable strain. The ultramontanes offered 'imaginative responses to the Church's myriad problems in this modern age, urging intellectual rigour and freedom, and an end to the anachronistic Constantinian ecclesiology still underpinning Catholic political thought'.[19] However, they encountered suspicion and criticism from Rome and the self-declared Catholic liberals alike.

Turning to the particular situation in Spain, Bernard Callebat studies the 'Historical and Ecclesiological Foundations of Spanish Catholic Liberalism'. He shows the influence of the Enlightenment and Jansenist thought on the Constitution of Cádiz of 1812. Although the constitution stipulated the Catholic confession of the State, it also introduced a 'slow and gradual process of secularity'.[20] This trajectory is illustrated by the fact that albeit a year later the infamous Inquisition promulgated in 1478 by Pope Sixtus IV was abolished. Once more, the argument is rightly made for a more nuanced picture to do justice to the complexity of Catholic liberalism. Callebat's analysis thus shows at the same time, how the plurality of critical and methodological positions within Catholic liberalism 'adds to the difficulties in identifying and defining it'.[21]

Francisco Javier Ramòn Solans analyses Catholic opposition in Spain to the liberal demands of religious freedom following the period after the constitution of Cádiz. He takes a new perspective and looks at the events of 1869 in the context of the Constituent Assembly. This chapter demonstrates how the liberals, many of whom still considered themselves as Christian, positioned themselves against the Catholics and thus alienated them from the new political arrangements rather than trying to integrate them into the new society. Circumstances in Spain were very different to the situation in France and Great Britain. However, Ramòn Solans' study shows that the debate we encountered with Newman was actually not that different from the positions held in Spain. The fundamental questions were the same, in particular regarding the vexed issue of freedom of worship. However, the positions of the Catholics in Spain were more intransigent, based on the idea of a Catholic definition of citizenship. It proved impossible to defend such an exclusive position, but the argument was made that any change of the concept of 'Catholic citizenship' was rather an abnormality and an exception. This demarcates a profound difference in comparison with the situation in France or Great Britain. The political discourse in Spain demonstrates that in view of the constitutional changes and the threat to the dominance of Catholicism, the Catholics embraced in a strategic move the language and practice of rights as well as the workings of parliamentary representation. In this regard, the rearguard action of the Catholics in Spain was not dissimilar from the strategies pursued by the Catholics in France and Great Britain.

In his case study, 'Sin, Grace and Secular History: Pierre Paul Royer-Collard's Criticism of the Anti-Sacrilege Law of 1825', Daniele Giuseppe Palmer shows that liberal Catholics should not be seen as one homogenous faction and did not follow a single political or theological agenda. Royer-Collard holds an original position, which was heavily influenced by Jansenism. It is important to reiterate that his criticism of the Anti-Sacrilege Law was informed by his theological convictions and was not meant to be a political stand. Palmer's comparative approach underscores the importance to 'take seriously the religious worlds these figures inhabited'.[22] A too narrow focus on the political field would not do justice to the sometimes sophisticated and often heated polemics on the Catholic side in post-revolutionary France.

The relationship between Church and State is at the heart of most debates between advocates of a secular State and those who argued for an active role of Catholicism in the State. The different approaches to find a place for the Catholicism of traditionalists and liberals within the Catholic Church are also brought to light in the chapter by Arthur Hérisson. He analyses the thought of Charles de Montalembert, who employed an interesting strategy to safeguard the Church's room for manoeuvre and influence within an increasingly heterogeneous society. Montalembert was a former disciple of Félicité de Lamennais and holds an important place within nineteenth-century liberal Catholicism. Montalembert argued for the independence of the Catholic Church, rather than trying to ally it with the State and curry favours and privileges from the State. This is a substantial reversal of the Gallican position and the Church's approach to access power during the *Ancien Régime*. At the same time, he warned of an absolute separation between Church and State, as this could equally lead to the suppression of the Church.[23] He presented the Catholic religion as a crucial palladium to counterbalance the increasingly far-reaching force of the State. The Church should find its place within the free and open organization of society. The Catholic creed inspired moral strength in the citizen and provided a counterweight to the encroachments of the State. The demand to break the monopoly of State education and to allow for Catholic education as well, independent of the structures of the State, was therefore one of the crucial demands. Hérisson rightly identifies Montalembert's original argumentation in the claim that only common liberties would allow the Church to prosper. A regime of privileges for the Church would make it dependent on the State and expose her to the arbitrariness of political rulers.[24] Montalembert rejected the intransigent hardening of European Catholicism of his time. However, his ideas remained largely in a minority position, before they gained significant influence and prominence in the next century.

The battle for education was also fought in the UK. In comparison to France, conditions were different in a country where the monarch was the head of the Anglican Church. Not only was the relationship between Church and State different, but more importantly for the context of this volume, Catholics were in a minority within the fabric of State and society.[25] To complicate matters further, Ireland was, however, a particular case within the political setting in the UK.[26]

In the concluding chapter of this volume Maud Besnard traces key aspects of this struggle in her contribution to this volume. She shows how Victorian society was receptive to a change in attitude. Even within the Anglican Church, this change was tangible. Broad Churchmen, one branch of Anglicanism, challenged religious dogma. They agreed that religious and theological matters could be subjected to critical study. Such an approach contrasted with the other branch of Anglicanism, the more conservative Anglo-Catholicism of the High Church. 'The High Churchmen firmly relied on the ecclesiastical and apostolic tradition and were hostile to any form of liberalism in religion, hence defended the Scriptures as the exclusive moral guidance of human conduct.'[27] Besnard shows how John Henry Newman fits into this debate about education. He challenged the belief that the development of moral virtue depended on intellectual improvement. He saw such an approach as dangerous. In Newman's view, it desacralized Holy Scripture and put it on a par with any random reading activity. Besnard shows how the question of education was key within the English debate of religion, politics and society. Newman's position contrasted sharply with that of Lord Henry Brougham, a Whig politician and co-founder of University College London in 1826, which was the first university in England that was indifferent to the religious beliefs of its staff and students. Brougham was a defender of religious liberalism, arguing that all religion was only a private matter. He maintained that religious instruction led to superstitious ideas and undermined the faculty of reasoning.

As this volume demonstrates in detailed case studies, Catholic liberalism does not define a specific political philosophy. It was rather a heterogeneous movement, which entailed different, sometimes competing, theological and ecclesiological positions, which in turn informed different intellectual and political attitudes. Catholic liberalism is difficult to determine as a whole. The prevailing importance and influence of religion in the nineteenth century should not be underestimated. Joseph de Maistre's assertion at the end of the eighteenth century that 'religion mingles in everything, animates and sustains everything,'[28] still had a valid point at the end of the nineteenth. Liberal Catholics sought new avenues to reconcile their faith with the emerging modern society, which was characterized by unseen economic dynamics and moral and religious scepticism, which fundamentally changed the social fabric. What was almost worse for them was that these new attitudes instrumentalized religion for moral and political thought,[29] which made it more difficult to preserve the original faith of the Catholic creed and to distinguish it from such an approach by preserving at the same time a liberal approach.

Notes

1. The early study by A. Leroy-Beaulieu, *Les Catholiques libéraux: l'Église et le libéralisme de 1830 à nos jours* (Paris, 1885) remains a valuable starting point. Recent pertinent studies with further references to the secondary literature include J. Darrell, ed., *Catholicism Contending with Modernity: Roman Catholic Modernism and Anti-Modernism in Historical Context* (Cambridge: Cambridge University Press, 2000) and E. Perreau-Saussine, *Catholicism and Democracy: An Essay in the History of Political Thought* (Princeton: Princeton, New Jersey, 2012).
2. See, E. Perreau-Saussine, 'French Catholic Political Thought from the Deconfessionalisation of the State to the Recognition of Religious Freedom', in *Religion and the Political Imagination*, ed. I. Katznelson and G. Stedman Jones (Cambridge: Cambridge University Press, 2010), 150–70. He traces the 'shift from a radical anti-liberalism to a certain type of liberalism' within the Catholic Church. Ibid., 150.
3. The impressive collection of essays on nineteenth-century political thought, for instance, does hardly discuss liberal Catholicism in the more than thousand pages of this volume. See in particular, 'Part IV: Secularity, Reform and Modernity', in *The Cambridge History of Nineteenth Century Political Thought*, ed. G. Stedman Jones/G. Clayes (Cambridge: Cambridge University Press, 2011), 603–933.
4. In 1869, Pius IX convoked the First Vatican Council, where among other issues the doctrine of papal infallibility was defined. This doctrine curtailed the role of the bishops to the advantage of the papacy. It was also a major challenge to the moderate position of the liberal Catholics. See the criticism by Gladstone of the dogmatically defined position of infallibility in his *The Vatican Decrees in Their Bearing to Civil Allegiance*. The actual text of the doctrine is accessible in the addenda to Gladstone's work. 'The Dogmatic Decrees of the Vatican Council concerning the Catholic Faith and the Church of Christ', in *The Vatican Decrees in Their Bearing to civil Allegiance*, ed. P. Schaff and W.E. Gladstone (New York, 1875), 167f.: 'the Roman Pontiff, when he speaks ex cathedra, that is, when in discharge of the office of pastor and doctor of all Christians, by virtue of his supreme Apostolic authority, he defines a doctrine regarding faith or morals to be held by the Church, by the divine assistance promised to him in blessed Peter, is possessed of that infallibility with which the divine Redeemer willed that his Church should be endowed for defining doctrine regarding faith or morals'.
5. Pius IX, Qui Pluribus, 9 November 1846. See the discussion by Maud Besnard in this volume.
6. See, H.W. Stratz and H. Zabel, 'Säkularisation, Säkularisierung', in *Geschichtliche Grundbegriffe: Historisches Lexikon zur politisch-sozialen Sprache in Deutschland*, ed. O. Brunner, W. Conze and R. Koselleck (Stuttgart: Klett-Cotta, 1984), vol. 5, 789–829 and I. Hunter, 'Secularization: the birth of a modern combat concept', *Modern Intellectual History* 12, no. 2 (2015) 'prior to the early 1800s nobody used the term "secularization" to refer to an epochal transition from a culture of religious belief

to one of rational autonomy'. Cf. also H. Blumenberg, *Die Legitimität der Neuzeit* (Frankfurt/Main: Suhrkamp, 1999), in particular part I, 9–134.

7   I. Hunter, 'Secularisation: Process, Program, and Historiography', *Intellectual History Review* 27, no. 8 (2017).

8   In his recent study, Robert Yelle also underscored this point from a different perspective. R.A. Yelle, *Sovereignty and the Sacred Secularism and the Political Economy of Religion* (Chicago: The University of Chicago Press, 2019), 71: 'genealogical excavation reinforces the challenge to modern secularism (…). If even Weber, the master of secularism, succumbed to latent theological biases, how can we be sure that we ourselves are free of similar biases?' On the general discussion regarding secularization in recent scholarship, see S.M. Dromi and S.D. Stabler, 'Good on Paper: Sociological Critique, Pragmatism, and Secularization Theory', *Theory and Society* 48 (2019): 325–50.

9   J.S. Mill, 'Autobiography', in *Collected Works of John Stuart Mill*, ed. J.M. Robson and J. Stillinger (Toronto: University of Toronto Press, 1981), vol. 1, 45: 'I am (…) one of the very few examples, in this country, of one who has, not thrown off religious belief, but never had it'.

10 See R. Carr, 'The Religious Thought of John Stuart Mill: A Study in Reluctant Scepticism', *Journal of the History of Ideas* 23 (1962): 475–95 and with references to further literature P. Schröder, '*Devoid of Faith, yet Terrified of Scepticism* – Die Bedeutung der Religion in John Stuart Mills politischer Theorie über Staat und Gesellschaft', in *Vom Nutzen des Staates. Das Staatsverständnis des klassischen Utilitarismus: Hume/Bentham/Mill*, ed. O. Asbach (Baden: Nomos, 2009), 229–46.

11 F. Lessay, 'Regards sur le libéralisme', *Commentaire* 6 (1979): 324: 'le libéralisme ne se laisse pas facilement appréhender, définir, "mettre à plat" pour les besoins de l'analyse historique ou philosophique'.

12 'The term "ultramontain" ("beyond the mountains" that is "beyond the Alps") was applied to those Catholics who maintained that the French Church was entirely subject to the authority of Rome'. E. Perreau-Saussine, 'French Catholic political thought', 153.

13 C. O'Siochru, 'Liberties before Liberalism: ultramontane political thought in England, c.1835–50' in this volume, 72–91.

14 For discussion of the relationship between religion and classical liberalism more generally, see N. Campagna, *Der klassische Liberalismus und die Gretchenfrage. Zum Verhältnis von Freiheit, Staat und Religion im klassischen politischen Liberalismus* (Stuttgart: Franz Steiner Verlag Wiesbaden GmbH, 2018) and L. Siedentop, *Inventing the Individual: The Origins of Western Liberalism* (London: Belknap Press, 2014).

15 Drawing on Blumenberg and Louis Dumont, Bourdin presents a sophisticated argument about the relationship between Christianity-modernity that relies on Ockham, and hence on a specific understanding of Christianity: 'To the notion of a hierarchical universal *ordo*, the Franciscan theologian opened the way to that of future political philosophies of the contract which only recognize individuals, free and equal by natural law and governed by a State (sovereign or executive power) wanted by themselves. The modern political concept of power is to Modernity ("modern ideology" [Dumont]) what the hierarchy was to Christianity before William of Ockham. Voluntarism and Ockhamist singularism are undeniably at the heart of the interpretative circle of Modernity by a certain type of Christianity'. B. Bourdin, 'Political modernity-Christianity: interpretative circles' in this volume, 11–27.

16 Ibid.

17 F. Libaud, 'John Henry Newman: an anti-liberal?', in this volume, 29–39.
18 C. O'Siochru, 'Liberties before Liberalism: ultramontane political thought in England, c.1835–50', in this volume, 72–91.
19 Ibid.
20 B. Callebat, 'Historical and ecclesiological foundations of Spanish Catholic liberalism. From the Jansenist imprint to the Constitution of Cádiz of 1812', in this volume, 93–109.
21 Ibid.
22 D. G. Palmer, 'Sin, Grace and Secular History: Pierre Paul Royer-Collard Criticism of the Anti-Sacrilege Law of 1825', in this volume, 129–147.
23 Cf. C.F. de Montalembert, *L'Église libre dans l'État libre. Discours prononcés au Congrès catholique de Malines* (Paris: C. Douniol et Didier, 1863), 143: 'Cette séparation absolue n'est pas du tout une condition essentielle de la liberté religieuse ou publique. Tout au contraire, elle peut très – bien se combiner avec une effroyable oppression'.
24 Cf. de Montalembert, *L'Église libre dans l'État libre*, 42: 'Ces symptômes du mal dont tous les peuples modernes sont atteints, éclatent sur tout dans les progrès constants et quotidiens de la centralisation, inventée par les princes pour faciliter le triomphe de toutes les révolutions, et qui, après avoir été le tombeau de la royauté du vieux droit, menace de devenir la prison, l'ergastule de la démocratie moderne'.
25 A.N. Wilson, *The Victorians* (London: Hutchinson, 2002) provides good overview of this period.
26 Besnard discusses the specific attempts by Prime Minister Peel to establish non-confessional university colleges in Ireland. She rightly points out that in October 1846 Pius IX officially condemned the non-confessional establishments in Ireland.
27 M. Besnard, 'J.H. Newman Facing the Spirit of the Day: A Focus on the Idea of Education in the Victorian Context' in this volume, 169–181.
28 J. de Maistre, *Considerations on France*, ed. R.A. Lebrun (Cambridge: Cambridge University Press, 1994), 42.
29 Again, Mill is a pertinent example for such a move. See J.S. Mill, 'Three Essays on Religion: Utility of Religion', in *Collected Works of John Stuart Mill*, ed. J.M. Robson and J. Stillinger (Toronto: The University of Toronto Press, 1969), 405: 'religion may be morally useful without being intellectually sustainable.'

Bibliography

Abellan, J.L. 'Del Barroco a la Ilustración (siglos XVII y XVIII)'. In *Historia crítica del pensamiento español*. Madrid: Espasa Calpe, 1988.
Acton, John Emerich (Lord). 'The Roman question'. *The Rambler*. January, 1860.
Acton, John Emerich (Lord) 'Cavour'. *Rambler* 5 July 1861, 141–65.
Acton, John Emerich (Lord) 'Nationality'. *HFR* 1 July 1862, 1–25.
Acton, John Emerich (Lord) 'Contemporary Literature'. *HFR* 2 January 1863, 278.
Acton, John Emerich (Lord) 'Ultramontanism'. *HFR* 3 July 1863, 162–206.
Acton, John Emerich (Lord) 'Conflicts with Rome'. 1864. In *Selected Writings of Lord Acton*, edited by J. Rufus Fears. Indianapolis: Liberty Fund, 1985–1988.
Acton, John Emerich (Lord). 'Döllinger on the Temporal power'. 1861. In *Selected Writings of Lord Acton*, edited by J. Rufus Fears. Indianapolis: Liberty Fund, 1985–1988.
Acton, John Emerich (Lord). 'Political thoughts on the Church'. 1859. In *Selected Writings of Lord Acton*, edited by J. Rufus Fears. Indianapolis: Liberty Fund, 1985–1988.
Acton, John Emerich (Lord). 'The Protestant Theory of Persecution'. 1862. In *Selected Writings of Lord Acton*, edited by J. Rufus Fears. Indianapolis: Liberty Fund, 1985–1988.
Acton, John Emerich (Lord). 'The Count of Montalembert'. 1858. In *Selected Writings of Lord Acton*, edited by J. Rufus Fears. Indianapolis: Liberty Fund, 1985–1988.
Acton, John Emerich (Lord). 'The History of Freedom in Antiquity'. 1877. In *Selected Writings of Lord Acton*, edited by J. Rufus Fears. Indianapolis: Liberty Fund, 1985–1988.
Acton, John Emerich (Lord). 'The History of Freedom in Christianity'. 1877. In *Selected Writings of Lord Acton*, edited by J. Rufus Fears. Indianapolis: Liberty Fund, 1985–1988.
Acton, John Emerich (Lord). *Lectures on the French Revolution*. 1895–1899. Edited by John Neville Figgis and Reginald Vere Laurence. London: Macmillan and Co, 1910.
Acton, John Emerich (Lord). 'Inaugural Lecture on the Study of History'. 1895. In *Lectures on Modern History*, edited by John Neville Figgis and Reginald Vere Laurence. London: McMillan and Co, 1906.
Acton, John Emerich (Lord). *Add MSS. 4869, 4948, Acton Papers*. Cambridge: Cambridge University Library. AEB Owen, *University Library, Cambridge, Summary Guide to Accessions of Manuscripts (other than medieval) since 1867*. Cambridge: Cambridge University Press, 1966.
Acton, John Emerich (Lord). 'Mr. Goldwin Smith's Irish History'. 1862. In *Selected Writings of Lord Acton*, edited by J. Rufus Fears. Indianapolis: Liberty Fund, 1985–1988.
Agnès, Benoît. *L'appel au pouvoir. Les pétitions aux parlements en France et au Royaume-Uni (1814–1848)*. Rennes: Presses universitaires de Rennes, 2018.
Alía Miranda, Francisco, and Antonio de Juan García, eds. *Centenario del Cardenal Monescillo (1897–1997)*. Cuenca: Ediciones de la Universidad de Castilla La Mancha, 1997.
Alonso, Gregorio. *La nación en capilla. Ciudadanía católica y cuestión religiosa en España, 1793–1874*. Granada: Comares, 2014.
Altholz, Josef. *The Liberal Catholic Movement in England: The 'Rambler' and Its Contributors, 1848–1864*. London: Burns & Oates, 1962.

Altholz, Josef, and John Powell. 'Gladstone, Lord Ripon, and the Vatican Decrees, 1874'. *Albion* 22, no. 3 (Autumn 1990): 449–59.

Anderson, M.L. 'Piety and Politics: Recent Work on German Catholicism'. *Journal of Modern History* 63, no. 4, (December 1991): 681–716.

Anderson, M.L. 'The Limits of Secularization: On the Problem of the Catholic Revival in Nineteenth-Century Germany'. *Historical Journal* 38 (September 1995): 647–70.

Andrés Gállego, José. 'Génesis de la acción católica española, 1868–1926'. *Ius canonicu* 13, no. 26 (1973): 369–404.

Andujar Castillo, F. 'La Corte y los militares en el siglo XVIII'. *Estudios: Revista de Historia Moderna* 27 (2001): 91–120;

Andujar Castillo, F. *Military poder elites: las guardias reales en el siglo XVIII*. In *La pluma, la mitra y la espada. Estudios de Historia institucional en la Edad Moderna*, edited by J.L. Castellano & ly, 65–94. Madrid: Marcial Pons, Editiones de Historia, 2000.

Anstey, T.C. 'Ozanam's *English Chancellors*'. *DR* 3 October 1837, 305–25.

Arenal, Concepción. 'La Sociedad de San Vicente de Paúl y la Revolución'. *La Voz de la Caridad*, 15 January and 1 February 1871.

Arendt, Hannah. *The Origins of Totalitarianism*. New York: Schocken Books, 2004.

Armenteros, Carolina. *The French Idea of History: Joseph de Maistre and His Heirs, 1794–1854*. Ithaca, NY: Cornell University Press, 2011.

Arnold, Matthew. 'The Function of Criticism at the Present Time'. *National Review* 19 (1864): 230–51.

Arnold, Matthew. *Schools and Universities on the Continent*. London: MacMillan and Co., 1868.

Arnold, Matthew. *Culture and Anarchy. An Essay in Political and Social Criticism*. London: Smith, Elder and Co., 1869.

Asociación de católicos en España. Noticia de su origen, organización, estado actual y gracias que le ha otorgado la Santa Sede, publicada por la Junta Superior de la misma. Madrid: Imprenta de la Compañía de Impresores y Libreros, 1878.

Aspden, Kester. *Fortress Church: The English Roman Catholic Bishops and Politics 1903–63*. Herefordshire: Gracewing, 2002.

Astorgano Abajo, A. 'La biblioteca jansenista del canónigo Mariano Lucas Garrido (1831), secretario de Meléndez Valdés'. *Dieciocho* 43 (2020): 103–36.

Astorgano Abajo, A.'Poesía y jansenismo en el Convento de los agustinos calzados de Salamanca en tiempos de Meléndez Valdés'. *Revista de Estudios Extremeños* LXXII, no. 1 (2016): 147–208.

Attuel-Hallade, Aude. *Thomas Babington Macaulay et la Révolution française. La pensée libérale whig en débat*. Paris: Michel Houdiard, 2018.

Aubert, Roger. *Le Pontificat de Pie IX (1846–1878)*. Paris: Bloud & Gay, 1952.

Aubert, Roger. 'L'intervention de Montalembert au Congrès de Malines en 1863'. *Collectanea Mechliniensia* 35 (1950): 525–51.

Aubert, Roger. 'Montalembert et Adolphe Dechamps. Contribution à l'histoire des relations de Montalembert avec la Belgique'. *Revue d'histoire de l'Église de France* 56, no. 156 (1970): 91–113.

Ayala Martinez, C. 'Política eclesiàstica de Alfonso X. El Rey y sus obispos'. *Alicante* IX (2014-2015): 41–105.

Ballanche, Pierre-Simon. *Ville des Expiations*. Paris: Hachette, 1907.

Barante (de), Propser, A. *La vie politique de M. Royer-Collard. Ses discours et ses écrits*. Paris: Didier et Cies, Libraires éditeurs, 1864.

Baridon, M. 'Lumières et Enlightenment. False parallel or true dynamic of the philosophical movement?'. *Dix-huit Siècle*, no. 10 (1978): 45–69.

Barmann, Lawrence. 'The Pope and the English Modernists'. *US Catholic Historian* 25 (Winter, 2007): 31–54.

Barney, C. 'La Nueva España in the crisis of 1808'. *Cuadernos de Historia del Derecho* 19 (2012): 49–63.

Barr, Colin. *Paul Cullen, John Henry Newman, and the Catholic University of Ireland 1845-1865*. Notre Dame: University of Notre Dame Press, 2003.

Barroche, Julien. 'Maurice Hauriou, juriste catholique ou libéral? *Revue française des idées politiques* 28, no. 2 (2008): 307–35.

Barry, William. 'Modern Society and the Sacred Heart'. *DR* 25 July 1875, 1–38.

Bauderot, Jean. 'Sécularisation et Laïcisation. Une trame décisive'. In *L'Histoire religieuse en France et en Espagne*, edited by B. Pellistrandi, 17–38. Madrid: Collection de la Casa de Velázquez, 2004.

Bauberot, Jean, and S. Mathieu. 'le Royaume-Uni: l'ébranlement du système de *Church and State*'. In *Religion, modernité et culture au Royaume-Uni et en France 1800-1914*. Paris: Editions du Seuil, 2002.

Baustert, Raymond. *Le Jansénisme et l'Europe. Actes du colloque international organisé à l'Université du Luxembourg les 8, 9 et 10 novembre 2007*, edited by R. Baustert. Tübingen: Narr, 2010.

Beauchesne. *Du Jansénisme au modernisme: la Bulle Auctorem fidei, 1794, pivot du magistère romain magisterium*, edited by J.B. Amadicu and S. Icard. Paris: Beauchesne, coll. 'Théologie historique', 2020.

Beaulieu, Anatole (de). *Les Catholiques libéraux: l'Église et le libéralisme de 1830 à nos jours*. Paris: Librairie Plon, 1885.

Beaumont, K. 'La place de la théologie dans un cursus universitaire selon l'Idée d'Université de John Henry Newman'. *Revue des sciences philosophiques et théologiques* 3, tome 92 (2008): 637–49.

Berranger, O (de). 'Conscience et infaillibilité dans l'*Apologia* de Newman'. *Nouvelle Revue Théologique* 129 (2007): 177–88.

Blas Martin, N. 'Un país más extranjero que la China: libros españoles en las librerías parisinas del siglo XVIII'. *Cuadernos de Ilustración y Romanticismo* 24 (2018): 388.

Blumenberg, Hans. *La Légitimité des temps modernes*. Paris: Nrf Editions, Gallimard, coll. 'Bibliothèque de philosophie', 1999.

Blumenberg, Hans. *Die Legitimität der Neuzeit*. Frankfurt/Main: Surhkamp Verlag, 1999.

Bodin, Jean. *Les Six livres de la République*, text revised by Christiane Frémont, Marie-Dominique Couzinet, Henri Rochais, Book I chap X. Paris: Fayard, 1986.

Boffa, Massimo. 'Contre-Révolution'. In *Dictionnaire critique de la Révolution française*, edited by F. Furet and M. Ozouf, 87–101. 1989. Paris: PUF, 2009.

Bossy, John. *The English Catholic Community, 1570-1850*. Darton: Longman and Todd, 1975.

Bourke, Richard. *Empire and Revolution. The Political Life of Edmund Burke*. Princeton NJ: Princeton University Press, 2017.

Boutry, Philippe. 'Une théologie de la visibilité: le projet *zelante* de resacralisation de, Rome et son échec (1832–1829). In *Cérémonial et rituel à Rome (XVIe-XIXe siécle)*, edited by M. Visceglia and C. Brice, 317–67. Rome: Ecole française de Rome, 1997.

Brown, Stewart Jay. 'The National Churches and the Union in Nineteenth-Century Britain and Ireland'. In *Bonds of Union. Practices and Representations of Political Union in the United Kingdom (18th-21st Centuries)*, edited by Isabelle Bour and Antoine Mioche. Tours: Presses Universitaires François-Rabelais, 2005.

Burke, Edmund. *Letter to the Chevalier de Rivarol*. 1 June 1791.

Burke, Edmund. *Reflections on the Revolution in France 1790*. Edited by J.G.A. Pocock. Indianapolis: Hackett Publishing Company, 1987.
Burke, Edmund. *Reflections on the Revolution in France 1790*. New Haven, CT: Yale University Press, 2003.
Busaall, J.B. *Le spectre du jacobinisme. L'expérience constitutionnelle française et le premier libéralisme espagnol*. Madrid: Collection of the Casa de Velázquez (56), 2012.
Butterfield, Herbert. *The Englishman and His History 1944*. Cambridge: Cambridge University Press, 1945.
Caffiero, Marina. *La politica della santità. Nascità di un culto nell-età dei Lumi*. Rome: Laterza, 1996.
Caffiero, Marina. 'La maestà del papa. Trasformazioni dei rituali del potere a roma tra XVII e XIX secolo'. In *Cérémonial et rituel à Rome (XVIe-XIXe siécle)*, edited by M. Visceglia and C. Brice, 281–316. Rome: Ecole française de Rome, 1997.
Calvio Tojo, M. 'Reconocimiento de la jurisdicción eclesiástica por el Estado español'. *Almogaren* 36 (2005): 350 et seq.
Campagna, N. *Der klassische Liberalismus und die Gretchenfrage. Zum Verhältnis von Freiheit, Staat und Religion im klassischen politischen Liberalismus*. Stuttgart: Franz Steiner Verlag, 2018.
Cândido Dos Santos. 'Catálogo das Obras de António Pereira de Figueiredo mandado fazer por ele mesmo a 28 de Junho de 1780. Torre do Tombo, manuscript da Livraria, b. 1938'. In *Padre António Pereira de Figueiredo. Erudição e polémica na segunda metade do século XVIII*, 373–7. Roma: Roma Editora, 2005.
Capellán de Miguel, Gonzalo. 'Más allá de la nación: religión, filosofía de la historia y humanidad en la España del siglo XIX'. *Rubrica contemporanea* 9, no. 17 (2020): 31–55.
Capellán de Miguel, Gonzalo 'El problema religioso en la España contemporánea. Krausismo y catolicismo liberal'. *Ayer* 39 (2000): 207–241.
Capes, J.M. 'Short Notices'. *Rambler* 3 November 1848, 211.
Capes, J.M. 'Communism'. *Rambler* 5 February 1850, 109–24.
Capes, J.M. *Reasons for Returning to the Church of England* (1871).
Capes, J.M. *To Rome and Back* (1873).
Capes, J.M. *What Can Be Certainly Known of God and of Jesus of Nazareth?* (1880).
Cárcel Ortí, Vicente. *Iglesia y revolución en España (1868–1874). Estudio histórico-jurídico desde la documentación vaticana inédita*. Pamplona: Eunsa, 1979.
Carr, R. 'The Religious Thought of John Stuart Mill: A Study in Reluctant Scepticism'. *Journal of the History of Ideas* 23 (1962): 475–95.
Cartwright, W.R. 'The Italian Question'. *Westminster Review* 71 April 1859, 444–83.
Cashdollar, C.D. *The Transformation of Theology, 1830–1890: Positivism and Protestant Thought in Britain and America*. Princeton, NJ: Princeton University Press, 1989.
Castano, S. R. 'La teoría de la traslación del poder en Suárez, entre tradición y ruptura'. *Mediaevalia. Revista de pensamiento medieval* 8, no. 2 (2015): 93–114.
Castelar, Emilio. *Discursos parlamentarios de Emilio Castelar en la Asamblea Constituyente*. Madrid: Editores A. De San Martin y Agustín Jubera, 1877.
Chadwick, Owen. 'Acton and Newman'. *Etudes Newmaniennes*, no. 11 (November 1995): 163–85.
Chadwick, Owen. *Acton and History*. Cambridge: Cambridge University Press, 1998.
Chadwick, Owen. *A History of the Popes, 1830–1914*. Oxford: Oxford University Press, 2003.
Ceretta, Manuela, and Mario Tesini, eds. *Montalembert Pensatore Europeo*. Rome: Studium, 2013.

Cezero Galan, P. *Religión y laicismo en la España contemporánea. Un análisis ideológico*. In *Religión y sociedad en España (siglos XIX y XX), Actas reunidas y presentadas por Paul Aubert*. Madrid: Casa de Velázquez, 2002.

Chantin, J.P. 'A la recherche des évêques constitutionnels jansénistes'. In *Gouverner une Eglise en Révolution. Histoire et mémoires de l'épiscopat constitutionnel*, edited by P. Chopelin. Paris, Lyon: LAHRA, 2017.

Chapman, H.S. 'The Canadian Question'.*Westminster Review* 3 July 1837, 79–113.

Chapman, H.S. 'The Irish in America'. *Westminster Review* 3 October 1837, 452–68.

Chapman, H.S. 'Principles of Colonization: New Zealand'. *Westminster Review* 34 (January, 1838): 67–96.

Chapman, H.S. 'Transatlantic Travelling'. *DR* 7 November 1839, 399–429.

Chinnici, J.P. *The English Catholic Enlightenment: John Lingard and the Cisalpine Movement*. Shepherdstown: Patmos Press, 1980.

Cicero. *De Officiis*. Edited and Translated by Walter Miller. Cambridge, MA: Cambridge University Press, 1975.

Clere, J.J. 'L'aboliton des droits féodaux en France'. *Cahiers d'Histoire* 94–5 (2005): 135–57.

Clive, J. *Macaulay: The Shaping of the Historian*. 1973. New York, Massachusetts: The Belknap Press of Harvard University Press Cambridge, 1987.

Col, Norbert. *Burke, Le contrat social et les révolutions*. Rennes: PUR, 2001.

Colantonio, Laurent. 'Daniel O'Connell. Un Irlandais au cœur du débat politique français, des dernières années de la Restauration à la Deuxième République'. Doctoral thesis, Université de Paris VIII, 2001.

Coleridge, Henry. 'The Liberalism of Lacordaire'. *The Month*, June, 1870, 641–64.

Constant, Benjamin. *De la religion*. In *Oeuvres complètes*, vol 1. Berlin/Boston: De Gruyter, 2013.

Conway. *Catholic Politics in Europe, 1918-1945*. Oxfordshire: Routledge, 1997.

Conzemius, Victor. 'Lord Acton and the First Vatican Council'. *Journal of Ecclesiastical History* 20 (October 1969): 247–9.

Corts I Blay, R. 'La figura episcopal y pública by Josep Climent en Barcelona (1766–1775)'. *Pedralbes* 26 (2006): 81–103.

Courtney, Cecil P. 'Burke et les Lumières'. In *La Révolution française entre Lumières et Romantisme*, 55–64. Caen: Université de Caen, 1989.

Critstobal de Gregorio, J. 'Los ilustrados y la Ilustración. Implicaciones ético-jurídicas'. *Boletín de la Facultad de Derecho de la UNED* 8–9 (1995): 125–46.

Cuchet, Guillaume, and Sylvain Milbach. 'The Great Fear of 1852'. *French History* 26, no. 3 (2012): 297–324.

Daly, Gabriel. *Transcendence and Immanence: A Study in Catholic Modernism and Integralism*. Oxford: Clarendon Press, 1980.

Daniel-Odon, H. 'Les Bénédictines de Saint-Maur et l'histoire au XVIIe siècle'. *Littératures classiques* 30 (1997): 33–50.

Darrell, J., ed. *Catholicism Contending with Modernity: Roman Catholic Modernism and Anti-Modernism in Historical Context*. Cambridge: Cambridge University Press, 2000.

Dayras, S., and D'Haussy. *Le catholicisme en Angleterre*. Paris: Armand Colin, 1970.

Deane, Seamus. 'Freedom Betrayed: Acton, Burke and Ireland'. *The Irish Review*, no. 30 (2003): 13–35.

De Blanca Torres, R. 'El fundamento ideológico de la Constuitución de Cádiz de 1812. Ilustración y romanticismo. El sentido de la presencia de los textos jurídicos medievales en la Constitución de cádiz de 1812'. *Revista de la Facultad de Ciencias Sociales y Jurídicas de Elche* 1, (2009): 158–67.

De Diego Garcia, E. 'The "Orgánica" of las Cortes 1810-1813'. *Cuadernos de Historia Contemporánea* 24 (2002): 31.
De Franceschi, S.H. 'L'autorité pontificale face au legs de l'antiromanisme catholique et régaliste des Lumières: Réminiscences doctrinales de Bellarmin et de Suàrez dans la théologie politique et l'ecclésiologie catholiques de la mi-XVIIIe siècle'. *Archivum Historiae Pontificiae* 38 (2000): 119-63.
De la Fuente, Vicente. *La pluralidad de cultos y sus inconvenientes*. Madrid: Imp. De La Esperanza, 1865.
De la Fuente, Vicente. 'Origen, desenvolvimiento, beneficios y estado actual de la Asociación de Católicos'. In *Crónica del Primer Congreso Católico Nacional Español. Discursos y trabajos presentados*. Madrid: Tipografía de los Huérfanos, 1889.
De la Fuente Monge, Gregorio. 'El enfrentamiento entre clericales y revolucionarios en torno a 1869'. *Ayer* 44 (2001): 127-50.
De la Hera Perez-Cuesta, A. 'The "Monarchia Catholica" española'. *Anuario de Historia del Derecho español* 67 (1997): 661-75.
DeLaura, David J. 'Pater and Newman: The Road to the Nineties'. *Victorian Studies* 10, no. 1 (1966): 39-69.
DeLaura, David J. *Hebrew and Hellene in Victorian England: Newman, Arnold, and Pater*. Texas: University of Texas Press, 1969.
Déloye, Yves. *Les voix de dieu. Pour une autre histoire du suffrage electoral: le clergé catholique français et le vote XIXe-XXe siècle*. Paris: Fayard, 2006.
Devas, C.S. *Studies of Family Life. A Contribution to Social Science*.1886.
Dippel, H. 'Constitucionalismo moderno. Introducción a una historia que necesita ser escrita'. *Historia constitucional* 6 (2005): 181-99.
Doria, Corinne. 'Le "juste milieu" entre le trône et l'autel. Pierre Paul Royer-Collard et la loi sur le sacrilège de 1825'. *Revue d'histoire ecclésiastique* 110 (2015): 1-2.
Doria, Corinne. *Pierre Paul Royer-Collard (1763-1845): un philosophe entre deux révolutions*. Rennes: Presses Universitaires de Rennes, 2018.
Dos Santos, C. *O Jansenismo em Portugal*. Porto: Faculdade de Letras da Universidade do Porto, Departamento de História e de Estudos Políticos e Internacionais, 2007.
Doyle, W. *Jansenism: Catholic Resistance to Authority from the Reformation to the French Revolution (Studies in European History)*. London: Palgrave Macmillan, 2000.
Dreyer, Michael. 'German Roots of the Theory of Pluralism'. *Constitutional Political Economy* 4, no. 1 (1997): 7-39.
Dromi, S.M., and S.D. Stabler. 'Good on Paper: Sociological Critique, Pragmatism, and Secularization Theory'. *Theory and Society* 48 (2019): 325-50.
Dufour, G. *Lumières et Ilustración en Espagne sous les règnes de Charles III et de Charles IV (1759-1788)*. Paris: Ellipses, 2006.
Dufour, G. '¿ Cuándo fue abolida la Inquisición en España ?'. *Cuadernos de Ilustración y Romanticismo* 13 (2005): 99-106.
Duggan, Jacob. 'Liberal Catholicism in the Church of England'. *The European Legacy* 27 (2021): 1-14.
Dumont, Jean-Noël. *Montalembert et ses contemporains*. Paris: les Éd. du Cerf, 2012.
Dumont, Louis. *Homo hierarchicus. Le système des castes et ses implications 1967*. Paris: Gallimard, 1975.
Dumont, Louis. *Essais sur l'individualisme. Une perspective anthropologique sur l'idéologie moderne*. Paris: Seuil, coll. Points Essais, 1991.
Dupont, Paul, ed. *Archives parlementaires*. Paris: J.Mavidal et E. Laurent, 1880, XLIV.

Durán Pastor, Miguel. 'De "El Conciliador" a la "Unidad Católica"'. *Bolletí de la Societat Arqueòlogica Lul·liana: revista d'estudis històrics* 42 (1986): 131–51.

Durán Pastor, Miguel. *Cartas de Vicente de la Fuente a Jose Mª Quadrado*. Palma de Mallorca: Obradors, 1981.

Egido, T. 'La religiosidad de los ilustrados'. In *La época de la Ilustración. El Estado y la cultura (1759–1808)*, edited by Mr Batllori, 418–26. Madrid: Espasa Calpe, 1987.

Faccarello, Gilbert. 'From the Foundation of Liberal Political Economy to Its Critique. Theology and Economics in France in the Eighteenth and Nineteenth Centuries'. In *The Oxford Handbook to Christianity and Economics*, edited by Paul Oslington, 73–94. Oxford: Oxford University Press, 2014.

Fears, Rufus, ed. *Selected Writings of Lord Acton* (3 vols). Indianapolis: Liberty Classics, 1988.

Fernandez de la Cigona, F. J. *El liberalismo y la Iglesia española. Historia de una persecución. Antecedentes*. Madrid: Speiro, 1989.

Fernandez Sarasola, I. 'La responsabilidad del Gobierno en los orígenes del constitucionalismo español: el Estatuto de Bayona'. *Revista de Derecho Político* 41 (1996): 177–214.

Fernandez Sarasola, I. 'La forma de gobierno en la Constitutión de Bayona'. *Historia Constitucional* 9 (2008): 64.

Figgis, J.N., and R.V. Laurence, eds. *Selections from the Correspondence of the First Lord Acton* (London: Longmans Green, 1917).

Finlason, W.F. 'Robberies of Religion, Ancient and Modern'. *Rambler* 10 November 1852, 381–99.

Finlason, W.F. 'Jansenism, Gallicanism and Jacobinism'. *DR* 37 September 1854, 96–189.

Flanagan, Thomas. 'The Church and Empire in the Thirteenth Century'. *Dublin Review* 17 December 1844, 487–516.

Flanagan, Thomas 'The Anglo-Saxon and Ancient British Churches'. *Dublin Review* 18 March 1845, 128–74.

Flanagan, Thomas. *Dublin Review* 19 September 1845, 195–229.

Franco Rubio, G.-A. 'El ejercicio del poder en la España del siglo XVIII. Entre las prácticas culturales y las prácticas políticas'. *Mélanges de la Casa de Velasquez* 35, (2005): 51–77.

Garcia-Baquero, A., and L.C. Alvarez Santalo. 'Riqueza y pobreza del clero secular en la Sevilla del Antiguo Régimen (1700–1834)'. *Trocadero, Revista de Historia Moderna y Contemporanea* 8–9, (1996–1997): 11–46.

García Cortés, Carlos. *El Cardenal García Cuesta (1803–1873). Un eminente arzobispo compostelano en la España liberal*. Santiago de Compostela: Cabildo Catedral de Santiago, 2006.

Garcia de Cortazar, F., and J.M. Gonzalez Vesga. *Breve historia de España*. Madrid: Alianza Editorial, 2016.

García Moscardó, Ester. 'La cruz como dogma del progreso: Democracia y religión en Roque Barcia Martí'. In *Dimensiones religiosas de la Europa del Sur: (1800–1875)*, edited by Rafael Serrano García, Ángel de Prado Moura, and Elisabel Larriba, 147–63. Valladolid: Universidad de Valladolid, 2018.

Gauchet, Marcel. *Le Désenchantement du monde. Une histoire politique de la religion*. Paris: Gallimard, 1985.

Gauthier, P. 'L'attitude pastorale de Newman à l'université'. *Revue des Sciences Religieuses*. tome 65, fascicule 3 (1991): 241–57.

Gazzaniga, Jean-Louis, and Philippe Ségur. 'Eglise'. In *Dictionnaire de philosophie politique*, 217–21. Paris: PUF, 2005.

Gengembre, Gérard. *La Contre-révolution ou l'histoire désespérante*. Paris: Edition Imago, 1989.
Gilley, Sheridan. 'Heretic London, Holy Poverty and the Irish Poor, 1830-1870'. *Downside Review* 89 (1971): 64-89.
Giovannoni, P.D. 'Il contesto italiano ed europeo'. In *Prospero Lambertini. Pastore della sua città, pontefice della cristianità*, edited by A. Zanotti, 15-33. Argelato: Minerva Edizione, 2004.
Gladstone, W.E. *The Vatican Decrees in Their Bearing on Civil Allegiance: A Political Expostulation*. Norderstedt: Hansebooks, 1874.
Gladstone, W.E. 'The Dogmatic Decrees of the Vatican Council Concerning the Catholic Faith and the Church of Christ". In *The Vatican Decrees in Their Bearing to Civil Allegiance*, edited by P. Schaff. New York, 1875.
Goldie, Mark. 'Priestcraft and the Birth of Whiggism'. In *Political Discourse in Early Modern Britain*, edited by Q. Skinner and N. Phillipson, 209-32. Cambridge: Cambridge University Press, 1993.
Gori, C. '*Scipione de' Ricci. Vescovo di Pistioa*'. *Il Covile* XV, no. 862 (2015): 13-15.
Gottfried, Paul. *Conservative Millenarians: The Romantic Experience in Bavaria*. New York: Fordham University Press, 1979.
Grasso, G. 'Pietro Tamburini difensore della Chiesa di Utrecht. Ruolo dell'edizione belga del "de tolerantia", Ghent, 1784'. *Revue d'Histoire ecclésiastique* 1-2, no. 114 (2019): 265-88.
Guerra, L. Lopez. *La Constitución de 1812: Edición conmemorativa del segundo centenario, introdución de L. Lopez Guerra*. Madrid: Edición Tecnos, 2012.
Hamburger, J. *Macaulay and the Whig Tradition*. Chicago: The University of Chicago Press, 1976.
Harris, Wendell V. 'Newman, Peel, Tamworth, and the Concurrence of Historical Forces'. *Victorian Studies* 32, no 2 (1989): 189-208, 192.
Harrison, Frederic. 'Rome Revisited'. *Fortnightly Review* 53, no. 317 (May 1893): 702-21.
Hawley, M.C. 'Newman's Immanent Critique of Liberalism: A Philosophical Argument against Liberal Hubris'. *Philosophy and Theology* 27, no. 1 (2015): 189-207.
Heimann, Mary. *Catholic Devotion in Victorian England*. Oxford: Clarendon Press, 1995.
Heimann, Mary. 'St Francis and Modern English Sentiment'. In *Christianity and Community in the West: Essays for John Bossy*, edited by Simon Ditchfield, 278-93. Aldershot: Taylor & Francis, 2001.
Hergenröther. *Catholic Church and Christian State. A Series of Essays on the Relation of the Church to the Civil Power*. Translated by C.S. Devas, 2 vols.,1876.
Hérisson, Arthur. 'Catholicisme intransigeant, progrès technique et modernité politique au milieu du XIXe siècle. La dystopie d'un "monde sans le pape" chez Juan Donoso Cortès et Louis Veuillot'. *Le XIXe siècle au futur. Penser, représenter, rêver l'avenir au XIXe siècle. Actes du VIIe Congrès de la SERD*, 2018. Online publication, https://serd.hypotheses.org/files/2018/08/He%CC%81risson_Congres-SERD_XIXe-siecle-au-futur.pdf.
Hérisson, Arthur. 'Louis Veuillot, *L'Univers* et l'intervention des laïcs dans les affaires de l'Église de France au milieu du XIXe siècle'. *Revue d'histoire de l'Église de France* 100, no. 245 (2014): 333-54.
Hérisson, Arthur. 'Les catholiques français face à l'unification italienne (1856-1871). Une mobilisation internationale de masse entre politique et religion'. Doctoral thesis, Université Paris 1 Panthéon-Sorbonne, 2018.
Hérisson, Arthur. 'Défendre Pie IX mais s'opposer à Veuillot. Les catholiques libéraux face à la question romaine'. In *Les forces de la modération. Ligne politique ou*

accommodements raisonnés dans les crises politico-religieuses européennes (XVIe-XIXe siècles), edited by Olivier Andurand and Albane Pialoux, 293–310. Bruxelles: Peter Lang, 2020.

Francheshi (de), Sylvio Hermann. 'Inquisición'. In *Diccionario de la Compañia de Jesús. Biográfico-Temático, III, Infanta of Santiago-Piatkiewicz*, edited by C.E. O'Neill and J. Ma Dominguez. Roma; Madrid: Institutum Historicum and Universidad Pontifica Comillas, 2001, col. 2035.

Francheshi (de), Sylvio Hermann. 'Les Derniers feux de la querelle de la grâce. Le jansénisme français et la question thomiste à la fin du XVIIe siècle'. *Ephemerides Theologicae Lovanienses* 8, no. 1 (2010): 27–81.

Francheshi (de), Sylvio Hermann. 'Agustinismo y molinismo del uso que los "Salamnticenses" (1631) hicieron de las enseñanzas de San Agustín contra las tesis de Luis de Molina'. *Criticón* 118 (2013): 81–97.

Hernandez Franco, J. 'Pasado y presente de Floridablanca como objeto de la Historia'. *Mixtures of Casa Velásquez* 39 (2009): 163–86.

Hildesheimer, F. *Le Jansénisme. L'histoire et l'héritage*. Paris: Desclée de Brouwer, 1992.

Hill, Roland. *Lord Acton*. Yale: Yale University Press, 2000.

Himmelfarb, Gertrude. *Lord Acton. A Study in Conscience and Politics*. Chicago: Chicago University Press, 1993.

Hohmann, Friedrich. 'Von der Jesuitenschule zum staatlichen Gymnasium Theodorianum'. In *Von der Domschule zum Gymnasium Theodorianum in Paderborn*, edited by Klemens Honselmann. Paderborn: Verein für Geschichte und Altertumskunde Westfalens, 1962.

Holmes, J.D. *More Roman than Rome: English Catholicism in the Nineteenth Century*. Oxfordshire: Burns & Oates, 1978.

Honoré, Jean. *La Pensée de J.H. Newman. Une Introduction*. Paris: Ad Solem, 2010.

Hoppen, K.T. 'Church, State, and Ultramontanism in Mid-Victorian England: The Case of William George Ward'. *Journal of Church and State* 18 (1976): 289–309.

Howard, T.A. *The Pope and the Professor: Pius IX, Ignaz von Döllinger and the Quandry of the Modern Age*. Oxford: Oxford University Press, 2017.

Hunter, I. 'Secularization: The Birth of a Modern Combat Concept'. *Modern Intellectual History* 12 (2015).

Hunter, I. 'Secularisation: Process, Program, and Historiography'. *Intellectual History Review* 27 (2017): 8.

Hutton, C.W. 'Roman Catholic Social and Economic Thought in England c.1880–c.1914. Some Tentative Steps towards a "Third Spring"?'. Oxford D.Phil Thesis, 2012.

Inarejos Muñoz, Juan Antonio. 'Sotanas, escaños y sufragios. Práctica política y soportes sociales del neo-catolicismo en las provincias castellano-manchegas (1854–1868)'. *Hispania sacra* 60, no. 121 (2008): 297–329.

Inglis, John. *Spheres of Philosophical Inquiry and the Historiography of Medieval Philosophy*. Leiden: Brill, 1998.

Isambert, F.A. *Le Sens du sacré, fête et religion populaire*. Paris: Ed. de Minuit, 1982.

Jacouty, Jean-François. 'Tradition et modernité dans la pensée politique de Royer-Collard'. *Revue française des idées politiques* 27, no. 1 (2008): 75–109.

Janse, Maartje. '"Association Is a Mighty Engine": Mass Organization and the Machine Metaphor, 1825–1840)'. In *Organizing Democracy: Reflections on the Rise of Political Organizations in the Nineteenth Century*, edited by Henk te Velde and Maartje Janse, 55–76. Basingstoke: Palgrave Macmillan, 2022.

Janse, Maartje. 'A Dangerous Type of Politics? Politics and Religion in Early Mass Organizations: The Anglo-American world, c. 1830'. In *Political Religion beyond Totalitarianism: The Sacralization of Politics in the Age of Democracy*, edited by Joost Augusteijn, Patrick Dassen and Maartje Janse, 55-76. Basingstoke: Palgrave Macmillan, 2013.

Jaume, Lucien. 'La Place du catholicisme libéral dans la culture politique française'. In *Charles de Montalembert. L'Eglise, la politique, la liberté*, edited by A. de Meaux and E. Montalembert. Paris: CNRS éditions, 2012.

Jaume, Lucien. 'Liberté et souveraineté politique dans le catholicisme. *Cités* 4, no. 12 (2002).

Jaume, Lucien. *L'Individu effacé ou le paradoxe du libéralisme français*. Paris: Fayard, 1997.

Jennings, Jeremy. 'Constitutional Liberalism in France: from Benjamin Constant to Alexis de Tocqueville'. In *The Cambridge History of Nineteenth-Century Political Thought*, edited by Gareth Stedman Jones and Gregory Claeys, 349-73. Cambridge: Cambridge University Press, 2011.

Jodock, Darrell, ed. *Catholicism Contending with Modernity. Roman Catholic Modernism and Anti-Modernism in Historical Context*. Cambridge: Cambridge University Press, 2000.

Jones, Emily. *Edmund Burke and the Making of Modern Conservatism, 1830-1914. An Intellectual History*. Oxford: Oxford University Press, 2017.

Kaiser, Wolfram. *Christian Democracy and the Origins of European Union*. Cambridge: Cambridge University Press, 2007.

Kaiser, Wolfram *The Cross and the Ballot: Catholic Political Parties in Germany, Switzerland, Austria, Belgium and the Netherlands, 1785-1985*. Boston: Humanities Press, 1999.

Kaiser, Wolfram 'Introduction: The European Culture Wars'. In *Culture Wars: Secular-Catholic Conflict in Nineteenth Century Europe*, edited by Christopher Clark and Wolfram Kaiser, 1-11. Cambridge: Cambridge University Press, 2003.

Kaucisvili Melzi d'Eril, Francesca, ed. *Carteggio Montalembert-Cantù (1842-1868)*. Milan: Editrice Vita e Pensiero, 1969.

Kent, W.H. 'Dr. Fairbairn on "Catholicism"'. *Dublin Review* 124 (April 1899): 384-407.

Ker, Ian. *John Henry Newman: A Biography*. Oxford: Oxford University Press, 2009.

Kerr, Dónal. 'Dr Patrick Murray (1811-1882)'. *Irish Theological Quarterly* 49 (1982): 229-50.

Laboa, J.M. 'La libertad religiosa en la historia constitucional española'. *Revista de Estudios políticos* 30 (1982): 157-74.

Laborde, Cécile. *Liberalims's Religion*. Cambridge: Harvard University Press, 2017.

La Mennais (de), Félicité. *Des progrès de la révolution et de la guerre contre l'Eglise*. Paris, 1829.

Lalouette, Jacqueline. 'Les catholiques libéraux français et l'idée de séparation des Églises et de l'État au XIXe siècle'. In *Charles de Montalembert: L'Église, la politique, la liberté*, edited by Antoine de Meaux and Eugène de Montalembert, 115-43. Paris: CNRS Éditions, 2019.

Lamberts, Emiel. *The Struggle with Leviathan. Social Responses to the Omnipotence of the State, 1815-1965*. Leuven: Leuven University Press, 2016.

La Parra, E. 'El eco de Lamennais en el progresismo español: Larra y Joaquín María López'. In *Libéralisme chrétien et catholicisme libéral en Espagne France et Italie dans la première moitié du XIXe siècle*, 323-42. Aix en Provence: Université de Provence, 1989.

Lasarte, J. 'Nota sobre José Alonso y López, diputado en las Cortes de Cádiz y del Trienio Liberal'. *Revista de Estudios Regionales* 98 (2013): 234–5.
Latreille, André. 'Les dernières années de Montalembert'. *Revue d'histoire de l'Église de France* 54, no. 153 (1968): 281–314.
Leighton, C.D.A. 'Finding Antichrist: Apocalypticism in Nineteenth-Century Catholic England and the Writings of Frederick Faber'. *Journal of Religious History* 37, no. 1 (March 2013): 80–97.
Le Guillou, Marie-Joseph, and Louis Le Guillou, eds. *La Condamnation de Lamennais*. Paris: Beauchesne, 1982.
Lebrun, Richard Allen, and Sylvain Milbach, eds. *Lamennais, a Believer's Revolutionary Politics*. Leiden: Brill, 2018.
Lecanuet, Édouard. *Montalembert*. 3 vols. Paris: C. Poussielgue, 1895.
Lefebvre, P., and Masson. *John Henry Newman – Doctor of the Church*. J.T. Ford: Family Publications, 2007.
Leon Navarro, V. 'Conflictos ideológicos durante los primeros años de don Francisco Fabián y Fuero en la mitra valenciana'. In *La catedral ilustrada. Iglesia, sociedad y cultura en la Valencia del siglo XVIII*, edited by E. Callado Estella, vol. 3, 137–85. València: Institucio Alfons el Magnanim, 2015.
Leonard, Ellen. 'English Catholicism and Modernism'. In *Catholicism Contending with Modernity: Roman Catholic Modernism and Anti-Modernism in Historical Context*, edited by Darrell Jodock, 248–74. Cambridge: Cambridge University Press, 2000.
Leroy-Beaulieu, A. *Les Catholiques libéraux: l'Église et le libéralisme de 1830 à nos jours*. Paris: Librairie Plon, 1885.
Lessay, Franck. 'Lord Acton, libéral et historien catholique'. *Commentaire* 4, no. 68 (1994): 941–6.
Lessay, Franck 'Burke et la nationalisation de la raison'. In *La Révolution française entre Lumières et Romantisme. Actes du colloque de novembre 1989. Cahiers de Philosophie politique et juridique (16)*, 67–82. Caen: Université de Caen, 1989.
Lessay, Franck. 'Regards sur le libéralisme'. *Commentaire* 2, no. 6 (1979): 324–9.
Levy, J.T. 'From liberal constitutionalism to pluralism'. In *Modern Pluralism: Anglo-American Debates since 1880*, edited by Mark Bevir, 21–39. Cambridge: Cambridge University Press, 2012.
Lopez Tabar, J. *Los famosos traidores. Los afrancesados durante la crisis del Antiguo Régimen (1808-1833)*. Madrid: Biblioteca Nueva, 2001.
Lothian, J.R. *The Making and Unmaking of the English Catholic Intellectual Community, 1910-1950* (Notre Dame, Ind.: University of Notre Dame Press, 2009).
Louzao Villar, Joseba. 'Catholicism versus Laicism: Culture Wars and the Making of Catholic National Identity in Spain, 1898–1931'. *European History Quarterly* 43, no. 4 (2013): 657–80.
Löwith, Karl. *Histoire et Salut. Les présupposés théologiques de la philosophie de l'histoire*. Translated from German by M.C. Challiol-Gillet, S. Hurstel, and J.F. Kervegan (1949/1953). Paris: Gallimard, 2002.
Lucas, Edward. *The Life of Frederick Lucas*. 2nd edition, 2 vols. 1887.
Lupano, A. 'Le Traité inédit "*Della povertà religiosa*"(1759): L'antiromanisme universitaire turinois selon Angelo Paolo Carena et son maître Carlo Sebastiano Berardi'. In *Droits antiromains XVIe-XXIe siècles. Juridictionnalisme catholique et romanité ecclésiale*, edited by S. de Franceschi and B. Hours, 149–68. Lyon: LAHRA, 2017.
Macaulay, Ambrose. *Dr Russell of Maynooth*. Darton: Longman and Todd, 1983.
Macaulay, Thomas Babington. 'Southey's Colloquies'. 1830. In *The Complete Works of Lord Macaulay*, edited by Albany edition. London: Longmans Green and Co, 1898.

Macaulay, Thomas Babington 'Parliamentary Reform'. 16 December 1831. In *The Complete Works of Lord Macaulay*, edited by Albany edition. London: Longmans Green and Co, 1898.
Macaulay, Thomas Babington 'Burleigh and His Times'. 1832. In *The Complete Works of Lord Macaulay*, edited by Albany edition. London: Longmans Green and Co, 1898.
Macaulay, Thomas Babington. 1833. In *The Complete Works of Lord Macaulay*, edited by Albany edition. London: Longmans Green and Co, 1898.
Macaulay, Thomas Babington 'Gladstone on Church and State'. 1839. In *The Complete Works of Lord Macaulay*, edited by Albany. London: Longmans Green and Co, 1898.
Macaulay, Thomas Babington 'T.B. Macaulay to Duncan Mclaren' (30 January 1841). In *The Letters of Lord Macaulay*, edited by Thomas Pinney. Cambridge: Cambridge University Press, 2009.
Macaulay, Thomas Babington 'The Church of Ireland'. 1845. In *The Complete Works of Lord Macaulay*, edited by Albany edition. London: Longmans Green and Co, 1898.
Macaulay, Thomas Babington. 'The History of England from the Accession of James II'. 1848–1861. In *The Complete Works of Lord Macaulay*, edited by Albany edition. London: Longmans Green and Co, 1898.
Magnouloux, H. 'Lord Acton face au Cardinal Newman'. *Etudes Newmaniennes*, no. 26 (November 2010): 9–66.
Maistre (de), Joseph. *Considérations sur la France*. 1796. Paris: Imprimerie Nationale Editions, 1994.
Maistre (de), Joseph de *Considérations sur la France*. Edited by P. Manent. Brussels: Editions Complexe, 1988.
Maistre (de), Joseph de. *Examen d'un écrit de J.-J. Rousseau sur l'inégalité des conditions*. Lyon: unknown, 1884.
Manent, Pierre. *Les libéraux*. Paris: Gallimard, coll. 'tel', 2001.
Manning, H. E. *The Temporal Power of the Vicar of Jesus Christ*. 1861.
Martina, Giacomo. *Pio IX*. 3 vols. Roma: Pontificia università gregoriana, 1974–1990.
Martina, Giacomo. 'Verso il *Sillabo*. Il parere del barnabita Bilio sul discorso di Montalembert a Malines nell'agosto 1863'. *Archivum Historiae Pontificiae* 36 (1998): 137–81.
Martínez Hoyos, Francisco. 'Cristianos liberales en la España decimonónica: el mito de la irrelevancia'. *Aportes* 98, no. 3 (2018): 115–47.
Martinez Millan, J. *La Inquisición española*. Madrid: Alianza Editorial, 2021.
Mathis, R. 'Diffuser le jansénisme au risque de la prison ? Les imprimeurs "jansénistes" et le pouvoir royal (1643–1712)'. In *Port-Royal et la prison*, edited by J. Lesaulnier, 197–211. Paris; Nolin: Université Port-Royal, 2011.
Maultrot, Gabriel-Nicolas. *Origine et étendue de la puissance royale, suivant les livres saints et la tradition*. Paris: Hachette, 1789.
Mayeur, Jean-Marie. 'Quelques rencontres entre les catholiques français et les catholiques belges'. *Le Mouvement social*, no. 178 (1997): 27–35.
Mc Connell, Mickael V. 'Establishment and Toleration in Edmund Burke's "Constitution of Freedom"'. *The Supreme Court Review*, 1995.
McCloskey, C. John. *Liberalism and Newman the Anglican: Vision and Response*, doctoral diss., Universidad de Navarra, 1982.
McElrath, Damian. *Richard Simpson, 1820–1876. A Study in XIXth Century Liberal Catholicism*. Louvain: Publications universitaires de Louvain, 1972.
Meaux (de), Antoine and Eugène de Montalembert, eds. *Charles de Montalembert. L'Église, la politique, la liberté*. Paris: CNRS Éditions, 2012.

Menendez Pelayo, M. *Historia de los heterodoxos españoles*. Alicante: Biblioteca Miguel de Cervantes, 2003.

Menozzi, Daniele. 'Tra riforma e restaurazione. Dalla crisi della società cristiana al mito della cristianità medievale (1758–1848)'. In *Storia d'Italia, Annali 9, La Chiesa e il potere politico dal Medioevo all'età contemporanea*, edited by Giorgio Chittolini and Giovanni Miccoli, 767–806. Turin: Giulio Einaudi Editore, 1986.

Menozzi, Daniele. *Chiesa e diritti umani. Legge naturale e modernità politica dalla Rivoluzione Francese ai nostri giorni*. Bologne: Il Mulino, 2012.

Menuet, M. 'The "*Nouvelles ecclésiastiques*" (1728–1750) face à leurs opposants: quelques polémiques autour du prêt à l'intérêt'. *Oeconomia* 8, no. 1 (2018): 29–44.

Mercader Riba, J. *José Bonaparte Rey de España (1808–1813). Estructura del estado español bonapartista*. Madrid: Consejo Superior de Investigaciones Científicas, 1983.

Mestre Sanchis, A. *Mayans y Siscar y el pensamiento ilustrado español contra el absolutismo*. León: Universidad de León, 2007.

Metz, Jean-Baptiste. *La foi dans l'histoire et la société*. Paris: Les Editions du Cerf, coll. 'Cogitation Fidei', 1979.

Meynell, Charles. 'The Philosophy of the Absolute'. *Rambler* 22 September 1858, 173–90.

Miccoli, Giovanni. 'Chiesa e società in Italia fra Ottocento e Novecento: il mito della cristianità'. In *Fra mito della cristianità e secolarizzazione. Studi sul rapporto chiesa-società nell'età contemporanea*, 21–92. Casale Monferrato: Marietti, 1985.

Milbach, Sylvain. 'Les catholiques libéraux et la presse entre 1831 et 1855'. *Le mouvement social* 215, no. 2 (2010): 9–34.

Milbach, Sylvain. 'Les catholiques libéraux et la Révolution française autour de 1848. 'Elle est toujours vivante: elle nous entoure, elle domine'. *Annales historique de la Révolution française* 362 (2010): 55–78.

Milbach, Sylvain. 'Catholicisme intransigeant et catholicisme libéral au XIXe siècle'. In *Histoire du christianisme en France*, edited by Alain Tallon and Catherine Vincent, 341–60. Paris: A. Colin, 2014.

Milbach, Sylvain. *Les chaires ennemies. L'Église, l'État et la liberté d'enseignement secondaire dans la France des notables (1830–1850)*. Paris: Honoré Champion, 2015.

Milbach, Sylvain. *Lamennais (1782–1854)*. Rennes: Presses universitaires de Rennes, 2021.

Mill, J.S. *Mill: The Spirit of the Age, on Liberty, the Subjection of Women*. Selected and edited by Alan Ryan. Oxford: A Norton Critical Edition, 1997.

Mill, J.S. 'Autobiography'. 1818. In *Collected Works of John Stuart Mill* vol. 1, edited by J.M. Robson and J. Stillinger. Toronto: University of Toronto Press, 1981.

Mill, J. S. 'Three Essays on Religion: Utility of Religion'. In *Collected Works of John Stuart Mill*. 33 vols. (vol. 10), edited by J.M. Robson and J. Stillinger. Toronto: University of Toronto Press, 1969.

Minnerath, Roland. 'Eglise-Etat'. In *Dictionnaire critique de Théologie*, edited by Jean-Yves Lacoste. Paris: PUF, 1998.

Miranda Alvarez, A. 'Siglo ilustrado y siglo de las luces, dos denominaciones a caballo entre dos siglos'. In *Actas del Congreso 'Enter Siglos. Cultura y literatura en España desde finales del siglo XVIII a principios del XIX"*, *Bordighera*, edited by E. Caldera and R. Frodli, 39–53. Roma: Bulzoni, 1993.

Monod, Jean-Claude. *La querelle de la sécularisation de Hegel à Blumenberg*. Paris: Librairie Philosophique J. Vrin, 2002.

Montalembert (de), Charles Forbes. *Du devoir des catholiques dans la question de la liberté d'enseignement*. Paris: l'Univers, 1843.

Montalembert (de), Charles Forbes. *Discours sur la question de la liberté de l'Église dans la discussion du projet de loi sur les fonds secrets*. Paris: Sagnier et Bray, 1844.
Montalembert (de), Charles Forbes. *Des Intérêts catholiques au XIXe siècle*. Paris: J. Lecoffre, 1852.
Montalembert (de), Charles Forbes. *Lettre à M. le Comte de Cavour*. Paris: C. Douniol, 1860.
Monsell, William. *A Lecture on the Roman Question, delivered at Limerick December 1st, 1859*. 1860.
Montalembert (de), Charles Forbes. *L'Église libre dans l'État libre. Discours prononcés au Congrès catholique de Malines*. Paris: Ch. Douniol et Didier et Cie, 1863.
Montero García, Feliciano. *El primer catolicismo social y la Rerum Novarum en España (1889– 1902)*. Madrid: CSIC, 1983.
Montero García. *El movimiento católico en España, 1889–1936*. Alcalá de Henares: Editorial Universidad de Alcalá, 2017.
Morales, A. 'El jansenismo en España y su carácter de ideología revolucionaria'. In *A Revolução francesa e a Península ibérica*. Coimbra: Instituto de Historia e Teoria das Ideas, Faculdade de Letras, 1988.
Moral Roncal, A.-M. 'La nobleza española en la política y diplomacia durante la edad contemporánea'. *Doors* 89, no. 30 (2015): 83–5.
Moran, M. 'Los diputados eclesiásticos en las Cortes de Cádiz: revisión crítica'. *Hispania Sacra* 42 (1990): 35–60.
Moran, M. 'Conciencia y revolución liberal. Actitudes políticas de los eclesiásticos en las Cortes de Cádiz'. *Hispania Sacra* 42 (1990): 485–92.
Morrow, John. 'Romanticism and Political Thought in the Early Nineteenth Century'. In *The Cambridge History of Nineteenth-Century Political Thought*, edited by Gareth Stedman Jones and Gregory Claeys, 39–76. Cambridge: Cambridge University Press, 2011.
Mucci, G. 'Newman e il liberalismo'. *Civiltà Cattolica*, no. 3849 (November 6, 2010).
Murphy, Dominick. 'The Reformation in Sweden. – Gustavus Wasa'. *Dublin Review* 19 September 1845, 229–65.
Navarro, V.-L. 'El grupo valenciano y el reformismo de Joaquin Lorenzo Villanueva anterior a las Cortes de Cádiz'. *Anales de la Universidad de Alicante. Historia Contemporánea*, 1983, 9–33.
Neale, R.S. 'Chapman, Henry Samuel'. *Australian Dictionary of Biography* (1969), accessed 6 February 2017, https://adb.anu.edu.au/biography/chapman-henry-samuel-3193.
Newman, John Henry. *Discussions and Arguments on Various Subjects*. London: Basil Montagu Pickering, 1872.
Newman, John Henry. *An Essay on Aid of a Grammar of Assent*. 1870. London: Longmans, Green and Co., 1917.
Newman, John Henry. *Letter to the Duke of Norfolk*. Paris: Newmanian Texts VII, Desclée de Brouwer, 1970.
Newman, John Henry. *The Idea of a University*. 1873. Reprinted with notes and introduction. Edited by I.T. Ker. Oxford: Clarendon Press, 1976.
Newman, John Henry. 'Tamworth's Reading Room'. *Etudes Newmaniennes*, no. 16 (November 2000): 7–68.
Newman, John Henry. *Apology pro vita sua*. 1864. Paris: Ad Solem, 2003.
Newman, John Henry. *Essay on the Development of Christian Doctrine*. 1845. Paris: Ad Solem, 2007.
Newman, John Henry. *University Sermons*. Paris: Ad Solem, 2007.
Newman, John Henry. *Grammaire de l'Assent*. Paris: Ad Solem, 2010.
Newman, John Henry. *Catholic Sermons*. Paris: Cerf, 2019.

Nunez, F. 'La imagen del "indio" en los debates de las Cortes de Cádiz (1810–1812)'. *Historia* 1 (2018): 16–23.

Oftestad, Bernt T. *The Catholic Church and Liberal Democracy*. London and New York: Routledge, 2019.

O'Hagan, Thomas. 'Ireland in 1853 – Hopes of Progress'. In *Occasional Papers and Addresses*, 271–312. 1884.

O'Malley, Martin. 'Currents in Nineteenth-Century German Law, and Subsidiarity's Emergence as a Social Principle in the Writings of Wilhelm Ketteler'. *Journal of Law, Philosophy and Culture* 3, no. 1 (2008): 26–30.

O'Sullivan, W. M. 'Henry Nutcombe Oxenham: "Enfant Terrible" of the Liberal Catholic Movement in Mid-Victorian England'. *Catholic Historical Review* 82, no. 4 (October, 1996): 637–60.

Oxenham, Henry Nutcombe. 'The Neo-Protestantism of Oxford'. *Rambler* 4 March 1861, 287–314.

Oxenham, Henry Nutcombe 'The Rival Bishops on the New Dogma'. *Saturday Review* (28 May 1870): 699–701.

Palacio Cerezales, Diego. 'Forjadas por los adversarios. Movilización católica en la era del liberalismo (1812–1874)'. *Historia y Política* 46 (2021): 175–206.

Pamparacuatro Martin, J. 'Lenguaje y moral en el siglo XVII: la controversia entre Jansenistas y Jesuitas'. *Pensamiento* 76, no. 289 (2020): 408.

Papencordt, Felix. *Geschichte der vandalischen Herrschaft in Afrika*. Berlin: Duncker und Humblot, 1837.

Papencordt, Felix. *Dublin Review* 6 May 1839, 289–325.

Papencordt, Felix. *Cola di Rienzo und seine Zeit*. Hamburg: Friedrich und Andreas Perthes, 1841.

Peel, Robert. *Inaugural Address, Delivered by the Righ Hon. Sir Robert Peel, Bart.MP., President of the Tamworth Library and Reading Room, on Tuesday, 19th January 1841*. 2nd edn. London: James Bain, 1841.

Pelletier, Gerard. *Rome et la Révolution française. La théologie et la politique du Saint-Siège pendant la Révolution française (1789–1799)*. Rome: Ecole française de Rome, 2004.

Pereiro, James. *Cardinal Manning: from Anglican Archdeacon to Council Father at Vatican I*. 1998. Leominster: Gracewing, 2008.

Perez, J. *Brève histoire de l'Inquisition en Espagne*. Paris: Fayard, 2002.

Perez-Magallon, J. 'Jansenio, agustinismo y la batalla propagandística entre Francia y el imperio hispánico'. *Criticón* 118 (2013): 137–49.

Perreau-Saussine, Emile. 'French Catholic Political Thought from the Deconfessionalisation of the State to the Recognition of Religious Freedom'. In *Religion and the Political Imagination*, edited by I. Katznelson and G. Stedman Jones, 150–70. Cambridge: Cambridge University Press, 2010.

Perreau-Saussine, Emile. *Catholicism and Democracy: An Essay in the History of Political Thought*. Oxford: Princeton University Press, 2012.

Petición dirigida a las Cortes constituyentes a favor de la Unidad católica en España. Madrid: Imprenta de 'La Esperanza', 1869.

Pezzimenti, Rocco. *The Political Thought of Lord Acton. The English Catholics in the Nineteenth Century*. Leominster: Gracewing, 2001.

Picton, H. 'De Newman à Colenso: Trollope et l'Église d'Angleterre'. *Etudes anglaises* 2, tome 59 (2006): 145–55.

Pierrard, Pierre. *Louis Veuillot*. Paris: Beauchesne, 1998.

Pignatelli, Giuseppe. 'Le origini settecentesche del cattolicesimo reazionario: La polemica antigiansenista del *Giornale ecclesiastico di Roma*'. *Studi Storici* 11, no. 4 (October-December 1970): 755-82.
Plongeron, Bernard. *Histoire du Christianisme. Les défis de la modernité (1750-1840)*. Paris: Desclée, T. 10.
Pocock, J.G.A. 'The Varieties of Whiggism from Exclusion to Reform: A History of Ideology and Discourse'. In *Virtue, Commerce and History. Essays in Political Thought and History, Chiefly in the Eighteenth century*, 215-330. Cambridge: Cambridge University Press, 1985.
Prélot, Marcel. *Le libéralisme catholique: textes choisis et présentés*. Paris: Armand Colin, 1969.
Printy, Michael. 'History and Church History in the Catholic Enlightenment'. *Modern Intellectual History* 18 (2021): 248-60.
Puyol Montero, J.M. 'Los proyectos de Napoleón y de José Bonaparte para la convocatoria de unas Cortes en Madrid (1808-1812)'. *Anuario de Historia del Derecho español* 85 (2015): 203 et seq.
Quadrado, José Maria. 'Naturaleza de estas asociaciones'. In *La Unidad católica*, no. 2, 14 March 1869. Reproduced in *Ensayos religiosos, políticos y literarios*. vol. IV, 22-23. Palma de Mallorca: Tipografía de Amengual y Muntaner, 1896.
Quinn, Dermot. *Patronage and Piety: The Politics of English Roman Catholicism, 1850-1900*. Basingstoke: Macmillan, 1993.
'Quirinus Nepos'. *Tablet*, 19 November 1921, 664-5.
Ramirez Aledon, L. 'Joaquín Lorenzo Villanueva y la polémica sobre la carta del obispo Gregoire contra la Inquisicíon española in 1798'. *Cuadernos de Ilustración y Romanticismo* 13 (2005): 13-54.
Ramón Solans, Javier. '"El catolicismo tiene masas". Nación, política y movilización en España, 1868-1931'. *Historia contemporánea* 51 (2015): 427-54.
Ramón Solans, Javier, and Raúl Alberto Mayoral Trigo. 'Sociología de los diputados por Aragón en las Cortes de Cádiz'. *Revista de historia Jerónimo Zurita* 87 (2012): 259-79.
Records and Recollections of St. Cuthbert's College, Ushaw. Preston: E. Buller & Son, 1889.
Régnier, Ph. *La Révolution française entre Lumières et Romantisme. Actes du colloque de novembre 1989. Cahiers de Philosophie politique et juridique (16)*. Caen: Université de Caen, 1989.
Rémond, René. *Lamennais et la démocratie*. Paris: Presses Universitaires de France, 1948.
Rémusat (de), Charles. 'Du Traditionalisme'. *Revue des Deux Mondes* 9 (1857): 241-71.
Revuelta Gonzalez, M. 'Negación de asilo a Jesuitas franceses refugiados en España en el dictamen del fiscal Campomanes en 1764'. *Miscelànea Comillas* 65, no. 126 (2007): 101-24.
Rey Castelao, O. '*Las relaciones entre la Monarquía y la Iglesia en el siglo XVIII ¿ La evolución de un modelo europeo ?*'. In Las monarquías española y francesa (siglos XVI-XVIII) ¿ Dos modelos políticos ?, edited by A. Dubet and J. J. Ruiz Ibáñez. Madrid: Casa de Velázquez, 2010.
Rials, Stéphane. *Révolution et Contre-révolution au XIXe siècle*. Paris: Édition Albatros et Duc, 1987.
Richardson, P.A. 'Serial Struggles: English Catholics and Their Periodicals, 1648-1844'. PhD Thesis, University of Durham, 2003.
Rickaby, Joseph. *Political and Moral Essays*. Chicago: Kessinger Publishing, 1902.
Robertson, J.B. 'Gerbet on the Eucharist'. *Dublin Review* 1 May 1836, 200-21.

Robertson, J.B. 'The Life and Writings of Görres'. *Dublin Review* 6 January 1839, 31–74.
Robertson, J.B. 'Summary of German Literature'. *Dublin Review* 6 January 1839, 282.
Robertson, J.B. 'Moral and Intellectual Condition of Catholic Germany'. *Dublin Review* 11 August 1841, 53–93.
Robertson, J.B. 'Religious and Social Condition of France'. *Dublin Review* 16 March 1844, 1–44.
Robertson, J.B. *The Philosophy of History; in a Course of Lectures delivered by Frederick von Schlegel, with a Memoir of the Author*. 1835, edited and translated by J.B. Robertson, 2 vols. 6th edn. London: Henry G. Bohn, 1848.
Robertson, J.B. 'Hurter on the Institutions, Manners, and Customs of the Middle Age'. *Dublin Review* 28 March 1850, 50–90.
Robertson, J.B. *Dublin Review* 33, December 1852, 418–66.
Rochini, Mr. 'Teologia politica ed ecclesiologia del piccolo numero: l'idea del martirio nel giansenismo italiano settecentesco'. *Rivista di Storia del christianesimo* 15 (2018): 359–76.
Rodriguez Fernandez, M. 'Las tres España of 1808'. *Revista Aequitas* 11 (2018): 50 et seq.
Rosa, M. 'Jesuitisme et antijésuitisme dans l'Italie du XVIIe siècle'. In *Les antijésuites. Discours, figures et lieux de l'antijésuitisme à l'époque moderne*, edited by P.A. Fabre and C. Maire, 587–619. Rennes: Presses Universitaires de Rennes, 2010.
Rosanvallon, Pierre. *La démocratie inachevée*. Paris: Gallimard, 2000.
Rosso, Mr. 'Feijóo et les frontières du savoir'. In *Soglie e interazioni. I linguaggi espanici nella tradizione e nella contemporaneità*, Atti del XXVI Convegno dell'AISPI, 473–86. Trento: Università degli Studi di Trento, 2013.
Royer-Collard, P.P. 'Discours de la Chambre des Pairs'. In Barante. *La vie politique de M. Royer-Collard*.
Rudé, George. *Europa en el siglo XVIII: La aristocracia y el desafío burgués*. Madrid: Alianza Editorial, 1978.
Rújula López, Pedro Víctor and Francisco Javier Ramón Solans. 'Representantes y representación: los diputados aragoneses en las Cortes de Cádiz'. *Trienio: Ilustración y liberalismo* 61 (2013): 7–28.
Rupert, Jane. *J.H. Newman on the Nature of the Mind. Reason in Religion, Science, and the Humanities*. Lanham: Lexington Books, 2011.
Saada, Julie. 'Critique du thomisme et construction de la loi naturelle chez Hobbes'. In *Hobbes, Spinoza or the Politics of Speech*, edited under the supervision of Julie Saada, 63–91. Lyon: ENS Editions, 2009).
Saarinen, Risto. 'Indéfectibilité de l'Eglise'. In *Dictionnaire critique de théologie*, edited by Jean-Yves Lacoste. Paris: PUF, 1998.
Saint-Arnaud, J.G.J. *Newman et l'incroyance*. Paris: Editions Desclée and Editions Bellarmin, 1972.
Salas Alvarez, J. 'La antigüedad clásica en la España Sagrada del Padre Henrique Flórez de Setién y Huidobro'. *Gerión* 27 (2009): 57–78.
Salvador, Carmelo Romero. *Caciques y caciquismo en España (1834–2020)*. Madrid: Catarata, 2021.
Sanchez Espinosa, L. 'Los libreros Ángel Corradi y Antoine Boudet y la importación de libros franceses para la Academia de San Fernando'. *Bulletin hispanique* 114, no. 1 (2012): 195–216.
Sandoni, Luca. "Un coup d'État de Dieu'. Approches catholiques du 2 décembre 1851, entre théologie et politique." *Revue d'histoire de l'Église de France* 103, no. 2 (2017): 247–70.

Santana Perez, J. M. 'Carlos IV ¿ El último gobierno del despotismo ilustrado y el primer fracaso del liberalismo en España ?'. *Presente & Pasado* 9, no. 18 (2004): 105.

Sanz de Diego, Rafael. *Medio siglo de relaciones Iglesia-Estado: el Cardenal Antolín Monescillo y Viso (1811–1897)*. Madrid: Universidad Pontificia Comillas, 1979.

Saranyana, J.A. 'La eclesología de la Revolución en el Sínodo de Pistoya (1786)'. *Anuario de Historia de la Iglesia* 19 (2010): 61.

Schettini, G. 'Confessional Modernity: Nicola Spedalieri. The Catholic Church and the French Revolution'. *Modern Intellectual History* 17, no. 3 (2020): 677–705.

Schiefen, R.J. 'Review [of McElrath, *Richard Simpson*]'. *Catholic Historical Review* 62, no. 4 (October 1976): 626–8.

Schmitt, Carl. *La visibilité de l'Eglise, Catholicisme romain et forme politique, Donoso Cortés* (four essays), presented by Bernard Bourdin, *Carl Schmitt: quelle théologie politique?*. Paris: Editions du Cerf, coll. 'La nuit surveillée', 2011.

Schneider, Bernhard. 'Insel der Märtyrer oder ein Volk von Rebellen? Deutschlands Katholiken und die irische Nationalbewegung in der Ära Daniel O'Connells (ca. 1820–1847)'. *Historisches Jahrbuch* 128 (2008): 225–75.

Schneider, Bernhard. 'Reform of Piety in German Catholicism, 1780–1920'. In *Piety and Modernity*, edited by Jarlert Anders, 193–224. Leuven: Leuven University Press, 2012.

Schröder, P. 'Devoid of Faith, Yet Terrified of Scepticism – Die Bedeutung der Religion in John Stuart Mills politischer Theorie über Staat und Gesellschaft'. In *Vom Nutzen des Staates. Das Staatsverständnis des klassischen Utilitarismus: Hume/Bentham/Mill*, edited by O. Asbach, 229–46. Baden-Baden: Nomos, 2009.

Sciutti Russi, V. 'Abolir l'Inquisition d'Espagne: une lettre de l'Abbé Grégoire'. *Annales de la Révolution française* 333 (2003): 121–32.

Shea, M. C. 'Ressourcement in the Age of Migne: The Jesuit Theologians of the Collegio Romano and the Shape of Modern Catholic Thought'. *Nova et Vetera* 15, no. 2 (2017): 579–613.

Siedentop, L. *Inventing the Individual The Origins of Western Liberalism*. Belknap Press: London, 2014.

Simmonds, Gemma. 'Jansenism (1640–1713): An Historico-Theological Account with Special Reference to One Twentieth-Century Response'. Doctoral diss., University of Cambridge.

Simpson, Richard. 'Mr Buckle's Thesis and Method'. *Rambler* 22 July 1858, 27–42.

Simpson, Richard. *Rambler*, February 1859, 113–25.

Skinner, Simon. *Tractarians and the 'Condition of England': The Social and Political Thought of the Oxford Movement*. Oxford: Clarendon Press, 2004.

Smidt, A.J. 'Piedad e ilustración en relación armónica. Josep Climent i Avinent, obispo de Barcelona, 1766–1775'. *Manuscrits* 20 (2002): 91–109.

Solez Pascula, E. 'Ocios de espanoles emigrados: Una revista del exilio londinense'. In *Disidencias y exilios en la espara moderna, Actas de la IV Reunión Científica de la Asociación Española de Historia Moderna, Alicante, 27–30 de mayo de 1996*, edited by A. Mestre-Sanchís and E. Gimenez-Lopez, 833–48. Alicante: Caja de Ahorros del Mediterráneo, Universidad de Alicante, 1997.

Southey, Robert. *Book of the Church*. 2 vols. 1824.

Spuller, Eugène. *Royer-Collard*. Paris: Hachette & Cie, 1895.

Stedman Jones, G., and G. Clayes, eds. *The Cambridge History of Nineteenth Century Political Thought*. Cambridge: Cambridge University Press, 2011.

Stella, P. *Atti e decreti del concilio diocesano di Pistoia dell'anno 1786* (Vol. I: Ristampa dell'edizione Bracali. Indici a cura di P. Stella; Vol. II: Introduzione storica e documenti inediti. A cura di Pietro Stella, Firenze, Olschki, Biblioteca storica toscana), Series II, vol. 9 (1986), vol. I: XII- XII: 256–144–32, con 2 tavv. F.T.; vol. II: VI–698 con 4 tavv. F.T.

Stratz, H.W., and H. Zabel. 'Säkularisation, Säkularisierung'. In *Geschichtliche Grundbegriffe: Historisches Lexikon zur politisch-sozialen Sprache in Deutschland*, edited by O. Brunner, W. Conze, and R. Koselleck, vol. 5, 789–829. Stuttgart: Klett-Cotta, 1984.

Suarez Cortina, M. 'Liberalismo, política y constitución en la España contemporánea (una miranda desde la historia constitucional'. *Historia y Política* 19 (2008): 292.

Suárez, Federico. *Santiago Masarnau y las Conferencias de San Vicente de Paúl*. Madrid: Rialp, 1994.

Suanzes-Carpegna, J.V. 'Las Cortes de Cádiz y la Constitución de 1812 (una visión de conjunto)'. *Anuario by Derecho Parlamentario* 26 (2012): 193.

Swidler, Leonard. 'Liberal Catholicism: A Lesson from the Past'. *Cross Currents* 21 (1971): 25–37.

Tackett, Timothy. *Par la volonté du peuple. Comment les députés de 1789 sont devenus révolutionnaires*. Paris: Albin Michel, 1997.

Taverneaux, R. *La vie quotidienne des Jansénistes*. Paris: Hachette, 1985.

Taylor, Charles. *L'Age séculier*. Paris: Edition du Seuil, 2011.

Tenbus, Eric. *English Catholics and the Education of the Poor, 1847–1902*. London: Pickering & Chatto, 2010.

Tern, J. 'J. H. Newman: From Fundamentalism to Tradition in the Church'. *Nova and Vetera*, July-August-September 2010, 281–97.

The Correspondence of Henry Edward Manning and William Ewart Gladstone. The Complete Correspondence 1833–91, edited by P.C. Erb, 4 vols. Oxford: Oxford University Press, 2013.

The Correspondence of Lord Acton and Richard Simpson vol. I., edited by Josef Altholz and Damian McElrath. Cambridge: Cambridge University Press, 1971.

The Correspondence of Lord Acton and Richard Simpson vol. II., edited by McElrath Altholz and J.C. Holland. Cambridge: Cambridge University Press, 1973.

The Correspondence of Lord Acton and Richard Simpson vol. III., edited by McElrath Altholz and J.C. Holland. Cambridge: Cambridge University Press, 1975.

Tocqueville (de), Alexis. *Oeuvres complètes (vol. XI)*, edited by J.P. Mayer. Paris: Gallimard, 1970.

Trevor, Meriol. *Newman. Light in Winter*. London: Macmillan, 1962.

Trevor, Meriol. *Newman: Pillar of the Cloud*. London: Macmillan, 1962.

Troeltsch, Ernst. *Protestantisme et modernité*, translated from German and prefaced by Marc B. de Launay. Paris: Nrf Editions Gallimard, coll. 'Librairie des Sciences Humaines', 1991.

Urigüen, Begoña. *Orígenes y evolución de la derecha española: el neocatolicismo*. Madrid: CSIS, 1986.

Vanden Heuvel, Jon. *A German Life in the Age of Revolution. Joseph Görres, 1776–1848*. Washington, DC: Catholic University of America Press, 2001.

Van Kley, D.K. 'From the Catholic Enlightenment to the Risorgimento: The Exchange between Nicola Spedalieri and Pietro Tamburini, 1791–1797'. *Past & Present* 224 (2014): 109–62.

Van Kley, Dale. 'Christianity as Casualty and Chrysalis of Modernity: The Problem of the French Revolution'. *American Historical Review* 108, no. 4 (October 2003): 1081–1104.

Van Kley, Dale. 'From the Catholic Enlightenment to the Risorgimento: The Exchange between Nicola Spedalieri and Pietro Tamburini, 1791–97'. *Past & Present* 224 (2014): 109–62.

Van Kley, Dale. *The Religious Origins of the French Revolution, 1560–1791*. New Haven: CT, 1996.
Varacalli, Joseph. *Toward the Establishment of Liberal Catholicism in American*. Washington, DC: University Press of America, 1983.
Vatican Apostolic Archive (VAA). 'Letter from the nuncio Franchi to Secretary of State Antonelli'. Nunciature in Madrid, box 463, title III, 23. Madrid, 1 December 1868.
Vatican Apostolic Archive (VAA). 'Draft of the Letter from nuncio Franchi to Secretary of State Antonelli (Madrid, 16 November 1868)', VAA, Nunciature in Madrid, box 463, title II, 17.
Vatican Apostolic Archive (VAA) 'Letter from Secretary of State Antonelli to the nuncio Franchi (Rome, 10 February 1869)', VAA, Nunciature in Madrid, box 463, title II, 17.
Verri, Carlo. *Controrivoluzione in Spagna. I carlisti nell'assemblea costituente (1869–1871)*. Rome: Viella, 2021.
Veuillot, Eugène, and François Veuillot. *Louis Veuillot*, 4 vols. Paris: V. Retaux, 1899.
Viaene, Vincent. *Belgium and the Holy See from Gregory XVI to Pius IX (1831–1859). Catholic Revival, Society and Politics in 19th Century Europe*. Leuven: Leuven university press, 2001.
Viejo Yharrassarry, J. 'El caso climent ¿ Ilustración católica o catolicismo ilustrado?'. *Hispania. Revista española de historia* LXXXI, no. 269 (2021): 651–81.
Vildósola, Antonio. *'Las' apariencias y la realidad de la fusión dinástica*. Madrid: Pérez Dubrull, 1869.
Villis, Tom. *Reaction and the Avant-Garde: The Revolt against Liberal Democracy in Early Twentieth-Century Britain*. London: Tauris Academic Studies, 2006.
Vincette, P. 'Presentation du dernier article de Newman: "La Révélation en rapport avec la foi"'. *Revue des sciences philosophiques et théologiques*, tome 87, no. 2 (2003): 313–40.
Voegelin, Eric. *Les religions politiques*. Paris: Editions du Cerf, col. 'Humanités', 1988.
Ward, Bernard. *The Dawn of the Catholic Revival in England, 1781–1803*. 2 vols. 1909.
Ward, Bernard *The Sequel to Catholic Emancipation: The Story of English Catholics Continued Down to the Re-establishment of the Hierarchy in 1850*, 2 vols. (1915).
Ward, Wilfrid. *William George Ward and the Catholic Revival*. 1893. 1912.
Ward, Wilfrid. *The Life and Times of Cardinal Wiseman*. 2 vols. 1897. 1912.
Ward, Wilfrid. *Problems and Persons*.1903.
Ward, Wilfrid. *Men and Matters*.1914.
Ward, W. G. 'Church and State'. *Dublin Review* 26 April 1876, 351–76.
Ward, W. G. *Dublin Review* 20 October 1877, 308–39.
Weber, Max. *L'Ethique protestante et l'esprit du capitalisme suivi de Les sectes protestantes et l'esprit du capitalisme*. Paris: Plon, 1964.
Weill, George. *Histoire du catholicisme libéral en France, 1828*–1908. Paris: Slatkine, 1979.
Wetherell, T.F. 'Thoughts on the Causes of the Present War'. *Rambler*, July 1859, 186–98.
Whitman, J.Q. *The Legacy of Roman Law in the German Romantic Era: Historical Vision and Legal Change 1990*. Princeton: Princeton University Press, 2014.
Wilson, A.N. *The Victorians*. London: Hutchinson, 2002.
Wilson, Bee. 'Counter-Revolutionary Thought'. In *The Cambridge History of Nineteenth-Century Political Thought*, edited by Gareth Stedman Jones and Gregory Claeys, 9–38. Cambridge: Cambridge University Press, 2011.
Wiseman, Nicholas. 'La vita ed il Pontificato di Gregorio VII, pubblicata da Sir R. Greisley, Baronetto'. *Annali della Scienze Religiose* 1, no. 2 (settembre-ottobre 1835): 267–77.
Wiseman, Nicholas. 'La vita ed il Pontificato di Gregorio VII …'. *Annali della Scienze Religiose* 1, no. 3 (novembre-dicembre 1835): 374–84.

Wiseman, Nicholas. *Lectures on the Principal Doctrines and Practices of the Catholic Church, Delivered at St. Mary's, Moorfields, during the Lent of 1836.* 2 vols.1836.

Wiseman, Nicholas. 'Authority of the Holy See in South America'. *Dublin Review* 5 July 1838, 233–56.

Wiseman, Nicholas. 'National Holydays'. *Dublin Review* 14 May 1843, 481–505.

Wiseman, Nicholas. *Essays on Various Subjects.* 3 vols. 1853.

Wiseman, Nicholas. *Recollections of the Last Four Popes and of Rome in Their Times.*1858.

Yelle, R.A. *Sovereignty and the Sacred Secularism and the Political Economy of Religion.* Chicago: The University of Chicago Press, 2019.

Index of Names

A

Acton, John Emerich Edward Dalberg (Lord) 4–6, 32, 41, 43, 45, 47–52, 54–8, 60–4, 74–6, 83–5, 185, 186
Alcala-Zamora y Caracuel, Luis 118
Alexandre, Noël 96
Anstey, Thomas Chisholm 79, 83
Antonelli 114, 118, 161
Archbishop of Santiago de Compostela 118, 120
Arenal, Concepcion 112
Arendt, Hannah 23
Arias, Veremundio 97
Arnauld, Antoine 96
Arnold, Matthew 177–8, 184
Aron, Raymond 23–4
Artois (d'), Charles-Ferdinand 134
Attuel, Cynthia 11, 29, 93
Attuel-Hallade, Aude 1, 11, 29, 41, 93, 185, 186

B

Bacon, Francis 132
Ballanche, Pierre-Simon 135
Barr, Colin 175
Bellarmine (Cardinal) 21
Belloc, Hilaire 75
Benedict XIV (Pope) 96
Benedict XVI (Pope) 36, 38
Benitez de Luco, Cayetano 96
Bentham, Jeremy 172
Berardi, Carlo Sebastiano 97
Berranger (de) Olivier 33
Berti, Alessandro Pompeo 97
Besnard, Maud 169, 188
Biard, Michel 47
Bishop of Jaén 113, 114, 118, 119, 120
Blumenberg, Hans 13–17, 19–21, 25, 184
Bodin, Jean 15
Boffa, Massimo 58

Bonald (de), Louis 78, 84, 130, 136
Bonaparte, Joseph 99
Bonaparte, Louis-Napoléon 150, 153, 154, 156–8
Bonaparte, Napoléon 2, 56, 150, 153, 161
Bossuet 79, 157
Bourdin, Bernard 11, 185
Boutry, Philippe 5, 77
Brougham, Henry (Lord) 170, 175, 188
Brown, Stewart Jay 46
Burke, Edmund 3, 41–4, 46, 47–60, 63–4, 81, 142, 185
Butterfield, Herbert 42

C

Caffiero, Marina 77
Callebat, Bernard 93, 186
Calvin, John 18, 19, 25
Capes, John Moore 75
Carbonero y Sol 122
Carlos IV 99
Carlyle, Thomas 172
Castelar, Emilio 111
Castlereagh 82
Chadwick, Owen 32
Chapman, H.S. 84
Charles I 53
Charles II 53
Charles IV 112
Charles X 133, 134, 136, 139, 141
Chateaubriand (de), François-René 142
Cicero 143
Clément, Jean-Charles Augustin 97
Clement XI 91, 96
Climent, José 97
Coke, Edward (Sir) 42, 81
Colenso, John William 36
Constant, Benjamin 22, 55, 57, 59, 60, 184, 185
Cortes, Juan Donoso 160

Count of Orgaz 122
Coux (de), Charles 78

D
Daens, Adolf 122
Deane, Seamus 55
DeLaura, David J. 178
Deschamps, Adolphe 6
Döllinger (von), Johann Joseph Ignaz 6, 36, 43, 51, 74, 75, 160
Dumont, Louis 13, 16–21, 23, 25
Dupac de Bellegarde, Gabriel 97
Dupanloup, Félix 43
Dupuy, Pascal 47

E
Egido, Teófanes 95
Eichorn, K.F. 82
Elizabeth I 53

F
Fabian y Fuero, Francisco 97
Fairbairn, A.M. 76
Febronius, Justinus 96
Feijóo, Benito Jeronimo 96
Ferdinand VII 1, 99
Fleury, Claude 95, 96
Flórez, Enrique 96
Franchi, Alessandro 114, 118
Froude, Hurrell 35, 79
Froude, James Anthony 177

G
Garcia Cuesta, Miguel (Cardinal) 118, 120, 121
Gauchet, Marcel 5, 22, 56, 57, 59
Gazzaniga, Jean-Louis 51
Gengembre, Gérard 59
Gerbet, Olympe-Philippe 79
Gierke (von), Otto 85
Gladstone, William Ewart 43, 45, 52–5, 59, 74
Godoy, Manuel 98
Goldie, Mark 44
Goldsmith, Oliver 48
Gorham 50
Görres, Josef 79, 81, 85
Graham, James 175
Grégoire, Henri (Abbot) 97

Gregory VII (Pope) 2, 20
Gregory XVI (Pope) 79, 149, 155
Grotius 101
Guizot, François 144

H
Hampden 50
Hegel 22
Heimann, Mary 76
Hérisson, Arthur 149, 187, 188
Hildebrand 84
Hobbes, Thomas 15, 21, 22, 52
Hume, David 42
Hus, Jan 20

I
Inglis, Robert (Sir) 175
Isabel II 114, 117

J
Jansen, Cornelius 136–7, 139, 143
Jaume, Lucien 56
Jehu 31
Jovellanos (de), José 100

K
Keble, John 35, 79
Kent OSC, W.H. 76

L
La Fuente (de), Vicente 112, 116, 117
Lacordaire, Jean-Baptiste Henri 4, 32, 76, 78
Lamartine (de), Alphonse 130
Lamennais (de), Félicité 4, 60, 74, 79, 83, 131, 134, 135, 143, 149, 150, 153, 156, 187
Laud, William 53
Leo X 56
Leo XIII (Pope) 29, 33, 38
Leopold II (Emperor) 44
Lessay, Franck 29, 56, 59, 64
Libaud, Frédéric 29, 185
Liberatore, Matteo 75, 84
Locke, John 21, 22, 54
Lopez y Noball, Alonso 102
Louis XIV 151, 156
Louis XVI 56
Louis XVIII 132, 133

Löwith, Karl 5, 11, 57, 58
Luther, Martin 20, 21

M
Macaulay, Thomas Babington 3, 41, 42, 43, 45–50, 52–5, 57–60, 63–4, 172, 185, 186
Maistre (de), Joseph 3, 56, 57, 60, 75, 78, 79, 81, 130–2, 134–6, 143, 152, 156, 162, 184, 188
Maitland, Samuel Roffey 81
Manning (Cardinal) 75, 84
Manso de Tapia, Pedro 96
Manterola, Vicente 118
Marquis of Mirabel 121, 122
Marquis of Viluma 114, 115
Marsilius of Padua 20
Masarnau, Santiago 116
Maultrot, Gabriel-Nicolas 139–41, 143
Mayans y Siscar, Gregorio 96
McConnell, Mickael 54
Mendizábal, Juan Álvarez 118
Mérode (de), Félix 152
Mésenguy, François-Philippe 96
Metz, Jean-Baptiste 24
Milbach, Sylvain 152
Mill, John Stuart 169, 172, 184
Milner, John 75
Minnerath, Roland 49
Monescillo, Antolin 118, 119, 122
Moñino y Redondo, José 100
Monsell, William 74
Montalembert (de), Charles 4, 5, 6, 32, 50, 74, 78, 117, 120, 149–62, 187
Müller, Adam 82
Murray (Dr) (Archbishop) 176

N
Newman, John Henry 5, 29, 30–8, 74, 75, 169, 171, 173, 174, 178, 179, 185, 187, 188
Nicole, Pierre 96
Noris, Enrico (Cardinal) 96
Novalis 82

O
O'Connell, Daniel 49, 54, 77, 79, 153, 155, 176
O'Hagan, Thomas 74

O'Siochru, Colm 73, 186
Ockham (of), William 14–17, 19, 20, 21, 185
Ortiz, Antonio Romero 112
Oxenham, Henry Nutcombe 74
Ozanam, Frédéric 79

P
Palgrave, Francis (Sir) 81
Palmer, Daniele Giuseppe 129, 187
Papencordt, Félix 82
Parisis, Pierre-Louis (Your Grace) 154
Peel, Robert 169, 170–3, 175–6
Pelayo, Menéndez 96
Pelletier, Gérard 77
Pereira de Figueiredo, Antonio 96
Phillips, George 81
Pidal y Mon 122
Pius VI 56, 97, 154
Pius VII 56, 150
Pius IX 2, 41, 61, 62, 121, 122, 149, 161, 176, 177, 183
Pufendorf 101
Pusey, Edward Bouverie 79

Q
Quadrado, José Maria 112, 114–16
Quesnel, Pasquier 95

R
Racine, Jean 96
Ramon Solans, Francisco Javier 111, 187
Ranke (von), Leopold 82
Rémond, René 5
Rémusat (de), Charles 129, 130–2, 136, 142
Rials, Stéphane 59
Rivarol, Viscount 44
Robert, Roberto 123
Robertson, John Burton 79, 81, 83
Robespierre, Maximilien 47
Rodriguez de Campomanes, Pedro 97
Rosanvallon, Pierre 132
Rousseau, Jean-Jacques 6, 21, 22, 44, 100, 130, 136
Royer-Collard, Pierre-Paul 129, 132–44, 187
Rupert, Jane 178
Russell, Charles William 78

S
Saint Augustine 4
Saint Paul 4, 119
Saint Thomas Aquinas 15, 16
Saint-Arnaud, Jean-Guy 30
Saint-Simon (de), Henri 132
Salinis (Your Grace) 156
Schlegel, A.W. 79, 82
Schlegel, Friedrich 80, 81, 85
Schmitt, Carl 11, 24
Schröder, Peter 183
Scipio of Ricci 97
Segur, Philippe 51
Selvaggio, Julio Lorenzo 96
Simpson, Richard 74
Soler, Juan 99
Southey, Robert 41, 49, 52, 53
Spinoza, Baruch 21, 22

T
Tamburini, Pietro 96, 97
Taylor, Charles 5
Thoyras (de), Rapin 42
Tillotson, John 54
Tocqueville (de), Alexis 58, 84, 135, 160, 184
Troeltsch, Ernst 18

V
Van Espen, Zeger Bernard 96
Van Kley, Dale 76
Veuillot, Louis 75, 84, 149, 154, 157
Vildósola, Antonio 117
Villanueva y Astengo, Joaquin Lorenzo 101
Villèle (de), Joseph 133, 134
Voegelin, Eric 23, 24
Voltaire 44

W
Walter, John 173
Ward, Wilfrid 76
Weber, Max 5, 11, 22
Wetherell, T.F. 74
Windischmann, Friedrich 79, 81
Wiseman, Nicholas 5, 77, 78, 79, 80, 82, 83, 84
Wycliffe, John 20

Y
Yearley 34

Z
Zola, Giuseppe 97

www.ingramcontent.com/pod-product-compliance
Lightning Source LLC
Chambersburg PA
CBHW052108300426
44116CB00010B/1576